ARKTOS

THE NEW SCIENCE SERIES:

- MAN-MADE UFOS: 1944—1994, 50 Years of Suppression
- UNDERGROUND BASES & TUNNELS
- THE FREE ENERGY DEVICE HANDBOOK
- THE FANTASTIC INVENTIONS OF NIKOLA TESLA
- THE ANTI-GRAVITY HANDBOOK
- ANTI-GRAVITY & THE WORLD GRID
- ANTI-GRAVITY & THE UNIFIED FIELD
- VIMANA AIRCRAFT OF ANCIENT INDIA & ATLANTIS

THE LOST CITIES SERIES:

- LOST CITIES OF ATLANTIS, ANCIENT EUROPE & THE MEDITERRANEAN
- LOST CITIES OF NORTH & CENTRAL AMERICA
- LOST CITIES & ANCIENT MYSTERIES OF SOUTH AMERICA
- LOST CITIES OF ANCIENT LEMURIA & THE PACIFIC
- LOST CITIES & ANCIENT MYSTERIES OF AFRICA & ARABIA
- LOST CITIES OF CHINA, CENTRAL ASIA & INDIA

THE MYSTIC TRAVELLER SERIES:

- IN SECRET TIBET by Theodore Illion (1937)
- DARKNESS OVER TIBET by Theodore Illion (1938)
- IN SECRET MONGOLIA by Henning Haslund (1934)
- MEN AND GODS IN MONGOLIA by Henning Haslund (1935)
- DANGER MY ALLY by Michell-Hedges

ARKTOS

The Polar Myth in Science, Symbolism, and Nazi Survival

Joscelyn Godwin

Adventures Unlimited Press

Arktos
The Myth of the Pole in Science, Symbolism, and Nazi Survival

This printing June 1996

ISBN 0-932813-35-6

Published by
Adventures Unlimited Press
One Adventure Place
Kempton, Illinois 60946 USA

Printed in the United States of America

Contents

Preface

Because of my interest in the Harmony of the Spheres, over the years I have read widely in that unclassifiable corner of literature sometimes described as "metaphysical," "esoteric," or "occult." In its earlier stages, my search was mainly for musical allusions and for understanding of their context. Later, when several themes forced themselves on me by sheer repetition from one text to another, I began to note them whenever I came across them, and the field of my research expanded commensurably.

One of these recurrent themes was the Pole. I came to it first because an interest in theories of the Harmony of the Spheres involves one in questions of cosmology, astronomy, and to a lesser extent astrology. Beside the more obvious themes that relate directly to the musical system, such as the twelve signs of the zodiac and the seven visible planets, I was struck by the repeated mention of some mystery concerning the poles, both those of the earth and of the heavens. Almost every major writer had something to say about it.

Once I started to concentrate on the polar theme, I quickly found that there was a school of thought which held that the earth's poles had shifted in the past, with significant results for whatever creatures were inhabiting it. Likewise, a group of authorities—more occult than scientific, in this instance—warned that the poles would shortly be shifting again. The investigation of this topic became the starting-point for the present book, and constitutes one of its major themes. The short first part (Chapters 1–2) outlines the situation that supposedly obtained before the poles shifted, which is closely allied to the mythology of a lost Golden Age.

One of the supposed results of a "non-shifted" pole, according to several sources, was that the Hyperborean or Arctic regions were formerly fit for human habitation. What manner of people lived there, and what has become of them? Asking these questions led me into waters that became progressively deeper and more perilous, and I have tried to replicate my experience in the arrangement of Part Two, "The Northern Lights." Step by step, it moves from theories of the Arctic, Aryan or Nordic race to the point at which respectable science discarded the idea, leaving it to be picked up and used as a political weapon by the pseudo-scientists of the Third Reich.

One might have thought that the idea of the "Aryan Race" died with Hitler in 1945, having contributed to the unforgettable cruelties of the Nazis toward Jews, Slavs, Gypsies, and other "non-Aryan" individuals. But not only has it survived the fall of the Third Reich: it has continued to inspire a worldwide group of esotericists who combine an engagement in the spiritual path with an attitude to Nazism ranging from compliance to enthusiasm.

The reader will find that the people in question are far from being semiliterate inhabitants of the lunatic fringe. They are highly intelligent, cultivated, and familiar with the literature and techniques of esotericism (yoga, meditation, alchemy etc.). However, they share, to a man, a certain combination of themes that are avidly cultivated in circles which my academic colleagues would shun like the plague. These include UFOs, extraterrestrials, the Hollow Earth, Hitler's survival, Nazi bases still existing in polar regions, and those "spiritual centers" called Agartha and Shambhala. Both the Arctic and the Antarctic loom large in this mythological mêlée, which is analyzed in Part Three (Chapters 7–10). Here I have tried above all to separate the sense from the nonsense, and to trace each rank growth to its roots. The reader may agree with me in suspecting that there is "something" behind all of this. Maybe he or she will know what it is: I do not, but I think that it is time to put up a warning sign saying "Watch this space."

The fourth part of the book (Chapters 11–13) is an attempt to come to terms with this material, using whatever tools the study of comparative religion and esoteric practice has provided. I believe that there are realities and truths that stand inviolate, whatever abuse is made of them for egotistic or political reasons. Christianity is one repository of such truths; the history of Christianity, an appalling example of such abuses. But it seems to me that there has been another spiritual stream in the West, parallel to Christianity, that I call the "Polar tradition." Having shown this at its worst in the Nazis, in Chapter Thirteen I give my impression of it at its highest, as exemplified by the mystical philosophers of medieval Persia.

Finally, and again in a spirit of "agnostic suspicion," this book returns to the theme of the polar shift, its history, mechanism, and causes. In presenting the mass of contradictory theories in Part Five (Chapters 14–18), I respect the examples of Charles Fort, the American collector of anomalies, who was content to document the facts that challenge "consensus reality"; and, more recently, Jacques Vallee, the writer on UFOs who emphasizes the seriousness of the phenomenon while discouraging emotional and premature conclusions. As in my profession, the teaching of undergraduates, my intention is to equip the reader for an informed and open-minded consideration of these ideas.

I take pleasure in thanking those who have found, lent, or given me books and articles used in writing *Arktos*: Christopher Bamford, Deborah Belle Forman, Janet Godwin, Nicholas Goodrick-Clarke, Hans Thomas Hakl, Seán King, Joan Matthews, and a Friend in Iowa. Especial thanks are due to Arthur Versluis and to my wife Janet for their comments on the manuscript, and to David Fideler and Cynthia Weber-Brownell at Phanes Press. I am also grateful for the indispensable help of David Hughes of the Colgate University Interlibrary Loan Service, and of the Library of Congress, which generously lent Landig's and Serrano's books when all other sources failed. Most of the research on Saint-Yves d'Alveydre, Agartha, and Shambhala was done in Paris and Lyon with the help of a Grant-in-Aid from the American Council of Learned Societies, a Travel to Libraries Grant from the National Endowment for the Humanities, and a grant from the Colgate University Research Council. An earlier version of part of Chapter Seven appeared in *The Hermetic Journal.*

This book is dedicated to my son Ariel, who worked side by side with me during most of its creation, and whose astronomical studies helped me understand what I was writing about.

—JOSCELYN GODWIN

PART I:
Prologue in Hyperborea

Chapter One:
The Golden Age

As one can see from the simplest globe, the earth does not sit erect in its orbit around the sun, but tilts at an awkward angle of about 23 1/2° from the perpendicular. Yet there is an oft-repeated story that our planet's situation was once far different; that it was a catastrophe that brought about its present state, and that some day it will be reinstated in the geometrical perfection of its origin. Whether literally or only symbolically true, this aspect of the polar archetype constellates the mythology of Fall and Redemption, Lost Eden and New Jerusalem. Its branches link with the ideas of cyclical development, evolutionary change, and every other effort to make sense of the course of history and prehistory. It is this that will frame our investigations.

Numerous authorities, who will be named later, assure us that in primordial times the earth was not tilted, but spun perfectly upright with its equator in the same plane as the ecliptic; or, which comes to the same thing, with its axis perpendicular to the plane of its orbit around the sun. They add, moreover, that the earth then orbited the sun in exactly 360 days. Under these circumstances there would be no seasons of summer or winter, spring or fall; all days would be alike. Near the equator, the climate would always be hot; near the poles, always cold. The distribution of sea and land (surely far different from today's) might affect the temperatures of certain regions, as the Gulf Stream now makes the climate of Northern Europe milder than that of other places in the same latitude, such as Newfoundland or Moscow. Lands high above sea-level, likewise, would be cold, as mountains always are. But the climate of every zone would be uniform throughout the year. Plants would sprout, blossom, seed, and die in obedience only to their innate rhythms. The characteristic vegetation of every land would always be present, in every state of its life-cycle, thus providing food all year round for whatever creatures might need it.

At the equator, the sun would appear at six o'clock each morning precisely in the east, rise vertically to reach the zenith at noon, and continue its journey to set due west at six p.m. Further to the north or south, it would rise at an angle to the horizon and reach less high at its noontime limit. Towards the poles, its angle would be so narrow that its twelve-hour journey would carry it no more than a few degrees above the horizon. But its rising and setting places would

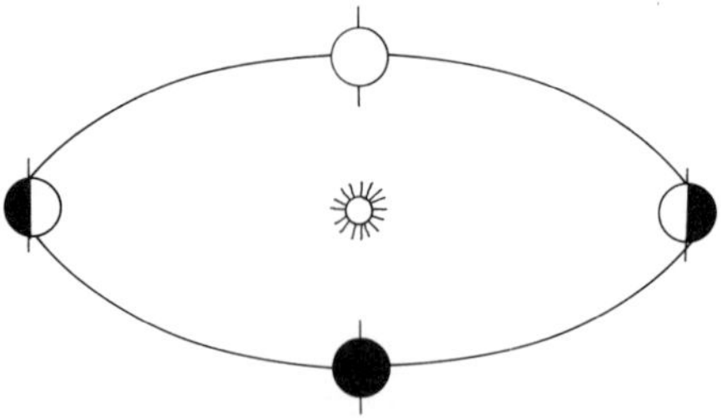

Illustration 1a: "Golden Age"—equinoctial conditions all year

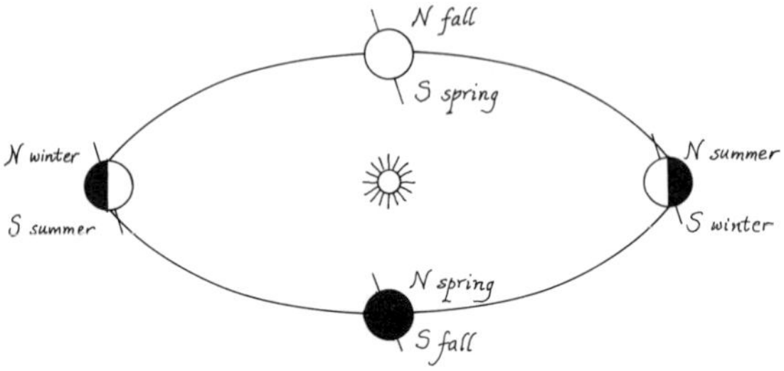

Illustration 1b: Present day—four seasons

never vary, and the lengths of night and day would invariably be equal. For that reason, one might well call this a time of perpetual spring, since it is only at today's spring and autumn equinoxes that equal day and night occur.

Unusual celestial conditions would obtain at the poles themselves. Assuming that the landscape was fairly even, the sun there would neither rise nor set, but half of its disk would be visible all the time, circling the horizon once a day. These areas, warmed by only half a sun, would necessarily be chilly and unwelcoming to animal life. Even if the earth produced its own heat, as in the volcanic springs that now warm Iceland, no food plants could flourish in a region so poor in the light needed for photosynthesis. It is hard to imagine the mythical land of Hyperborea (the "land beyond the North Wind") ever inhabited by humans like ourselves. Nevertheless, the absence of seasons would make the earth habitable, and even comfortable, to much higher latitudes than is the case today. With heat and cold alternating daily but not annually, there would be no months-long night in the Arctic or Antarctic regions, during which all life now becomes dormant. Aided as might be by ocean currents and by the inner heat of the earth, twelve hours of sunlight would permit fertility to a very high latitude. Even today, the low sun of the Arctic spring brings forth an astonishing variety of vegetable, insect, and animal life, while the Antarctic seas swarm with krill and the creatures that live on it directly and indirectly. With the upright axis, this would be the norm all year round. There would be no need for energy to be spent on migrations; animal young could be raised at any time of year, and the food for it would never be wanting. As for the rest of the earth, from temperate to tropical zones, it would indeed enjoy a Golden Age.

If the annual cycle had no consequences for the earth's climate, the year would be purely a cosmic phenomenon. The sun would rise and set each day against a slightly different background of stars, and after 360 days would complete the circle of the zodiac. More noticeable (to any beings inclined to notice such things) would be the annual changes in the night sky. Each night the stars would rise, and each morning they would set, moving in a trajectory exactly matching that of the sun. At the equator, the whole bowl of heaven would swing up and overhead as if it were pivoting on the northern and southern horizons. In the temperate zones, the motionless pivot might be visible if it happened to coincide with a polar star; the swing of the other stars would be at an angle to the horizon. Nearer the poles the angle would diminish, and the pivotal point rise higher and higher, until at the poles themselves the pivot would be directly overhead, and the stars would move around it like a bowl spun on a finger.

The keen observer, however, would notice that each day a different star first became visible above the eastern horizon as the sun set in the West. The daily cycle of the stars would seem to be suffering a slight slippage, amounting to one degree. By the end of 360 days, the slippages would have added up to one entire circle, and the next annual cycle would begin. Yet with no solstices or equinoxes to punctuate the year, its "beginning" would be no fixed point, but merely the reappearance at dusk of whatever star was chosen as an aid to reckoning.

There is no telling how the moon would have behaved at this time: whether its orbit was also in the equatorial plane, whether its period of revolution around the earth was a mathematically satisfying 30 days, or, as some of our authorities will question, whether the moon was there at all. If it shared the same plane as the earth, each month would be marked, at the dark of the moon, by an eclipse of the sun, and each full moon would disappear for a few hours into the shadow of the earth. In a world without seasons, these monthly eclipses would be the most prominent markers of the course of time.

Time itself would have little meaning in this primordial Paradise. As Jean Phaure writes in *Le Cycle de l'humanité adamique* (The cycle of adamic humanity, 1988):

> In the Golden Age, "Time" in all its plenitude was closer to Eternity than to duration. On coming out of Paradise, we fell into time, and our ongoing flight is merely our Fall, gradually accelerating. Our measuring instruments are the signs of our anguish. A being that lives in harmony with the environment in which it flourishes has no need for a wrist-watch: the courses of the stars are enough. It experiences growing old only as a happy ripening; it participates in the music of the spheres.[1]

Some may feel that all this is mere hypothesis: interesting as an imaginative exercise, but not grounded in historical certainty, much less in scientific proof. Rather than dismissing it as a wild speculation about prehistory, such readers should consider it as a Platonic Idea of how the earth "ought" to be—knowing well that the geometrical perfection of the ideal realm is unattainable in the corporeal world. Perhaps it is not even an attractive picture, used as we are to creatively dealing with the world's imbalances and disharmonies. Real or ideal, however, it must be accepted that this is a recurrent hypothesis in the history of ideas, and that those who have held it command a hearing. To them we now turn.

The Cycle of the Ages

The memory or imagination of a Golden Age seems to be a particularity of the cultures that cover the area from India to Northern Europe.[2] In the Americas, the most fully developed mythologies of history were those of the Mayas and Aztecs, for whom there was no past era unclouded by the threat of cyclical destruction by fire or flood. Nor does the philosophy of Buddhism have any place for nostalgia, although in practice it absorbed the idea of declining ages from its Indian surroundings. But in the ancient Middle East there is an obvious relic of the Golden Age in Genesis, as the Garden of Eden where humanity walked with the gods before the Fall. The Egyptians spoke of past epochs ruled by god-kings. Babylonian mythology, as reported by Berosus, had a scheme of three ages, each lasting while the vernal equinox precessed through four signs of the zodiac; the first of these, under the dominion of Anu, was a Golden Age, ended by the Flood. The Iranian Avesta texts tell of the thousand-year Golden Reign of Yima, the first man and the first king, under whose rule cold and heat, old age, death and sickness were unknown.

The most fully-developed theory of this kind, and probably the oldest one, is the Hindu doctrine of the Four Yugas. The Sanskrit names for these four ages refer to their relative durations: Krita or Satya Yuga (four units), Treta Yuga (three), Dvapara Yuga (two), and Kali Yuga (one), the whole tenfold period making up one Mahayuga. A modern scholar thus describes the first of these ages:

> In the first kritayuga, after the creation of the earth, Brahman created a thousand pairs of twins from his mouth, breast, thighs, and feet respectively. They lived without houses; all desires which they conceived were directly fulfilled; and the earth produced of itself delicious food for them, since animals and plants were not yet in existence. Each pair of twins brought forth at the end of their life a pair exactly like them. As everybody did his duty and nothing else, there was no distinction between good and bad acts.[3]

After the Krita or Satya Yuga, things get progressively worse: each successive yuga sees the human race falling into increasing unhappiness and vice, until at the end of the Kali Yuga (mercifully, the shortest of the series) the world is set on fire, deluged with water, and then reborn.

Western culture first learned this cyclical conception of ages from the Greeks. The farmer-poet Hesiod (flourished circa 700 BCE), in his *Works and Days*, tells of the history of the human race in five ages: Gold, Silver, Bronze, Heroic, and Iron. (He had to add the Heroic Age so as to fit Greek history into the traditional scheme.) In the first of these, mankind lived under the rule of Kronos (Saturn), free from hard work, pain, and old age. "The fruitful grainland yielded its harvest to them of its own accord; this was great and abundant, while they at their pleasure quietly looked after their works, in the midst of good things, prosperous in flocks, on friendly terms with the immortals."[4] Plato, in his *Statesman*, wrote similarly about the reign of Cronus that preceded the present reign of his usurper Zeus:

> When God was shepherd there were no political constitutions and no taking of wives and begetting of children. For all men rose up anew into life out of the earth, having no memory of the former things. Instead they had fruits without stint from trees and bushes; these needed no cultivation but sprang up of themselves out of the ground without man's toil. For the most part they disported themselves in the open needing neither clothing nor couch, for the seasons were blended evenly so as to work them no hurt, and the grass which sprang up out of the earth in abundance made a soft bed for them.[5]

Centuries later, the Roman Ovid, in the first book of his *Metamorphoses*, gave a more elaborate account of the cycle of ages, likewise imagining the Golden Age as a pastoral paradise where "springtide lasted all the year"[6] and mankind was free from the two greatest ills of Ovid's, or of any time: war, and the threat of famine.

Although not universal in the classical world, there was a predominant idea of time as proceeding in one or more cycles of decline: the world and its inhabitants had been created in a state of careless innocence and had fallen by degrees into a worse and worse condition. Plato, in the same dialogue, has the young Socrates instructed by a "Stranger" on the governance of the world during two alternating types of era:

> In the one era it is assisted on its way by the transcendent divine cause, receiving a renewal of life from its creator, an immortality of his contriving. In the other era, when it has been released, it moves by its innate force [...][7]

The meaning of this passage, like so much of Plato's mythology, is debatable, but one likely interpretation allies it to the cycle of ages. The first era would then be the Satya Yuga or Golden Age, maintained by the "divine cause," and the other era the subsequent ages, falling under the law of entropy as the gods leave the earth and its inhabitants to their own devices. However, if this is not a single cycle but part of a larger movement, then there is hope. At the end of the Iron Age, at the uttermost nadir of dereliction, the world will suddenly experience a reversion to its original golden state. Like a clock rewound that has been left to run down, the cycle of the ages will begin anew. Virgil, court poet of Caesar

Augustus, announced the advent of such a renovation in his Fourth Eclogue—over-optimistically, as it has turned out.

The three Abrahamic religions each have their own adaptation of the myth of declining ages and restoration. Judaism, Christianity, and Islam all begin with Adam and Eve in Paradise. They all believe in a Fall, and in the sending of prophets to recall the human race to its duties and virtues. Each looks forward to the end of a present time in which none finds much to praise: Jews, to the coming of the Messiah; Christians, to the second coming of Christ; Muslims, to the Day of Judgement. For the elect, what follows will be more glorious even than Paradise. But exoterically speaking, that is the end of the history of the world, if not of the universe. In comparison to the Oriental or Greek system, the Abrahamic religions consider only a single turn of the wheel of time. It is this turn that the Christian esotericist Jean Phaure calls the "Cycle of Adamic Humanity," lasting some 64,000 years, while allowing that other cycles have happened and will happen in the future.

The obvious psychological interpretation of the myth of a returning Golden Age—which may well be true without for that reason being exhaustive—sees it as a projection serving to alleviate present sufferings: first, by the eternal pessimism that assures us that things have never been worse than they are today; second, by the eternal optimism that they might suddenly get better. However, our concern here is with cosmology as well as mythology, and in particular with the elusive and subtle point at which they meet. If, as so many testify, the earth once enjoyed the situation described at the beginning of this chapter, then the memory of the Golden Age may be founded on more than wishful thinking.

Chapter Two:
The Imperishable Sacred Land

We will hear in Part Five many voices which assure us that the present position of the axis is abnormal, and offer reasons for the earth's fall from grace. Far fewer are those in modern times who pretend to any acquaintance with its original state. Two writers in particular stand out as willing to share such knowledge with their readers, which they admit to having acquired through other than the usual channels: these are H. P. Blavatsky (1831–1891) and René Guénon (1886–1951), arguably the two most authoritative esotericists of modern times.

We turn first to Blavatsky's account of the lost epochs of Hyperborea and Atlantis. For this it is necessary to sift and sort the remarks scattered in her masterwork of "initiatic science" *The Secret Doctrine*, which takes the form of a commentary on the cryptic "Stanzas of Dzyan," an otherwise unknown text of traditional cosmogony. Blavatsky is not always consistent, whether through haste and incompetence, as her opponents naturally assumed, or else through her deliberate confusing of the reader through placing "blinds" along the way, lest the Secret Doctrine prove too easy of access.[1] But the main lines of her story of humanity can be reconstructed thus, as the sequence of seven Root-Races on seven continents:

1. The first continent of this Manvantara (a period of many millions of years) was the "Imperishable Sacred Land."[2] Although little can be said of it, it "capped over the whole North Pole like one unbroken crust..."[3] This was the home of the First Race of mankind, which "had neither type nor color, and hardly an objective, though colossal form."[4] These, our first ancestors, had ethereal, not physical bodies, and could not be injured or destroyed by death.[5] (The parallel with Plato's deathless and non-breeding race will be noticed.)

2. The second continent extended southward and westward from the North Pole;[6] it may have included Baffin Bay, as well as a horse-shoe shaped continent stretching from Greenland to Kamschatka.[7] On it appeared the Second Race, of monstrous, androgynous, semi-human beings; they were "the first attempts of material nature at building human bodies."[8] The bulk of them perished in the first great cataclysm, as Greenland and the other northern "Edens with their eternal spring" were transformed into "hyperborean Hades."[9]

3. For the third continent, stretching from the Indian Ocean to Australia,[10] Blavatsky borrowed a contemporary geologist's term, Lemuria. This was the time of the Third Race, a "Golden Age" when the "gods walked the earth and mixed freely with the mortals." [11] In the course of the Lemurian era, the first of the truly human races appeared, as they gradually developed from androgynous egg-layers into two distinct sexes.[12] This was the "Fall of Man," [13] and occurred about 18 million years ago.

4. Lemuria was destroyed in its turn, and its survivors gave birth to the Fourth Race,[14] whose home was Atlantis. The Atlanteans divided from their earliest tribes into the righteous and the unrighteous.[15] Their continent sank about 850,000 years ago.

5. The Fifth, brown-white Race (Aryan) appeared in Asia. Since then, many lands have appeared and disappeared, of which the last was Plato's "Atlantis," a fragment of the great continent which sank some 12,000 years ago.[16]

6, 7. Two more races are to follow before the end of this Manvantara.

To sum up, Blavatsky says: "We believe in the seven 'continents,' four of which have already lived their day, the fifth still exists, and two are to appear in the future." [17]

The account preserved in the Hebrew *Sepher Bereshith* (Book of Genesis) can readily be interpreted to agree with Blavatsky's first four races. It begins with the creation by the Elohim of a "male-and-female," spiritual Adam (Genesis 1.27). The second creation story, generally accepted as an alternative version drawn from the Jahwist source, tells of a more materialized being made from dust of the earth plus the breath of life (2.7), and placed in "Eden." Third comes the separation into sexes (2.21–22); lastly, the definitive entry into physical bodies (the "coats of skin" of Genesis 3.20) and exclusion from Eden (or the polar homeland). Thence the human beings, now fully resembling ourselves, proceed to breed the variously colored races and populate the globe.

In the Hindu Puranas, which are another of Blavatsky's primary sources, the land of Hyperborea is called *Svita-Dvîpa*, the "White Island," and has as its mythical center Mount Meru. This mountain, according to the *Haimavatchanda*, has four enormous supports: the east one is of gold; the south one, iron; the west one, silver; the north one, brass. From it flow four rivers which all derive from the celestial Ganges issuing from the feet of Vishnu, near the Pole Star.[18] (One perceives the similarity with the four rivers of the Biblical Eden.) Blavatsky wrote that this sacred land "is the only one whose destiny it is to last from the beginning to the end of the Manvantara throughout each Round" [19]—possibly symbolized by its four supports made from the metals of the four ages.

Much is written about Meru in Hindu texts and in the modern commentaries on them, beginning with Francis Wilford's *Essay on the sacred isles in the West*,[20] which patriotically tried to situate the White Island in Britain. Orientalists, and also Indians, have strained to reconcile the geography of Meru—supposedly 672,000 miles high—with some specific place on earth. Blavatsky's Hyperborea is ambiguous in this regard: it is geographical, being situated at the North Pole, yet it is immaterial, meaning that one will probably not find it if one looks for it there with mortal eyes. A recent evaluation of the Vedic cosmology by a scientist, Richard L. Thompson, makes the bold suggestion that many readers will appreciate: that the places described in the Vedas, impossible to situate or accommodate with the known dimensions of the earth, are part of a broader, multi-leveled cosmos occupying the same space as our own, which was perceptible to beings of the earlier yugas.[21]

Guénon on Hyperborea

One could scarcely choose two more different characters than the volatile Russian aristocrat, whose life is a web of intrigue and mystery, yet whose work is a mine of esoteric wisdom; and the coolly intellectual Frenchman, who held in disdain Madame Blavatsky, all her followers, and all she stood for, while teaching in many instances exactly the same things. Blavatsky got her knowledge through wide reading and through the oral teaching of "Masters" who have never been conclusively identified.[22] Guénon derived his from different but analogous sources: there are rumors of mysterious Hindu contacts in his early life. He left his readers in no doubt that he spoke with authority derived from initiatic teachings, and not merely from scholarship or personal philosophy. In an article on "Atlantis and Hyperborea" (1929), Guénon says of another writer on the subject:

> We consider him as a "seeker" (and that is in no way to denigrate him), who offers explanations according to his personal views, sometimes quite adventurous ones: which is his perfect right, since he is not attached to any currently living tradition and is not in possession of any data received by direct transmission. In other words, we may say that he is doing archeology, whereas we ourselves are doing initiatic science; and those are two points of view which, even when they touch on the same subjects, cannot coincide in any way.[23]

René Guénon's account of Hyperborea resembles Blavatsky's in many ways, but is conceived on a far more restricted time-scale. He concerns himself with epochs far anterior to any historical times, but nevertheless belonging to the same Mahayuga, or series of four ages, as all of known history. (Guénon also calls this period a Manvantara, although usually that denotes a much longer period containing seventy-one Mahayugas.[24]) Calculating on the basis of the numbers given in the Hindu Puranas, Guénon suggests that its duration might be 64,800 years, "corresponding very well to the actual age of present earthly mankind."[25]

This Adamic cycle, which Guénon believed to be now nearing its close, began in the Hyperborean land called Tula—the same name as the Greek and Latin Thule. It was "the first and supreme center for the whole of the current Manvantara [...] the archetypal 'sacred island,' and its situation was literally polar, at the origin."[26] What manner of beings lived there, Guénon does not say, but he gives one to understand that our cycle of humanity began there, under the primordial law and tradition given it by the Vaivasvata Manu or spiritual founder of the Manvantara. ("Tradition" is used in a special sense by Guénon and his followers to denote the complex of esoteric knowledge, symbolism, initiation, and ritual practice of which a religion constitutes the exoteric side.)

Later than this Hyperborean center, and quite distinct from it, according to Guénon, came Atlantis, the land now sunk beneath the waves of the Atlantic Ocean. He surmises that the Atlantean civilization might have lasted for a "Great Year" of 12,960 years, equal to half the period of the precession of the equinoxes.[27] As for our own post-Atlantean epoch, he says that it received its tradition from a dual source: first, directly from the Primordial tradition in the North; second, from the Atlantean in the West.[28] The first of these is at the origin of Hinduism, which Guénon regarded as the closest of all current traditions to the primordial one, while the second took root both in ancient Egypt and in America. It seems from his essays on symbology that Guénon did not regard Meru as an actual mountain situated at the North Pole,[29] but rather as a symbol of the earth's axis that passes through the pole and points to the *Arktoi*, the constellations of the Great and Little Bears.

Only in a passing footnote does Guénon mention the inclination of the earth's axis, "which, according to certain traditional data, has not existed from the beginnings, but is a consequence of what in Western language is called the 'Fall of Man' ";[30] but his readers will know that his most pregnant hints are often tucked away in notes. On the whole, Guénon's interest in this material was in expounding the symbolism and mythology of the Pole, to which we will return in Chapter Eleven. It is important to realize the degree to which he was stepping outside the normal boundaries of his teaching in even mentioning such things as Hyperborea and Atlantis. Most of his work is about symbolism and metaphysical doctrines, especially as transcending the boundaries between the different religions and as revealing their unanimity at the esoteric level. Atlantis, it is true, was described by Plato and has been the subject of hundreds of books; it is a marginally respectable topic, though geologists regard an Atlantic location for it as a discredited idea. Hyperborea is less acceptable, particularly in the interpretation Guénon gives of it. For whereas there have been scholarly attempts, from Jean-Sylvain Bailly to Jürgen Spanuth, to identify the legendary Atlantis with some actual territory in the far North, Guénon does not do so: he makes it abundantly clear that Hyperborea is not the same as Atlantis, but an earlier continent situated fairly and squarely at the North Pole.

It is, admittedly, difficult for the present-day mind to imagine a purely ethereal First Race such as Madame Blavatsky places at the Pole; and the question will naturally arise of why the remains of her Second and Third Races have not been discovered by paleontologists. Guénon, though he generally avoids such topics as too sensational, touches on them when he writes in *The Reign of Quantity and the Signs of the Times* of the progressive solidification of the world and its inhabitants[31]—adding, à propos modern science, that far from having pushed back the boundaries of the known world, it has shrunk them as never before by reducing the world and man to "mere corporeal entities, deprived, by hypothesis, of the smallest possibility of communication with any other order of reality!"[32] Earlier in the Manvantara, he explains, the descent into matter had not gone so far as it has today. Some of his followers[33] agree with the Theosophists in saying frankly that this is why we do not disinter the bones of our Hyperborean ancestors: their bodies were simply not materialized to the extent that ours are, and consequently have not been preserved.[34]

This easily disposes of the objection based on the polar climate as being too cold and dark for human beings. As Blavatsky says:

> We men have learned to live in every climate, whether frigid or tropical, but the first two Races had nought to do with climate, nor were they subservient to any temperature or change therein. And thus, we are taught, men lived down to the close of the Third Root-Race, when eternal spring reigned over the whole globe [...][35]

Jean Phaure has developed Guénon's hints into a version of prehistory that brilliantly reconciles four disparate chronologies: Guénon's 64,800-year cycle of our present humanity, due to end in the fairly near future; the Hindu system of four Yugas; the astrological ages (of which more will be said in Chapter Twelve); and the "Great Years" of the Greeks. His scheme is as follows:

> circa 62,800–36,880 BCE: Golden Age (Krita Yuga), duration 25,920 years (one full precessional cycle, beginning with the Age of Leo)
> Earthly Paradise before incarnation
>
> 36,880–17,440 BCE: Silver Age (Treta Yuga), duration 19,440 years (nine astrological ages, Leo to Sagittarius)
> Fall into incarnation; Hyperborea. Possibly Mu and Lemuria.
>
> 17,440–4,480 BCE: Bronze Age (Dvapara Yuga), duration 12,960 years (half a precessional cycle, Scorpio to Gemini)
> End of Atlantis circa 10,800 BCE; Atlantean colonies; Noah's Flood; beginning of writing.
>
> 4,480 BCE–2000 CE. Iron Age (Kali Yuga), duration 6,480 years (Ages of Taurus, Aries, Pisces)
> "Classical" history; birth of Christ marks the beginning of the Piscean Age.[36]
>
> Millenium; Aquarian Age; Parousia; Judgement; Beginning of a new cycle of humanity.

In Phaure's book, this scheme is preceded by very extensive documentation to bring it into line with scientific views of prehistory, which cannot possibly be summarized here. But like Richard Thompson, he holds views broader than those of materialistic science. While the first race is not even physical, Phaure is unperturbed by the consequences of incarnating his "Silver Age" humanity in the Arctic, in the middle of an Ice Age:

> Might there have existed there, on the scale of a small continent, a "micro-climate" maintained by sources of energy that are mysterious to us because they are spiritual? This humanity of the beginning of the Silver Age was incarnated, certainly, but still endowed with immense psychic and gnostic powers. It is possible that, given mastery of their own bodily energies and particularly of the Kundalini, the "post-primordial" humans of the Silver Age might have found their ideal habitat in a land too cold for us. Right up to recent years, some Tibetans have borne witness to these same "powers," living almost unclad at very high altitudes and radiating heat sufficient to dry soaked and frozen garments almost instantly! Besides, how can one forget the analogous tradition of a Primordial Paradise depicted as *surrounded* by sparkling walls of ice? Who knows what might be revealed by an exploration of the soil of Greenland (the "green land"), difficult as it would be?[37]

The accounts of Blavatsky and Guénon are compatible to a certain extent, but their fundamental differences show that the matter is far from being settled, even among those working mainly from Hindu sources. Obviously Blavatsky's idea of a Manvantara, in accordance with that of Hindu dating, is immensely longer than Guénon's, lasting millions of years as against his thousands. Compared to her chronology, Guénon's "Hyperborea" and "Atlantis" are mere incidents within the history of the Fifth Race. However, these two uneasy companions are united in their radical opposition to the picture presented by modern evolutionary theory. The human race, in their view, did not struggle up from ape-like ancestors and continue to progress in knowledge and power up to its present level. On the contrary, its origin was divine and its first state a non-physical one; only as the cycle proceeded did it enter as fully into the physical world as we find ourselves today. It is not the "ascent of man," as Darwin put it, but a descent that is traced through these prehistoric phases.

I well remember the impact of discovering these authors and their many followers, and suspecting for the first time that the "scientific" view of history with which nearly every youngster is brainwashed might be completely wrong. To realize that we could be at the trough of a cycle, not riding the crest of an ever-rising wave, frees one from the existential anguish of our time, which clings to the broken reed of faith in human "progress" against the overwhelming evidence to the contrary.

PART II:
The Northern Lights

Chapter Three: *The Arctic Homeland*

Our preliminary investigations have left us uncertain as to whether any facts lie behind the theories and fantasies of a Golden Age. Part Five will be devoted to this question. By contrast, the next part of the book has to do with facts of the most concrete kind. The chapters that follow chart one thread of the intellectual and mythical complex that gave birth to Nazism and its ideologies, in order to demonstrate how armchair speculations, when fueled by the energy of an archetype, can lead to unimaginable consequences.

We begin by revisiting the Arctic homeland, the "Hyperborea" of Blavatsky and Guénon. Such an idea could not have occurred in a culture that subscribed to the veracity of the Book of Genesis, which has all the races of the world descending first from a Mesopotamian Eden, then from Noah and his sons. It required an infusion from the East to enable the Western imagination to entertain so different a view of human origins. This came first from Jesuit missionaries like Père Amiot,[1] and later from British colonial administrators such as Sir William Jones.[2]

It took the many-sided talents of Jean-Sylvain Bailly (1736–1793), "astronomer, mystic, and revolutionary," as his biographer calls him,[3] to collate the newly-discovered eastern sources with those of classical antiquity and the Bible, and to weigh them all against the certainties of modern astronomy. Bailly's studies convinced him that ancient Egypt, Chaldea, China, and India were rich in genuine scientific knowledge, but that this was merely the half-remembered residue of a far superior culture: that of the antediluvian North.

> It is a very remarkable thing that enlightenment appears to have come from the North, against the common prejudice that the earth was enlightened, as it was populated, from South to North. The Scythians are one of the most ancient nations; the Chinese descend from them. The Atlanteans themselves, more ancient than the Egyptians, descend from them...[4]

One indication of this, to Bailly's penetrating mind, was the report of the Greek astronomer Eudoxus (4th century BCE): that the solstices and equinoxes were situated at the fifteenth degrees of Aries, Cancer, Libra, and Capricorn.

Bailly calculates that this would indeed have been the case in about 1353 BCE, but points out that it would have made nonsense to invent a zodiac in which the crucial points of the year fell in the middles of signs, rather than at their junctures. He deduces that in the original zodiac, these points must have corresponded with the beginnings of certain signs—but which ones? Since the zodiacal signs were already known in 3,000 BCE, Bailly favors the next earliest coincidence of the spring equinox with the first degree of a sign: that of Gemini, in around 4,600 BCE, and it is to that epoch that he dates the invention of the zodiac.[5] Since the spring point would have moved immediately to the 30th degree of Taurus, modern parlance would identify Bailly's epoch with the beginning of the "Taurean Age," on which more will be said in Chapter Twelve.

Bailly admitted that this was several centuries before the conventional dating of Noah's Flood. Who, then, could have been responsible for such an invention in so remote a time? Bailly was an inveterate euhemerist: all the gods, titans, and demigods of antiquity were human kings and sages to him. Therefore he attributes the codification of astronomy before the Flood to an Oriental "Hercules," after whom he says the Greek hero was later named.[6] Hercules's twelve labors had long been recognized as emblematic of the sun's annual journey through the twelve signs of the zodiac, so this hero seemed the most likely candidate for mankind's first astronomer.

As humanity began to reconstitute itself after the Deluge (to continue with Bailly's account), the purest stream of civilization descended from northern Asia into India, which to this day carries evidence of having the most ancient astronomical system on earth. Thus Bailly introduces the idea of a northern homeland for humanity, or at least for what he considered the most important branch of it. One of his favorite arguments for this was the fable of the Phoenix, which is found both in Egypt (reported by Herodotus, II,73) and in the poetic Edda, the epic poem of the North. The version Bailly prefers is the Nordic one:

> [The Phoenix's] head and breast are the color of fire; its tail and wings sky-blue. It lives for 300 days, after which, followed by all the birds of passage, it flies off to Ethiopia and nests there; it burns itself together with its egg, from whose ashes there emerges a red worm, which, after having recovered its wings and the form of a bird, takes flight again with the same birds towards the North.[7]

Since the Phoenix is by general consent a solar symbol, its death and rebirth imaging the eternal return of the sun, Bailly explains the strange details of its legend as referring to the annual disappearance of the sun in regions beyond the Arctic Circle. The alternation of 300 days of sunlight with 65 days in which the sun does not appear occurs at the latitude of 71° (for example, at Baffin Bay, or the very north of Norway). Following the erudition of Olaus Rudbeck (1630–1702), author of *De Atlantica* (and not to be confused with Olaus Magnus, 1490–1558, author of *Historia de gentibus septentrionalibus*), Bailly compares the Nordic Phoenix to the image of Janus, the Roman god of time and the year, who reputedly holds the number 300 in his right hand, and the number 65 in his left. Thus, he says, "one cannot avoid thinking that Janus is a northern god, imported to the South through the emigration of peoples."[8] As a further instance, the Edda has a story of the goddess Freia and her husband, the chief god Odin: they have a contract which allows the husband to absent himself from the nuptial bed for 65 days of the year, on condition that he is present for the remaining 300.[9]

These three coincidences are certainly striking. But to complete Bailly's version of prehistory, it required relics of other stages of the southward migration. One that seemed to refer to a still more northerly latitude was the legend of Adonis, sentenced by Jupiter to spend four months of the year with him on Olympus, four with Venus, and four with Persephone in Hades. Bailly relates this to latitude 79°, where the sun is absent for four months of the year. He saw the same situation reflected in the myth of the earth-goddess Freia, clothed by turns in black, green, and white garments; also in the "year" of four months apparently still kept by the inhabitants of Tartary.[10]

Bailly found records of subsequent stages of the great racial migration in the mythology of Egypt and Syria, where the dying and resurrected gods Osiris and Adonis were mourned for forty days: this would correspond to the sun's annual absence at 68th degree of latitude, he says—but surely not quite accurately, since that is practically on the Arctic Circle.[11] Again, in the *Zend-Avesta*, the sacred book of the Persians which had recently (1771) been translated by Anquetil Duperron, Bailly read that the longest day of the year is twice as long as the shortest. This is the case at 49°, by no means an Arctic latitude but still far to the north of Persia. The natural conclusion was that these various legends preserved the racial memory of an origin in the far North and a gradual migration to the South.

Bailly showed his work before publication to the Comte de Buffon, who discovered a marked analogy with his own theory of the cooling of the earth. Buffon had dared to extend the age of the earth on a scale hitherto unthought-of, calculating with sanguine exactitude that it was 34,770 1/2 years old by the time its surface was cool enough to touch, and counting 74,832 years from its separation from the sun until the present day (he was writing in 1749).[12] Buffon also maintained that the polar regions must have been the first to cool sufficiently for life to exist,[13] and had placed the first civilizations in northern and central Asia, east of the Caspian Sea.[14]

Bailly did not go so far as Buffon in his estimate of the earth's age, since he stolidly avoided the religious controversy that the question aroused. But he was emboldened to move the cradle of mankind even further to the North. "We did not have the intention," says Bailly, "of transporting [the origin of knowledge] to the Pole itself, but there are perhaps some fables, and even some astronomical facts, that gain thereby a natural explanation."[15] Foremost among these is the myth of Proserpine, who spends six months on earth, alternating with six months in the underground realm of Pluto. The inhabitants of Kamschatka, he adds, still have a "year" of six months. Later, as Bailly surmises, the migrations would have passed through the latitudes corresponding to the myths of the triply-divided year (79°); of the Phoenix and of Janus (71°); then to that of Osiris and Adonis (68°). Only when they reached the region between 60° and 50°, outside the Arctic circle, does Bailly think that humanity was able to assimilate the observations of its long winter nights and to understand fully the earth's roundness, the obliquity of the ecliptic, and the revolutions of the planets around the zodiac,[16] thus laying the foundations of ancient cosmology.

Temperate climates, according to Bailly, are conducive to science, whereas tropical ones only encourage indolence. Always fleeing before the gradual cooling of the earth, the vigorous migrants eventually came to Chaldea, India, and China. Then their progress halted. Their knowledge was preserved, but without understanding: all that was left was servile tradition. Having said as much, Bailly pulls himself up short, noticing that the age of the earth is not nearly long enough for such a movement to have taken place. Nevertheless, he believes that he has established the existence of "this people, extremely able and enlightened, which was the ancestor of all the peoples of Asia, or at least the source of their knowledge; and of its home in northern Asia, at the 50th or 60th parallel of latitude."[17]

Bailly's history of ancient astronomy is still a valuable source for its subject. Its prestige ensured that the theories of the Arctic homeland and the migration into Central Asia were introduced into the erudite world. The second of these theories, as we will see in the next chapter, had a brilliant career in the nineteenth century. The first, however, was too strange to be generally adopted, and it was over a century before another scholarly study was devoted to the subject.

Warren's Polar Paradise

The Rev. Dr. William F. Warren, President of Boston University and member of several learned societies, restated the theory of the polar origin of mankind in a book of 1885, *Paradise Found.* Its thesis was "That the cradle of the human race, the Eden of primitive tradition, was situated at the North Pole, in a country submerged at the time of the Deluge."[18] Warren tested his hypothesis against the current state of knowledge in all the relevant sciences and in comparative mythology—he was particularly well-versed in German scholarship—and found that it emerged triumphant.

Although there is nothing occult or theosophical about Warren's book, as a Christian and an anti-Darwinian he utterly rejected the image of mankind as evolving from the ape through a state of primitive savagery. The earliest men, in his view, were the noblest and the longest-lived; only after the Deluge and the ensuing Ice Age did they take on the feeble lineaments of ourselves. As for their polar homeland, Warren devotes many pages to showing how mistaken one would be in imagining it as cold, dark, and disagreeable. One well knows (he says) how long the sky is light before dawn and after sunset; well, at the Poles there is likewise twilight while the sun is within 20° beneath the horizon. This means that for two months at each end of its six-month "day" there is still sunlight, even though the sun itself is not showing.[19] Even during the remaining two months, when there is no sunlight at all, the polar region is by no means dark, for in addition to the moon and stars, which by all accounts shine there with unrivalled splendor, there is the almost nightly play of the Aurora Borealis.[20] Warren waxes eloquent on the subject:

> Whoever seeks as a probable location for Paradise the heavenliest spot on earth with respect to light and darkness, and with respect to celestial scenery, must be content to seek it at the Arctic Pole. Here is the true City of the Sun. Here is the one and only spot on earth respecting which it would seem as if the Creator has said, as of His own heavenly residence, "There shall be no night there."[21]

Warren's Golden Age, then, owes nothing to the vertical axis favored by our authorities on Hyperborea. He rejects the idea that the obliquity of the ecliptic has ever changed, but, being a good scholar, he presents the ancient and modern arguments in favor of it. Warren's explanation is that after the survivors of the polar Flood settled in their north Asian exile, they found the skies tilted in respect to the way they had known them: the North Star was no longer overhead. The first exiles understood perfectly why this was so, but "their rude descendants, unfavored with the treasures of antediluvian science, and born only to a savage or nomadic life in their new and inhospitable home, might easily have forgotten the explanation,"[22] and thought that instead of the human horizon, it was the earth itself that had shifted. This resembles Bailly's picture of the withering of knowledge as migration proceeded southwards, but for entirely the opposite reason: for the Frenchman, it was the warm climates of the South that made people soft and indolent, while for the Bostonian, the Pole was pleasant and even warm, while the steppes of Central Asia were cold and unconducive to natural philosophy.

We cannot do justice in this summary to the wealth of evidence Warren summons up to support his theory, nor to his persuasive and engaging argument. But while he believed that he had clinched the matter once and for all, he failed to consider the possibility that the myths and legends of many lands might not be simple records of material history. Later, in Chapter Thirteen, we will learn from Henry Corbin and the theosophers of Iran that a polar "homeland" does not even need to be on earth. The innumerable symbols that Warren takes as referring to his polar Paradise,[23] such as Atlas's Pillar, the Spine of the Earth, the Churning-stick, the Trunk of the Cosmic Tree, the Lance of Alexander, the Irminsul Pillar, the Tower of Kronos, the Spindle of Necessity, and the Seven-runged Ladder of Mithraic initiation, do not require any human being to have set foot in the Arctic regions, but merely to have understood something of cosmology.

Tilak's Arctic Home

Another sort of evidence was marshalled by Bâl Gangâdhar Tilak (1856–1920), famous as a pioneer of Indian independence from British rule around the turn of the century. At an early age, Tilak met the remarkable Sri Govindananda Bharati, known as the Shivapuri Baba (1826–1963),[24] who in the latter's words "taught him some astronomy." It is not known whether this included the essentials of the theory which Tilak published later in his first astronomical work, *Orion, or Researches into the Antiquity of the Vedas* (1893). He showed there that the positions of the heavens mentioned in the Vedas could be dated precisely with reference to the precession of the equinoxes, consequently placing the oldest Vedic period around 4500 BCE, which was much earlier than the British scholars allowed.

In 1897, Tilak was jailed for anti-British writings in the newspaper which he edited, *The Kesari*. Thanks to the influence of the eminent orientalist Max Müller (who, incidentally, had accepted the dedication of Warren's book), the distinguished prisoner was able to spend his sentence profitably in study of the Vedas, and after an early release he wrote a much larger work: *The Arctic Home in the Vedas*, finished in 1898 though not published until 1903.[25] Tilak writes that he hesitated to publish it, having touched therein on so many subjects in which he was not an expert; he bemoaned the fact that in India he did not have the access to the best authorities in every field that a British scholar could take for granted. Moreover, his patron Müller died in 1900. However, Tilak had the advantage over most Europeans of a perfect mastery of the language of the Vedas, and an encyclopedic knowledge of them, and on this he based his work.

Tilak makes two main points in his *Arctic Home*. One concerns the age of Vedic civilization, the other its original location. Here is his summary of the chronology, now much more daring than that of *Orion*:[26]

> circa 10,000 or 8,000 BCE: destruction of original Arctic home by the last Ice Age; commencement of post-glacial period.
>
> 8,000–5,000 BCE: Aditi Period or Krita Yuga, age of wandering. Migration to northern Europe and Asia, ending with pre-Orion Period, with vernal equinox in Purnavasü (Gemini).
>
> 5,000–3,000 BCE: Orion Period, with vernal equinox in the constellation of Orion. Vedic hymns composed. First calendar reform and sacrificial system.
>
> 3,000–1,400 BCE: Krittikä Period, with vernal equinox in the Pleiades (Taurus). Period of the *Taittirîya Samhitâ* and the *Brahmanas*. Traditions of the Arctic home dim and misunderstood; hymns less intelligible.
>
> 1,400–500 BCE: Pre-Buddhistic Period. Sutras and philosophic systems.

Tilak credits William Warren and John Rhys (see Chapter Four) for anticipating his theory. He begins from the well-known fact of warm-weather remains in the Arctic regions, which proves beyond a doubt that their climate was far different during the interglacial periods. He rejects at least six reasons that had been proposed for this in the nineteenth century: (1) the sinking of the Isthmus of Panama, diverting the Gulf Stream; (2) the earth's going through hot and cold regions of space; (3) variations in the heat put out by the sun; (4) alteration in the obliquity of the ecliptic (this, he says, would involve a change in the equatorial bulge, which is not observed to have happened); (5) sudden changes in the distribution of land and water; (6) eccentricity of the earth's orbit.[27] Nevertheless, he says, scientists do concede the existence, in the distant past, of a warm circumpolar continent, and the circumstances there would not have been nearly as unfavorable to human existence as is commonly imagined. He then continues with a description of the polar twilight, the Aurora Borealis, and more, in terms very similar to Warren's.

The ancient Indian texts, as Tilak read them, point unmistakably to a "realm of the gods" where the sun rises and sets once a year, showing at least that their writers could understand the astronomical conditions obtaining at the North Pole.[28] But it is the Vedic hymns to the Dawn that argue most persuasively for actual experience of those regions. The hymns are full of images that make nonsense in the context of a daily sunrise, such as the "Thirty Dawn-Sisters circling like a wheel," and the "Dawn of Many Days" preceding the rising of the sun. If, however, they are applied to the Pole, they fall perfectly into place.[29] The light of the sun circling beneath the horizon would be visible for at least thirty days before its annual rising. One can imagine the sense of anticipation felt by the inhabitants, as the wheeling light became ever brighter and the long winter's night came to an end.

Unlike Warren, Tilak did not think of life at the Pole as having been one of unmitigated delight: the night, though far less than six months long, was not pleasant. The *Rig Veda* speaks of the darkness as sheltering the enemies of Indra: there are prayers that one may safely reach the end of the night whose "other boundary is not seen."[30] A normal night of a few hours hardly answers to such a description. Lastly, Tilak proposes an original interpretation of the Devayâna and the Pitriyâna, traditionally the two alternative paths that the soul may take upon death: the Way of the Gods (*devas*) and the Way of the Ancestors (*pitris*). He says that since the oldest Vedic year, corresponding to polar conditions, had only two divisions, they were given these names and correlated with the Day and Night of the Gods.

In India it is considered inauspicious to die during the Pitriyâna: in the *Mahabharata*, for example, Bhîshma waits on his deathbed until "the sun turns north" after the winter solstice, which now marks the beginning of the Devayâna.[31] But the original Devayâna would have begun at the Spring Equinox, when the sun first appears for its six-month polar "day." Only later, when astronomical circumstances no longer justified it, was the date changed and the Devayanâ revised to correspond to the period of the sun's increase.[32]

Tilak's theory, though of little impact in the West, remained very much alive in India. When the learned Zoroastrian H. S. Spencer wrote his book *The Aryan*

Ecliptic Cycle (1965), which is a development of Tilak's work, he was able to obtain endorsements from Sir Ramaswami Aiyer and Sir S. Radhakrishnan, then President of India, as well as from dignitaries of the Theosophical Society in Adyar and the Sri Aurobindo Ashram in Pondicherry. Spencer goes much further than Tilak in tracing the progress of the Aryans from the North to their new homes, and the schisms that beset them on the way—notably that of the Persian from the Indian stream. His method is to apply Tilak's approach not to the Vedic but to the Zoroastrian scriptures, drawing out from them allusions to successive positions of the sun during the precessional cycle. This enables him to give precise dates for all the events he chronicles, though whether there is any truth behind the smokescreen of his scholarship, I am not competent to say. That Spencer was no conventional scholar is evident from his references to *Oahspe, the Kosmon Bible* (a work "revealed" to an American in 1881), and to séances and visions of his own, which he then found confirmed by study of the sources.

The "Aryan ecliptic cycle" of the title runs from 25,628 BCE to 292 CE, beginning with the residence of the Aryans in their polar homeland during the Inter-glacial Age. Spencer insists that they must have been there long before the earliest dates mentioned by Tilak, in order to have made the religious "progress" evident from the Vedic Hymns. Eventually they were forced to leave their happy home of Aryano-Vej by "the presence of huge reptiles and the advent of intense cold and snow,"[33] as the Ice-Age spread a "glacial flood" around the Pole. This happened around 10,000 BCE, and was just one of the several results of the natural cataclysms of that time, which destroyed three other ancient civilizations in Atlantis, Lemuria, and around the Gobi Sea.[34] The Aryans gradually battled their way against the forces of nature and the indigenous races of Asia, suffering a period of enslavement to the Turanians, until by about 8,500 BCE they were supreme over all their neighbors, ruling from the seat of their empire at Balkh in Bactria.[35]

Spencer's Aryans had worshipped Mazda as supreme god from at least the nineteenth millenium BCE, but only as first among equals; what he calls "full-orbed monotheism" was only achieved after the teaching of Zarathustra (7129–7052 BCE).[36] Only the Persian branch, says this keen Zoroastrian convert, remained true to the faith. The Indian branch, succumbing to native polytheism, had to wait for their conversion until Zarathustra's reincarnation as Krishna in the fourth millenium BCE; the European Aryans, until the return of the same spirit as Jesus. But everywhere the Aryan influence was felt: it moulded the religions and cultures of Egypt, Sumer, Babylon, and of the Semites in both their Hebrew and Arab branches, hitherto worshippers of the Female Aspect of the Godhead. Spencer sums up:

> The most important consequence resulting from these influences is the substitution in the basic religious concept of these non-Aryan races, of the supremacy of the Purusha or Male Concept of God over the Female Concept.

> It is a change which is the inevitable result of the permeation of monotheistic doctrines in their basic religious thought.[37]

We will notice that the masculine religion is one of the hallmarks of the Aryan attitude, as we turn to those who sought to define the race that perhaps made this heroic journey from the North Pole, and to the almost incredible consequences of what might seem little more than the fantasies of a few outdated scholars.

Recent research in geology, while it has nothing to say about human occupation of the Arctic area, at least provides a viable scenario for the events which Tilak and Spencer have envisaged. Two senior geologists, Wallace Broecker and George Denton, showed in 1990 that, while the changes in earth's climate are linked to astronomical cycles (see Chapter Eighteen), their immediate cause is the generation of warm water in the North Atlantic, and its circulation as deep currents around the oceans of the world.[38] This "North Atlantic deep water current," they say, was shut off until the end of the last Ice Age, 14,000 years ago. By 9,000 BCE, the retreat of the glaciers was well under way, and temperatures had risen to interglacial levels. "Suddenly, in as little as 100 years, northern Europe and northeastern North America reverted to glacial conditions."[39]

The probable cause of this little ice age, according to Broecker and Denton, was the overflowing of Lake Agassiz, a prehistoric lake in northern Canada larger than any of the present Great Lakes, that had been emptying southwards into the Gulf of Mexico via the Mississippi River. The retreat of the ice unblocked an alternative, northern outlet, down the Saint Lawrence River, and Lake Agassiz forthwith poured into the North Atlantic. The lake surface fell by forty meters, and its fresh water reduced the salinity of the ocean surface to such a degree that the upper levels no long sank to the bottom. This stopped the "conveyor belt" system of circulating warm water, with the consequent chilling of the whole region. The ensuing period, known as the Younger Dryas (after an Arctic flower), witnessed a cooling of 6° Centigrade, as shown by the Greenland ice cores. About 1000 years later—circa 8,000 BCE—a lobe of ice advanced to block the Saint Lawrence exit again: the system re-started, and the cold spell ended abruptly, in as little as twenty years.

In Broecker's and Denton's work we have a scientific explanation for the "glacial flood" and the minor ice age that are supposed to have forced the polar inhabitants out of their homeland in about 9,000 BCE: the date, more or less, of the fall of Atlantis according to Plato.

Chapter Four:
The Aryan Myth

Bailly's tentative guess at a polar homeland was short-lived, being perhaps too bizarre a concept for any but the esotericists. But the time was ripe for the idea of a wise and heroic race descending from the north, especially for those who considered themselves its progeny. We now trace the fortunes of this "Aryan Race," from its birth from the heads of German philologists.

The prehistory of the Aryans lies in such speculations as we have summarized from French scientists of the Enlightenment: Bailly, Buffon, and also Bailly's Masonic brethren Court de Gébelin (author of *Le Monde Primitif*) and Voltaire. The freethinking authors of the *Encyclopédie* and their kind, keen to dissent from any biblical notions that might favor the Middle East as the site of Eden, welcomed an alternative location of humanity's cradle in Asia.[1] But Voltaire could not believe that the preceptors of humanity could have been the rough "Scythians," a catch-all name for the many peoples inhabiting Central Asia. In a letter to Bailly he cynically observes:

> Nothing has ever come to us from either European or Asiatic Scythia but tigers who have devoured our lambs. True, some of these tigers were amateur astronomers when they had the leisure, after sacking all of northern India; but are we to believe that they set out from their lairs with quadrants and astrolabes?[2]

Voltaire confessed to Bailly that he was convinced that everything—including astronomy, astrology, and metempsychosis—had come to us from the banks of the Ganges.[3]

The Germans who looked across the Rhine for their *Aufklärung* adopted similar views. Immanuel Kant was attracted by Voltaire's idea of Indian origins, but preferred for the birthplace of primitive humanity the higher ground of Tibet. Likewise, Johann Gottfried von Herder (1744–1803), the court preacher at Goethe's Weimar to whom the Bible was but a copy of some legendary "natural revelation," placed the cradle of mankind in the primitive mountains of Asia. In his encyclopedic work on the philosophy of history (1784–91), Herder expressed his disappointment that the present inhabitants of this region, the

Kalmucks, Buriats, and Mongolians, were such poor and ugly specimens of humanity in comparison with the noble Kashmiris and gentle Indians.[4]

There had long been a tendency to place the origin of humanity in mountains. The biblical tradition, of course, had Noah's brood descending from Mount Ararat, and even the scientific adaptors of the Deluge legend admitted that high ground would have been the first to become habitable after a large-scale flood. The primordial origin of humanity, however, remained an enigma for those who rejected biblical authority; scientists like Buffon were content with vague deistical notions, happy to discuss whether humanity was born in one place or in several, but coy about its exact manner of "birth."

Herder's Indophilia had a considerable effect on the German Romantics, several of whom became Oriental scholars in their own right. Nostalgia for the East also made itself felt in two authors who did not much care for India, but admired the Persia of the *Zend-Avesta* and of the Sufi poets: hence Goethe's *West-ostlicher Divan* and Nietzsche's *Also sprach Zarathustra*. Further East, it was Buddhism that inspired the philosophy of Arthur Schopenhauer, and, through him, attracted Richard Wagner. This Orientalism reflected the struggle of the German Romantics, in the words of Léon Poliakov, to free themselves from Judeo-Christian fetters.[5]

But although the Orient and its philosophy might be admired from a distance, something was lacking before Germans could actually identify themselves with it. Simultaneously with their oriental leanings, the Romantics cultivated a new respect for the German *Volk*, its folklore, and its spirituality, reaching back to the pre-Christian Teutonic tribes of whose character and customs Julius Caesar and Tacitus had written with guarded admiration, and to their descendants, the Goths, whose vigor had dealt the death-blow to the decayed Roman Empire. Looking around them with new eyes, the Romantics noticed as if for the first time the greatest art-work of Christendom, the "Gothic" cathedrals, so different from the Classical architecture that they had been brought up to regard as exemplary.

But where had those noble and gifted tribes come from? Were they, too, sons of Noah, or dared one sunder them from the biblical genealogy? The time was ripe to do so. The French Encyclopedists had set the precedent of contempt for the Hebrew scriptures as a source of accurate information. The British School of Calcutta, with their *Asiatic Researches*, had revealed another world, surely more learned, and to many minds philosophically and morally superior to that of Moses. If the Germans could link their origins to India, then they would be forever free from their Semitic and Mediterranean bondage.

Proof of Indian or Himalayan origins was lacking so long as Hebrew was still believed to be the original language of mankind. But the British Sanskritists had done sufficient groundwork to suggest that the languages of classical Europe might have had a wholly different origin, namely the "classical" Hindu language of Sanskrit. Friedrich von Schlegel (1772–1829) was already an established classical scholar when he decided to take the logical step of learning Sanskrit,[6] under the tutelage of the London professor Alexander Hamilton. Thenceforth Schlegel regarded India as the source of all culture and religion, including that of Egypt. He believed that Moses, raised in Egyptian wisdom, could not have been ignorant of the Oriental doctrines, but had refrained from teaching his people those of metempsychosis and the immortality of the soul because of the gross superstitions that had become attached to them.[7] Friedrich's brother, August Wilhelm von Schlegel (1767–1845), though more of a poet and critic than a philosopher, also became a Sanskrit scholar and published in later life editions of the *Bhagavad-Gita* (in Latin) and the *Ramayana*.

Friedrich von Schlegel was prompted to wonder, in his influential book *Über die Sprache und Weisheit der Indier* (On the language and wisdom of the Indians, 1808), how the Indian influence could have reached so far as to mould the languages of Scandinavia. But he recalled that the Indians had a high veneration for the North, and for the wonderful mountain of Meru at the North Pole. The Indian tribes must at some distant time have been driven northwards, not from mere necessity, "but by an almost supernatural idea of the majesty and glory of those regions."[8] Their language and traditions proved that the Indians and the Nordics formed a single race. In 1819 Schlegel provided an alternative name for them: they were all "Aryans." The word had been borrowed from Herodotus' *Arioi* (an early name of the Medes[9]) by Anquetil Duperron, who applied it to the ancient Persians. Now that people, too, could be situated as a link in the human chain that reached from India to Scandinavia. In an epoch-making sally of emotionally-laden etymology, Schlegel connected the word Aryan with *Ehre*, the German word for honor.[10] So the Germans and their ancestors, the ancient Indians, were preeminently the people of honor, the aristocracy of the human race.

Léon Poliakov, author of the fundamental book *The Aryan Myth*, writes of the many philosophers and philologists who contributed to the Indo-Germanic myth in the first half of the nineteenth century: besides those mentioned, he cites Joseph von Görres, Georg Friedrich Creuzer, Friedrich von Schelling, Georg Wilhelm Friedrich Hegel, and Jacob Grimm. Johann Gottfried Rhode, in 1820, was the first to propose Central Asia as the Indo-Germanic homeland, and to extol the teaching of Zoroaster over that of Moses. A still more obscure, but crucial figure was Christian Lassen, a protégé of the Schlegel brothers, who elaborated the myth in his *Indische Altertumskunde* (Ancient teachings of India, 1847) by contrasting the honorable Indo-Germans with the "egotistic and unphilosophical" Semites. His fantasy had all the ingredients of master-race thinking: biological superiority, the triumph of the strongest, an emphasis on youth (hardly appropriate, one would have thought, for a race claiming primordiality!), and the primacy of the White Race.[11]

In the 1850s and 1860s, the great philologist Max Müller, who founded the still unsupplanted series of *Sacred Books of the East*, was urging upon his British readers the use of the term "Aryan" in place of "Indo-Germanic," which seemed to exclude the French, the English, and all the other peoples who could trace the ultimate root of their language to Sanskrit. By about 1860, as Poliakov says, the Aryan-Semitic division was accepted as dogma and formed part of the intellectual baggage of all cultivated Europeans.[12] The dogma was simple enough: (1) Europeans were of the Aryan Race; (2) This race had come from the high plateaus of Asia. There had dwelt together the ancestors of the Indians, Persians, Greeks, Italians, Slavonians, Germans, and Celts, before setting off to populate Europe and Asia. Müller writes in an essay of 1853 that "at the first dawn of traditional history we see these Aryan tribes migrating across the snow of the Himâlaya southward towards the 'Seven Rivers' [...] and ever since India has been called their home."[13] He thought that the purity with which the Hindus had preserved the Aryan language and religion showed that the Aryans who went to India had probably been the last to leave their highland home.

By the time Müller was writing, the ideas of Charles Darwin had conquered the intellectual world, and the "struggle for existence" and "survival of the fittest" were readily applied to the races of humanity. But whereas Darwin's was a basically optimistic philosophy, seeing the best strains predominate over inferior ones, it could be applied in the contrary sense. A signal example of this is Comte Joseph Arthur de Gobineau's *Essai sur l'inégalité des races humaines* (Essay on the inequality of human races, 1853–55), which concluded that the natural superiority of the White Race had been lost by miscegenation, and that only further decline could be expected for it. Of course, one might argue that it was not too late for a "re-purification," and this, as we shall see, would become the case.

Max Müller's influence was felt in France in the 1860s through his friend Ernest Renan, author of the tremendously influential *Vie de Jésus* (Life of Jesus, 1863). It seemed perfectly obvious to Renan that the Aryans were at the top of the human pyramid; the Semites, admirable enough in their own time, had passed them the torch of progress, along with Christianity. In one of his philosophical dialogues, entitled *Rêves* (Dreams, 1876), Renan writes about the history of mankind and its possible future. Humanity's purpose, he says, is to produce great men. He dreams of an "aristocracy of reason, a papacy truly infallible." And what is this new church? It is Science, of course, the tawdry god of nineteenth-century rationialism.

Renan saw a great future opening up for biology. Through selective breeding, he says, nature could be improved and "gods" and "devas" produced. "One can imagine an age when the production of a deva would be evaluated at a certain capital expense, representing difficult and costly work."[14] His eugenic nightmare continues:

> A factory of Ases [Scandinavian heroes], an *Asgaard*, might be reconstituted in the center of Asia. If one dislikes such myths, one should consider how bees and ants breed individuals for certain functions, or how botanists make hybrids. One could concentrate all the nervous energy in the brain [...] It seems that if

> such a solution should be at all realizable on the planet Earth, it is through Germany that it will come."[15]

Grimly prophetic words, as we can see in an era of genetic manipulations!

We will return in Chapters Seven and Eight to this Central Asian "Asgaard" and its enigmatic developments in the minds of the occultists. To these we now turn, and specifically to the compilations of popular science and ancient religion in Blavatsky's *Isis Unveiled* and *The Secret Doctrine*, whose translations into French and German were available by the turn of the century.[16]

Aryanism and Theosophy

Blavatsky wrote in *Isis Unveiled* of a vast inland sea that once existed in Central Asia, north of the Himalayas—the region which "science now fully concedes to have been the cradle of humanity."[17] In that sea was an island, beautiful beyond compare, reached not by water but by underground passages in every direction, of which outlets survive in the ruins of Ellora, Elephanta, and the caverns of Ajanta. This island was the home of the "last remnant of the race which preceded ours," who had a perfect mastery of the environment. These were the "Sons of God," the Elohim of the Bible, the educators of mankind.[18] Blavatsky concurred with Baron Bunsen,[19] who in *Egypt's Place in Universal History* reckoned that the Deluge occurred about 10,000 BCE, and added that this changed the whole face of Central Asia.[20] She implies that it was from this time and place that the Aryans spread and settled in India, the Middle East, and Egypt, whose peoples adapted the Aryan myths and religions according to their lights. One therefore has a vague picture from *Isis Unveiled* of the Aryans as nurtured by superhuman beings on an island in the Gobi Sea, and forced by geological changes to leave their homeland and become the first Brahmins.

The truth about the races of mankind "had to be concealed at that incipient tentative stage of the Theosophical Society"[21] represented by *Isis Unveiled*. In 1882 it was ready to be revealed by the Masters Koot Hoomi and Morya, in their correspondence with A. P. Sinnett and A. O. Hume known as the *Mahatma Letters*. The nature and origin of these letters remain enigmatic, much as the skeptics have tried to slough them off as another of Blavatsky's deceptions. Koot Hoomi wrote to Sinnett in June 1882 that "most of the peoples of India—with the exception of the *semitic* Moguls—belong to the oldest branchlet of the present *fifth* Human race, which was evoluted in Central Asia more than one million of years ago."[22]

In October of the same year, Koot Hoomi wrote the longest of his letters to Sinnett—over thirty pages in print—and specified further about this "branchlet":

> [...] the highest people now on earth (spiritually) belong to the first sub-race of the fifth *root* Race, and those are the Aryan Asiatics; the highest race (physical intellectuality) is the last sub-race of the fifth—yourselves the white conquerors. The majority of mankind belongs to the seventh *sub*-race of the fourth *Root*

> *race*—the above-mentioned Chinamen and their off-shoots and branchlets (Malayans, Mongolians, Tibetans, Javanese, etc., etc., etc.) and remnants of other sub-races of the fourth—and the seventh sub-race of the third race. All these, fallen degraded semblances of humanity are the direct lineal descendants of highly civilized nations neither the name nor memory of which have survived except in such books as *Popalvul* and a few others unknown to Science.[23]

The study of the Theosophical system of Rounds, Root Races, and Sub-races is a recreation reserved for the few. But here, in Koot Hoomi's statement, we have one of the most important elements of it. In Chapter Two we reviewed Blavatsky's system of the seven Root-Races of humanity: (1) [Invisible], (2) Hyperborean, (3) Lemurian, (4) Atlantean, (5) our present one, and (6,7) two others still to come. Each of these is subdivided into seven "sub-races." Following the principles enunciated in the *Mahatma Letters*, Blavatsky in *The Secret Doctrine* attributes the present-day Black Africans, Dravidian Indians, and Australian Aborigines to the Lemurian Root-Race ("the seventh sub-race of the third race" in the above quotation); the Yellow peoples of Asia and the Native North and South Americans to the Atlantean Root-Race ("the seventh sub-race of the fourth Root race"); and the Indians, Persians, Middle-Easterners, and Europeans to the various sub-races of the Fifth Root-Race, which had its beginnings a million years ago in Central Asia.

It would be futile to argue about whether such a doctrine is "racist" in the present-day usage of the term. Modern Theosophists pointedly avoid the subject, being among the least racially prejudiced of people and mindful of the original objects of the Theosophical Society, first and foremost of which is "Universal Brotherhood." Once in India, Madame Blavatsky and Colonel Olcott scandalized the impeccably racist British community by fraternizing with, even sitting at the feet of, Indians and Sinhalese. But they were still children of their time, and it was a time when the racial explanation had become so firmly fixed in the European and American consciousness as to be virtually ineradicable. To regard human history in terms of great racial movements accorded well with Darwinism, and provided answers to innumerable questions posed by the sciences and very inadequately answered by the Hebrew Bible. The nineteenth century, moreover, believed in progress, and in the White Race as the acme of human achievement in science, the arts, and philosophy. The Victorians had only to look around them to convince themselves of how much further they had "progressed" than the poor colored races whom they were busy colonizing!

The originality of the Theosophists was to administer a snub to Western complacency by pointing out that civilizations in the distant past had achieved as much, and more, in technology, while being infinitely superior to ours in wisdom. But those ancient races were out of reach: one could learn about them only from Masters and their pupils, who either possessed secret histories given in initiation, or else were able to penetrate the veils of the past through clairvoyance.

The unoriginality of the Theosophists was to place themselves and their Indian allies—Aryans all—at the vanguard of humanity, in an alliance of the highest spirituality with the highest "physical intellectuality" (which simply means technology), while classing the Black, Yellow, and Red races as laggards who had passed their zenith hundreds of thousands of years ago—though they are seldom as harsh as Koot Hoomi, in the above quotation, which was included in Sinnett's *Esoteric Buddhism* (1883). Another early leak of the Theosophical racial system, before Blavatsky gave it its definitive form in *The Secret Doctrine*, was in *Man: Fragments of Forgotten History*, by "Two Chelas" (1885), which contains such remarks as the following:

> Physically the Aryan of the period with which we are dealing was superior to his present representative. His body was free from disease, and not subject to untimely death; while the natural term of his life was a great deal longer than it is now. The complexion of the early Indian Aryans was not like that of the present generation of Hindus—various shades of brown—but almost pure white, with a slight tinge of gold. Taken altogether, the epoch which witnessed their rise and development will stand for all ages as the most remarkable era known in the history of the world.[24]

One wonders what psychological and sexual complications lay behind the need for these authors—a young English woman and a young Indian man—to color their Aryans white.

The Many Homes of the Aryans

By the time *The Secret Doctrine* was published in 1888, scientific opinion was already shifting on the matter of Aryan origins. So many and various were the theories proposed that we show them on a map. Some scholars were even returning to the idea of a homeland in the Euphrates Valley, near the traditional site of the Garden of Eden.[25] In 1883 two books were published which turned the whole theory of Aryan migration backwards, placing its origins in Europe. Karl Penka's *Origines Ariacae* argued on anthropological grounds for a Scandinavian homeland. "The pure Aryans," he maintains, "are represented only by the North Germans and Scandinavians, a most prolific race, of great stature, muscular strength, energy, and courage, whose splendid natural endowments enabled it to conquer the feebler races to the East, the South, and the West, and to impose its language on the subject peoples."[26] Otto Schrader, in *Sprachvergleichung und Urgeschichte*, arguing from philology, proved that the Aryans must have come from what is now the Ukraine, in an area bounded by the forests and swamps of Volhyria to the North, the Danube and the Black Sea to the South, the Dnieper to the East, and the Carpathian Mountains to the West.[27]

Learned as they were, these German professors had very likely not read the *Histoire philosophique* of Fabre d'Olivet, whose theories of cataclysmic change will be described in Chapter Fourteen. If they had, they would have found that

Illustration 2: The Many Homes of the Aryans

lonely pioneer already identifying the Hyperboreans with the ancestors of the White Race, whose origins he placed at the Boreal Pole, and having them migrate southwards into Europe.[28] As Fabre d'Olivet tells it, at the time of the arrival of the Whites, the Black Race was much stronger, and the Whites were enslaved by them. Later the tables were turned, and the white, boreal "Celts" became the dominant race of Europe. Their spiritual leader Rama took their doctrines to India, and there, in about 6729 BCE, he founded the Universal Empire of prehistoric times.[29] This version of the great racial movements was also adopted in the *Mission des Juifs* (Mission of the Jews, 1884) of Saint-Yves d'Alveydre,[30] who in turn had probably not read the German professors since virtually the only book he quotes from is Sinnett's *Esoteric Buddhism*. Still, one notes the synchronicity of the idea's appearance in 1883–84 in such very different contexts.

The Germans soon found a following in the English-speaking world. John Rhys, in the 1886 Hibbert Lectures, suggested that the Aryans might have originated within the Arctic Circle, somewhere to the north of Finland.[31] Gerald H. Rendall, a Liverpool professor, identified the Aryans in 1889 as the "blond dolichocephalic race that was cradled on the Baltic shores."[32] He imagined that they had suddenly picked up and left, after 10,000 years of settlement whose mute witnesses are the massive "kitchen middens" of the southeastern Scandinavian coasts. They had become dolmen builders, leaving monuments to mark their trail through France, Spain, and North Africa to the very shores of the Nile.

Charles Morris, another classicist, wrote in 1888 that "The Aryan stands as the type of intellectual man, the central outcome of the races, in which the special conditions of dark and light, North and South, emotional and practical, have mingled and combined into the highest and noblest states of mind and body."[33] Basing his argument on the words which are the same in both the Indian and European groups of languages, Morris identifies the parent Aryans as a people who occupied a cold region; lived near a large inland body of water; were agriculturalists; and knew the fauna and flora of Europe, but not the lions and tigers of India. His deduction is that they lived first as nomads in southeastern Russia, then in the Caucasus where they somehow acquired their fair complexion, formed their language, learned agriculture, and developed their political and religious systems.[34]

Despite the mounting pressure of evidence, the aging Max Müller still held out for an Oriental Aryan homeland; but in 1887 he could only say that it was "somewhere in Asia, and no more."[35] Isaac Taylor, writing in the following year, was virulently opposed to Müller and the Orientalists, nor did he accept the Scandinavian or Russian hypotheses. He felt that the difficulties of Aryan origins were removed if one assumed that their lineal descendants were the "Celtic race of Central Europe."[36] And so the arguments continued.

No serious scholar now writes about the "Aryan Race." In tracing its origins to so many different places, the nineteenth-century theorists succeeded in destroying it as an entity. Only in the German-speaking world did it live on, with consequences that would have appalled everyone mentioned in the present chapter.

Chapter Five:
The Thule Society

We come now to the mythology that has grown up around the Arctic homeland in the twentieth century, fed by the dual currents of esotericism and scientific theory. In order to distinguish this essentially racial concept from that of Hyperborea, the primordial center of humanity as defined in Chapter One, I will call it by the name of Thule.

Our voyage to the mythical land of Thule departs, appropriately enough, from Atlantis, queen of all the lost realms. For centuries, mainly on the authority of Plato, Atlantis was believed to have risen in the middle of what is now the Atlantic Ocean. It was Olaus Rudbeck, in the late seventeenth century, who first dissented from this common view, and identified the lost domain with his native Sweden. Rudbeck's assiduous reader Jean-Sylvain Bailly, after writing the history of ancient astronomy from which we quoted in Chapter Three, had a correspondence with Voltaire in which he persuaded himself,[1] if not his correspondent, that Atlantis had indeed been in the far North, probably on the islands of Spitzbergen, Greenland, and Nova Zemlya. When the earth was younger, Bailly says, its interior heat was greater, and life in the Arctic may well have been more tolerable than elsewhere; besides, the earth's movement being less rapid near the poles, the atmosphere was probably less turbid, and so the legend of a perpetual spring may well have been true.[2] Bailly's "Atlanteans" were thus the same as the "Hyperboreans" of classical legend,[3] having originated in the "Garden of the Hesperides" near the Pole, and left evidence of their once happy climate in the fossil flora and fauna of the Arctic Circle.[4]

The oceanographic explorations of the nineteenth century and the laying of transatlantic telegraph cables from 1858 onwards failed to produce any evidence for a lost continent having existed in the mid-Atlantic Ocean at any time within reasonable human memory. Perhaps this is one reason why those still drawn to Plato's legend leaned towards the idea of an Atlantis in the far North. Could it have been the same as the mysterious land of Thule, first charted by Pytheas of Massilia? (We will meet him again in Chapter Fifteen, measuring the obliquity of the ecliptic.) At some time between 340 and 285 BCE, Pytheas made an adventurous voyage to the North, which took him to Scotland and for six days' sailing beyond. He observed that the longest day in northern Britain was nineteen hours, which shows that he must have reached the North Shetland Islands. His additional trip to "Thule" is less easily mapped: it may have been to Iceland, or else in the opposite direction, to Norway. In any case, Pytheas reported that one day north of Thule, he reached a frozen sea.[5]

Classical writers tended to disbelieve Pytheas because of their own ignorance of the geography and conditions of the North.[6] Tacitus, for example, could scarcely believe that people would live, from choice, in the rigorous climate of Germany.[7] Yet there was a persistent tradition of a warm and open polar sea, and of a clement and habitable Hyperborean climate with warm summers: a tradition which, as the Arctic expert Vilhjalmur Stefansson says, has always been believed by explorers, and always doubted by stay-at-home experts.[8] Christopher Columbus himself knew of such traditions, and claimed to have sailed three hundred miles north of Iceland, which very few people were willing to credit, the northern zone being deemed impenetrable.[9] For centuries after, the history of Arctic exploration is the chronicle of Columbus' successors in the search for a westward passage to the Orient.

What concerns us in this chapter is the Thulean revival of the nineteenth and twentieth centuries, and the manner of its adoption into National Socialist mythology. The meticulous groundwork of Nicholas Goodrick-Clarke's *The Occult Roots of Nazism* (1985) allows us to summarize the story, while adding some details of our own.

The ideology of the Nazis connected the myth of polar origins and Aryan supremacy with that of the German race, to whom the Roman historian Tacitus had given every reason to believe themselves especially favored:

> I concur in opinion with those who deem the Germans never to have intermarried with other nations; but to be a race pure, unmixed, and stamped with a distinct character. Hence a family likeness pervades the whole, though their numbers are so great: eyes stern and blue; ruddy hair; large bodies...[10]

But for all their admiration of the tall, blond-haired, blue-eyed, Nordic Aryans, most of the Nazi leaders—and, conspicuously, Adolf Hitler himself—were of the darker, shorter physique typical of Alpine and Central Europe. The Nordic physique was seen as the ultimate aristocratic ideal, as the result of a hundred years of science and pseudo-science which had begun and ended by placing the cradle of the master-race in the far North.

The three godfathers of the Nazi Thule were Guido von List (1848–1919), Jörg Lanz von Liebenfels (1874–1954), and Rudolf von Sebottendorff (1875–1945). It is significant that all three decided at some point to adorn their plain bourgeois names with the particle *von* (which in German suggests noble descent even when it is not further defined by *Graf*, *Baron*, etc.). One of the hallmarks of master-race philosophy is that no one is known to have embraced it who does not consider himself a member of that race. And what is more tempting, having once adopted the belief that one's own race is chosen by Nature or God for preeminence, than to put oneself at its aristocratic summit?

The Viennese Jörg Lanz, a former religious of the Cistercian Order, was the founder in 1907 of the "Order of the New Templars" (ONT), a chivalric, gnostic, and ritualistic order with the most extreme of racist ideals.[11] There can be little doubt that the ONT, with its lodges in ruined castles, was the prototype for Heinrich Himmler's *Schützstaffel* (the notorious "SS"), as it was transformed after 1930 to become the training- and breeding-ground for the masters of a New Age of Aryan supremacy. Lanz was a very copious writer on biblical exegesis, astrology, antifeminism, and many other topics. One of his earliest creations, in about 1900, was Theozoology: a new "science" inspired by H. P. Blavatsky's *Secret Doctrine*.

Blavatsky had explained the origin of the anthropoid apes,[12] not as remnants of the ancestors of mankind, but as the descendants of bestiality committed by the Third Race (Lemurians) with monstrous animals. Lanz applied this principle in the most perverted way: the non-Aryan races, he said, were the result of bestiality on the part of the ancient Aryans, after their departure from the northern Garden of Eden. To deal with these peoples, thus regarded as only semi-human, Lanz recommended variously: enforced sterilization and castration; deportation to Madagascar; enslavement; incineration as a sacrifice to God; and use as beasts of burden. As Goodrick-Clarke comments, "Both the psychopathology of the Nazi holocaust and the subjugation of non-Aryans in the East were presaged by Lanz's grim speculations."[13]

It is no surprise that Lanz had a theory about the original homeland of the Aryans: it was a vanished polar continent called Arktogäa (from the Greek: "northern earth").[14] This was adopted by his older acquaintance Guido von List, another Viennese mythomaniac who, more than anyone else, laid the foundations for the romantic blend of ideas that links these proto-Nazis uncannily with the Greens and New-Agers of today: an interest in natural living, vegetarianism, anti-industrialism; an appreciation of prehistoric monuments and the wisdom of those who built them; a feeling for astrology, earth energies, and natural cycles; a religious outlook vaguely resembling that of Theosophy. The generic name given to this kind of thinking was *völkisch*, an untranslatable word on the borderlines between nationalistic and folkloric.

Around 1910, according to Goodrick-Clarke, some activists of these persuasions began to hatch the idea of a secret quasi-masonic lodge, to counter the "Jewish conspiracy" in which they had come to believe.[15] The chief result of this underground movement was the *Germanenorden* ("Order of Germans"), founded in 1912 and soon operating lodges in many cities. Applicants were examined for their racial characteristics and ancestors, while handicapped and "unpleasant looking" persons were excluded.

More information comes from Jean Mabire, a prolific writer on Germany and an enthusiast for Thulean ideals. He is too biased to be a wholly reliable witness, but one is sometimes obliged, in these studies, to make use of such sources, under all reservations. Mabire quotes a specialist in the history of ideas, living in

Göttingen, whose identity it is impossible to confirm. This man reportedly opened his dossiers to him, from which it was possible to reconstruct an important conference that the Germanenorden held at Pentecost, 1914, in the small town of Thale [!] in the Harz Mountains.[16] The purpose of the meeting was to unite all the disparate groups of *völkisch*, pangermanic, and anti-Judaic persuasions which acknowledged the Nordic heritage and the myth of Thule. The historian told Mabire that out of this Pentecost conference was born a *Geheimbund* ("secret band"), whose mission was to revive the true Nordic tradition and coordinate all the efforts of the *völkisch* groups towards it. Mabire comments on how irrelevant it might have seemed, at this Pentecost meeting, to be earnestly discussing Hyperborea and Thule while all the countries of Europe were massing for war. Yet it is here that he situates the essential beginnings of the movement that was to arise from the ashes of Germany after 1918.

There is no doubt that the Germanenorden was still active during the war. From the middle of 1916, its newsletter displayed a curved-armed swastika superimposed on a cross,[17] and it placed advertisements in newspapers inviting "fair-haired and blue-eyed German men and women of pure Aryan descent" to join it.[18] One of these advertisements came to the notice of Rudolf von Sebottendorff, and he decided to contact its leader, Hermann Pohl.[19] The Saxon-born Sebottendorff had had a genuinely adventurous career, much of it spent in Turkey where he had studied Islamic mysticism, apparently reconciling it with his Aryan ideals;[20] he called himself a Rosicrucian, a Muslim Brother, and an Odinist,[21] and he had somehow acquired a fortune through manufacturing. Mabire's historian makes Sebottendorff the one who defined the ultimate goal of the Germanenorden: the creation of a spiritual community which he called *Halgadom*. These are his words, of which the opening sentence is worth remembering as we proceed through the coming chapters:

> This temple of *Halgadom* is simultaneously spiritual and material. It belongs to earth and to heaven, to the past and the future. It is the Hyperborean equivalent of the Ark of the Covenant of the Israelites. *Halgadom*, in Sebottendorff's mind, far surpasses that Second Reich which Wilhelm's Germany had incarnated since 1871. It is the empire of all the Germans. Those who live between the Rhine and the Vistula, between the Baltic and the Alps, are only the heart of an immense territory inhabited by other heirs of ancient Thule. To this *Halgadom* belong not only the Germans, but also many other Europeans: the Scandinavians, faithful to their Nordic origins; the Netherlanders, more German than the Germans; the British, divided between Celts and Saxons; the French, heirs of the Franks and regenerated by the Normans or the Burgundians; the Italians, in whose veins runs the blood of the Lombards; the Spaniards, who still carry many an imprint of the Visigoths. And also the Russians, whose country was founded by the Swedish Varegs, those Vikings of the rivers and steppes.[22]

Towards the end of World War I, when German defeat was inevitable, Rudolf von Sebottendorff was in Munich, busily organizing a Bavarian branch of the Germanenorden. His colleague Walter Nauhaus, an artist invalided out of the war and given to occult study, suggested a new name for the order: the Thule Gesellschaft ("Thule Society"), whose ceremonial foundation duly took place on 17 August 1918. Its emblem was a dagger, its blade wreathed in oak leaves, with a curved-armed swastika around the hilt emitting rays of light. At the very eve of the Armistice, on 9 November 1918, Sebottendorff exhorted the Thuleans to fight for Germanic and Aryan ideals, not against the British or French victors, but against "our deadly enemy, Judah"; to fight "until the swastika rises victoriously out of the icy darkness."[23] In his important historical study of Nazi origins, *Bevor Hitler kam* (Before Hitler came, 1964), Dietrich Bronder gives the names of sixteen members of the Thule Society: "Most of these Thule men," he says, "had become Catholics; seven had Jewish origins or relations."[24]

The Thule Society, which met at the Hotel Vierjahreszeiten in Munich, was a hotbed of political agitation, carried on under the presiding myth of the Arctic homeland and the pure race that had issued therefrom. When seven of its members, including Nauhaus, the Countess Hella von Westarp, and the Prince of Thurn und Taxis, were brutally executed by Communist rebels on 30 April 1919, the society's status grew commensurably. While the Thule membership was predominantly upper- and middle-class, Sebottendorff also reached out to the working classes through popular journalism, forming a subgroup within the National Socialist Party (NSP) of Anton Drexler, which on 5 January 1919 became the German Workers' Party (DAP). This, in turn, was transformed at the end of February 1920 into the National Socialist German Workers' Party (NSDAP), of which Adolf Hitler would soon become the President. All three groups used the swastika as their emblem.[25]

The Swastika in Russia

The swastika has been forever sullied: it can never be used again without arousing memories of the most uncomfortable kind. Originally it was an elegant and decorative symbol, capable of infinite variation and embodying profound meanings that we will explore in Chapter Eleven. Besides its adoption as the special sun-sign of the Aryan Race by German anti-Judaic groups in the late nineteenth century, it also played a strange part in linking the events in Germany with the no less momentous ones in Russia.

Alexandra, the last Empress of Russia, inscribed the left-handed swastika (see Chapter Eleven for definition), with the date 1918, on the wall of the house in Ekaterinburg where she and her family were murdered by the Bolsheviks.[26] Henry Rollin, in his study of modern antijudaism, *L'Apocalypse de notre temps* (1939), offers several possible explanations: (1) the Empress had adopted the swastika as her talisman as the result of Theosophical contacts in her native Darmstadt or in Russia; (2) she had received it from her physician Badmaieff, a practioner of Tibetan medicine; (3) she had seen it on holiday in the Baltic, where the peasants use it to decorate their houses; (4) she could have got it from one of the gypsies summoned to the imperial court for fortune-telling.[27]

However, the swastika served the Empress not merely as a talisman, but also as a secret sign of recognition in her correspondence.[28] It was used, too, by a group of Russian monarchists who had taken refuge in Kiev and were collaborating with the German occupiers of the Ukraine; their plots for rescuing the Imperial Family were one of the reasons that the latter were removed to Ekaterinburg.

Upon the defeat of Germany and the triumph of the Bolsheviks, a number of these Germanophilic Russians—several of them of Baltic origin—gravitated to the entourage of General Ludendorff, protector of Hitler. Among them was Lieutenant Chabelski-Bork, who had been at Ekaterinburg at the moment of discovery not only of the Empress' swastika, but also, in the pathetic handful of possessions left behind, her copy of Serge Nilus' *The Great in the Small*: the work that contained the infamous forged "Protocols of the Elders of Sion."[29] So here was "proof," for those eager for it, that the Imperial Family had fallen victim not merely to the Communists but to the great Jewish conspiracy described in the "Protocols," of whom the Bolsheviks were agents.

Chabelski-Bork would be instrumental in distributing the "Protocols" outside Russia; in Germany, their publication was exactly what was needed to fan to a flame the smouldering antijudaism kindled by the Aryan theorists. In 1919, the swastika served as flag for the Baltic uprising against the Bolsheviks, led by General von der Goltz. In Berlin, the following year, it flew over the abortive Kapp Putsch. In the summer of 1920, Hitler chose the right-handed swastika as the symbol of his dual struggle against Jewry and Communism.[30] And the rest, as they say, is history.[31]

The Occult Roots of Nazism

Adolf Hitler had ample opportunity to learn the Thulean mythology in 1924, during his imprisonment in Landsberg jail with Rudolf Hess (1894–1987), who was the most committed of the early Nazis to the kind of ideals that List, Lanz, and Sebottendorff were propagating. Hess was as *völkisch* as could be: he ate biodynamic food and was interested in Rudolf Steiner's Anthroposophy, magical topics, astrology, the doctrine of correspondences, and herbalism.[32] One would know much more about the political and even the occult machinations of this period, so integral to an understanding of the twentieth-century's greatest tragedy, if Hess had been encouraged to speak instead of being held incommunicado in Spandau prison for over 40 years.

The first book to present the many connections, real and imagined, between the Nazis and the occult was *The Morning of the Magicians* by Louis Pauwels and Jacques Bergier, first published in France in 1960. Many were the eager readers who first met there the names of Guénon and Gurdjieff, Haushofer and Hörbiger, and fell under the powerful spell cast by these ingenious authors. A number of those readers went on to write books of their own, more or less pillaged from the original. Most of them were French; and it is true to this day that the "Nazis and the Occult" genre is most avidly cultivated in France, while in Germany it is virtually shunned. There are good reasons for this. A German scholar and churchman, Ekkehard Hieronimus, writing about the nostalgic dream of primordial cultures, explains:

> It has always fascinated me to see how everything that was actually created by the Germans in the Romantic era was not taken seriously by them, but wandered off into France or Italy. The most important book about the "black" or demonic side of Romanticism was the work of the Italian, Mario Praz [reference to *The Romantic Agony*]. The significant thing to realize in all of this is that the Frenchman's relationship to thought is very different from the German's. I would not dare to enter the lofty reaches of categorical thought: that would raise the theme [of primordial cultures] to an abstract level, which is exactly what I wanted to avoid. Everything would then end up in philosophy again—but we no longer have this possibility. I am sorry, but behind us lies all the blood that has been shed in the name of this dream, and that is deadly serious.[33]

In other words, the Latins still play innocently with abstract ideas, even demonic ones, whereas the Germans have become wise—after the event—to the dangers of so doing.

Readers of Pauwels and Bergier will have come across another, more secret society supposed to lie at the roots of Nazism: the Vril Society, apparently founded by a group of Berlin Rosicrucians after hearing a lecture by Louis Jacolliot,[34] or else directly illuminated by the Brahmins of India,[35] and in any case fiercely anti-Christian.[36] The sole primary source is an article by Willy Ley, a German rocket engineer who came to the United States in 1933 and became an author of popular scientific books—excellent ones, I might add. In an article called "Pseudoscience in Naziland," based on his own admittedly limited knowledge, Ley writes:

> The next group [after Lanz's Ariosophy] was literally founded upon a novel. That group which I think called itself *Wahrheitsgesellschaft*—Society for Truth—and which was more or less localized in Berlin, devoted its spare time looking for *Vril*. Yes, their convictions were founded upon Bulwer-Lytton's "The Coming Race." They knew that the book was fiction, Bulwer-Lytton had used that device in order to be able to tell the truth about this "power." The subterranean humanity was nonsense, *Vril* was not. Possibly it had enabled the British, who kept it as a State secret, to amass their colonial empire. Surely the Romans had had it, inclosed in small metal balls, which guarded their homes and were referred to as *lares*. For reasons which I failed to penetrate, the secret of *Vril* could be found by contemplating the structure of an apple, sliced in halves.
>
> No, I am not joking, that is what I was told with great solemnity and secrecy. Such a group actually existed, they even got out the first issue of a magazine which was to proclaim their credo.[37]

Pauwels and Bergier, who had apparently talked to Willy Ley but learned no more from him than he wrote here, continued their researches and discovered—how, they do not say—that "this Berlin group called itself *The Luminous Lodge*, or *The Vril Society*."[38] They add that Karl Haushofer had been a member of it, citing Jack Fishman's *The Seven Men of Spandau* (where there is no such information). Haushofer had been in the Far East and possibly in Tibet; he was the mentor of Rudolf Hess at the University of Munich; the inventor of the science of Geopolitics, one of the established doctrines of Nazi academia, and hence the designer (according to one interpretation of his work) of the Germano-Japanese plan for world-domination. Hess was carrying the visiting-cards of Haushofer and his son Albrecht when he landed in Scotland in 1941. Albrecht was executed as one of the plotters against Hitler's life in 1944, and, according to Pauwels and Bergier, Karl Haushofer himself committed suicide, Japanese fashion, on 14 March 1946.[39] His supposed membership of the "Vril Society" completed the mythical network by connecting the Nazis with the underground world of Lytton's *Coming Race*, and with the mysteries of Asia, of which we will have more to say when we come to the subject of Agartha in Chapter Seven; and the ritual *hara-kiri* bore unmistakable witness to a deep spiritual connection with the Far East, elaborated by the rumors of a Tibetan colony in wartime Berlin.

Actually, there is no cause to imagine sinister proto-Nazi plots hatching in this group. The exercise of contemplating an apple, presumably cut in half horizontally to reveal a five-pointed star, merely suggests that the "Truth Society" had learned something from Rudolf Steiner, who recommends similar meditations in his handbook *Knowledge of Higher Worlds and Its Attainment*. The interest in Vril was a commonplace among Theosophists, all of whom knew of Bulwer-Lytton's work; it was equated by some to Reichenbach's "Od" force, or to Eliphas Levi's "Astral Light." And to set the record straight, it should be mentioned that Haushofer did not die "Japanese fashion" but from arsenic poisoning on 10 March 1946, as has been documented by his interrogator, Father Edmund Walsh.[40]

The Veilleurs

At the same time as Rudolf Hess was studying with Karl Haushofer, an Alsatian chemist called René Schwaller (1887–1961) was organizing some of his Theosophical friends in Paris into a group with the motto "Hierarchy, Fraternity, Liberty." Its first public appearance, in 1919, was with a review, *L'Affranchi*, numbered so as to seem like a continuation of the Theosophical Society's magazine of prewar days.[41] The articles, signed by pseudonyms, treated the themes of social and spiritual renewal in the context of internationalist and somewhat mystical politics. There was praise for Woodrow Wilson's League of Nations, and discreet allusions were made to a coming Messiah.

Within the Affranchis were two inner circles: one a "Centre Apostolique," Theosophical in nature; the other, formed in 1918, called the "Mystic Group *Tala*," a word that René Guénon translates as "the link." We know nothing of its activities, but can scarcely pass over the similarity of the name with Thule—and Thale. Another coincidence: in his very first book, *Les Nombres* (1916), Schwaller had discussed just one symbol, beside the numbers and basic geometrical figures: the swastika, which he calls an accentuation of the cross within a circle, representing the archetypal formative movement of any body around its axis.[42] There are other parallels between Schwaller's group, renamed in July 1919 "Les Veilleurs" (the Vigilants), and the Thule-descended parties organized by Hess and eventually headed by Hitler: their warrior mentality, their antijudaism,[43] their uniform of dark shirts, riding breeches and boots (which Schwaller claimed to have designed),[44] their messianism, and the title of *Chef* given to their leaders.[45] Then there is Schwaller's chosen name "Aor" (Light), first signifying a mystic source of illumination, later his preferred mode of address. A euphonic relationship, at the very least, exists with the rune "Ar" which, in Sebottendorff's words, "signifies Aryan, primal fire, the sun and the eagle."[46] Finally, one might ask why it was that Prince Matila Ghyka should have had a conversation on Egyptian mathematics with a certain "Pytheas," who "speaks for Monsieur de Lubicz,"[47] if it was not that the yacht-sailing Schwaller identified himself with the legendary voyager to Thule.

It was Pierre Mariel (alias Werner Gerson), yet another French writer with a fund of unusual information but a sometimes careless way with sources, who proposed the vital link between the ambitious chemist and the future Reichsminister: he wrote that the young Rudolf Hess was a member of the Veilleurs.[48] I cannot be sure whether to believe this or not; but it is worth considering. Hess, whose movements in 1919 are virtually uncharted, was certainly aware of what was going on in Paris. The difference of language would have presented no difficulty either to Schwaller or to the young Hess, raised in Alexandria and educated in Switzerland. It is thinkable that, on his return to Germany, Hess set himself to create, upon the foundations of the Thule Society, a veritable parody of the Veilleurs. Likewise it is not merely thinkable but definite that Schwaller's world of ideas intersected at many points with that of Thule: a circumstance that has troubled more than one admirer of this Hermetic master.[49]

Another member of the Affranchis and Veilleurs was Schwaller's friend, the Lithuanian poet and Hermetic philosopher Oscar Vladislas de Lubicz Milosz (1877–1939), who in a gesture of spiritual fatherhood bestowed his patronymic on the younger man. As a representative of the newly-created state of Lithuania to the 1919 Peace Conference, and later as Chargé d'Affaires in Paris and Brussels, Milosz worked hard for the nation whose language he could not speak, and to which he only half belonged (his mother was Jewish).[50] Milosz wrote much around this time for another journal of the Veilleurs group, *La Revue Baltique*, having convinced himself that Lithuania and Latvia were "the mothers of this Indo-European race, the spiritual center of the modern Aryan world,"[51] and the key to European peace. So again we have the myth of Aryan origins on the "Amber Coast" of the Baltic Sea. Milosz's cry in the wilderness of 1918 has a strangely prophetic ring, now that we have seen these insignificant republics spearheading the breakup of the Soviet Union. Later, in 1927, Milosz would write of the Indo-Europeans that "they had, for thousands of years, led a nomadic existence on the steppes of mysterious southern Russia, a land which in the night of prehistory seems to have influenced decisively the destiny of the Aryan race." [52]

The Myth of the Twentieth Century

The Aryan homeland theory, almost discarded in the English-speaking world, was still flourishing in Germany after World War I. Herman Wirth gave it a fresh and definitive form in his enormous work, *Der Aufgang der Menschheit* (The rise of mankind, 1928), largely based on the comparison of runic and other symbols from all the northern regions. Wirth had found in the geological work of Alfred Wegener the physical justification for believing in the Nordic and Iranian myths, and in the polar origin of the northern peoples. What had made the Arctic regions uninhabitable since those times was not the cooling of the earth, as Bailly thought—that was now untenable—but the shifting of continents and the wandering of the poles. Wirth's Arctic Race had separated from the apes some millions of years ago, then about half a million years ago had begun its southward wanderings, moving in reponse to the various ice ages. Pockets of comparatively high culture had remained all round the Arctic Ocean, until the fall of Atlantis in about 9000 BCE; remnants of them survive in the blond, bearded Eskimos found by the Danish "Thule Expedition" of Knud Rasmussen (1906–07).[53]

Wirth's theories made him an obvious candidate for the *Ahnenerbe*, the academy of revisionist science founded by the SS chief Heinrich Himmler. But he fell victim to Himmler's rivalry with Alfred Rosenberg, the chief mythographer of the Third Reich, and, according to Miguel Serrano, narrowly escaped ending his days in a concentration camp. Wirth's ideological crime may have been his matriarchal conception of the ancient Aryans: he imagines them in an ideal state, governed by a Magna Mater ("Great Mother").[54]

Alfred Rosenberg (1893–1945) was the author of *Der Mythus des 20. Jahrhunderts* (The myth of the twentieth century, 1930).[55] Coming from obscure ancestors in the Baltic region, he began humbly enough as an Estonian architectural student who, like Hitler, supported himself in hard times as a watercolorist. After World War I he ended up in Munich, where he quickly made contact with Thulean circles. Rosenberg's *Mythus* was second only to *Mein Kampf* as a non-fictional best-seller in Nazi Germany, its sales reaching over a million copies by 1944.[56] Those who felt obliged to buy this stout work of pseudo-scholarship, but could not struggle past the first chapter, would at least have read the following passage which neatly summarizes the myth which we have been tracing:

> The geologists show us a continent between North America and Europe, whose remains we can see today in Greenland and Iceland. They tell us that

> islands on the other side of the Far North (Novaia Zemlya) display former tide marks over 100 meters higher than today's; they make it probable that the North Pole has wandered, and that a much milder climate once reigned in the present Arctic. All this allows the ancient legend of Atlantis to appear in a new light. It seems not impossible that where the waves of the Atlantic Ocean now crash and pull off giant icebergs, once a blooming continent rose out of the water, on which a creative race raised a mighty, wide-ranging culture, and sent its children out into the world as seafarers and warriors. But even if this Atlantean hypothesis is not thought tenable, one has to assume that there was a prehistoric northern center of culture.[57]

Hitler definitely did not accept Rosenberg's book as party orthodoxy.[58] He had had little time for the whole Thule business, once it had carried him where he needed to be, on his release from jail in 1924. Guido von List's revival of the Hyperborean or Odinic religion did not excite him: he could see the political worthlessness of paganism in Christian Germany. Neither did the Führer's plans for his Thousand-year Reich have any room whatever for the heady love of individual liberty with which the Thuleans romantically endowed their Nordic ancestors.[59] Jean Mabire suggests that Rudolf Hess's quixotic flight to Britain was the last attempt of the old Thule Society—long dissolved, or driven underground—to affect world politics in the face of a Führer who had escaped their clutches and completely deformed their visions. His Göttingen historian offered this alternative version of Third Reich history:

> Hess knew of the projected attack on Russia. He wanted to warn the English. It has been said that he dreamed of a reversal of alliances. I believe that it was even more complicated. He simply wanted peace. He hoped to defuse this bomb, more fatal than the atomic bomb. He knew the inner workings of the regime well enough to know that the Führer was not only going to attack the East, but that he could only be following the most stupid of politics. Hess had understood that it was certainly not the spirit of Thule that was reigning in Germany, but the narrowest pangermanism. All these Gauleiters from South and West Germany understood nothing of the Slavic world. Have you already noticed how little importance the North and East Germans had in this Third Reich, which considered itself so "nordic"? I think that the Baltic Germans would not have allowed such elementary and, to be honest, such criminal foolishness.[60]

Julius Evola

Not long after the publication of Alfred Rosenberg's book of universal history, a far superior effort appeared from the other end of the "Axis"—the significantly-named alliance that transfixed Europe from the Baltic to Sicily. This was Julius Evola's *Rivolta contro il mondo moderno* (Revolt against the modern world, 1934, also published in German in 1935). Baron Giulio or Julius Evola was born in 1898, crippled in the bombardment of Vienna in 1945, and died in 1974. Jean Mabire remarks that Evola has aroused too much hatred not to have been a "Luciferian," that is, a light-bringer;[61] and certainly no one who has heard of him is without an opinion, whether or not they have read his books. *Rivolta*, his key work, is the manifesto of a romantic return to "Tradition" in the sense that René Guénon gave to the word, and a paean to the tradition not of the Brahmins but of the Kshatriyas (respectively the priestly and the warrior castes of Hinduism), by an author who criticized Rosenberg as "lacking all understanding of the sacred and transcendent dimension." [62]

Whereas those traditionalists whose ultimate values were those of Advaita Vedanta, such as Guénon and A. K. Coomaraswamy, looked to Manu and the original Brahmins (the priestly and learned caste) as the supreme arbiters of our cycle, Evola reversed the hierarchy of castes by placing the Kshatriyas (the warrior caste) at the top. He attributed to them an entirely different religion from that of the Brahmins: an essentially Nordic tradition of solar worship and masculine values that, he says, will always be in opposition to the feminine cults of the South.

We met a similar idea at the end of the previous chapter. It was Fabre d'Olivet who first proposed it as an explanation for the earliest traditions of mankind:[63] he described it in his *Histoire philosophique* as a schism, occurring in prehistoric times, between the devotees of the First Cause as a male principle and those for whom it was female. (No one, it appears, could leave it as neuter, perhaps because French—like Italian—lacks that gender.) The religious schism soon led to wars, migrations, and the establishment of masculine and feminine civilizations with their respective cults. For Evola, the Golden Age was that of the warriors and their Sun-god; the Silver Age, that of the goddesses of Earth and Moon, their priests and priestesses. He leaves one in no doubt whatsoever of his own sympathies, and would later write a *Metafisica del Sesso* (Metaphysics of sex, 1983) to elaborate on them.[64]

Evola's version of prehistory is couched in a form that has become so familiar that a series of extracts will serve well as a summary of our theme so far, besides giving a sampling of a book that is unlikely to be translated into English in the near future. After quoting Guénon on the symbolism of the Pole, Evola writes as follows:

> The memory of this Arctic seat is the patrimony of the traditions of many people, in the form either of real geographic allusions, or of symbols of its function and original significance, often transferred—as we shall see—to a super-historical significance, or else applied to other centers that may be considered as copies of the original one. [...] Above all, one will notice the interplay of the Arctic theme with the *Atlantic* theme, of the mystery of the North with the mystery of the West, because the principal seat that succeeded the original and traditional pole was actually situated in the Atlantic. It is known that the astrophysical phenomenon of the inclination of the earth's axis causes

> a change of climate from one epoch to another. Moreover, as tradition tells, this inclination took place at a given moment, and in fact through the alignment of a physical and a metaphysical fact, as if a disorder in nature were reflecting a certain situation of a spiritual order. [...] At any rate, it was only at a certain moment that ice and eternal night descended on the polar region. Then, with the enforced emigration from that seat, the first cycle closed and the second opened, initiating the second great era, the Atlantean Cycle.[65]

As far as the emigration of the Boreal Race is concerned, two distinct major streams issued forth, one from north to south, and the other, later one from west to east. Carrying everywhere the same spirit, the same blood, the same body of symbols, signs, and words, groups of Hyperboreans first reached North America and the northern regions of the Eurasian continent. Tens of thousands of years later, a second great emigration seems to have thrust as far as Central America, but to have settled principally in a vanished land situated in the Atlantic region, founding there a center in the image of the polar one. [...] In this regard one should properly speak of a "Nordic-Atlantic" race and civilization.[66]

> From the spiritual point of view, just as from the anthropological one, two components have to be considered, one Boreal and the other Atlantean, out of the vast fund of traditions and institutions to which the primordial center gave place in turn. One refers directly to the light of the North, maintaining the original Uranian and "polar" orientation as far as it can be approximated; the other hands down the transformation brought about by contact with the Southern powers.[67]

In Evola's view, the latter, Atlantean stream became polluted with telluric and demonic elements from the even more ancient Lemurians, whose distant descendants survive in the dark races. From this blending came the cults of the Mother and of the Earth, which would forever remain in opposition to the original cult of the Sun, preserved by the purer Nordic stream. The Atlantean tradition thus opened a new cycle, the Silver Age, "a mixture—which already has the sense of degeneration—of North and South."[68] As for the Nordics, they never lost the imprint on their souls of the polar homeland and its sun-worship:

> Especially during the period of the long icy winter, it was natural that in the northern races the experience of the Sun, of Light, and of Fire itself should have acted in a spiritually liberating sense. Hence natures which were Uranian-solar, Olympian, or filled with celestial fire would have developed much more from the sacral symbolism of these races than from others. Moreover, the rigor of the climate, the sterility of the soil, the necessity for hunting, and finally the need to emigrate across unknown seas and continents would naturally have moulded those who preserved inwardly that spiritual experience of the Sun, of the luminous sky, and of fire into the temperament of warriors, of conquerors, of

> navigators, so as to favor that synthesis between spirituality and virility of which characteristic traces are preserved in the Aryan races.[69]

> Thus also in the esoteric domain, the antithesis of North and South is reflected in two types: the Hero and the Saint, the King and the Priest [...]. In every historical epoch since the decline of the Boreal races, one can recognize the action of two antagonistic tendencies, repeating in one form or another the fundamental polarity of North and South. In every later civilization we have to recognize the dynamic product of the meeting or collision of these tendencies [...] victory or defeat falling to one or the other of the spiritual poles, with more or less reference to the ethnic streams which originally knew the "Northern Light," or else capitulated to the sorcery of the Mothers and the ecstatic abandon of the South.[70]

The reader will see that the basic outlines of Evola's prehistory resemble those of Theosophy, with Lemurian, Atlantean, and Aryan root-races succeeding each other, and a pole-shift marking the transition from one epoch to another. Evola did not, however, go back as far as H. P. Blavatsky's immaterial Hyperboreans. His story began, as did René Guénon's, with a physical race in the Arctic, intimately involved with the catastrophe that destroyed Atlantis some 11,000 years ago. One part of this Nordic, Borean, or Aryan Race fell victim to miscegenation and the pollutions of the feminine South; another part preserved its blood and solar traditions intact. It was the latter branch, we are to understand, that populated Europe and India. Evola was not troubled by the controversies of the scholars concerning the location of the Aryan Race's home, because his Aryans all originated at the North Pole, migrating southward in every direction. Thus in 1935, in Fascist Italy, we have identified a further link in the long chain of savants, philosophers, and seers (Evola was all three) who have adhered to the polar homeland theory.

A Sicilian baron could hardly be expected to show much adulation for the owners of blond hair and blue eyes. Not surprisingly, Evola belonged to those who argued for a broader conception of the Aryan Race. His idea of it, in fact, was based much less on race than on caste: on the dominance of the warrior mentality, wherever and whenever it occurs. This allowed him to inscribe the ancient Romans on the honor-roll of the Kshatriyas, and to approve Mussolini's efforts to revive the past glories of his nation.

Evola's relationship with Fascism and National Socialism was, as one would expect, ambiguous. At one point the Nazis had looked him over: he was given a tour of the SS castles in 1938, whereupon he praised the Order's "spiritual solidarity, which might become supra-national."[71] But this very remark shows how distant he was from the pangermanism cultivated in the *Ordensburgen*. Philippe Baillet, the author of a scholarly investigation of Evola's connections, reckoned that the Baron saw the Fascist and Nazi movements as counter-revolutionary, hence as the last chance for putting an end to the European decadence marked by the revolutions of 1789, 1848, and 1917.[72] But he himself was spiritually and intellectually far too fastidious to join any such movement, especially one which had reneged on the authentic Thulean ideals of which Evola considered himself the most authoritative mouthpiece.

Mircéa Eliade, who is as likely to know as anyone, said that Evola went to fight on the barricades against the Russian advance into Vienna, and was shot "in the third chakra—and don't you find that significant?"[73] Evola has been described as a heroic, yet at the same time a pathetic figure, sitting paralyzed in his apartment on the Corso Vittorio Emmanuele, nursing his increasingly lonely revolt against the modern world: a Thulean born out of time. Yet his intellectual progeny is more numerous now than ever, especially in France, where his many books can be read in translation. (Only two of them have been published in English.[74]) His uncompromising refusal of a modern world that few esotericists can bring themselves to admire, combined with the illumination he brings to every subject he touches on, make him the spiritual master of the New Right, as Guido von List and Lanz von Liebenfels were of the Thule Society.

Chapter Six: *The Black Order*

This chapter addresses some examples of "Thulean" ideology from modern Germany, France, and Chile, in order to show something of the murky and seamy fabric into which the polar and Aryan archetypes are being woven in the postwar period. Unlike the Thule Society itself, which is dead and gone, the myth of a surviving "Black Order" is very much alive in that twilight zone between fact and fiction: the most fertile territory for the nurturing of mythological images and their installation in the collective imagination.

The admirable work of Walter Kafton-Minkel, *Subterranean Worlds* (1989), gives much information on the myth of underground Nazi survival as it appears in crank periodicals and tabloid newspapers, as well as in more credible sources.[1] However, being more interested in the philosophical aspects, I turn in this chapter to a few ambitious and encyclopedic works which place the myth in a context of comparative religion and universal history. Thus we will close the cycle that opened in Chapter Three with Bailly's wise Antediluvians descending from the Arctic Circle.

Foremost among these recent books is Wilhelm Landig's *Götzen gegen Thule*, published in Hannover in 1971 by the same house (Hans Pfeiffer Verlag) as had issued Bronder's *Bevor Hitler kam*. The title translates, awkwardly enough, as "Godlets against Thule," referring to Thule's perpetual battle with the petty divinities of the other races of mankind. Landig subtitles his novel "a fiction full of facts" (*Ein Roman voller Wirklichkeiten*), and tells the reader at the outset that it contains authentic information on secret military technology, and on the multi-leveled "conflict of symbols" that even now is taking place.[2] In the course of the book, he mentions Evola, Wirth, Gobineau, Tilak, Hörbiger, Wegener, and Otto Rahn, enabling the enterprising reader to go and explore Landig's sources at first hand, while the digressions within the framing adventure story are sufficient to furnish a grounding in most of the themes that we have been examining.

Götzen tells the story of two German airmen with the allegorical names of Recke ["Brave warrior"] and Reimer ["Rhymer" or "Poet"], who find themselves sent, near the end of World War II, to a secret base that has been prepared in the remotest regions of Arctic Canada. The existence of this polar base, "Point

103," is unknown not only to the Western governments, but even to most German authorities. It is a large underground complex with all the benefits of a technology superior to anything yet operating in Europe. Supplies are fetched mainly from the United States, where sympathizers in influential positions have been looking after Thulean interests, confident that they represent a force of opposition to "certain forces in the Reich government, identified by the number 666."[3]

Other peoples evidently share this concern, for a motley international group is described as attending a great conference in the temple-like assembly room of Point 103: a Tibetan lama, Japanese, Chinese, and American officers, Indians, a Black Ethiopian, Arabs, Persians, a Brazilian officer, a Venezuelan, a Siamese, and a full-blooded Mexican Indian.[4] All have donned their national costumes for the occasion, and many of them make speeches identifying their national ideals with those of Thule.

To transport all these envoys to the Arctic in early 1945 might have presented insuperable problems, were it not for the advanced technology for whose reality Landig has vouched. Travel to and from the base is by the V7: a vertical take-off aircraft shaped like a sphere with a glass dome, surrounded by a rotating ring of turbine blades. We gather—and there is every reason, outside the novel, to believe this[5]—that a very few prototypes of this V7 have been built in German and Czech factories, but not yet put into production or war service.[6] One of the purposes of the heroes' later mission, when they are sent to Prague in the very face of the Allied advance, is to prevent this technology from falling into Russian or American hands. But after the capitulation, Point 103 declares itself independent and undefeated, and substitutes for the German markings on its planes its own symbol of the Black Sun: a disk that is not exactly black, but the very darkest red, like congealed blood.[7]

Reimer and Recke are rescued from an airplane crash in the Arctic wastes by Gutmann ["Good man"], an officer of the Waffen-SS, who thereafter becomes their guide and philosophical instructor. Here is a summary of the Thulean philosophy, adapted from Gutmann's many discourses.

The light of Thule comes not from the East but from the North. Its tradition is "Uranian," being derived from Uranos, lord of the cosmic world order and of the primordial Paradise of the Aryan Race, situated at the North Pole. It was Uranos's usurping son Saturn who brought upon this originally happy and unified humanity the dubious gift of the egoic state. The temptations consequent upon this change in the human constitution lead to the loss of primeval unity and, eventually, the destruction of Saturn's realm, Atlantis. Thereupon the warm climate of the secret island of the Hyperboreans was suddenly replaced by bitter winter. The primordial races of the Arctic and of the Nordic Atlantis both lost their homes, and were forced to migrate southwards. Wherever they settled—in Europe, Persia, India, and elsewhere—they tried to remake their lost Paradise, and in their myths and legends cherished the memory of it.[8]

While Uranos and Saturn appear to have personified forces or events whose influence is limited to this earth, the Thulean pantheon was actually headed by a

Father God, a spirit of the universe beyond time and space. Beneath this unmanifested One is "God's Son," through which the Father is revealed. But far from being a personal deity, the Son is none other than the laws of the cosmos and the natural order itself. Since in ancient times this was experienced notably in the course of the sun and the eternal return of the year, the Son of God took on the lineaments of a solar divinity and became the Sun of God (the pun works in German, too). The Hyperborean solar Apollo of the Greeks, lord of the cosmic order, is just one example; another is Mithras, who represents the sun as marking off the great cosmic years through the precession of the equinoxes: thus he is shown slaying the Bull, to mark the end of the Age of Taurus, in the central icon of the Thuleans' underground temple.[9] Landig prefers not to add the Johannine identification of Christ with the Logos, the "Word" that structured the cosmos at the beginning, but obviously that could be assimilated to this traditional theology. We will have much to say on Mithras in Chapter Twelve.

Given this universalist belief, Landig's Thuleans are far from being narrow racial suprematists. They are aware of "an esoteric world-center or headquarters of the ethically positive forces. It is the true Ultima Thule, not just of the Aryan peoples, but of the whole world." Only a few know of its location, but it is not far—in global terms—from the polar base of Point 103. Other groups are in communication with it through telepathy. The ancient Egyptians knew it as the northern mountain, On; the Tibetans call it Ri-rap-hlumpo.[10]

The supreme center manifests through phenomena called Manisolas, which have been held since the earliest times in religious awe. An entirely different kind of UFO from the German disc-planes, the Manisolas are "bio-machines" which live, reproduce, and die through a seven-part life-cycle. They begin as circles of pure light, then crystallize into a metallic form with a high zirconium content. This is the female form, "*mater*-ialized." It then develops a masculine, phallic element, which brings it to the condition of androgynic equilibrium. Thereupon a regeneration process begins, and the nucleus of a new Manisola grows in its womb. For the sake of UFO buffs, I translate the continuation of this account:

> The regenerated part is expelled by the remaining mother-nucleus as a new energetic circle of light, corresponding to a birthing technique. This new circle enters on the same seven developmental stages, while the expelling maternal element rolls itself into a ball, which then explodes. The metallic remains contain particles of copper. The optical impressions that eyewitnesses of these Manisolas have had up to now are basically quite uniform. In the daytime they display an extremely bright gold or silver luminescence, sometimes with traces of rose-colored smoke which then often condense into greyish-white trails. At night the disks shine in glowing or glossy colors, showing on occasion long flames at the edges and red and blue sparks, which can grow so strong as to wreathe them in fire. Most remarkable is their power of reaction against pursuers, like that of a rational creature, far exceeding any possible electronic self-steering or radio control.[11]

As the novel continues, the Germans are sent on a mission halfway round the world, charged with establishing contact with individuals and groups whose ideals are in tune with those of the Thuleans: they pass through France, Spain, Syria, Iraq, Kuwait, Iran, Pakistan, India, and Tibet. Early in their journey they meet near Montségur a French *collaborateur* named Bélisse [from Bélisane, sun god of the Gauls]. His allegiance is to the Cathar tradition of his region, identifed with the guardianship of the Holy Grail. Bélisse is one of those few who have preserved the Cathar heresy despite centuries of Catholic persecution, and he recognizes the Germans as spiritual brothers. It is he who gives them the above explanation of the Manisolas' life-cycle.

Everywhere the Manisolas are mentioned as having been seen in the sky, and recognized as a manifestation of the White Power and a harbinger of the new, Aquarian Age.[12] Each people has its own mythology associated with them. To the Cathars of the Middle Ages, the Manisolas were connected with the Grail, which seems to have been of the same intermediate nature. "It was a material object," says Gutmann, "which not only symbolized the physical, physiological, and spiritual potencies, but must have possessed them in consequence of its special construction." He adds that "the disks of the Mani were in Provence and Languedoc the signatures of the highest love [*Minne*]." [13] Thus Landig enrolls the Cathars and the cult of love of the medieval Troubadours on the side of the "White Light," supported by flying saucers which seem to be creatures of another order of existence, nonetheless dedicated to the ideals of unity and love.

Landig's Thuleans, as is only to be expected, have their shadow, and it is Israel. Their rivalry goes back far into prehistoric times, to an interregnum during which the Nordic Atlanteans were enslaved by black magicians of Semitic origin. (Compare Fabre d'Olivet on the temporary enslavement of the Boreal Race by the Blacks, and Spencer's enslavement of the Aryans by the Turanians.) The Jewish tendency to migrate to places North and West of Israel embodies a nostalgia, a folk-memory of this time of their dominance, and a desire once more to rule from the North[14]—thus says the SS-officer Gutmann, whose fund of odd information is seemingly inexhaustible. To a wise old Sephardic Jew in Toledo, Reimer complains that Israel has worshipped *Götzen*, "godlets"; "You put the world on the two pillars of your cult, so as to rule it like a household. We do not build, but we place ourselves under the harmonious laws of the cosmos, and are thereby lords of it." [15] Yet as Gutmann adds, we are not enemies, just each bound to the laws of our blood.

The atmosphere becomes more occult as Gutmann reveals the nature of the battle between Israel and Thule. The Ark of the Covenant, apparently, was and is an astral accumulator designed for magical operations.[16] "The Hebrew magicians steal and conceal the force-field of the Aryans. They capture in their Ark of the Covenant the fertilizing elements of the Aryan tradition, whose bearers were the original races of the Arctic North and the Atlantean North with their later mixed variations, and filter the energy streams of the Aryan mission through the Hebraic Pole, so as to pervert it and make it work for them." [17] The same Ark, or the same type, is used by the American Shriners [!], whose headquarters in Chicago controls all the Masonic lodges devoted to One World Government. Roosevelt and Churchill belong to this brotherhood, and have always been working for its aims. In their Ark or Shrine, the Shriners "keep the magic personified by Yahweh as the energy-center of a partly racial, partly cosmopolitan active substance, which is effective in both directions." [18]

There is no telling exactly what Landig means by this, but some readers will make associations with ideas in the even more popular occult literature on "lost arks" and similar topics. As the new symbol of this usurpation of Thulean energies, Landig's characters mention with contempt the flag of the United Nations, which shows a map of the earth centered on the North Pole, in the "Israelite" colors of blue and white.[19]

When the Thuleans find themselves in Tibet, other dimensions of world conspiracy begin to reveal themselves. There they meet their long-separated companion Recke, and another German, Juncker ["Aristocrat"], who tells them of the plan for a Yellow world empire. The Yellow peoples, he says, are awaiting the coming of a new Great Khan out of the underground realm, Agartha.[20] A little later, the companions hear a more authentic version of the story from a Tibetan lama, the Ngön-kyi Padma Dab-yang.

> The source of material energies of the left hand, which have their seat in Shambala, is the upper-earth city of power and might, which is ruled by a great King of Fear. But it is the same seat of Shambala that a part of the western secret brotherhoods and lodges regards as their point of origin, from which come the promises and warnings of a Lord of the World. This Shambala is a searchlight of our will! Then there is the second source: Agartha, the inner, underworld realm of contemplation and its energies. There too is a Lord and King of the World, who promises his domination. At the proper moment, this center will lead good men against the evil ones; and it is firmly connected with Brahytma, that is, God. And that is the king to serve, the one who will set up our empire and rule over the others. When you said before, Lama from the West, that a treaty was broken, that was no break, but the fault of the men in your Reich, who joined themselves with the energies of Shambala, of pure force, and in their secret way worked against the other men of your Reich. [...] And behind these energies which manifest themselves in Shambala stands the Caucasian, Stalin-Dugaschvili! He knew everything, he knew the men of the circle in your Reich and he played his own cards with them as if they were their own. Stalin-Dugaschvili had the support of the Lord of Fear and Power against your Reich![21]

Gutmann objects to this, saying that he thought it was the Tibetans in London who had been feeding Germany secret information all through the war. Yes, says the lama: we have helped you, and we have also destroyed you. The right hand of Agartha helped you, until that group of men gave themselves into the hands of Shambala. "The left-hand source is good, so long as it is combined with the right hand. He who serves the left alone is lost."[22] And he adds that Tibet has lost years of patient work through the defection of the Reich; that Stalin is now working against Tibet, too, and that the shadows are gathering over it. Yet "the secret realm lives still in the Asian wastes, its throne is the Roof of the World, and here it will come to life and visible manifestation, when the promised time is fulfilled. And it is near, my White Lamas from the West. It is near!"[23]

Once again, we hear the theme of the attempted revival of the Polar tradition in the earlier twentieth century, and of its subsequent perversion. Landig's thesis, in short, is that Hitler's meteoric rise to power was the result of Thulean assistance, but that when he "went wrong," he and all of Germany were left in the lurch, as befitted (to use Landig's terms) the devotees of the materialistic, power-hungry Shambala, marked by the Beast whose number is 666.

Finally, Landig gives a third point of view, putting it into the mouth of a Gyud-Lama, a magician-monk who is not a Mongol but a native of Hind. He takes no part, he says, in the rivalries within Tibetan Buddhism, or in the string-pulling by the Dalai Lama on the one hand, and the Hutukhtu in Urga on the other. He is not interested in a great world empire, for everything to him is Maya (illusion) except the eternal Atma-Brahman and the Peace of Buddha. Yet, he allows, the West is also seeking the Devayana, the Way of the Gods; "your light comes from the Midnight Mountain, whence you come and whither you must return. And because that is your vocation, you can partake neither of Buddha's peace, nor of the storms of Asia's steppes."[24]

The Germans, held courteously but against their will, eventually succeed in slipping away from Tibet, always hoping to rejoin the Arctic center, Point 103. But their fate is to be captured in India by the British, and because of their lack of papers and of a convincing story of where they have been, they languish long in a prisoner-of-war camp. When they are eventually repatriated to Germany and Austria, they find a world ruined and demoralized. Point 103 seems to have forgotten them: they ruefully admit, during a reunion in Salzburg, that if it still exists, it has probably had to isolate itself completely from the world of today. It is the Thuleans, it seems, who have become the "new Ahasuerus" (traditional name of the Wandering Jew). All that remains to them is to constitute a "Fourth Reich in exile," patiently waiting for the Age of Pisces to reach its inevitable end. And as the Fish Age passes, so St. Peter's religious tyranny in Rome will crumble, and the black magic of the Shriners' and the Jewish Arks will lose its potency.[25] Then, says Landig, the blue and gold banner of the Aryans will fly again, and the Black Sun of their nigredo will turn to silver.[26]

Götzen gegen Thule is in one sense a massive work of revisionism, or, to put it plainly, of whitewashing the Nazis. Juncker claims quite coolly, for example, that the pictures of heaps of bodies supposedly taken in the concentration camps were actually the stripped victims of the Allied air-raids on Munich, piled up and photographed for propaganda purposes.[27] In another sense, *Götzen* is the philosophy of Evola's *Rivolta contro il mondo moderno* adapted for the novel-reading public, educating them in the myths of Arctic Thule and in its politics, and decorated with other powerful myths of our time, such as those that link the UFOs (man-made or otherwise), the Underground Kingdom, the Cathars and Albigenses, the Holy Grail, Nazi survival, Himalayan masters, and international conspiracy both political and occult.

Chasing the Black Order

The discovery of a North Canadian hideout of Nazi survivors reappears in a French book of uncertain credentials,[28] *Le Renversement, ou La Boucane contre l'Ordre Noir* (The reversal, or La Boucane against the Black Order, 1984), by R. P. (=Révérend Père) Martin. Because this work is better-known than Landig's, and has been summarized and discussed in several books,[29] we need not treat it at such length. Presenting itself in every regard as factual, and thoroughly anti-Nazi in its sentiments, Martin's book tells of the discovery in 1971 that a group of ex-Nazis is working behind the scenes towards world domination. This "Black Order" (originally the sobriquet of the SS) is developing its own advanced technologies, especially aircraft and methods of seismological and meteorological control, that will soon give it complete global power. It has a worldwide network of bases from which it destabilizes Western nations through terrorism, the encouragement of vice and of racism. Above all, it works with the right-wing governments of Central and South America towards the eventual federation of that continent under its rule.[30]

Le Renversement is structured around a voyage from Hudson Bay to Cape Horn, as the Black Order's ship, the *Sankt Pauli*, is surreptitiously tracked and eventually robbed of its treasure, just as it is nearing its unknown base called "Asgärd." Martin comments:

> If the Arctic location of the mythological Asgärd refers directly to the polar origin of the Primordial Tradition, evoked by René Guénon, the *Sankt Pauli*, in heading for the Antarctic, would soon indicate that a true "REVERSAL of the poles" had taken place, *stricto sensu*.[31]

Martin's book presents the issue as an unambiguous contest between the forces of evil, represented by the Black Order, and those of good, represented by a Christian warrior élite founded by General de Gaulle, which was the subject of his preceding book, *Le Livre des Compagnons Secrets* (The book of the secret companions, 1982). The ideals of the latter, called simply "The Order," seem to owe as much to Lord Baden-Powell as to the General: cleanliness in thought, word, and deed; simple piety, patriotism, and fairness in fighting; and the brotherhood of all races and classes. Its spiritual masters are René Guénon and... Teilhard de Chardin, bugbear of the Traditionalists; its intellectual ones, Pierre Dunoyer de Segonzac (one of de Gaulle's generals) and... Mao Tse-Tung![32] Far from being obsessed with racial purity, this Order includes the story's hero, Napoléon La Boucane, who is the son of a French Canadian father and a

Cherokee Indian mother, and the captain of the expedition, a mulatto from Guadeloupe.

In comparing Martin's book with Landig's, it is perhaps disconcerting to realize that, however different their roots, the ex-Nazis of Point 103 cherish exactly the same moral ideals as those of the Gaullist Order. One happens to be pagan, the other Gallican Christian, but they share a common revulsion for the "Reign of Quantity" as exemplified by the United States and its European vassals; for leaders without philosophy and without vision, serving only the interests of party politics and moneymaking.

Serrano Glorifies the Führer

An extreme case of the reversal of all accepted views is that of Miguel Serrano (born 1917), who was Chile's Ambassador to India (1953–62), Yugoslavia (1962–64), and Austria (1964–70), and member of various international commissions. His postings enabled him to meet many distinguished people, including Hermann Hesse and C. G. Jung, on whom he wrote in his book *C. G. Jung and Hermann Hesse: A Record of Two Friendships*. Six other books of Serrano's, published in English, treat of Yoga and Tantra, mystical love, and his own travels as a seeker of wisdom in India, South America, and the Antarctic.

Serrano is a major figure, which makes it all the more important to know what really lies behind his polished and poetic work. This is to be found in his 600-page philosophical *summa*, entitled *Adolf Hitler, el Último Avatãra* (Adolf Hitler, the last avatar, 1984), which is dedicated "To the glory of the Führer, Adolf Hitler."

El Último Avatãra is probably the fullest modern statement of the Thulean philosophy in any language. We are to understand the title quite literally: Serrano means that Hitler is the Tenth Avatar of Vishnu, the Kalki Avatar, who has incarnated to bring about the end of the Kali Yuga and usher in a New Age.[33] In the terminology of Buddhism, Hitler is a Tulku or a Bodhisattva, who having previously emancipated himself from bondage to the circles of this world has taken on voluntary birth for the sake of mankind. Therefore he is beyond criticism. I write "is" because Serrano is a firm believer in the Hitler Survival Myth: he thinks that the Führer left Berlin in 1945, probably in one of the German flying saucer planes, to assume an invisible existence in the subterranean realm of the South Pole,[34] from which, now that the Exoteric War is over, he continues to direct the Esoteric War.[35]

But to understand the necessity for such an avatar, it is necessary to go far back in time, to the beings who arrived on earth from outside the galaxy and founded the "First Hyperborea." There has been an enormous conspiracy to conceal their origins, says Serrano: the last documents were destroyed along with the Alexandrian Library.[36] There is also a conspiracy to misrepresent them as "extraterrestrials" coming in spaceships or UFOs. True, if we were to see them they would appear as disks of light; but we have lost the senses that would enable us to perceive them properly.[37] Their center on earth, the First Hyperborea, was immaterial, not limited to geographic zones, and outside the "Circle of Circles," that is, the realm ruled by the Demiurge who was and is the lord of this planet.[38]

An inferior kind of godlet, this Demiurge had managed to create human beings of a sort: low, robotic types of whom we find remnants in Neanderthal Man.[39] The Demiurge's plan for his creatures was that on death they would take the *pitriyana*, the Way of the Ancestors, and return to earth again and again. For the Hyperboreans, on the other hand, this kind of involuntary reincarnation, trapped in the Demiurge's circles, was abhorrent: at death they take the *devayana*, the Way of the Gods, returning to the world only if they choose, as Tulkus or Bodhisattvas.[40] These Hyperboreans commanded the power of *Vril* and possessed the Third Eye; they did not reproduce sexually, but through plasmic emanation from their own bodies,[41] while through their veins coursed the light of the Black Sun.[42] It was their great adventure to incarnate for the purpose of combating the mechanical universe of the Demiurge.[43]

As the divine beings entered into this holy war, a Second Hyperborea was made, at first invisible, later as a circular continent around the North Pole. This was the place of the Golden Age or Satya Yuga, ruled by Saturn (the god who "devours time") and his consort Rhea.[44] Generously, the Hyperboreans began training the planet's lower races to help bring them out of their semi-animal state; they gave to the Black, Yellow, and Red races a particle of immortality, and began to spiritualize the earth.[45]

Then came the catastrophe. As Genesis 6.4 puts it, "the sons of God came in to the daughters of men, and they bore children to them." The Hyperboreans made the mistake of mingling their blood in intercourse with the Demiurge's creatures, and in this sin of racial mixture, Paradise was lost.[46] The physical cause was the fall of a moon or comet, as a result of which the North and South Poles changed position, and Hyperborea became invisible again.[47] Before the cataclysm, some Hyperboreans had already taken refuge at the South Pole. Others were driven southwards by the Ice Age: we known them historically as the fine and artistic Cromagnon Man, whose sudden appearance in Europe is a puzzle to anthropologists. One group of exiles founded a great civilization in the Gobi Desert, then a fertile place.[48]

Henceforth the world became the battleground between the Demiurge and the Hyperboreans, the latter always in danger of diluting their blood. "There is nothing more mysterious than blood. Paracelsus considered it a condensation of light. I believe that the Aryan, Hyperborean blood is that—but not the light of the Golden Sun, not of a galactic sun, but of the light of the Black Sun, of the Green Ray."[49]

We have already met the Black Sun as the symbol of Landig's Point 103, and later in this book we will perhaps reach some understanding of the nature of the Green Ray. Serrano practiced yoga, and he devotes much of his book to esoteric anatomy based on the chakras, to which he assimilates the Nordic runes. An unnamed Master tells him that at a certain point of yoga, one leaves one's body, goes through the mystical death, past the Golden Sun to the Black Sun, and sees a new light: the Green Ray. Then one knows that one lives in the astral body.[50] This appears to be the key to his "extra-galactic" mythology: his Hyperboreans do not belong anywhere in the physical universe, but in a parallel state of being which they can occupy simultaneously with earthly consciousness, so as to carry on their combat in two or more worlds.[51] However, this kind of transcendence is limited to those whose blood preserves the memory of the ancient White, Hyperborean race. Serrano praises the Brahmins of India for preserving their blood, and thus the memory of the time before the destruction of the Gobi civilization; he cites the theories of Tilak on the Arctic home of the Brahmins.[52] One hardly need add that the same purposes are ascribed to the "Aryan" principles of the Nazis.

In a way, one could appreciate Serrano's vista of hierohistory as an epic on the scale of J. R. R. Tolkien's *The Silmarillion*, or the Book of Genesis, or *The Secret Doctrine*, believing or disbelieving as one chose but admiring the scope and the coherence of the whole. However, a detached reading is just not possible in this instance, which becomes more than obvious as we continue.

The Demiurge, who is Jehovah or Yahweh, is anything but tolerant of the meddlings of the Hyperboreans, and from the beginning he has waged merciless war on them. His main tool in this resistance is the Jewish people: an "anti-race" responsible for the Great Conspiracy to which Serrano constantly refers. The Jews, we are told, are behind all the institutions of this world: ecclesiastical, political, hermetic, exoteric, and esoteric. Serrano hates Christianity, as he hates Freemasonry, seeing both as elements of the Jewish Conspiracy. Hitler himself was betrayed by the aristocratic Christian and Masonic generals, so as to "lose the most just war of this Dark Age, the only one which might have redeemed the planet, breaking the Circle of Circles."[53]

The Thule Society, in this perspective, was a revival of the Hyperborean ideals via Germanic myth and the science of runes. It may have had some element of English ancestry, going back to John Dee, on whose researches Serrano writes some interesting pages.[54] Likewise, it belonged to the same "golden thread" as the Templars. These knights, he says, had discovered the Hyperborean tradition for themselves and broken with their Judeo-Christian origins: an event celebrated by their rupture from the "Priory of Sion." Some of them, like Hitler, fled the ruin of their order and probably came to America in 1307, the date when their fleet disappeared from La Rochelle.[55] (I notice parenthetically that the 600th anniversary of this exodus was marked by Lanz von Liebenfeld's foundation of the Ordo Novi Templi in 1907, and by the command of "Jacques de Molay" received in Paris early in 1908 to found a new Order of the Temple with René Guénon as chief.) Nearer the Thuleans' own time, there was evidently a link with the Hermetic Order of the Golden Dawn, but Serrano says that it was perverted by the degeneracy of Aleister Crowley and the Jewish Bergsons.[56] (Moira Bergson, sister of the philosopher Henri, was the wife of S. M. McGregor Mathers and channel for his rituals.) So the Thule Society was succeeded by the SS, the shock-troops of an effort to reverse the direction of human devolution.

During the earlier part of Hitler's campaigns, according to Serrano, his intention had simply been to reconquer the ancient territories of the Aryans or Hyperboreans. Rudolf Hess's flight to England in 1941 was the last stage of this effort, intended through renewed contacts with the Golden Dawn to unite Germany with her Aryan cousins, the British, and encourage them also to purify their race.[57] But after the apparent failure of this mission, Hitler took up his avataric destiny of total war on all fronts against international Jewry and the Demiurge,[58] attacking them in their most powerful creation, the Communist Soviet Union. As for Hitler's attacks on Jewry within his own created frontiers, Serrano denies the "Myth of the Six Million," and writes that the German is heroic, but never cruel: cruelty, he says, is typical of races of mixed blood.[59]

Unknown to almost everybody, Hitler's major energies during the World War went into experiments in "magical realism," which included the construction of flying saucers, dematerialization, submarine exploration of the Arctic, discreet contact with Tibet, and the pursuit of advanced science in the Antarctic or Arctic fastnesses.[60] Then, with the fall of Berlin, he escaped through an underground passage that Albert Speer had designed, connecting the Bunker with Tempelhof Airfield, and entered another world. Serrano now joins hands with the Hollow Earthers, whom we will meet again in Chapter Thirteen:

> Had the German submarines discovered at the North Pole or in John Dee's Greenland the exact point through which one penetrates, as through a black funnel, going to connect with the Other Pole, emerging in that paradisal land and sea that are no longer here, yet exist? An impregnable paradise, from which one can continue the war and win it—for when this war is lost, the other is won. The Golden Age, Ultima Thule, Hyperborea, the other side of things; so easy and so difficult to attain. The inner earth, the Other Earth, the counter-earth, the astral earth, to which one passes as it were with a "click"; a bilocation, or trilocation of space.[61]

It is one thing to read such stuff in that peculiar corner of literature that unites UFO and Hollow Earth enthusiasts with Nazi revisionists: for example, the publications of Ernst Zündel, *UFOs: Last Secret of the Third Reich* and *Secret Nazi Polar Expeditions*.[62] It is quite another thing, and a more disturbing one, to find the identical mixture spilling from a man in full command of the esoteric field and familiar with the corridors of worldly power. Serrano's latest book is called *Nacionalsocialismo, única solución para los pueblos de América del Sur* (National socialism: The only solution for the peoples of South America).[63] It gives one the uneasy feeling that Père Martin may have been onto something in his analysis of neo-Nazi activity in the countries concerned.

Marching with the Dead: the case of Jean Parvulesco

For a last and most ambiguous word on the Black Order, I turn to *La Spirale Prophétique* (The prophetic spiral, 1986), the work of Jean Parvulesco, a poet and novelist of Rumanian origin who writes in French.

Parvulesco shares many themes with Serrano, in particular his obsession with the Black Sun, the Green Ray, Nazism, and sexual yoga. However, he is not an admirer of Hitler, seeming rather to agree with Landig when he pronounces, in his peculiar style, the following verdict on the Third Reich:

> Thus it fell out that Hitler's Germany missed the mark, and it is very fortunate that it missed it; for it was necessary that things should have happened as they did, and not otherwise. Why should the Europe of the End have been a German Europe? The Europe of the End must be European, and it will be so; the Europe of the End cannot be otherwise than European. For such is the sole question that is truly and totally revolutionary at the present time, the sole liberating question: when the time comes (and it is already here), will the European nations find, in their deepest selves, the burning reality of the "nation before all the nations," the transcendental legacy of the "Indo-European nation" of our former origins?

Parvulesco's enthusiasms range far and wide, uniting some seemingly incompatible objects: he is most obviously an admirer of Evola, but also of Saint-Yves d'Alveydre, René Guénon, G. I. Gurdjieff, Raymond Abellio, Henry Corbin, the Nazi apologist Savitri Mukherji, the stigmatic priest Padre Pio, Charles de Gaulle, Pope John Paul II, and the present Dalai Lama. He finds equally inspiring, indeed "mediumistic,"[64] certain writers of fiction who supposedly reveal the occult subcurrents of our century: the Viennese novelist Gustav Meyrink, the Franco-Irish Raoul de Warren, and three English authors commonly classed as purveyors of rollicking adventure for teenage boys and adults of arrested development: John Buchan, Talbot Mundy, and Denis Wheatley. Out of all this he constructs a spell-binding work that, true to its title, never quite comes to the point, but traverses an intellectual landscape of breathtaking variety and strangeness.

In Chapter Five I quoted the words of Pastor Hieronimus on the French proclivity for the dark side of Romanticism. In *La Spirale Prophétique*, and even more in Parvulesco's long novel, *Les Mystères de la Villa "Atlantis"* (The mysteries of the villa "Atlantis," 1989), one senses, beneath the scintillating surface of erudition and the power of subliminal association, a deep will to violence, particularly against the feminine. In this Parvulesco is by no means alone.

It is the nature of woman, said Evola, to be subservient to man and to come to whatever spiritual realization she is capable of through him. Thus Evola in 1934 defended such institutions as the burning of widows in Hinduism, the harem in Islam, and sacred prostitution in ancient times.[65] Thus the forefather of the Veilleurs, O. V. de Lubicz Milosz, trumpeted: "A great spirit's education requires cruel sacrifices: in this matter, woman, the being of feeling, must be sacrificed. She is indispensable for our education, but pity must not stop Me."[66] Miguel Serrano writes of how woman has no chakras and no soul, but "sacrifices herself voluntarily, immolating herself in order to give her eternity to her lover, in the anxious yet serene hope that he will bring her back to life."[67] And thus the hero of Parvulesco's novel starts out by making a retreat to practice Eliphas Levi's "Dogma and Ritual of High Magic" with the "dogmatic assistance" of a mindless female companion. In the course of the book he flits from affair to affair, haunted by the strangulation of a woman in the Bois de Boulogne, which he may or may not have done himself. And all this is supposed to concern the mystic preparation for the return of the "Great Monarch" at the End of Time.

It might seem unfair to blame an author for the actions of his fictional self, but in *La Spirale Prophétique*, Parvulesco deforms other authors and their plots to bend them to exactly the same mentality. The heroines have no existence in themselves, but are there solely to provide the heroes with the opportunity to exercise, like the narrator of *Les Mystères de la Villa "Atlantis"* and the tantric adepts of Evola's treatises, the "amorous science" necessary for a particular kind of masculine power.

Parvulesco's rendering in *La Spirale Prophétique* of Talbot Mundy's *Om: The Secret of Ahbor Valley* (in French, *L'Oeuf de Jade*) is a case in point. This novel of 1924 concerns the discovery by an English adventurer, Cottswold Ommony, that high initiates, hidden in a remote corner of Tibet, have been nurturing and educating a feminine avatar of English birth. The lama-guardian of this woman has been told by his guru that when she comes to the West "there will come to you a man of her own race, who can serve her better than you when his turn comes. He will know less, but he will have the qualities she needs." The guardian tells Ommony: "I offer you my place, as [her] protector and servant, to guard her that she may serve the world."[68] That is all there is in Mundy's text, but it serves Parvulesco as the springboard for high flights of imagination, masquerading as summary: he describes the young woman as belonging to "the virginal line of priestesses consecrated to the *amorous science* and destined to sustain, to illuminate from within, with their living flesh and their living breath, the Western advent of the New Savior awaited in this very century"; she is to "serve nuptially the coming of the New Savior of the End," her Hermetic spouse whom she will meet in France after being admitted beneath the sky of "pure steel" of the Polar Star.[69]

Steel skies, the Black Sun, the Green Face, and the cold light of Arktos illuminate Parvulesco's bewitching but equivocal *oeuvre*. Revolted by, and revolting against the modern world, his allegiance is to the "supreme, transcendental center of the Black Order, [...] the philosophical snows of the imperial, immaculate, and most hermetic Asgärd." But, he warns,

> ...the surest way of understanding nothing of the present business is to go on to confuse the Black Order, as it should be, with its political counterfeits, of which one, as one knows only too well, ended in the most abject nightmare.[70]

In other words, Himmler's black-uniformed and esoterically-trained SS was but an imitation of the true Black Order to which the highest initiates belong.

Like the companions of *Götzen gegen Thule*, returned from their Odyssey to find themselves abandoned like wandering Jews among the devastation of their hopes, Parvulesco sees himself as a lonely hero. Referring to his late friend and mentor, the esoteric novelist Raymond Abellio (another "Bélisanian" pseudonym), he writes:

> Soldiers already lost in a war that becomes ever more total, ever more occult, we bear at the very edges of this world the spiritual arms and the most enigmatic destiny of military honors from the Beyond. In the ranks, both visible and invisible, of the Black Order to which we belong, those whom death has struck down march on side by side with those who are still standing.[71]

There will always be men who find psychological fulfillment in war or in fantasies of war, but to advertise this as a "spiritual" mission is grossly pretentious. Krishna in the *Bhagavad-Gita* teaches Arjuna what should be the attitude of the man forced against his will to fight and kill his fellow humans. By casting Arjuna's own relatives as his enemy, the author prevents the dehumanization of the opponent that is the ugliest feature of war. But the warriors of the Black Order are not of Arjuna's kind. They are not unwilling, nor do they see their enemies as their own flesh and blood—far from it! That is why theirs is a war against humanity, and why we should take every opportunity to expose their pretensions.

PART III:
The Hidden Lands

Chapter Seven: *Agartha and the Polaires*

The displacement of the world's spiritual center from the Arctic, which up to now has been one of our constant themes, implies that it has moved to somewhere else. Miguel Serrano thought that it had gone to Antarctica, an idea that we will examine in due course. Others have suggested a location in Central Asia or South America. Wherever it is, the spiritual center is now hidden from the profane, though it remains "polar" in the operative sense of directing the world's development and the destiny of humanity.

Two names tend to crop up whenever the hidden center is mentioned: Agartha and Shambhala (I use the simplest of their many spellings). They were named in the last chapter by Wilhelm Landig as two rival sources of occult power, the first good and idealistic, the second evil and materialistic. In saying this, Landig was unwisely relying on Louis Pauwels and Jacques Bergier, who write as follows in *The Morning of the Magicians*:

> According to the legend with which Haushofer no doubt became acquainted in 1905, and the version which René Guénon gave of it in his *Le Roi du Monde*, after the cataclysm of Gobi the lords and masters of this great center of civilization, the All-Knowing, the sons of Intelligences from Beyond, took up their abode in a vast underground encampment under the Himalayas. There, in the heart of these caves, they divided into two groups, one following the "Right Hand Way," and the other the "Left Hand Way." The first of these had its center at Agarthi, a place of meditation, a hidden city of Goodness, a temple of non-participation in the things of this world.
>
> The second went to Schamballah [sic], a city of violence and power whose forces command the elements and the masses of humanity, and hasten the arrival of the human race at the "turning-point of time." The Wise Men, leaders of the peoples of the world, would be able to conclude a pact with Schamballah, which would be sealed with solemn oaths and sacrifices.[1]

One would like to be able to pinpoint the original source of this scenario of Agartha-Shambhala rivalry, but it does not seem possible. Pauwels and Bergier say that Haushofer "no doubt" became acquainted with it—which means that they are guessing—in 1905, from a Vril Society for which there is no evidence before World War I. That leaves René Guénon as the implied source. Yet there is not a word in *Le Roi du Monde* about any of this: the name of Shambhala does not appear there (in any spelling), nor do the Gobi cataclysm, the caves beneath the Himalayas, or the schism in the underground world.

No matter: the myth was launched, and would be repeated by most of the French authors of the genre, even ones with a pretension to scholarship.[2] Here is a baroque version from Jean-Claude Frère's *Nazisme et sociétés secrètes* (1974). After the cataclysm that made Hyperborea uninhabitable, perhaps 6000 years ago, the inhabitants migrated to the region now covered by the Gobi Desert and there founded a new seat: Agartha. People flocked from all directions to this "center of the world," which enjoyed 2000 years of brilliant civilization. Then another catastrophe occurred, its cause unknown: the surface of the region was devastated, but Agartha survived underground. Thither the great initiates traveled—Frère mentions Pythagoras, Apollonius of Tyana, and Jesus—to receive orders from the Masters of the World. The Aryan people migrated in two directions: one went north and west, hoping to return to their Hyperborean homeland and to conquer their lost territories. A second group went south, to the Himalayas, and there founded another secret center in underground caverns.[3]

Jean-Claude Frère concludes his tale thus:

> the sons of the Outer Intelligences are said to have split into two groups, one following the "Right-hand Path" under the "Wheel of the Golden Sun," the other the "Left-hand Path," under the "Wheel of the Black Sun." The first group preserved the center of Agartha, that undefined place of contemplation, of the Good, and of the Vril force. The second supposedly created a new place of initiation at Shambhala, the city of violence in command of the elements and of human masses, hastening the arrival of the "charnel-house of time."[4]

This, Frère says, is the doctrine that the early Nazis learned between 1920 and 1925; and he points to their power over the German masses as typical of Shambhala's methods.

One can see by comparing Frère's version carefully with Pauwels' and Bergier's that although the conclusion is the same—the schism of Agartha and Shambhala—every detail leading up to it is different. To cite further versions would be to compound the chaos. Instead, having outlined the problem, this chapter will trace the history of Agartha, and the next that of Shambhala, in the hope of clarifying what they are and what they are not.

The use of "Agartha" or some phonetically similar name for a hidden land is surprisingly recent, whatever popular writers and cranks may give their readers to believe. It had not been used before the 1870s, when Ernest Renan wrote about an "Asgaard" in Central Asia, as told in Chapter Three. But although that name came straight from Nordic mythology, it is curious how close Renan's utopian land was, both phonetically and geographically, to the "Asgartha" which another French freethinker, Louis Jacolliot, was writing about at the same time.

To Jacolliot (1837–1890) must go the dubious credit of creating the Agarthian myth. He was a magistrate in Chandernagor, South India; among his many popular books, he produced a trilogy on Indian mythology and its relationship with Christianity. In one of these books, *Le Fils de Dieu* (The Son of God, 1873), Jacolliot tells of how he made friends with the local Brahmins, who allowed and helped him to read ancient texts such as the *Book of Historical Zodiacs* in the Pagoda of Villenoor, took him to see a Shaivite orgy in an underground temple, and told him the story of "Asgartha."

Jacolliot's Asgartha was a prehistoric "City of the Sun," the seat of the "Brahmatma" who was the chief priest of the Brahmins and the visible manifestation of God on earth, to whom even kings were as slaves. The Brahmatmas ruled India at least from the accession of Yati-Rishi in 13,300 BCE, a date which Jacolliot claims to have fixed astronomically; it corresponds to the spring equinox occurring in the first degree of Libra.[5] Their solar capital, Asgartha, was of a splendor unparalleled, and there the Brahmatma lived, "invisible among his wives and favorites in an immense palace," only appearing to the people once a year.[6] To the anticlerical Jacolliot, a Deist who loathed all constraints on social and religious liberty, the Brahmatma's theocracy was anything but admirable. But if there was anything worse, in his eyes, than ancient Indian theocracy, it was the pretensions of the Christian religion, which in the companion volumes of his trilogy, *Christna et le Christ* (Krishna and Christ, 1874) and *Le Bible dans l'Inde* (The Bible in India, 1872), he tries to debunk as nothing but an ape of the ancient oriental religions.

Far from crediting this prehistoric high culture of India to the Aryans, Jacolliot says that it was there long before them. The Aryans were originally Brahmins, who for 3000 years or more formed a separate caste whose name simply meant "honorable" or "illustrious." Towards 10,000 BCE, they attempted to unseat the priestly authorities, and Asgartha was taken. The priests managed to forge an alliance with the victorious Aryans, who henceforth became the warrior caste of Kshatriyas.[7] Only much later, around 5000 BCE, was Asgartha actually destroyed, by the brothers Ioda and Skandah who invaded Hindustan from the Himalayas. Driven out by the Brahmins, they returned whence they had come, continued northwards, and became immortalized in the names "Odin" and "Scandinavia." The Norsemen, says Jacolliot, conserved so well the memory of their flight from India and their pillage of Asgartha that, when they prepared to march on Rome, they sang: "We go to sack Asgar, the City of the Sun."[8]

Thus the myth was born, very much in the spirit of a century which had seen many a fanciful theory about the Aryan Race, its antiquity, and its geographical origins.

Soon after the appearance of Jacolliot's trilogy, a strange anonymous work called *Ghostland, or Researches into the Mysteries of Occultism* (1876) was published under the auspices of Emma Hardinge Britten, a well-known medium and a founding member of the Theosophical Society. The narrator of these "autobiographical sketches," while in India, finds his way to initiation into a certain "Ellora Brotherhood," whose secret meeting-place is near the famous rock-temples of that name. Here is part of his luxuriant description of it:

> I stood in a subterranean temple of immense extent, fashioned in the shape of a horse-shoe, the large oval of which was arranged as an auditorium, with luxuriously cushioned seats in ascending circles, on the plan of an amphitheatre. The lofty roof was surrounded with highly-wrought cornices, sculptured with emblems of Egyptian and Chaldaic worship, interspersed with sentences emblazoned in gold, in Arabic, Sanskrit, and other Oriental languages. In the midst of the roof which sloped upwards, was a magnificent golden planisphere, formed on an azure plane, and so skilfully designed that the interior of the temple was illuminated from the representations of the heavenly host that gleamed and sparkled above my head. [...]
>
> Ranged in a semicircle midway on the platform were seven tripods supporting braziers, from which ascended colored flames and wreaths of deliciously perfumed vapors, whose intoxicating odors filled the temple. Behind each tripod, seated on thrones fashioned of burnished silver, so as to represent a glittering star, were seven dark-robed figures, whose masked faces and shrouded forms left no opportunity of judging of their sex or semblance. Around me, some reclining, some sitting in Oriental fashion, were multitudes of men attired mostly in European, but with some Hindoo costumes. Their faces were concealed, however, for they all wore masks.[9] [...]
>
> The whole temple was furnished with fine metallic lines, every one of which converged to six powerful galvanic batteries attached to the silver thrones by six of the adepts. These persons, adepts in the loftiest and most significant sense of the term, received their inspiration from the occupant of the seventh throne, a being who, though always present, was not always visible, although as on the first night of my attendance a presence from the realms of supernal being was always there.[10]

It was through the electrical system of this "complex battery," the positive pole of which was formed by the seven adepts and the negative by the assembled neophytes, that the narrator and his fellows were mentally impressed with vivid images of cosmic events, covering several pages in his description. The author compares the process to experiments in the electric transmission of thought made by himself with his friend Emma Hardinge Britten. But the adepts of the Ellora Brotherhood were not mere purveyors of a kind of Wagnerian synaesthetic show: we are given to understand that they radiate an unknown force to affect public opinion throughout the world.[11]

Ghostland does not use the name of Agartha, but it is as if Jacolliot's prehistoric center here takes on a new incarnation, as the seat of living adepts who are the hidden masters of world events. And such people do not even have to journey to

Ellora to work their powers: the narrator says that once he was made an adept, he was able to occupy the seventh, presiding throne while his body lay sleeping hundreds of miles away.[12] What is missing, however, is the single dominating figure, represented by Jacolliot's Brahmatma, whose powers make him the clandestine ruler of the world.

Saint-Yves d'Alveydre

Did the Asgartha myth of Jacolliot really come from a secret Indian tradition? One would readily dismiss it, were it not for the testimony of Saint-Yves d'Alveydre (1842–1909), whose theories on prehistoric earth changes we will meet in Chapter Sixteen.

Saint-Yves was a self-educated Christian Hermetist who had made a successful marriage, enabling him to publish his theories of world history and government and to cultivate political ambitions. In his quest for universal understanding, he decided in 1885 to take lessons in Sanskrit, the classical and philosophical language of India. He learnt far more than he expected. Saint-Yves' tutor was a certain Haji Sharif (or Hardjji Scharipf, 1838–?). Nobody knows who he was, or what became of him later, though the gossip current among Saint-Yves' disciples and René Guénon's circle of friends had him leaving India at the Sepoy Revolt of 1857, and working as a bird-seller at Le Havre.[13] However, there is no doubt that he existed, and that he was responsible for putting the Agarthian idea into Saint-Yves' brilliant but unbalanced mind.[14]

The manuscripts of Saint-Yves' Sanskrit lessons are preserved in the library of the Sorbonne, written in exquisite script by Haji and embellished by philological comparisons from Hebrew and Arabic. On the very first lesson (8 June 1885), Haji signed his name with a cryptic symbol and styled himself "Guru Pandit of the Great Agarthian School." Elsewhere he refers to the "Holy Land of Agarttha" (his favored spelling) and its protector the "Master of the Universe." In due course he informed Saint-Yves that this school preserves the original language of mankind and its 22-lettered alphabet: it is called Vattan, or Vattanian. From references to Agartha and Vattan in the Sanskrit lessons and in Saint-Yves' own notebooks, it is plain that the conversations with Haji, during 1885 and 1886, centered on this hitherto unknown alphabet and its homeland—which, far from having been destroyed thousands of years ago, was supposedly still in existence.

Saint-Yves could not get close enough to Agartha through his teacher, but he possessed other means of access: he had mastered the art of disengaging his astral body, and in this way was able to visit Agartha for himself. The detailed report on what he found there became the crowning volume of his series of politico-hermetic "Missions": *Mission des Souverains*, *Mission des Ouvriers*, *Mission des Juifs*, and now *Mission de l'Inde* (The Mission of India).[15] Printed at his own expense, like all his works, it was dated 1886 and styled "Third Edition": a common deception aimed at making a new book look like a best-seller.

No sooner were the sheets off the press than Saint-Yves became nervous: had he gone too far? Later writers would claim that his Indian informants had threatened him with death if he published the secrets of Agartha. In the event, the entire edition was destroyed before publication, with the exception of two copies, one kept by Saint-Yves himself and the other secreted by the printer.

Mission de l'Inde, to put it bluntly, takes the lid off Agartha. We learn that it is a hidden land somewhere in the East, below the surface of the earth, where a population of millions is ruled by a "Sovereign Pontiff" of Ethiopian race, styled the Brahmatma. This almost superhuman figure is assisted by two colleagues, the "Mahatma" and the "Mahanga" (who had not appeared in Jacolliot). His realm, Saint-Yves explains, was transferred underground and concealed from the surface-dwellers at the start of the Kali-Yuga, which he dates around 3200 BCE. Agartha has long enjoyed the benefits of a technology advanced far beyond our own: gas lighting, railways, air travel, and the like. Its government is the ideal one of "Synarchy" which the surface races have lost since the schism that broke the Universal Empire in the fourth millenium BCE, and which Moses, Jesus, and Saint-Yves strove to reinstate. Now and then Agartha sends emissaries to the upper world, of which it has perfect knowledge. Not only the latest discoveries of modern man, but the whole wisdom of the ages is enshrined in its libraries, engraved on stone in Vattanian characters. Among its secrets are those of the relationship of soul to body, and of the means to keep departed souls in communication with incarnate ones. When our world adopts Synarchical government, the time will be ripe for Agartha to reveal itself and to shower its spiritual and temporal benefits on us. To further this, Saint-Yves includes in the book open letters to the Queen of England, the Emperor of Russia, and the Pope, inviting them to use their power to hasten the event. There is much more in the book of an extremely bizarre nature, rather as if Bacon's *New Atlantis* had been rewritten by Jules Verne and C. W. Leadbeater.

Perhaps the oddest thing is Saint-Yves' own stance. Far from presenting himself as an authorized spokesman for Agartha, he admits that he is a spy. Dedicating the book to the Sovereign Pontiff and signing it with his own name in Vattanian characters (just as Haji had written it out for him), he expatiates on how astounded this great dignitary will be to read the work, wondering how human eyes could have penetrated the innermost sanctuaries of his realm. Saint-Yves explains that he is a spontaneous initiate, bound by oath of secrecy to no one, and that the Brahmatma, once over his shock, will admit the wisdom of what he has dared to reveal.

Hints about Agartha and the Brahmatma were leaked in Saint-Yves' own poems as well as in Papus' writings and letters. The small coterie of French esotericists who held Saint-Yves in awe thus had some inkling of it before the posthumous publication of *Mission de l'Inde* in 1910.[16] As for the question of Saint-Yves' sources, besides Jacolliot there is an obvious resemblance to the novel of Bulwer Lytton, *The Coming Race* (1871), which tells of a subterranean realm of highly developed beings who possess the mysterious "Vril force" and will one day emerge from their caverns and dominate us—no doubt for our own good. Saint-Yves was close to Bulwer Lytton's son, the Earl of Lytton, a former

Ambassador to France and Viceroy of India who translated Saint-Yves' *Poème de la Reine* (The poem of the queen, 1892) and presented it to Queen Victoria.[17] But a work like *Mission de l'Inde* cannot be explained away by literary influences alone. I believe that Saint-Yves did "see" what he described, and that he did not consider himself, to the slightest degree, to be writing fiction or deriving anything from anyone else. The proof is in his utter seriousness of character, and in the publications and correspondence of the rest of his life, which take Agartha and its Brahmatma for unquestionable realities. But it is quite another matter to accept his Agartha in all the actuality and physicality that he attributed to it.

Here is an extract from Saint-Yves' description of the subterranean city of Agartha, offered for comparison with the semicircular auditorium of the Ellora Brotherhood and its spectacles:

> Thousands, even millions of students have never penetrated beyond the first suburban circles; few succeed in mounting the steps of this formidable Jacob's ladder which lead through initiatic trials and examinations to the central cupola.
>
> The latter, a work of magical architecture like all of Agarttha, is lit from above with reflecting panels that only allow the light to enter after it has passed through the entire enharmonic scale of colors, in comparison to which the solar spectrum of our physics treatises is merely the diatonic scale.
>
> It is there that the central hierarchy of Cardinals and Archis, arranged in a semicircle before the Sovereign Pontiff, appears iridized like a view from beyond the Earth, confounding the forms and bodily appearances of the two worlds, and drowning in celestial radiances all visible distinctions of race in a single chromatic of light and sound, singularly removed from the usual notions of perspective and acoustics.[18]

Mission de l'Inde insists that there really is a "Coming Race" beneath the surface of the earth, technologically and spiritually superior to ourselves, and that they, or their leader, are the true rulers of our world. A couple of years before writing *Mission de l'Inde*, Saint-Yves had come across another version of the idea of hidden masters: that of the Himalayan Mahatmas Morya and Koot Hoomi who wrote, at Madame Blavatsky's behest, the "Mahatma Letters" to A. P. Sinnett, A. O. Hume, and others. Here, too, were preternaturally wise men, safe in their mountain fastnesses, in command of psychic powers and secret knowledge that gave them a lofty contempt for the science of the modern West. Saint-Yves welcomed Koot Hoomi's letters ecstatically on their appearance,[19] but after his investigations at first hand he soon found them redundant.

The notion of a secret realm where the Wise live and work had existed since the mid-eighteenth century in the Freemasonry of the Strict Observance, with its "Unknown Superiors." Baron von Hund, in founding this order, doubtless had in mind the Rosicrucians of the early seventeenth century, presented as moving surreptitiously among humanity and, incidentally, having their central shrine in an underground vault. The rumor, repeated by Guénon,[20] that after the end of the Thirty Years' War, in 1648, the Rosicrucians abandoned Europe for Asia is the very link needed to identify the hidden masters of the East with those who, like the Count of Saint-Germain and Alessandro Cagliostro, had attempted the renovation of the West.

What became of Agartha after Saint-Yves? A few Parisian occultists kept its memory alive in the face of the stronger attractions of the Theosophical Society, which knew no more of it than what Madame Blavatsky had read in Jacolliot.[21] Here is a new definition, taken from a series of articles by one "Narad Mani," which supplied the backbone of Guénon's own hostile study of the Theosophical Society:

> The true Hindu Center, spiritual in essence, which none of the leaders of Blavatskyism have ever been in touch with, is "AGARTTHA." And let him who has ears, hear: it is located, so said Saint-Yves d'Alveydre, in "certain regions of the Himalayas, among twenty-two temples representing the twenty-two arcana of Hermes and the twenty-two letters of certain sacred alphabets," where it forms "the mystic Zero, the Unfindable. The Zero is All or Nothing: All for harmonic Unity, nothing without it; all through Synarchy, nothing through Anarchy."
>
> Another center masks this one: it is the Masonry of the Taychoux-Marous, unknown to the Blavatskyians, whose branches spread secretly in Asia and in many Christian countries. [Note] This Masonry, whose headquarters is in the temple of J..., is composed of 33 Lodges. Each Lodge is composed of a master and 33 workers. Each worker has 33 pupils. Behind the 33 Lodges, there is an occult Committee, at the summit of which is the Dalai Lama, currently a prisoner of the English in Calcutta, and who, according to the customs of the country, should have been dead for 22 years. The Dalai Lama is called Tuldan-Gyatso.[22]

Such statements may intrigue, but they do not help to clarify the nature of Agartha, nor its relations to Tibet past or present. The whole idea might well have been forgotten after World War I and the death of Papus, always the most energetic proponent of Saint-Yves' discoveries. But in 1922, the Polish scientist Ferdinand Ossendowski wrote in a sensational travel and adventure book, *Beasts, Men and Gods*, that he had heard tell in Mongolia of a subterranean realm of 800 million inhabitants called "Agharti"; of its triple spiritual authority "Brahytma—the King of the World," "Mahytma," and "Mahynga," its sacred language "Vattanan," and many other things that seemed to corroborate Saint-Yves. The book ended on a somber note of prophecy from one of Ossendowski's informants; that one day (the year 2029, to be exact) the people of Aghardi [sic] would issue forth from their caverns and appear on the surface of the earth.[23]

Any unprejudiced reader, finding in three chapters of Ossendowski's book a virtual précis of the "Agarttha" described in *Mission de l'Inde*—not omitting the most improbable details—would conclude that he had capped an already good story with a convenient piece of plagiarism, altering the spellings so as to make his version, if challenged, seem informed by an independent source. But Ossendowski denied this indignantly, asserting in the presence of René Guénon that he had never even heard of Saint-Yves d'Alveydre before 1924. Guénon's interest was kindled, and in 1925 he wrote that he had no reason to doubt Ossendowski's sincerity.[24] More than that, Guénon was moved to write his own book on the subject and its ramifications, which appeared in 1927 as *Le Roi du Monde* (The king of the world). He began by saying that "independently of Ossendowski's testimony, we know from quite different sources that tales of this kind are current in Mongolia and all of Central Asia."[25] Guénon does not tell us what these sources are, nor what degree of similitude is meant by "tales of this kind." His Agartha, whose name means "the inviolable," is the spiritual center of the world, ruled by a "King of the World" who is not to be confused with the Satanic "Princeps huius mundi." To prove its reality, Guénon spins one of his most fascinating webs of connections, correspondences, and multi-faceted symbols taken from the myths and religious traditions of East and West. But is there any physical truth behind it, such as Saint-Yves claimed there to be? Near the end of the book, Guénon faces the ontological question of Agartha:

> Now, should its placement in a definite region be regarded as literally true, or only as symbolic, or is it both at the same time? To this question we simply reply that, for us, the geographical facts themselves and also the historical facts have, like all others, a symbolic value; which moreover evidently does not remove any of their own reality in so far as they are facts, but which confers on them, beyond this immediate reality, a superior significance.[26]

So Guénon at the very least did not count out a geographical Agartha: if one were proved to exist, it would only bolster the superior reality of the symbolic one. Guénon's biographer Jean-Pierre Laurant comments on this that "the two interpretations have in fact nothing contradictory about them: they can even join with an appetite for the marvelous that Guénon did not repudiate, his life long."[27] And the late Marco Pallis, the traveler in Tibet, writer on Buddhism, and translator of Guénon, who wrote an article discrediting Ossendowski's sources,[28] called *Le Roi du Monde* "disastrous" in conversation with this author, because the great metaphysician had let himself wander off into sensationalism.

The Polar Fraternity

The same trait led Guénon in 1927 to lend at least temporary support to a most extraordinary enterprise: the founding of the "Polaires." The history of this movement is said to date back to 1908,[29] when a young Franco-Italian, Mario Fille, met a hermit who lived in the hills near Rome. Going by the name of Father Julian, this hermit confided to Fille a sheaf of old parchments, telling him that they contained an Oracle. Consultation of this Oracle took place through word and number manipulation, but the processes called for were painstaking and lengthy, and Fille did not bother with them until about twelve years later (that is, about 1920), at a time of personal crisis. Thereupon he followed the instructions, which were to phrase one's question in Italian, adding one's name and the maiden name of one's mother, turn them into numbers, and make with them certain mathematical operations. At the end of several hours' work, a final series of numbers emerged which, when retranslated into letters, gave a cogent and grammatically correct answer to one's question. Fille was amazed. Apparently the Oracle never failed to behave with perfect reliability, though its answers were sometimes in English or German. Obedient to Père Julian's command, Fille alone possessed the key to its manipulation.

One of the first questions to ask such an oracle is "Who are you?" Working with his friend and fellow-musician Cesare Accomani, Fille learned that this was called the "Oracle of Astral Energy": that it was not a method of divination like some Kabbalistic oracles or the *I Ching*, but an actual channel of communication with the "Rosicrucian Initiatic Center of 'Mysterious' Asia," situated in the Himalayas and directed by the "Three Supreme Sages" or the "Little Lights of the Orient,"[30] who live in—Agartha. These at first included Father Julian, then, after his passing on 8 April 1930, purported to come from a "Chevalier Rose-Croix" who was guessed to be a favorite of the neo-Theosophists, the "Master Racoczy," sometime incarnated as Roger Bacon, Francis Bacon, and the Comte de Saint-Germain.[31]

Fille and Accomani settled in Paris, where the Oracle was demonstrated to a group of journalists and writers in the hope that they would publicize it. Some were favorably enough impressed to contribute to Accomani's book about it: *Asia Mysteriosa*, published in 1929 under the pseudonym of "Zam Bhotiva." One of these was Fernand Divoire, editor of *L'Intransigeant* and author of *Pourquoi je crois à l'occultisme* (Why I believe in occultism, 1929). Another was Maurice Magre: poet, novelist, and author of *Pourquoi je suis Bouddhiste* (Why I am a Buddhist, 1928). Implicitly equating the Oracle's source with that of Blavatsky's Theosophy, Magre wrote that "The existence of this brotherhood, variously known as 'Agarttha' and as the 'Great White Lodge,' is what it has always been, but unproven by those 'material evidences' of which the Western mind is so fond."[32] And after paying further respects to Blavatsky and her Masters, he adds that "The revelations of Saint-Yves d'Alveydre in *La Mission de l'Inde*, despite their apparent improbability, must contain part of the truth."[33]

A third supporter of *Asia Mysteriosa* was Jean Marquès-Rivière, who had written on Tibetan Buddhism and Tantrism. In his Foreword, he mentions that both Emmanuel Swedenborg and the early nineteenth-century visionary Anne-Catherine Emmerich had believed in a spiritual center in Tibet or Tartary. He continues:

> Now, the center of transhuman power has a reflection on the earth; it is a constant tradition in Asia, and this Center (a terrestrial one? *I do not know to what degree*) [his emphasis], is called in Central Asia *Agarttha*. It has many other

different names which there is no point in recalling here. This Center has as its mission, or rather as its reason for existence, the direction of the spiritual activities of the Earth.[34]

If the Polaires' center was somewhere in Asia, then one might ask what was "polar" about them. The *Bulletin des Polaires*, 9 June 1930, explained:

The Polaires take this name because from all time the Sacred Mountain, that is, the symbolic location of the Initiatic Centers, has always been qualified by different traditions as "polar." And it may very well be that this Mountain was once really polar, in the geographical sense of the word, since it is stated everywhere that the Boreal Tradition (or the Primordial Tradition, source of all Traditions) originally had its seat in the Hyperborean regions.[35]

For a mouthpiece of the spiritual center of the whole earth, associated if not identified both with Blavatsky's White Brotherhood and Saint-Yves' Agartha, the Oracle fell sadly short of expectations. Its answers were elaborate, but not always conclusive. For example:

Q. Do the Three Supreme Sages and Agarttha exist?
A. The Three Sages exist and are the Guardians of the Mysteries of Life and Death. After forty winters passed in penitence for sinful humanity and in sacrifices for suffering humanity, one may have special missions which permit one to enter into the Garden, in preparation for the final selection which opens the Gate of Agarttha.[36]

Few of its statements provided any precise occult or mystical knowledge. One point of interest, however, is that it shared with René Guénon a strong aversion to the theory of reincarnation. One of the "Little Lights," Tek the Wise, says that:

They are without number, the planets which must be traversed in innumerable existences; but what is certain is that there is no return to the same planet.[37]

A fourth article in support of the Oracle was to have been contributed by Guénon himself. He had been interested, he said, by its enigmatic aspects, and had tested it by posing certain doctrinal questions. But the Oracle's responses were vague and most unsatisfactory, and moreover, between Guénon's question and the arrival of its answer, Fille and Accomani founded "a society dressed up with the baroque name of 'Polaires'," whereupon Guénon dissociated himself from them.[38]

Others who briefly accepted the Oracle's authenticity and are cited in *Asia Mysteriosa* include Arturo Reghini, the Italian writer on oriental traditions and alchemy, who was responsible for introducing Julius Evola to the works of

Guénon;[39] and Vivian Postel Du Mas,[40] who had been a member of Schwaller de Lubicz's "Veilleurs" after World War I, and in the 1930s led an esoteric-political group whose doctrines were based on the Synarchy of Saint-Yves.[41] Maurice Girodias paints a lively picture, in his autobiography *The Frog Prince*, of the vaguely Theosophic community run by Du Mas and Jeanne Canudo, and of their efforts to fight Hitler and Mussolini on the astral plane by directing thought-waves,[42] just as the Polaires had tried to influence world events and heal lost souls by mental projection.[43]

A more famous associate of the Polaires was Sir Arthur Conan Doyle, creator of Sherlock Holmes and propagandist for spiritualism; but his connection began only after his death on 7 July 1930. As a result of mediumistic communications on both sides of the English Channel, Zam Bhotiva (Accomani) got in touch with Grace Cooke, a London medium, in January 1931. Through her he heard Conan Doyle promising that the Polaires were "destined to help in the moulding of the future of the world... For the times are near." [44] Mrs. Cooke's spirit guide, another Tibetan Sage named White Eagle,[45] told her that Bhotiva had come because of instructions from Tibet. The Chevalier Rose-Croix added that Conan Doyle was now going to help the Brotherhood: "See—the star rises in the East—it is the sign of the Polaires, the sign of the two interlaced triangles!" [46]

On a very different front from English Spiritualism, the Polaires also seem to have had some connection with Krishnamurti, at least in their own opinion. Christian Bernadac, a novelist who wrote an important book on Otto Rahn (see below), states simply that Krishnamurti was "the Polaires' Messiah." [47] Maurice Magre and Fernand Divoire had in fact contributed in 1928 and 1929 respectively to the *Cahiers de l'Etoile*, a Krishnamurti-centered publication; and many of the Polaires must have been Theosophists, too. A member of the White Eagle Lodge also hinted to me in 1987 that the Polaires had taken over the Order of the Star, complete with its symbol, when Krishnamurti dissolved it on 3 August 1929. It would be quibbling, perhaps, to mention that Krishnamurti's order had used a five-pointed star, and the Polaires a six-pointed one.

During 1929 and 1930, the Polaires are said to have made excavations and archival researches in the Cathar country: the region south of Toulouse which suffered from the Albigensian Crusade, from 1209 to the final fall of Montségur in 1245. According to a local newspaper,[48] the Polaires had found traces of Christian Rosenkreutz' passage through the area, in the ruined castle of Lordat. This is probably the same episode as was recounted, rather cynically, by Pierre Geyraud: he tells of how Zam Bhotiva discovered through the Oracle the "Wand of Pico della Mirandola," which was supposed to tremble when it approached gold. Zam set off with his lady companion to find the lost treasure of Montségur, but having no success either there or in Spain, left the group in discouragement.[49]

It was surely not mere chance that the Polaires' investigation coincided both in time and place with that of Otto Rahn (1904–1939), which would result in his best-selling book, *Crusade against the Grail*. Rahn, who was a member of the SS from 1936 and possibly long before,[50] was largely responsible for the mythological complex that associated the Cathars and Montségur with the Holy Grail and its Castle. We have already touched on this myth in summarizing Landig's *Götzen gegen Thule*, where Bélisse was its spokesman. To this day, it fuels a profitable pilgrimage and tourist industry in the Ariège region, and is cultivated with particular zeal by the "Lectorium Rosicrucianum" founded in Haarlem, Netherlands by Jan van Rijckenborgh.

One possible link between Rahn and the Polaires was in the person of the Comtesse Pujol-Murat, one of Rahn's main patrons in the Ariège, who had been associated with the order.[51] The elderly Maurice Magre also retired to the region. Like Bélisse, Rahn regarded the French and Germans not as natural enemies but as separated families. His work describes a succession of noble peoples persecuted by the Roman Catholic Church who include the Aryan Visigoths, the Albigenses, the Protestants expelled from France in 1685, and the Camisards.[52] This is another version of the familiar theme of opposition between the Polar tradition and Judeo-Christianity, casting the latter as the oppressors. But whatever Rahn may have got from the gentle and harmless Polaires, and whatever value his work may have for the equally beneficent Rosicrucians and neo-Cathars of today, it was soon polluted by the influence of the Thulean blood-mythology. Here is an extract from his second book, *Luzifers Hofgesind* (Lucifer's court, 1936), written at the command of Heinrich Himmler:

> By the name of "Lucifer's Courtiers" I mean those who are of Nordic blood and who, faithful to this blood, have chosen as the supreme object of their quest for the Divine a *Mount of Assembly* situated in the farthest midnight North, and certainly not Mount Sinai, or Mount Sion, in the Middle East.[53]

Returning to the Polaires, we find them regrouping after Accomani's departure as a more popular movement with an emphasis on practical magic, astrology, and herb-lore. By 1936 there were separate groups for men and women in Paris, and sister groups in Geneva, New York, and Belgrade, all working under Mario Fille's direction in a well-meaning but woolly-minded way for the welfare of humanity.[54] One cannot say much more about them because the Polaires' documents, deposited at the Theosophical Society's headquarters in Paris, were looted during the Occupation, along with the archives of many Freemasonic and esoteric organizations. Christian Bernadac surmises that Alfred Rosenberg wanted these materials for his academy at Frankfurt, which was supposed to establish a historical basis to justify the Nazi movement.[55]

Who should have denounced the Polaires but their erstwhile friend, Jean Marquès-Rivière, who had now become an active collaborator with the German Occupation? This former student of Mahayana Buddhism organized an exhibition on *Le Juif et la France* (The Jew and France, September 1941), wrote the script of a long film on the ritual crimes of Freemasonry, and worked to establish a "Permanent Museum of Secret Societies,"[56] after the model of the Nazi's exhibitions of degenerate art. He is another disconcerting example of a man of evident spiritual knowledge seduced by the Black Order.

A Brahmatma in Charenton

Subsequent developments of the Agarthian myth evoke more pity than terror. There is, for example, the story of Madeleine V., born in 1889 to a comfortable French family.[57] Like many visionaries, she experienced angelic visitations even as a child of seven. After marriage, motherhood, and the death of her husband, she gave herself fervently to Catholic mysticism. In about 1930, she became aware of René Guénon and his circle, read all his books, and entered into a correspondence with Marcel Clavelle (=Jean Reyor), Guénon's chief agent in France after his move to Cairo. After an exchange of about a thousand letters, Clavelle called a halt, whereupon, in 1937, Madeleine went to Rome to see the Pope. Frustrated by her failure to obtain an audience, she addressed God directly and was rewarded by an interior vision of the Holy Spirit as a dove flying from her head. A voice called "Roi du Monde, Roi du Monde," and in her vision there appeared the great Pontiff, who invested her with the Ark of the Covenant as the Lord of the World.

Back in France, believing she had attained what Guénon called the "supreme identity" or "deliverance," she again saw Clavelle, who initiated her into the Order of the Divine Paraclete in 1938. In 1942 she performed a ritual for her dying son, which left her and him no longer distinct: she was henceforth androgyne. Little more is known about her until her committal as a mental patient in 1951, except that she lectured, published poems, and spent her inherited capital. Thereupon began the first year of the Brahmanic Era, as she set up in the asylum of Charenton as "The Divine Brahmatma," imagining Guénon as the Mahatma on her right hand and her husband Pierre on her left. Her internment she believed to be the result of a Freemasonic plot; it did nothing to lessen her influence, in her own eyes, as she directed the secret society "Agartha 8" and the Brahmanic Action Front, with its 15 million members in France. Giving audiences like a *grande dame* in her room, decorated like a fortune-teller's booth, and wearing a tiara of gold paper, she elaborated her vast plans for world government. When the students marched up the Champs Elysées in May 1968, she believed that it was a demonstration by her own party, and that the plans to erect her statue in the Place Victor Hugo had only just been foiled by her opponents. A close follower of the news, she kept her finger on the pulse of world affairs, and wrote constantly: symbolic treatises, letters to the United Nations and the authorities, plans for the union of religions, and the like. Every two weeks, her children would take her out to a restaurant.

Madeleine's story, which is told in the medical doctoral thesis of Jean François Allilaire, might be read as a cautionary tale: but to whom? Her beliefs and interests are within a hair's breadth of Saint-Yves d'Alveydre's: they share the Catholic mysticism, the Agarthian myth, the political involvement, the twin-soul theme. Her feeling of supreme identity and her general happiness are not questioned by Dr. Allilaire: yet she is classified as insane, while Saint-Yves was merely eccentric. And what of Guénon, whose writings planted the seeds of delusion in an already sensitive head? Did not he, too, believe in the King of the World and in the uniqueness of his own mission, offering what his biographer Jean Robin called "the last chance of the West" before the end of the cycle?

Another case-study could be made of Robert Ernst Dickhoff, (1904?–) the self-styled "Ph.D., D.D., Mystic, Adept, Mason of High Degree, Sungma Red Lama, Sa-Ish-Ka-Te (Red Fire), Messenger of Buddha, Grand Lama of the White Lodge of Tibet, Section of New York," not forgetting "Ufologist."[58] The author of a book, *Agharta* (1951), Dickhoff at least cannot be accused of plagiarism from Pauwels and Bergier. His Agartha is "the Holy abode of the Buddhist world, located in the Sangpo Valley, China." We realize that we are scraping new depths when we read this:

> Before Agharta became the recognized Holy City to be used by Buddhist Lamas it had to be cleansed of a remnant of Venus serpents masquerading in convenient human bodies, who had held the terminal city for many eons and from which stronghold they spread evil propaganda, designed to fight the Martian wizards' mentality, who also had selected human bodies via the principle of reincarnation.
>
> I am told that the cleansing was done by 500 Lamas who were instructed by the Grand Lama to march on the stronghold of the Evil Master of evil masters, who called himself "King of the World."[59]

We will meet these serpents again when we come to Antarctica. For now, it is enough to say that Dickhoff had probably been reading *Amazing Stories* rather than Guénon.[60] He had certainly been keeping dubious company, consorting with Prince Om Cherenzi-Lind, who had given him the title of Most Reverend Red Lama,[61] and with Walter Siegmeister, who regarded him as the Maitreya.[62] Cherenzi-Lind was a notorious pretender of the 1930s and 1940s, whose modest claim was to be the current incarnation of Koot Hoomi, Regent of Agartha, and Director of the Great White Brotherhood.[63] "Aghartha," Cherenzi-Lind writes unhelpfully, "has its principal seat in a well-known place, *Agharthi*."[64] At present, he adds, it is in the Great World Sanctuary Ch'an Cheng Lob, in Tien Shan (Tartary), where the Regent usually lives and keeps in telepathic contact with his colleagues. Siegmeister wrote as "Raymond Bernard" on the hollow earth, UFOs, underground realms in South America, and many other topics: he is probably responsible for the idea that Agartha (he spells it *Agharta*) is the interior of the globe, where the flying saucers come from, and that Shamballah is its capital city. We will return to him in Chapter Nine.

Whatever else one may say about Agartha, it does seem to have been a source of delusion, if not of certifiable insanity, to almost everyone who has written about it. Like the archetype of polar origins, to which it is closely linked, it seems to wield a power that is not always for the good. Here, at the end of this chapter

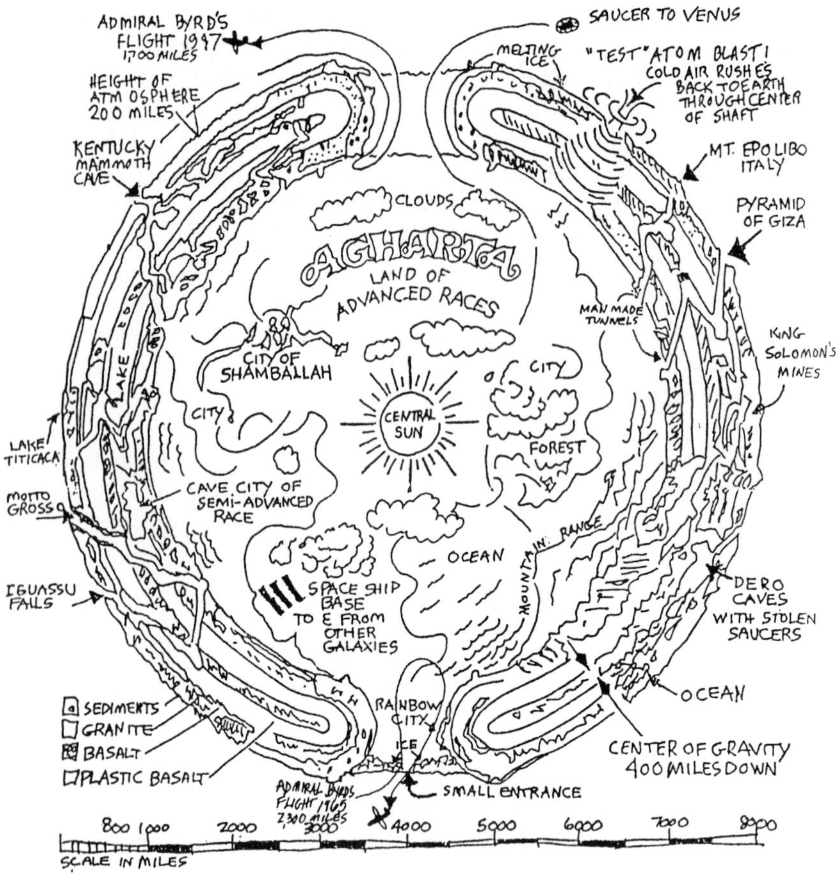

Illustration 3: Agartha and Shambhala (Bernard)

I have just lifted the lid of a Pandora's Box into which we will have to peer more closely when we come to the theme of the hollow earth and the polar openings. But first we must scrutinize Agartha's double, or ally, or deadly enemy (depending on who one listens to): the city or realm of Shambhala.

Chapter Eight:
Shambhala

Since Shambhala is a Tibetan term, in order to define it one cannot possibly do better than to consult the Tibetans themselves. The present, Fourteenth Dalai Lama gave the following explanation in 1981 to a group undergoing initiation into the Kalachakra Tantra:

> The *Kalachakra Tantra* [...] has been intimately connected with the country of Shambhala—its ninety-six districts, its kings, and retinue. Still, if you lay out a map and search for Shambhala, it is not findable; rather, it seems to be a pure land which, except for those whose karma and merit have ripened, cannot be immediately seen or visited. As is the case, for example, with the Joyous Pure Land [Tibetan terms omitted], Sky Territories, the Blissful Pure Land, Mount Da-la, and so forth, even though Shambhala is an actual land—an actual pure land—it is not immediately approachable by ordinary persons such as by buying an airplane ticket. Perhaps, if, in the future, spacecrafts improve to the point where they can proceed faster than light, it might be possible to arrive there, but the tickets might be expensive! In fact, we can consider the tickets to be meritorious actions, and thus it takes someone rich in merit to arrive there.[1]

The Dalai Lama's words indicate that Shambhala is not a physical place in any normal, geographical understanding of the term. The Kalachakra Tantra itself, "a system for transforming mind and body into purity,"[2] is used by some of its numerous initiates with the object of ensuring a future rebirth in the pure land of Shambhala. Since Buddhism does not limit the possible rebirths of human beings to fleshly bodies, life in a realm that, from the physical point of view, is immaterial, is a distinct possibility and may even be a desirable one.

One of the Dalai Lama's secretaries, Khamtul Jhamyang Thondup, contributed a description of Shambhala to a book by Andrew Tomas which fills out the picture a little more. "Its appearance," he says, "depends on one's spiritual status [...] therefore it is difficult to define it precisely."[3] However, the Kalachakra teachings say that Shambhala is made from atoms of the five elements with their potentialities, projected into the center of unconditioned empty space. The result, as Thondup describes it, is the typical palace of fantasy, with pillars of precious gems, wish-fulfilling cows, and more, inhabited by gods and god-kings.

The Tibetan idea of Shambhala conforms to the world view of Mahayana Buddhism. Thondup's words about its appearance being dependent on one's spiritual status are a key to its comprehension. What is said of Shambhala is just as true of New York or London. One perceives the city as one's state—perhaps a better word than "status"—permits one to perceive it. To some it is Hell, to others Heaven, or at least Purgatory. In his guidebook for pilgrims (in whatever sense), *The Way to Shambhala* (1775), the Third Panchen Lama puts it like this:

> Jambudvipa [the earth] always remains the same, yet one can see it in completely different ways; hence the parable that a beaker of water has a completely different appearance for three different kinds of beings, gods, men, and pretas [hungry ghosts]. For gods, there is pure nectar in it; for men, water; and for pretas, pus and blood.[4]

Since to the Buddhist all existence, even that of the gods in their heavens, is illusory, the distinction between a "real" city that one can find on a map or at the end of a road, and an "unreal" one like Shambhala, is not as clear-cut as it seems to the materialist. Neither is there so sharp a division between materiality and immateriality, the world of stuff and the world of mind: for what is any city but the result of hundreds of years of thought, on the part of millions of people? It takes on the lineaments of their creative ideas, be they noble or ignoble. From the ultimate point of view, both New York and Shambhala are equally real to their perceivers, or equally unreal to those who can see through the veil of Samsara.

What is the experience of those pure enough, as the Dalai Lama might define it, to visit Shambhala and see for themselves what manner of place it is? To the naive visionary, perhaps it is full of gem-encrusted halls where priceless treasures are piled in heaps: a place where there is no suffering, and every wish comes true. In Tibetan Tantric practice, the meditator may summon up such places in all their detail, and endow them with a sense of reality that may even become palpable to others. The Kalachakra Tantra itself is a very complex meditation of this kind. But the practitioner also knows that, however realistic the visionary experience, it is not ultimately real. If success is reached in the meditative creation of cities and landscapes, gods and demons, then the practitioner gains the corresponding capacity for the "de-creation" of the material, everyday world, that is, for the awareness that earthly cities, like Shambhala, are mind-created illusions. Given these assumptions, it is thinkable that Shambhala has never existed as a physical place, but that the possibility, even the frequency, of visionary journeys there have made it a familiar locale to Tantric initiates. Perhaps there is an analogy with *Ghostland*, where we read of the narrator traveling while his soul slept hundreds of miles away to preside over gatherings of the Ellora Brotherhood in an Indian underground temple; and with *Mission de l'Inde*, in which Saint-Yves d'Alveydre said that he witnessed the life and ceremonies of subterranean Agartha, while we know that he never set foot outside Europe.

It is no wonder, then, that the Tibetans are impossible to pin down on the subject of Shambhala's geographical location. *The Way to Shambhala* is written in such as manner as to confuse rather than guide the profane pilgrim. The Panchen Lama III there gives several different versions of its geography, with details that hint clearly enough that it is a mythical world—in the real sense:

> The people who live on the fringes of the snowy mountains have their bodies halved, such that on their right thighs they have male generative organs, but on their left, female ones. There too grow exclusively the paradise-trees of Jambudvipa. Then comes a wood, called Samantasubha, and beyond it stretches the great realm of Shambhala. [...]
>
> This great wonderland is quite circular, and its border is surrounded by a wreath of glaciers.[5]

Yet if Shambhala is now beyond the confines of materiality, it may not always have been so. Jeffrey Hopkins, writing his historical introduction to the Dalai Lama's Commentary, explains that the Kalachakra Tantra traditionally goes back to Gautama Buddha himself, who expounded it at the request of Suchandra, "King of Shambhala." Subsequent kings are said to have kept the Kalachakra initiation alive in Central Asia, so that it could be brought to India in the tenth century CE, and to Tibet in the eleventh.[6] The Italian Tibetologist (and friend of Evola), Giuseppe Tucci, says that tradition places this kingdom near the river Sita, which he equates with the Tarim, a large river flowing eastwards through Chinese Turkestan (Sinkiang), north of Tibet.[7] The Panchen Lama wrote that the "wide realm of Shambhala" extends between Mount Kailas (in the south of Tibet, about 700 miles from the Tarim) and the "nearby River Sita."[8] Then again, Lama Thondup calls Shambhala one of the six regions of the "central continent of the south," these being in order from the north: (1) the Land of Snow, (2) Shambhala, (3) China, (4) Ho-T'ien [South Sinkiang], (5) Tibet, and (6) India.[9] This would appear to place it in southern Siberia, or possibly in western Mongolia.

Shambhala in the Gobi

Moving now to Western authorities, we find the Theosophists unanimous in identifying Shambhala with a lost civilization of the Gobi Desert. There is an early allusion to it in Blavatsky's *Isis Unveiled*, where she says that long before Adam and Eve there was a vast inland sea extending over Central Asia. "An island, which for its unparalleled beauty had no rival in the world, was inhabited by the last remnant of the race which preceded ours." [10] Later, in the *Secret Doctrine*, she corrected this statement: it was the last race but one, the Lemurians, who had taken refuge in this place. Here is the relevant passage from the Commentaries on the Book of Dzyan, with Blavatsky's additions in italics:

> The last survivors of the fair child of the White Island (*the primitive Svera-dwipa*) had perished ages before. Their (*Lemuria's*) elect, had taken shelter on the sacred Island (*now the "fabled" Shamballah, in the Gobi Desert*), while some of their accursed races, separating from the main stock, now lived in the jungles and underground ("*cave-men*"), when the golden yellow race (*the Fourth*) became in its turn "black with sin." From pole to pole the Earth had changed her face for the third time...[11]

Elsewhere she says that this sacred island, "according to belief, exists to the present hour; now, as an *oasis* surrounded by the dreadful wildernesses of the great Desert."[12]

After Blavatsky's death and the schisms in the Theosophical Society, there were many who emulated her style of prehistory, based on sources inaccessible to the common scholar. Annie Besant and Charles W. Leadbeater, who together led the Adyar Theosophical Society in the first decades of our century, relied on Leadbeater's clairvoyance, which he would exercise in genial fashion, sitting comfortably around a table with his amanuenses, and discussing tricky points with Besant and others less psychically eloquent.[13] In *Man: Whence, How and Whither* (1913), which catalogues the results of these historical investigations, "Shambhalla" appears as a city founded in about 70,000 BCE by the Manu (priest-king-founder) of the Aryan Race, on the shores of the Gobi Sea, with the White Island opposite it.[14] There is no suggestion that it still exists, because after all the Masters of the Theosophical Society were well known to have their base in Shigatse, possibly in an esoteric school attached to the monastery headquarters of the Panchen Lama.[15]

Another who found her own route to the "akashic records" was Alice A. Bailey, channel for one of the junior Theosophical Mahatmas, Djhwal Khul. She, or rather he, wrote in one of their first books, *Initiation, Human and Solar* (1922):

> The central home of this Hierarchy is at Shamballa, a centre in the Gobi desert, called in the ancient books the "White Island." It exists in etheric matter, and when the race of men on earth have developed etheric vision its location will be recognised and its reality admitted.[16]

Bailey's Shambhala is the seat of the "Lord of the World," who has made the sacrifice (analogous to the Bodhisattva's vow) of remaining to watch over the evolution of men and devas until all have been "saved" or enlightened.[17] This is perhaps the earliest use of the title "Lord of the World," referring to the spiritual being presiding over earth's evolution from an invisible but still geographical center. The comparison of place and function with René Guénon's Agartha and its "King of the World" is too obvious to need underlining. And in Alice Bailey one also finds the theme of this great initiate's annual appearance,[18] just like that of Jacolliot's Brahmatma. No wonder, then, that some have simply equated Shambhala with Agartha. Nicholas Roerich, whom we will treat at length below, hints at this, while Alec MacLellan and Jean Angebert plainly assert the identity of the two.[19, 20]

Just as Agartha is believed by some to have a physical existence underground, so there are those who maintain that Shambhala is more than an etheric location on the surface of the earth. A Dr. Lao Tsin wrote in the *Shanghai Times* in 1925 that he had toured Shambhala, a warm valley in the wilderness of Tibet, and seen its advanced laboratories, but had promised not to reveal its whereabouts.[21] Such reports, hovering between fact and fancy, recall the Tibetan hideout of Talbot Mundy's novel *Om*, where the feminine avatar of a new age is being prepared; the Shangri-la of James Hilton's *The Lost Horizon* (1933); and the Asian center of Wilhelm Landig's *Götzen gegen Thule*.

One chooses the kind of Shambhala that one wants to believe in. But of all the varieties, that of Pauwels and Bergier is most at variance with the Tibetan model. It must have taken a peculiar perversity on the part of their source or informant to turn the materialistic Agartha of Saint-Yves, with its two-tongued race, inflatable mattresses, underground railroads, and threats to invade us, into the place of actionless meditation; and the pure land of Tibetan Tantra into the violent and earthly power-house. Among all their progeny, perhaps the ultimate degradation is that of Trevor Ravenscroft's *The Spear of Destiny* (1973), a blood-curdling work of historical reinvention which makes Agartha and Shambhala into the centers of Luciferic and Ahrimanic influence, respectively. These are the twin sources of evil in the cosmology of Rudolf Steiner, who had little regard for the wisdom of Tibet. "The Initiates of Agarthi," writes Ravenscroft, "specialised in astral projection and sought to inspire false leadership in all civilizations in the world. The Adepts of Schamballah sought to foster the illusion of materialism and lead all aspects of human activity into the abyss."[22] Often one can detect the source of someone's Shambhala and Agartha theories simply through examining their spelling of the names: Ravenscroft evidently relied on Pauwels and Bergier.

The Roerich Family

On quite another plane is the contribution to the Shambhala mythologem made in the 1920s and 1930s by the Roerich family: Nicholas, the painter and worker for world peace; Helena, his wife and channel for the Master Morya; and their son George, later a professor at Yale University. The Roerichs made an expedition through China and Mongolia to the borders of Tibet in 1925–1928, as the result of which they published several books of travel and reflections, one of them, by Nicholas, entitled precisely *Shambhala*.[23]

Nicholas Roerich saw in Shambhala the symbol of the coming age of world peace and enlightenment, and it is only just to say that he adapted what he learned at first hand in Mongolia to his own world-view. His expedition had a deep spiritual, even a magical intention—and a political one, too. But it never reached Lhasa. The Roerichs were forced by the temporizing of the Tibetan government to spend the winter of 1927–28 waiting for permission to proceed, during which several people and most of the animals died of exposure. It is no wonder that Roerich's writings show a contempt for the Lhasa government and even for the Dalai Lama XIII, balanced by sincere admiration of the exiled Panchen (or Tashi) Lama IX, the holder of the Kalachakra tradition.

Roerich writes of Shambhala:

> Shambhala itself is the Holy Place, where the earthly world links with the highest states of consciousness. In the East they know that there exist two Shambhalas—an earthly and an invisible one. Many speculations have been made about the location of the earthly Shambhala. Certain indications put this place in the extreme North, explaining that the rays of Aurora Borealis are the rays of the invisible Shambhala.[24]

But this is incorrect, he continues: Shambhala is only north in relation to India, being perhaps on the Pamir, in Turkestan, or in the Central Gobi.

Roerich found his way into esotericism through the Theosophical Society, and he always remained a friend to Madame Blavatsky and her Masters. He regretted that the conception of the Great Mahatmas had become separated from that of Shambhala, to which, he said, it is very close.[25] He also associates it with the conceptions of the subterranean city "Agharti," and of the White Island.[26] Blavatsky's island refuge in the Gobi Sea was reachable only by subterranean passages;[27] Roerich's "Splendid Valley" is reached by passages from the Himalayas.[28] The underground caverns of Central Asia are inhabited to this day, he tells us, by the people called the Agharti or the Chud. Throughout Asia he heard tales of this vanished tribe, peaceful and highly civilized, who were forced to take refuge underground when the "White Tsar" and his cruel warriors (that is, the Mongol hordes) invaded the Altai region. When the time of purification comes, say the legends, they will emerge in their glory.[29]

Although he was ready to listen to such tales, and to believe that mysterious things are concealed underground, Roerich lacked the credulity of an Ossendowski concerning a subterranean Agartha. He comments that "although the legend [of the Chud] speaks of the time of the Tartar yoke, you can distinguish that the essential bases [sic] of the legend is far more ancient and you can distinguish the traces of the typical effects of migration. [...] When you collect all the fairy-tales of lost and subterranean tribes, will you not have before you a full map of the great migrations?"[30] When he found in the Altai mountains menhirs, stone circles, and alignments just like those of Britain and Brittany, and when he saw among the inhabitants features that could have been those of Frenchmen or Spaniards, Roerich concluded that the migration had in fact taken the best and most courageous of the Central Asian people on a journey to the shores of the Atlantic.[31] Agharta, in short, was not of great interest to him except as a facet of the Shambhala myth.

The religion of Roerich's Shambhala, if one can call it that, centered around

Fire. Nicholas connects it with the ancient cults of Fire and the Sun, whose Swastika symbol he found repeatedly carved on rocks and painted on tankas. He was certainly aware of the history of this symbol as associated with the Aryan Race. But it disturbed him very much to find it in the temples of the Bön-Po religion as well as in Buddhist ones—indeed, to find that this "black faith" reveres what he calls "some mysterious gods of Swastika." He tried to rationalize its usage by saying that the Bön-Po drew the symbol of Fire counter-clockwise, in the reverse direction from the Buddhists.[32] But every serious study of the Swastika symbol shows that whenever it appears in ancient iconography, it turns indifferently either way.[33]

Just as for Madame Blavatsky, Tibet's indigenous, pre-Buddhist religion of Bön-Po signified for Roerich the worst kind of sorcery and black magic. Even within Buddhism, the sympathies of these Theosophists were limited to the Yellow-Hat (Gelugpa or Reformed) sect to which the Dalai and Panchen Lamas belong, causing Blavatsky and her master K.H. to regard the Red-Hats as ministers of evil.[34] With the best will in the world, then, one cannot altogether respect their interpretations of Tibetan religion. Had Roerich known the present Dalai Lama XIV, he would surely not have been so quick to denigrate the office of the Dalai Lama in favor of the Panchen Lama;[35] but he could have known only of the ill-starred Dalai Lama XIII, whose sole achievement (as Narad Mani pointed out cynically in Chapter Seven) seems to have been to avoid getting murdered by the Chinese before his majority. Could Roerich and Blavatsky see the present-day flowering of Western Buddhism, of which they were pioneers, they might be more friendly to the red-hatted Karmapa lineage, and even to Bön-Po as assimilated by the Dzogchen Tantric school.

Like the *Treatise on Cosmic Fire* of Alice Bailey and Djhwal Khul, Helena Roerich's and Morya's books on "Agni Yoga" are devoted to explaining, with more elaboration than clarity, what the Agni or Fire of Shambhala is, and how it will function in the New Era: it is the "great eternal energy, this fine imponderable matter which is scattered everywhere and which is within our use at any moment."[36] This could be a definition of Bulwer Lytton's Vril force. In the 1940s, Roerich says, "energies of cosmic fire will approach the earth and create many new conditions of life."[37] Alas, they did indeed! If Nicholas Roerich, the indefatigable worker for world peace, had known the form in which Agni would be compelled to manifest in 1945, he might have been more cautious in recommending it, and in identifying it as the core of the Kalachakra teaching. But a man who could get excited when the Mongolians said, on looking at his photographs of New York City, "this is the land of Shambhala!"[38] had evidently not fully descried the nature and the trajectory of the modern West.

On 5 August 1927, in the Kukunor district, the Roerich party witnessed a classic UFO, twenty years before the "official" beginning of the phenomenon with Kenneth Arnold's sighting in 1947. Although it is now a commonplace in the better class of UFO literature, I give the fullest of his accounts here:

> We all saw, in a direction from north to south, something big and shiny reflecting the sun, like a huge oval moving at great speed. Crossing our camp this thing changed in its direction from south to southwest. And we saw how it disappeared in the intense blue sky. We even had time to take our field glasses and saw quite distinctly an oval form with shiny surface, one side of which was brilliant from the sun.[39]

The lama with the party remarks: "A very good sign. We are protected. Rigden-jyepo himself is looking after us!"[40] In the Roerichs' books, Rigden-jyepo is the prophesied Lord of the New Era of Shambhala, who is currently preparing an invincible army. He is the "Ruler of the World," and none less than Maitreya, the Last Avatar who brings the Kali Yuga to an end and opens the new Krita or Satya Yuga.[41] The Roerichs did not expect to have to wait long for this apocalyptic event: Helena, writing in 1930 as "Josephine Saint-Hilaire," gave the heralds of Northern Shambhala five years to arrive;[42] a lama in Nicholas' *Heart of Asia* said "someone of greatness will come" in 1936.[43] We learned in Chapter Six who was cast in this role by Miguel Serrano, an admirer of Roerich's paintings and a sharer of much of his philosophy. A saner alternative might refer to Tenzin Gyatso, who was born in 1935 and identified as the incarnation of Chenrezig, hence as Dalai Lama XIV, in 1937.

There is a hint that the Roerich Expedition had an active part to play in this changing of the Ages. It concerns a Stone from a distant star that belongs to Shambhala; it is likened to the *lapsit exillis*, the Grail Stone of Wolfram von Eschenbach's romance *Parzival* (IX, 469), as also to the Philosophers' Stone of Western alchemy.[44] "The greater portion of this stone remains in Shambhala, while part of it is circulating throughout the Earth, retaining its magnetic link with the main stone."[45] The latter is said to be "on the tower of the Rigden-jyepo," whence it radiates for the benefit of humanity.[46] Andrew Tomas, who says that he heard from Professor [George] Roerich that the stone supposedly came from Sirius, interprets the broad hints in Helena Roerich's *On Eastern Crossroads* to mean that a small fragment of the central Stone had been sent to Europe to aid in the foundation of the League of Nations, and that it was returned to Shambhala by Nicholas Roerich on his expedition.[47] Several of his paintings, on the Chintamani theme, seem to refer to this secret mission. Likewise in Ossendowski there is the Mongolian legend of an oracular Black Stone, sent to the Dalai Lama by the King of the World; until a hundred years ago, it used to be in Urga (now Ulan Bator, capital of Mongolia).[48] This may be the same fragment, reputedly owned by King Solomon, Emperor Akhbar, a Chinese Emperor, and Tamerlane the Great.[49]

Urga, rather than Lhasa, seems to have been Roerich's choice for the future spiritual center when Shambhala becomes manifest on earth. When he passed through the city, he saw a site prepared for the chief Temple of Shambhala.[50] He thereupon presented his painting "The Ruler of Shambhala" to the Mongolian Government, who undertook to build a shrine for it.[51] One wonders, if the story of the fragment of stone is true, whether Urga was where Roerich surrendered it, and whether the shrine was intended to contain more than just a painting. That there were people in the Mongolian capital competent to discuss such matters is clear from George Roerich's account of an esoteric astrological college there, which also maintained the Kalachakra tradition.[52]

Were there also people in the know within the Theosophical Society? A secondary theme of Talbot Mundy's *Om*, published in 1924 while the Roerich Expedition was making its preparations in Sikkim, was the return of a stolen fragment of the great green jade stone which resided in the secret Asiatic center. Mundy, a member of the Point Loma Theosophists, published several popular books in the 1920s and 1930s on themes which bridge the gap of which Roerich complained, between the idea of the Theosophical Masters and that of Shambhala. It is not within our scope to investigate the links between these and other personages of the 1920s, but it does seem that Theosophists, semi-Theosophists, and even anti-Theosophists like René Guénon, whatever their internal dissensions, constituted a group dedicated to the ideal of Shambhala taken in its broadest sense: that of reverence for a center in the Orient from which comes the impulse for the imminent renewal of humanity, and to a Lord, King, or Ruler of the World who is neither Christ nor Lucifer.

Their allegiance to a living, spiritual pole in Asia stands in stark contrast to the nostalgia of the Thuleans for their dead Arctic homeland. In this lies the vital difference between the universalism of Nicholas Roerich and other Theosophists, and the racism of Guido von List, Lanz von Liebenfels, Rudolf von Sebottendorff, and their Nazi pupils.

The Shaver Mystery

Returning to the theme which opened this chapter, if one were to insist on contrasting Shambhala with Agartha, our investigations would favor the contrary conclusion: it is obviously Shambhala which is the "hidden city of Goodness" reached through meditation, while Agartha is the material, subterranean realm threatening us with eruption. Their relationship is akin to that between the states of the soul in meditation and after death, and the gross images of those states as presented by Dante and others, whose Inferno appears as a physical place under the earth.

This contrast can be seen with exemplary clarity in what is known as the "Shaver Mystery."[53] Richard Sharpe Shaver (1910–1975) contributed from 1943 onwards a number of articles to *Amazing Stories*, a science-fiction magazine, that told of an underground cave-world inhabited by "abandonderos": the cunning but degenerate remnant of a race which had left the earth 12,000 or more years ago,[54] and whom he held responsible for all the evil experienced by us surface-dwellers. Shaver, who spent his life in menial jobs, insisted that he had lived eight years in the caves as a prisoner of these "deranged robots" or "Deros." He knew from experience of their machinations, of the efforts by another underground race, the "Teros," to counteract them, and much more that inevitably included sex and violence—necessary ingredients in any pulp magazine. The editor of *Amazing Stories* was Ray Palmer, who immediately saw the commercial potential of Shaver's stories and put them into acceptable prose. In due course he learned that Shaver had spent years not in the caves, exactly, but in a mental hospital.[55] In the meantime, Palmer had discovered *Oahspe*, the "New Bible" revealed to John Ballou Newbrough in 1881, and found there many parallels with Shaver's tales—only with the difference that in *Oahspe*, the scenario was not the inside of the earth, but the astral world surrounding it. Without for a moment denying the subjective reality of Shaver's experiences, Palmer decided that they must have taken place in a state of psychic dissociation, and that Shaver's vagrant consciousness had witnessed in the deros and their depravity the "wandering spirits of darkness and evil," as *Oahspe* calls them, or the souls of the dead that dwell in the lower astral realms of the spirit world.[56] He did not add that "Teros" is given as a name for protective psychic energy in Helena Roerich's *Agni Yoga* (1929).[57]

For all the intellectual gulf between Shaver and Palmer on the one hand, and Saint-Yves and Roerich on the other, one can see the same contrast in each pair of the material versus the immaterial explanation. Shaver was an adamant materialist and a disbeliever in everything psychic or occult.[58] The sufferings of humanity were only explicable, and tolerable, to him when he could blame them on the Deros. Palmer, on the other hand, had other dimensions to his character: crippled as a child and nearly always in pain, he had become a success in worldly terms through his writing and editing, and had discovered the reality of intuition and the power of mind over matter.[59]

Both types no doubt exist in Central Asia, as they existed in medieval Europe—for Dante himself surely did not understand his *Inferno* and *Purgatorio* in a literal, geographic sense. Many people are constitutionally incapable of imagining anything outside material reality, and the great religions have kindly made allowances for them in their cosmologies. Even those who are gifted, or afflicted, with the capacity of "astral travel" are not always exempt from this tendency: some, like Shaver and Saint-Yves, will refuse to take their visions in any but a terrestrial sense. Not knowing that whatever they experience is a projection of their own spiritual state, they will find not the Shambhala of purified consciousness, but only the deceptive and glamorous Agartha.

Finally, Shambhala furnishes an illuminating parallel to the various interpretations of the primordial Paradise and the Arctic homeland discussed in Chapters Two and Three. Some situate them on the physical earth, others in what to us is an immaterial or etheric state, attainable only by beings of like nature, or by humans exceedingly "rich in merit." The Way to Shambhala as the Dalai Lama has described it is precisely the return to that primordial condition, which, irrespective of outer conditions, brings about in the individual the transition from the Iron to the Golden Age.

Chapter Nine:
The Hole at the Pole

Our study of Agartha and Shambhala has raised a group of themes that seem, especially in the popular literature, to travel in company: lost races, underground realms, conspiracy theory, the mystic East, the Holy Grail, UFOs, Apocalypse, and more. Ekkehard Hieronimus, who was quoted in Chapter Five, cautions against the dismissal of popular beliefs, reminding us of how Hörbiger's absurd "World-Ice Theory" rocketed to official status under the Third Reich. He writes:

> This makes me very wary. What is going on in the lower reaches of society is probably very much more potent and effective than what happens in intellectual circles. We think, of course, that it is the intellectuals—now in the broadest sense of the term, in which I include the scientists—who define our life. But lately the intellectuals have been rather like a film of oil on a great puddle of water: it shines mischievously and thinks that it is the whole thing, but it is only one molecule thick. I can see quite definite things coming towards us. The things going on in the so-called cultural underground, or the so-called subculture, are very strange.[1]

Anyone who shops in a supermarket is made well aware of this subculture of belief by the headlines of the tabloid newspapers. I am looking now at a double-page, colored montage of Doric columns arising from a frozen seascape, captioned: "Ruins of Atlantis found in the Arctic."[2] Apparently a joint French-Soviet research expedition to the North Pole has discovered this floating city, says the *Sun* reporter, while a British scientist predictably scoffs at it. Untold millions of shoppers have seen this headline and dozens like it: the archetypes it evokes are churning away somewhere in their psyches. In some fuzzy, unexamined way they all believe in Atlantis, in UFOs, in reincarnation, in the survival of Hitler and of Elvis Presley. Already in this book we have seen how unexamined belief in certain archetypal themes helped to lay the ground for National Socialism. One has to be thankful that our tabloids are not proclaiming Aryan supremacy or describing Jewish ritual murder; but one may well ask what collective attitudes are being formed by the currents in the "great puddle" of popular occultism.

As the natural sequence to the idea of an underground Agartha, this chapter is concerned with the theory that the earth is hollow, with holes opening at one or both poles. We cannot possibly review all the modern writing on the subject, which makes up in quantity what it lacks in intellectual and literary quality. Walter Kafton-Minkel's *Subterranean Worlds* can again be recommended to the reader as a delightful travel guide to this cloud-cuckoo land. Here it will suffice to trace the sources of the idea in the seventeenth century, and to analyze some of the different forms it has taken since then.

The Jesuit polymath Athanasius Kircher (1602–1680), in his treatise on the Subterranean World (*Mundus Subterraneus*, 1665), wrote of how the preceding two centuries had witnessed the exploration of the whole world, with the exception of the polar regions. Whether this would ever be remedied was doubtful to Kircher, because navigators in those parts had encountered such adverse conditions of wind and current that further progress north or southwards seemed impossible. This deficiency of practical experience could, however, be made up by logical reasoning in combination with tradition. Kircher knew the medieval geographers well, as also the classical writers from whom they had borrowed. The one he cites in particular is the thirteenth century friar, Bartholemew of England (Bartholemaeus Anglicus), who says confidently that at the North Pole there is a black rock some 33 leagues in circumference, beneath which the ocean flows with incredible speed through four channels into the subpolar regions, and is absorbed by an immense whirlpool.[3] Since by Kircher's own admission there was no way that Bartholemew could have been drawing on empirical experience, Kircher suggests (perhaps tongue in cheek) that he was transported to the Pole by magical arts. But the learned Jesuit agreed in principle with this mystical geography. He explains that the four channels are actually on a much larger scale, passing into the open polar sea through the Bering Straits, on the two sides of Greenland, and east of Spitzbergen. At the Pole itself, the waters enter a great whirlpool, then proceed through the body of the earth in "unknown recesses and tortuous channels" until they emerge in the open sea of the South Pole. Flowing outwards from the South, their currents likewise prevent any access by explorers. In confirmation of his theory, Kircher mentions some other medieval authorities, and among later ones Pierre-Jean Fabre's *Panchymici* (1646) and the report of the explorer Purchas, who said that the seas near the North Pole are both rapid and summer-like. He also tells the tragic story of Henry Hudson's expedition and death.

Kircher's rationale for his extraordinary theory of the polar vortices has two parts. The first is rather scholastic, for he states that everything in the universe has to be in motion, or else it will stagnate and die. Consequently, if the ocean were left immobile, it would soon become putrid like standing water, and all animals and men would die from its foul exhalations. Moreover, if the polar seas were not in motion, they would remain perpetually frozen, hence static. Happily this is not the case, since the Architect and Maker of the World has used the influxes of sun, moon, and stars to set the oceans in perpetual motion, both on the surface and within the earth's body.

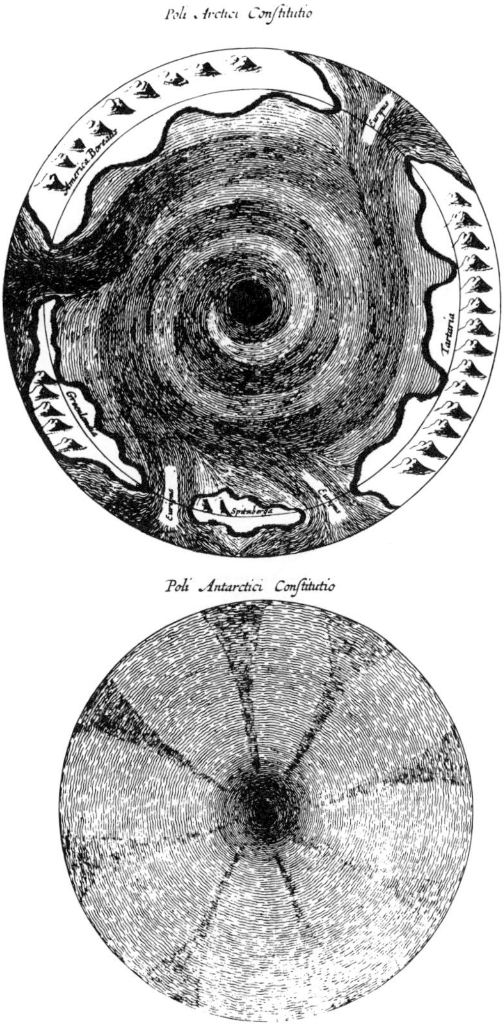

Illustration 4: The polar vortices (Kircher)

Kircher's second argument is through analogy of the seas' movement through the earth with human anatomy. After they have been absorbed at the North Pole, they are cooked in the earth's interior by the subterranean fires which, in Kircher's geology, permeate the earth's body and occasionally break out in volcanoes. The elements in the sea-water are extracted by this process, to be used for the generation of metals. The undigested remains are then expelled at the nether end, the South Pole. As a further analogy with animal anatomy, Kircher likens the circulation of waters to the recently-discovered circulation of the blood.[4] Thus he implies that the earth is constructed and behaves like a living creature. This was quite the contrary view to the one that science was tending to adopt in the later seventeenth century, but like many of Kircher's ideas it is enjoying a certain revival today, in what is currently called the "Gaia Hypothesis."

Thomas Burnet's *Sacred Theory of the Earth* also had the waters flooding out of the earth's interior through a cavity at the North Pole, but there the resemblance stopped: Burnet's was a mechanical earth, its periodical changes obedient only to the divine will, not to a self-sustaining process. A more obscure divine, Alexander Colcott of Bristol, adopted Burnet's idea in 1768; but instead of having the earth filled with water like a balloon, he took the step—and perhaps he was the first to take it—of positing a hollow globe whose inner surface was coated with an ocean. The Deluge was caused when this flowed out through the polar rift.[5]

The indefatigable Willy Ley unearthed three scientists of the same period who also toyed with the idea of a hollow sphere with a central sun. One was Sir Edmund Halley (of comet fame), who in 1692 published in the *Philosophical Transactions* of the Royal Society the hypothesis of an earth of three closed concentric hollow spheres with a hot spherical core at the center. The shiftings of these spheres were his explanation for the shifting of the earth's magnetic poles.[6] Halley's theory sounds like a brainstorm of outmoded science, yet if one were to deck it out in contemporary language, it would strangely resemble that of Donna Jurdy, outlined in Chapter Seventeen, who accounts for "True Polar Wander" by the slippage of the mesosphere inside the lithosphere. A second theorist was Sir John Leslie, who posited two inner suns called Pluto and Proserpine; a third, the mathematician Leonhard Euler, who thought there was but one. However, none of these eminent persons went so far as to suppose that the inner earth could be reached through a hole at either pole.

The apparent impossibility of attaining the poles allowed hollow earth and polar opening theories to command serious attention well into the nineteenth century. It also gave rise to a lively vein of imaginative literature, beginning with the anonymous *Passage du pôle arctique au pôle antarctique par le centre du monde* (Passage from the Arctic Pole to the Antarctic Pole via the center of the earth), a novella of 1721.[7] This is a very peculiar fantasy, telling of incredible events in absolutely deadpan style. The narrator sails from Amsterdam, but his vessel is swept up by a storm which forces it to the uttermost North. On reaching the Pole, the ship is sucked into a Kircherian whirlpool, and the narrator mercifully loses consciousness. When he comes to, he finds that his ship has been disgorged, still intact, in the Antarctic Ocean. Most of his account is devoted to the strange phenomena of the far South, which, since Antarctica had not yet been discovered, allowed full rein to the author's imagination.

While medieval theology, as celebrated in Dante's *Divine Comedy*, had found the interior of the earth to be a suitable location for Hell, later writers began to imagine quite the contrary. The universal philosopher Guillaume Postel, in his *Compendium Cosmographicum* (1561),[8] and the topographer Georg Braun, in his *Urbium praecipuarum totius mundi* (1581),[9] suggested that God had made the Earthly Paradise inaccessible to mankind by stowing it beneath the North Pole. Among the early novels on the theme of a Utopia beneath the surface of the earth are the

Chevalier de Mouhy's *Lamékis, ou les voyages extraordinaires d'un Egyptien dans la Terre intérieure* (Lamékis, or the extraordinary voyages of an Egyptian in the inner earth, 1737), and Ludvig Baron von Holberg's *Nicholas Klim* (1741), the latter much read in Holberg's native Denmark.[10] Giovanni Jacopo Casanova, the adventurer and libertine, also situated Paradise inside the earth. In *Icosameron* (1788), a work supposedly translated by him from the English, he describes the twenty-one years passed by his heroes Edward and Elizabeth among the "megamicros," the original inhabitants of the "protocosm" in the interior of our globe. One way into this realm is through the labyrinthine caves near Lake Zirchnitz, a region of Transylvania. The megamicros issue from bottomless wells and assemble in temples, clad in red coats. Their gods are reptiles, with sharp teeth and a magnetic stare. As Michel Lamy remarks after giving the summary from which I borrow here, *Icosameron* is "pure Lovecraft"![11]

The literature of the Romantic era, needless to say, is rich in fantasies of polar mysteries and lands within the earth. The best known works are probably George Sand's *Laura ou le voyage dans le crystal* (Laura, or the voyage in the Crystal); Edgar Allen Poe's *The Narrative of Arthur Gordon Pym*; Alexandre Dumas' *Isaac Laquédem*; Bulwer Lytton's *The Coming Race*; Jules Verne's *Voyage au centre de la terre* (Voyage to the Center of the Earth) and *Le Sphinx des glaces* (The Sphinx of the Ice). Novels by later and less distinguished authors include William Bradshaw's *The Goddess of Atvatabar* (1892), Robert Ames Bennet's *Thyra, a Romance of the Polar Pit* (1901), Willis George Emerson's *The Smoky God* (1908), and the Pellucidarian stories of Edgar Rice Burroughs, creator of Tarzan.[12]

First, however, we must render his due to the one man who lived and died for the hollow-earth theory: John Cleves Symmes (1780–1829; not to be confused with his uncle of the same name, who made the Miami Purchase in Ohio). Symmes was born in New Jersey and, after a "good common English education,"[13] enlisted in the United States Army where he rose to the rank of Captain, distinguishing himself in the French and Indian Wars. In 1808 he married Mary Anne Lockwood, a widow with five children, whose patrimony he conscientiously conserved as he raised them, together with another five of his own. When the army disbanded in 1816, he set up as a supplier for the troops and trader with the Fox Indians in St. Louis. Although his first proclamation to mankind has been frequently reproduced, it is irresistible to quote it again here:

CIRCULAR

Light gives light to discover—*ad infinitum*

St. Louis, Missouri Territory, North America
April 10, A.D. 1818

To all the World:

I declare the earth is hollow and habitable within; containing a number of solid concentric spheres, one within the other, and that it is open at the poles twelve or sixteen degrees. I pledge my life in support of this truth, and am ready to explore the hollow, if the world will support and aid me in the undertaking.

Jno. Cleves Symmes
Of Ohio, late Captain of Infantry.

N.B.—I have ready for the press a treatise on the principles of matter, wherein I show proofs of the above positions, account for various phenomena, and disclose Dr. Darwin's "*Golden Secret.*"

My terms are the patronage of THIS and the NEW WORLDS.

I dedicate to my wife and her ten children.

I select Dr. S. L. Mitchell, Sir H. Davy, and Baron Alexander Von Humboldt as my protectors.

I ask one hundred brave companions, well equipped, to start from Siberia, in the fall season, with reindeer and sleighs, on the ice of the frozen sea; I engage we will find a warm and rich land, stocked with thrifty vegetables and animals, if not men, on reaching one degree northward of latitude 82; we will return in the succeeding spring.

J.C.S.

This circular was sent to every learned society in the United States and Europe, every main town, and various distinguished individuals. It caused some hilarity in the popular press, but the only response seems to have been that of Count Volney, author of *Les Ruines des Empires*, supporter of the solar theory of religious origins, and President of the Académie des Sciences in Paris—who decided that it was unworthy of further consideration.

In the following year, 1819, Symmes moved to Newport, Kentucky, and, presumably, wrote the novel *Symzonia: A voyage of discovery*, published in 1820 under the name of "Captain Adam Seaborn." Soon after, he persuaded the State Senator, Richard M. Johnson, to submit a petition to Congress on 7 March 1822, requesting support for his proposed expedition to discover the lands within the earth. A second petition, to both Houses, was made in December 1823; and a third one, to the General Assembly of the State of Ohio, in January 1824,[14] the year in which Symmes settled on the farm which his uncle had left in Hamilton, Ohio. In the meantime, he published at least eight papers.[15]

Symmes had begun lecturing on his theory in 1820, in nearby Cincinnati. Perhaps encouraged by the Russian Government's granting of permission to start his expedition from Siberia—if he could underwrite and organize it, that is—he made a lecture-tour of the northeastern states in September 1825. He was accompanied by Jeremiah Reynolds, a young lawyer whom he had converted to the theory and who was one of the few to defend it in print.[16] But the strain of the tour brought on ill health, and Symmes retired to live in his native New Jersey until 1829, when he made the difficult journey back to Cincinnati. There he died on 29 May, and was buried in old Hamilton cemetery, beneath a monument erected by his son Americus, depicting the hollow globe which he had striven to explain to mankind.

Walter Kafton-Minkel surmises that Symmes got his ideas from reading about

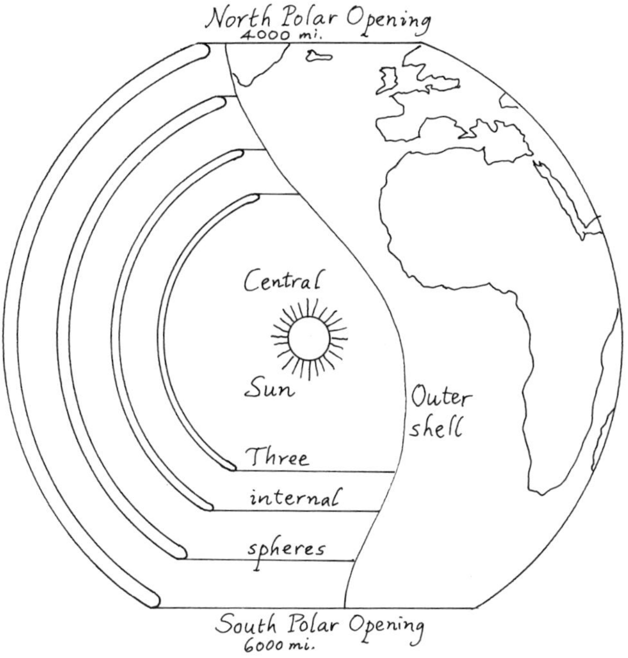

Illustration 5: Symmes's hollow globe

Halley's theory in Cotton Mather's *Christian Philosopher*, but his devotion to it betokens a more than literary influence. Symmes was no scholar, but a practical soldier, trader, and farmer. Something had utterly convinced him that the earth was a hollow shell, pierced by vast circular holes at each pole: 4000 miles across at the North, 6000 at the South (see diagram). These holes had never been noticed by sailors because of their enormous scale: to sail from our outer surface, round the inner rim, into the concave ocean within, was a matter of some 1500 miles, during which the changes of direction were very gradual. Certainly, mariners had experienced weird meteorological and magnetic conditions when venturing onto this in-between zone—but no one had yet gone further.[17] If any were deliberately to do so, they would discover not only the concave world on the underside of our own, but another globe suspended inside, also hollow and opening on to three further globes, like the nested spheres of Chinese ivory-carvers. In between there is space, filled with a light gas like hydrogen, which gives the spheres their buoyancy.[18] The whole inner world is lit with a perpetual day, thanks to the refraction of sunlight percolating through the holes.[19]

Symmes adduced several proofs of his theory. There was the unquestionable evidence of sailors that the North Polar region was something other than solid ice. Cosmogonically speaking, there was the observation that Nature likes to construct with hollow cylinders and concentric rings. Another proof was the phenomenon of earthquakes, which were impossible, Symmes thought, if the globe were solid right through; likewise, the strange behavior of tides and currents could best be explained by passages piercing the shell. (Kircher had also depicted underground channels to account for these.) Symmes made a very muddled analogy with Saturn and Jupiter, somehow interpreting their rings and belts, respectively, as signs that they were sets of hollow spheres. Light and dark circles around the poles of Mars, and the blunted south horn of the crescent Venus, completed his astronomical analogies: all the planets, he said, were made on the same pattern as the earth.[20] An early critic, Thomas J. Matthews, replied that Symmes' astronomical statements do not even stand up to observation; Newton's laws suffice to disprove the supposed refraction of light inside the spheres; while the diminished weight of Symmes' hollow earth would invalidate all the Newtonian laws of gravity. But he concurs that the Government should adopt Symmes' proposal, since even if his region is a fairyland, they might discover the North-West Passage.[21] Apparently it was enthusiasm for Symmes' ideas that was largely responsible for the US Exploring Expedition of 1838–1840, led by Charles Wilkes, which first determined that the Antarctic was of continental dimensions.[22]

It is easy to laugh at Symmes and his holes. But researchers in the occult will recognize him as a familiar type: the man with a military background (or the daughter of one), sane and competent in worldly terms, who nurtures a secret belief, perhaps founded on a moment of inexplicable revelation, that is the antithesis of his outward persona. Some psychologists would say that the more disciplined the mask, the more repressed and fantastic might be the inner life of such a person. We might add how symbolically appropriate this particular theory is, concretizing, as it were, the subliminal contents of the mind, and crying out for their exploration!

Psychometrists and Prophets

The open Arctic sea, perhaps surrounding an anomalously warm continent or island, was an obsession of nineteenth-century explorers. The appearance of driftwood floating south between Greenland and Spitzbergen, and the blowing of non-icy North winds, were two pieces of evidence that the climate does not necessarily get colder as one proceeds towards the Pole. While explorers from several nations spent the latter part of the nineteenth century crossing Greenland and northern Canada, the Bostonian family of William Denton was making its own investigations.

Mrs. Denton was a psychometrist, who could hold a rock or a bone in her hand and tell whence it came and what had befallen its owner. Here is the account of a sitting she gave while in Québec.

> One evening in December, 1862, when trying a crystal of amethystine quartz from St. Catherine's Bay, on the Saguenay, a tributary of the St. Lawrence, Mrs. Denton seemed to obtain, very readily, comprehensive views of the country to the north of there, and eventually appeared to pass into the polar regions,

though nothing of the kind was anticipated when the experiment commenced.

"The Hudson's Bay region is a great deal warmer than I supposed. I see lakes and streams over such a wide surface that they seem like pictures. I had no idea that these extreme northern regions had as temperate a climate as they seem to me now to possess. [...] It really seems warmer than it does here. It is so strange, it appears like another world. It seems a long way beyond the boundary of this continent. I fancy that must be the very pole itself. There is water between me and it. It does not seem as cold as I should have expected to find it, and I see neither snow nor ice. The heat seems to come from the interior, and yet I cannot think it possible. There seem to be boiling springs there." [23]

The Denton's son Sherman shared his mother's gift. At the age of thirteen, in 1869, he was induced to "visit" the extreme North, with the help of a map, and found islands there with plants, ferns, and animals. "If [the explorers] could push on through the thick ice, which is about a mile wide, they could get to the open sea; but they will stick before they get there," he said.[24] He also gave a description of the Antarctic regions, which he found as warm as the northern: there were brown men there, living in "quite decent" houses of sticks among a vegetation of monstrous leaves, and lit by the southern lights.[25] To complete the researches of this talented family, Mr. Denton's sister, Mrs. Cridge, was able to visit the same region. She also found a warm sea and a land beneath the North Star, "and a light rising continually, apparently from the water. It must be a current of electricity. It gives light continually; so that it is lighter here." Mrs. Cridge evokes the old myth of the magnetic mountain, adding: "There is a great deal of metal here that I think must be iron." [26]

The Dentons' findings could well have been appropriated as evidence by the hollow-earthers, who would say that the warm sea and the new, populated lands were really on the inside of the globe. Then, if there seemed something paradisal about this realm, it was hardly to be wondered at.

The inner Paradise reappears in a work by H. M. Howell, *The Kosmic Problem Solved* (1895). In the autumn of 1875, Howell had been brooding on biblical geography and studying the globe of the earth, when he was struck by the parallels that could be drawn between the ocean currents and the four rivers mentioned in Genesis 2.10–14 as flowing out of Eden. Symmes' theory furnished him with the clue he needed: "Eden" must be the concave side of the globe, the waters of its oceans welling out through the hole at the South Pole "as a great river, which subsequently washes the shores of the several continents with its purifying branches." [27]

Captain Symmes' son Americus, his father's biographer and faithful disciple, remarked in a postscript to his book dated 23 September 1880 that recent explorations seemed to prove the Symmes Theory true beyond a shadow of doubt. Apparently an English captain called Wiggins and an old American whaling master, Captain Tuttle, actually claimed to have visited "Symmzonia." A Mr. Seebohm, who had accompanied them, had read a paper at the Society of

EDEN RESTORED AND PARADISE FOUND.

HEAVEN REVEALED AND NEW JERUSALEM REALIZED.

Illustration 6: The four rivers and the polar paradise (Howell)

Arts in London, describing a country rich in gold, animals, and tropical flora. It was peopled by a race with a dark complexion, black hair, and "Roman noses"; they were seven or eight feet tall, and they spoke Hebrew. Were these not (said Mr. Seebohm) the lost tribes of Israel who went up the Euphrates to the North, and dwelt in a land where never man dwelt before?[28] Captain Tuttle is supposed to have corroborated Wiggins' and Seebohm's account in every detail.

I have not found other evidence of this delightful yarn: probably a couple of old sea-dogs were trying to "pull a fast one," perhaps in the hope of getting financial support for another expedition. The mythological dimension of the story is the most interesting one, as it admits the Lost Tribes of Israel to a Paradise—Howell also calls it Eden, the Third Heaven, and the New Jerusalem—inaccessible to the rest of us. It is the antithesis of the Lost Tribes theories so much bandied about in that period, which sought to identify them with Americans, British, or other surface-dwellers.

Americus Symmes, like his father, was no mystical dreamer. He immediately grasped the economic possibilities of the new world. Like a businessman summing up the potential market of an undeveloped nation, he points out that up to now, the Symmzonians have been marketing their produce ridiculously cheaply to the Chinese, with whom they must have some secret channels of communication; only this can explain how China is able to support so many people. The aptly-named Americus looks forward to the day when Symmzonia will be properly discovered and exploited. What an immense migration there will be! Nor does he ignore the medical benefits, in an age of tuberculosis and the longing of smog-ridden city-dwellers for warm, dry climates. All invalids, says Americus, should go to the interior world for their health.

But what if we were already there? This was the view of Cyrus or "Koresh" Teed (1839–1908) founder of Koreshanity. One of the many products of that breeding-ground of spiritual eccentricities, Upstate New York, Teed received his illumination in 1869 from an angelic Anima figure who appeared in his alchemical laboratory in Utica.[29] In 1870, he "announced the discovery of the cosmogonic form, which he then declared to be cellular, the surface of the earth being concave, with a curvature of about eight inches to the mile."[30] In other words, we live on the inside surface of a sphere.

Koresh taught that the earth was a laminated shell, a number of miles thick, formed from layers of the seven noble metals, with gold as the outermost one. The sun and stars move within the sphere, as also "the reflections called the planets and the moon."[31] In the center, as it appears from his diagrams, there is a black counter-sun which provides the obscurations of night (see diagram). All the planetary and terrestrial movements, including the precession of the equinoxes, were apparently explicable within the new scheme, which is not surprising, considering that they could be explained pretty adequately by the pre-Copernicans, before their universe was turned inside-out.

Koresh connected the precessional cycle of 24,000 years with the Incarnation of the "Son of God, who is Father, Mother, and Son." He came first in Adam,

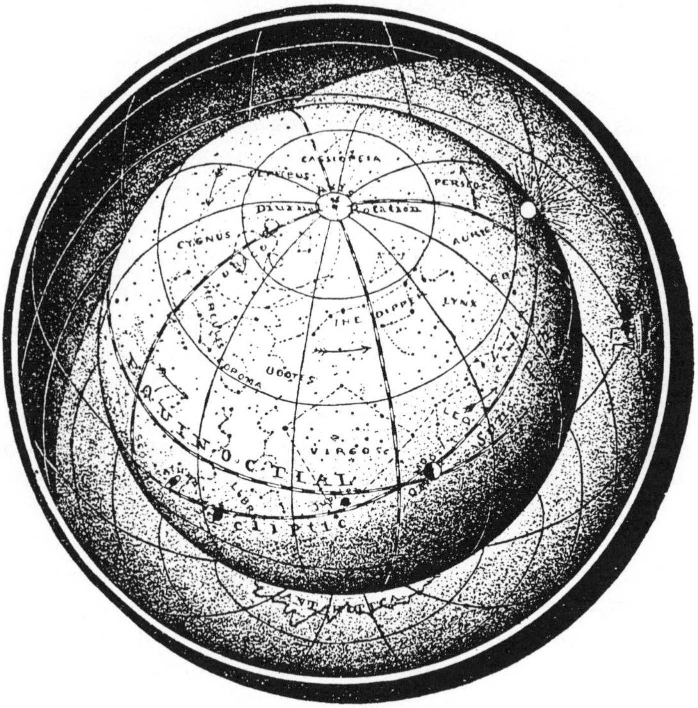

Illustration 7: The heavens as a sphere inside the concave earth (Koresh)

then, 24,000 years later, in Jesus Christ. Koresh explains:

> The Lord was not only the reincarnation of Elijah (God the Lord), of Moses, of Abraham, of Noah, of Enoch, and of Adam, in a direct line, but of all who died looking to his coming as the Messiah and Son of God in the indirect lines of reincarnation. He gathered into himself the spirits of the past. He was also the pole of influx from the heavenly worlds, and constituted the rolling together of the heavens as a scroll. He was the Word infolded and sealed.[32]

Koresh's own messianic role is indicated in the following prophecy:

> We are now approaching a great biological conflagration. Thousands of people will dematerialize, through a biological electro-magnetic vibration. This will be brought about through the direction of one mind, the only one who has a knowledge of the law of this bio-alchemical transmutation. The change will be accomplished through the formation of a biological battery, the laws of which are known only to one man. This man is Elijah the prophet, ordained of God, the Shepherd of the Gentiles and the central reincarnation of the ages. From

> this conflagration will spring the sons of God, the biune offspring of the Lord Jesus, the Christ and Son of God.[33]

Meeting with the usual reaction to home-grown cosmologies and provincial messianism, Teed eventually determined to prove his point on the scientists' own terms. In 1897, on the beach of Naples, Florida, he and his followers staged an experiment with equipment designed to produce an absolutely straight "air-line," free from the distortions of perspective that lead one to think that the earth curves convexly. Sure enough, the line, beginning 128" above water level, came closer and closer to the surface, eventually hitting the water in a little inlet, just over four miles down the beach. The world was indeed a concave sphere.

There are lively sketches of Teed's career in Kafton-Minkel,[34] as well as in two other compulsively readable books, Martin Gardner's *Fads and Fallacies in the Name of Science*[35] and John Michell's *Eccentric Lives and Peculiar Notions*.[36] There one can learn of his experiments and of the survival of his community in Florida to the present day. Teed emerges as an engaging personality, heading an efficient and hard-working celibate community which, true to its androgynous theology, showed an admirable respect for women. Michell remarks on the success of his experiments, which can hardly have been deliberately faked: "Perhaps the answer lies in the malleable, obliging nature of the universe, which reflects every image projected upon it and gives every experiment a tendency to gratify the experimenter."[37] I would concur, adding that it does not really matter whether the world is concave, convex, flat, or hollow: what matters is how people behave in or on it. There were plenty of decent folk in Antiquity and the Middle Ages who lived useful, even philosophical lives under the firm conviction that the earth was as flat as a pancake.

The hollow-earth revelation of Cyrus Teed in 1869 coincided with one on the other coast of America. Prof. William F. Lyon, of Sacramento, California, was visited in mid-September 1868 by a mysterious Dr. M. L. Sherman, who told him that he, Lyon, was the man he had been looking for.[38] Beginning on 1 January 1870, Sherman and his wife revealed the "seals" and "keys" of a mysterious book which they beheld in mediumistic trance, and which Lyon worked during 1870 into a lengthy treatise: *The Hollow Globe; or The World's Agitator and Reconciler* (1871).

> The first seal is supposed to allude to the great fact that this globe is a hollow or spherical shell with an interior as well as an exterior surface, and that it contains an inner concave as well as outer convex world, and that the inner is accessible by an extensive spirally formed aperture, provided with a deep and commodious channel suited to the purposes of navigation for the largest vessels that float, and that this aperture may be found in the unexplored open Polar Sea.[39]

Lyon was a practical man, of scientific bent. He reckoned that the inside of the globe would provide just the territory needed by an ever-expanding American or Anglo-Saxon race, likely to attain 400 million by 1971; and that Divine wisdom (always solicitous of the needs of superior races!) had provided for its discovery at precisely the right moment.[40] The Shermans' mystic book also promised the earth a second moon to appear within the century, to siphon off the excess electricity from the poles, thus warming them, and "to render still more cheerful the evenings of all the future generations, until our great mother shall so far unfold her inherent powers, as to be entirely independent of outside influences for the light her children require."[41] It seems that the Lyon-Sherman team had plugged into a similar source of inspiration to that of Charles Fourier, for whom the acquisition of extra moons and the self-luminosity of the earth were also promises of the future. Could it be that the "astral world," or wherever one imagines these revelations and channeled teachings to come from, is just as confused and confusing a place as the material world, where rival theories on the nature and history of the universe are continually being developed and discarded?

Modern Hollow-Earthers

With that sobering thought we proceed to 1906, when, amidst the anticipation of an imminent attainment of the North Pole, William Reed published his book *The Phantom of the Poles*. He called them a phantom in the sense that they do not exist as points on the earth's surface, as generally supposed, but merely as loci in space. Since Arctic exploration had progressed considerably since Symmes' time, Reed had to place the rims of his polar holes much further to the North and South, making openings of only a few hundred miles (see diagram). Nevertheless, he believed that all the recent polar explorers had made their way a certain distance around the rim, or even inside the cavity.

Reed's earth contains a central fire but no nesting spheres; the Arctic ocean continues round the rim into an inner world of lands and seas. Equipped with this scheme, he is able to find ingenious answers to the problems set by polar explorers and theorists:[42]

1. Why is the earth flattened at the poles? (Because the holes effectually cut it off)
2. Why have the poles never been reached? (There are none as such)
3. Why is the sun invisible so long in winter near the farthest points north or south? (Because one is already over the rim)
4. What is the Aurora Borealis? (Reflection of an interior fire)
5. Where are icebergs formed, and how? (As warm water flows out at the holes and freezes)
6. What produces a tidal wave? (Huge icebergs plunging into the ocean)
7. Why do meteors fall more frequently near the poles and whence do they come? (From interior volcanos)
8. What causes the great ice-pressure in the Arctic Ocean during still tide and calm weather? (Tidal waves from the interior—see 6)

GLOBE SHOWING SECTION OF THE
EARTH'S INTERIOR

Illustration 8: Sailing into the hollow earth (Reed)

9. Why is there colored snow in the Arctic region? (Pollen and volcanic dust from the interior)

10. Why is it warmer near the poles than six hundred to one thousand miles away from them? (Assuming that the earth is hollow, the interior should be warmer)

11. Why is ice in the Arctic Ocean frequently filled with rock, gravel, sand, etc.? (From volcanos exploding near where the iceberg was formed)

12. Does the compass refuse to work near the poles? (Yes, because it does not point to the Pole, but to the rim).

Reed's book defined the hollow-earth theory for the new century, and subsequent authors such as Marshall B. Gardner (*A Journey to the Earth's Interior*, 1913; revised and enlarged 1920) did little to improve on its classic simplicity. Adherents of the doctrine were, and are, little moved by any evidence to the contrary. If one can accept a hollow and habitable earth, it takes little additional effort to believe in a world-wide conspiracy to suppress knowledge of it, through the muzzling of explorers and, more recently, the falsification of satellite photographs.

Mention of suppressed evidence brings us to one of the most curious twists in this tale of polar holes. It begins in October 1926, when the student Amadeo Giannini had an epiphany while walking in the woods of New England.

> He journeyed to the celestial beacons on the wings of extrasensory perception's limitless necromancy. That magic permitted breaking through the long-established barriers of deduction, hypothesis, and theory. It disdainfully pushed aside the ice barriers of the terrestrial North Pole and South Pole assumed Earth ends [sic]. And there, beyond the Poles, the most fascinating creative secrets were divulged. Throughout the ages, they had been held in sacred trust for the doubter and true seeker who ventured that way. The secrets then disclosed provided knowledge of land courses into all the land areas of the Universe. Hence, to discerning consciousness, it was plainly shown there are no ends to the Earth.[43]

As is all too plainly shown by this extract, Giannini was no writer. But if *Worlds Beyond the Poles* is all but unreadable, Giannini deserves a place in this gallery of those fortunate enough to have been tapped on the shoulder by an angel when they were young—and unfortunate enough to have become frozen in the knowledge of that moment.

With admirable self-confidence, the young Amadeo took his cosmological vision in turn to a Professor of Astronomy, then to the Cardinal Archbishop of Boston, and in 1928 to numerous scientific and media people in California, whom he names in his book.[44] In 1930, he released an illustrated statement to the scientific editors of press syndicates in New York City. And so, like a reincarnation of Symmes, Giannini pursued his lonely mission until 1935, trying to find a wealthy patron to finance a stratospheric balloon ascent or a polar voyage to prove his cosmology.

What, precisely, was this cosmology, expressed in confusing prose and contradictory diagrams (to say nothing of his verse)? Giannini says that he has not explained but only hinted at it, and that "if the hint does not serve, modern civilization is not entitled to know the structure of the Universe."[45] The essential facts are these: (1) There is perfect analogy and physical continuity between what we know as earth, and what we see as the heavens when we look upward. (2) All the heavenly bodies except the sun are actually distorted appearances of the underside of the heavenly sky. The heaven-dwellers (plants, animals, and humans like ourselves) would see the same if they looked "down" towards us. (3) The heavenly surface and the earthly surface are separated by, or enclosed in, a dark stratosphere that is all our space vehicles could ever explore. (4) The apparent motions of the sun and heavenly bodies are caused by complex rhythmical movements of the earth's surface, which rises and falls like the breathing of a living creature. (5) The way to get from the earthly surface to the heavenly one is by continuing due north or south past the polar barriers of ice and snow. Once that is done, an infinite physical field lies open to exploration.

Giannini does not seem to have had a cosmological picture susceptible to being drawn or visualized. A pervasive theme of his book is the unreliability of optics, and the distortions caused by lenses including that of the eye. Sometimes he seems to be talking of a flat, hollow world, like the inside of a infinite sandwich, with heaven one side and earth the other. At other times, it makes more sense to imagine this world bent in torus shape, with communication at the poles. Then again, he evokes the image of an infinite plain on which a flat earth is circumscribed by "polar" ice and snow-barriers, with heaven extending beyond. One thing he never mentions is Relativity.

Whatever his cosmology, Giannini was convinced that access to the heavenly world had opened up in his time, in consequence of Sir George Hubert Wilkins' discovery of land beyond the South Pole on 12 December 1928, and Admiral Richard Byrd's discovery of land beyond the North Pole in February 1947. Young Giannini had managed to accost Wilkins before the latter departed on his expedition, and to explain his theory to the older man. Wilkins said to him: "You know, before leaving England I was advised that if I succeeded in penetrating beyond the South Pole point I would be drawn to another 'planet' by the suction of its movement," and promised that if Giannini would show him the route to the land claimed to exist beyond the South Pole, he would continue on in spite of all obstacles.[46] Giannini says that as a result, Wilkins' 1928 expedition, unlike those of Peary, Amundsen, and other explorers who claimed to have reached the poles but then turned back, "did penetrate beyond the South Pole point in a *southerly direction* and discovered that land extended at least five thousand miles BEYOND the original mathematized 'end' of the Earth."[47]

Parallel to Wilkins' achievement, in Giannini's view, was the expedition of Rear-Admiral Richard E. Byrd, who said in a radio announcement from his Arctic base in February 1947: "I'd like to see that land beyond the Pole. That area beyond the Pole is the center of the great unknown." Giannini analyzes this statement carefully, believing that it can only mean the celestial land, since none other is to be found in the Arctic ocean. Thus he describes Byrd's epoch-making flight:

> The admiral's airplane pursued a course on the horizontal from the North Pole point to a point 1,700 miles beyond the Earth. Then the course was retraced to the Arctic base. At no time did he "shoot up," or out, from the Earth level. As progress was made beyond the Pole point, there was observed directly under the plane's course iceless land and lakes, and mountains where foliage was abundant. Moreover, a brief newspaper account of the flight held that a member of the admiral's crew had observed a monstrous greenish-hued animal moving through the underbrush of that land beyond the Pole.[48]

Finally, Giannini records a radio announcement that "On January 13 [1956] members of the United States expedition accomplished a flight of 2,700 miles from the base at McMurdo Sound, which is 400 miles west of the South Pole, and penetrated *a land extent of 2,300 miles beyond the Pole*." Admiral Byrd, on his return, remarked that "The present expedition has opened up a vast new land."[49]

Giannini's book was not widely advertized, but it did come to the notice of Ray Palmer, now editor of *Flying Saucers*, who wrote a reflective review of it in

December 1959. It supplied exactly what had been missing ever since the Shaver Mystery had simmered down as a source for pulp material. Thus Byrd's discovery of land beyond the poles entered the repertory of popular myths. It was cited at least a dozen times, beginning with the title-page, in Raymond Bernard's *The Hollow Earth* (1964, rev. ed. 1969), the definitive document of the hollow-earth school.

The late Raymond Bernard (not to be confused with his living French homonym) was the author of over forty books and pamphlets which were marketed in mimeographed form during the 1960s by the Fieldcrest Publishing Co., New York (later by Health Research in California). Most of them concerned health, sex, organic living, and the problem of Christian origins. Because some have even doubted Bernard's existence, it may be mentioned that he attended the School of Education of New York University, earning the M.A. in 1930 and the Ph.D. in 1932, under the name of Walter Siegmeister.[50] In 1956 he moved to Joinville, Santa Caterina State, Brazil, to found a idealistic community and avoid the nuclear war that he felt to be inevitable before 1965.[51] Although he never claimed to have discovered them himself, he heard in many reports from friends and strangers about tunnels leading to an underground realm, and the emergence of flying saucers from them.[52] He then joined Dickhoff, "Doreal," "Brother Philip," George Adamski, George Hunt Williamson, and Ray Palmer's stable of writers as a proponent of the interplanetary invasion theory that was to be given the widest currency by Robert Charroux and Eric van Däniken.[53]

Some readers will already have wanted to object that Admiral Byrd was not at the North Pole in 1947, as stated in *Worlds Beyond the Pole* and *The Hollow Earth*, but in Antarctica. These are his activities there, as chronicled in *Quest for a Continent* by Walter Sullivan, the journalist who accompanied Byrd both on this and on his 1956 expedition. In the 50 hours beginning on 13 February 1947, ten flights were made in clear, cold weather, during which more unknown areas were sighted than ever before in such a period. In this "Operation Highjump," Byrd was seeking the answer to the question of whether Antarctica was one continent or two. On February 14, he flew to the South Pole and went 140 miles beyond it, in the direction of the Indian Ocean. On the 15th, Byrd decided to try for his other goal, the "Pole of Inaccessibility," 1000 miles from all sea-coasts, at about 84°S, 65°E. He flew over that point and on for 80 to 100 miles into the unknown hinterland beyond.[54] (See maps, p. 128.)

The 1956 expedition, "Operation Deepfreeze," comprised nine major flights between January 3–14. It revealed no great mountain range or hot springs area, but a featureless ice plateau more than 14,000 feet high. However, relatively little of the Antarctic continent was covered—its area far exceeds that of the United States—and there was much room for undiscovered mountains.[55]

So much for Byrd's rumored penetration of the hollow earth: his "land beyond the Pole" was nothing other than the unexplored part of the Antarctic continent, "beyond" the South Pole from the point of view of the U.S. base on the Ross Ice

Shelf. Probably the error sown by Giannini and repeated by Palmer and Bernard will flourish for years to come. Giannini himself excused it by claiming that Byrd had made a second, clandestine trip to the Arctic in 1947.[56] Then again, perhaps someone will even point out that Admiral Byrd is not such a trustworthy witness either, since circumstantial evidence points to his having faked his 1926 flight over the North Pole, and, with the help of his senator brother, to have broken the career of Bernt Balchen, the only man who knew it.[57]

Chapter Ten:
Antarctica

Kircher's analogy of the earth's body with that of an animal places the South Pole in a most undignified position. It may be that this is not merely northern chauvinism, for the earth itself presents a marked contrast between its two polar regions, which from the human point of view is a qualitative one. In the north, cities such as Oslo, Helsinki, Tallinn, and Leningrad cluster around the sixtieth parallel, to say nothing of Reykjavik at 64°N. To their north extend vast tracts of useful land, supporting agriculture and abundant forest life. Coal and other minerals are mined on Norway's Svalbard Islands (Spitsbergen), which reach beyond the 80th parallel. In the rosy days of the Thulean period, the Canadian explorer Vilhjalmur Stefansson claimed that "there is no northern boundary beyond which productive enterprise cannot go until North meets North on the opposite shore of the Arctic Ocean as East has met West on the Pacific" [1]—and he should know, having spent five months marooned on an ice-floe. Nowadays ice-breakers open the Northwest Passage every spring for a busy sea traffic; airplanes crisscross the Pole, and nuclear submarines pass beneath the thin ice of the Arctic Ocean, even breaking through at the North Pole itself, as the USS *Skate* did in March 1959.

In the South, things are quite different. As Charles Fort phrased it, "History, like South America and Africa, tapers southward. [...] Preponderantly peninsulas are southward droops." [2] Cape Horn, the last landfall of Chile, has drooped away by 56°S, and by the sixtieth parallel one is nearing the uninhabited South Orkney Islands, the first straggling harbingers of the Antarctic Peninsular. There are beautiful things about Antarctica, still miraculously free from mining and territorial claims; one can enjoy real and imaginary pictures of its unspoilt scenery and largely untroubled wildlife. But the unattractive things about this continent, as big as the United States and Europe combined, are such that none but scientists want to live there. It is hard to reach, being surrounded on all sides by seas of notorious roughness. It is much colder than the Arctic, thanks to the absence of warming currents like the Gulf Stream; the eccentricity of the earth's orbit, which makes the Antarctic summer a week shorter than that of the north; and the perpetual rolling down of chilled air from the icecap that covers the continent to a depth of up to three miles. Finally, apart from the creatures on its

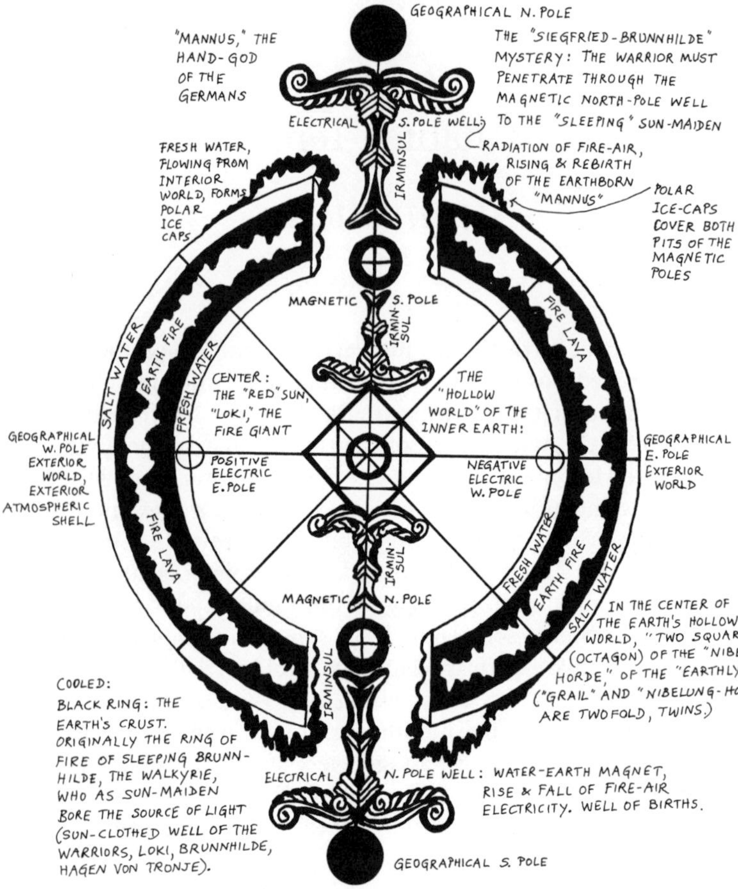

Illustration 9: Nordic mythology and the hollow earth (redrawn from Serrano)

fringes supported by the krill—whales, seals, penguins, gulls, mites, etc.—virtually the only life of its interior is the alien one of clouds and frozen water.

At least, that is the view in educated and scientific circles. But the kind of people who write about Commander Byrd's flight beyond the pole into the hollow earth are also quick to ascribe to him the sighting of lushly vegetated lands, preferably with a mammoth blundering through the undergrowth. The German Antarctic expedition to Queen Maud Land in 1938–39 made some surprising discoveries, including "a group of low-lying hills sprinkled with many lakes and completely free of ice and snow," resembling the barren hot springs region of Iceland.[3] Claiming this Norwegian sector with swastika flags, the Germans renamed it *Neuschwabenland* (New Swabia).

According to Miguel Serrano, the Germans also found there a way of communication with the Hollow Earth and its secret cities, where the First

Hyperboreans had taken refuge from the disaster that reversed the Poles.[4] There a secret base was prepared during the war years, and thither Adolf Hitler escaped in a *vimana* (flying saucer plane) to direct the "esoteric war" to this day. Serrano states this as fact in his philosophical testament, and supplies a diagram that blends the physical with the mythological: partly a cutaway diagram of the inner earth such as we met with in the previous chapter, it is also an explanation of the subtle currents at the two poles and their complementarity.

But Serrano was only repeating a favorite theme of neo-Nazi and sensational literature. In his well-documented study *The Hitler Survival Myth* (1981), Donald McKale identifies the earliest source of the myth of Hitler's escape to the southern hemisphere as the unexpected surrender of a German submarine in early July 1945 at Mar del Plata, Argentina. Several Buenos Aires newspapers, in defiance of Argentine Navy statements, said that rubber boats had been seen landing from it, and other submarines spotted in the area. One paper, *Critica*, carried on 17 July 1945 the report that Adolf Hitler and Eva Braun had landed from a U-530 in Antarctica, and mentioned the 1938–39 expedition, as a result of which a "new Berchtesgaden" was "likely to have been built." This report received wide distribution through quotation in *Le Monde* and the *New York Times* on 18 July; on the 16th, the *Chicago Times* had carried a sensational article on the Hitlers having slipped off to Argentina.[5]

The myth of an Antarctic refuge, armed with flying saucers, reached its apotheosis in W. A. Harbinson's thriller *Genesis* (1980). This develops the Jules-Vernian theme of a "Master of the World" who, thanks to the Nazi régime, has become a technocratic power before which even Washington and Moscow must quail. Harbinson supplements his fiction with an excellent list of factual sources about Nazi saucer-planes and Antarctic explorations.[6] Another version of the myth appears in *Opération Orth* (1989), a strange and surely an ironic work by Jean Robin, one of the foremost authorities on René Guénon and no lover of the "Counter-initiation" of which he holds Hitler to have been a primary, if unconscious, agent.

Jean Robin writes, supposedly on the evidence of a friend who had been there, of a subterranean complex of high technology entered near Valparaiso by a *vimana* which could pass through solid rock. There was found the new Asgard or Agartha, the headquarters of the Black Order, where 350,000 initiates await "Him Who Shall Come."[7] A mysterious green flame suspended in a niche of stone and called the *Cheskin* serves to recharge their energies and focus their cult.[8]

Is Adolf Hitler "He Who Shall Come," as in Serrano? No: in Robin's book Hitler died in this subterranean retreat in 1953, and his body is enshrined and visible in a hexagonal casket—side by side with that of Raoul Wallenberg, the Swedish diplomat who saved thousands of Hungarian Jews during the war, and was "kidnapped" by the Soviets in Budapest.[9] This dual presence, Robin's friend was given to understand, poses no problem to the many Jews who belong to the Black Order: they blame their fellows for their "refusal to collaborate" with the evolutionary process.[10]

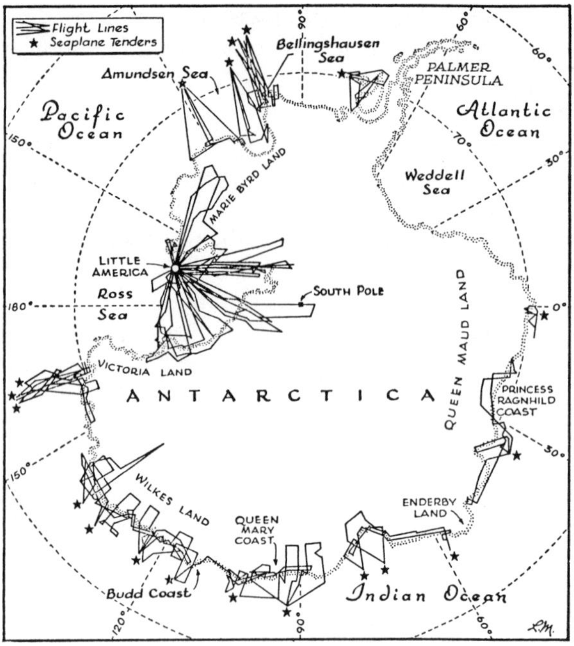

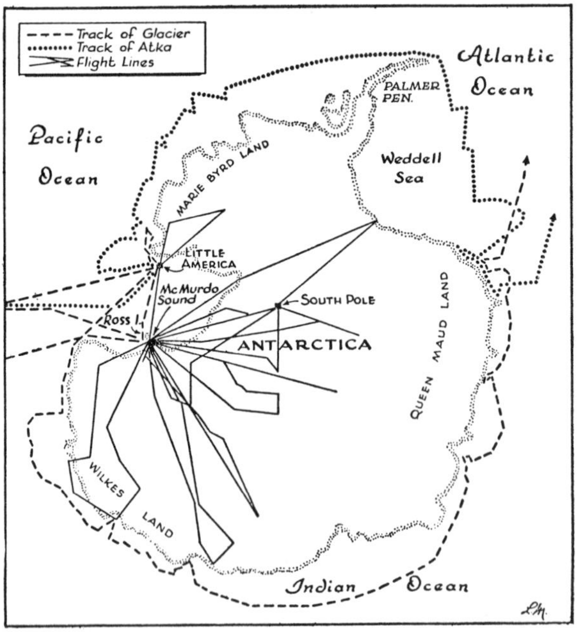

Illustration 10: Richard Byrd's exploratory flights

Opération Orth poses every manner of problem, however, to the reader, who can only wonder what prompted Jean Robin to present the shocking images of Hitler and Wallenberg reconciled, and the casual dismissal of the Holocaust by the Jews of his Black Order. In the context of Guénonian attitudes, which are nothing if not respectful of the Jewish people and their tradition, there is nothing to be said, unless it be that Robin actually accepts his friend's account, and is warning us of the Counter-initiation's final obscenity.

Those who believe in the Nazi Antarctic bases, with or without Hitler alive or dead, will find it significant that Richard Byrd went there in 1946–47, and again in 1956, on expeditions massively supported by the United States Navy. But here is the most extraordinary thing: according to the official maps of his many flights,[11] Byrd's expeditions left Queen Maud Land absolutely unvisited. The conspiratorial literature has no difficulty in explaining this: Byrd was scared away by the protective power demonstrated by the secret center, and after losing four planes, kept his distance.[12]

Poe, Verne, Lovecraft

Writers of fictions about Antarctica seem anxious for their work to be mistaken for fact. This was a common affectation in nineteenth-century fiction, and often used by the first great imaginative writer on Antarctica, Edgar Allen Poe (1809–1849). The South Pole appears in the short story *MS. Found in a Bottle* (1833), which employs the common literary device of a ship blown off course to discover new worlds. Poe's narrator, of course, goes one better: his own ship wrecked, he is hurled onto the rigging of a grotesquely antique, oversized galleon, manned by the living dead, which heads straight for the Pole. Scribbling frantically in the face of certain doom, he writes of his descent into a gigantic whirlpool:

> Oh, horror upon horror!—the ice opens suddenly to the right, and to the left, and we are whirling dizzily, in immense concentric circles, round and round the borders of a gigantic amphitheatre, the summit of whose walls is lost in the darkness and the distance. But little time will be left to me to ponder upon my destiny! The circles rapidly grow small—we are plunging madly within the grasp of the whirlpool—and amidst a roaring, and bellowing, and thundering of ocean and of tempest, the ship is quivering—oh God! and—going down![13]

Poe, who tried to be accurate in his facts, later felt obliged to add a note to the end of this tale, saying that it was only many years afterwards that "I became acquainted with the maps of Mercator, in which the ocean is represented as rushing, by four mouths, into the (northern) Polar Gulf, to be absorbed into the bowels of the earth; the Pole itself being represented by a black rock, towering to a prodigious height."[14] Poe would make good his error in *A Descent into the Maelstrom*, which is set in the North. But his polar masterpiece, and the longest piece of fiction he ever wrote, was *The Narrative of Arthur Gordon Pym* (1838).

At the time of Poe's writing, Antarctica had been touched on but not yet "discovered" in any real sense. Captain James Cook, in 1775, had reported after his circumnavigation of Antarctica that "no continent was to be found in this ocean but must lie so far south as to be wholly inaccessible on account of ice."[15] Subsequent explorations by the British and Russians were inconclusive, and mostly limited to the islands and peninsular. In 1825, John R. Reynolds of Ohio began vigorous agitations in favor of an American Antarctic expedition, twice addressing the U.S. Congress. (One notes circumstantially that Symmes' petition to explore the hollow globe had been made to the General Assembly of Ohio, in 1824.) Public opinion eventually came to his aid, and in 1836 an Exploring Expedition was authorized. After all manner of controversies and delays, the expedition set sail in August 1838 under Charles Wilkes. Poe's *Narrative* thus appeared in serial form in the full light of public interest and excitement about the Antarctic.

The Narrative of Arthur Gordon Pym is too well-known a literary work to delay us long. Suffice it to recall that the narrator discovers, beyond the ice-floes, a warm land inhabited by disagreeable black-toothed savages who bring about the deaths of all but himself and the half-breed Dirk Peters. The natives of this black land have a superstitious horror of anything white, which draws from them the cry *Tekeli-li!* Although they now live in the most primitive of shelters, Pym discovers a system of underground passages that seem to have been made in significant shapes, and also records what may be archaic script from the wall of one of the chambers. After the usual privations and hair-raising adventures, the two men escape and enter a calm polar sea that becomes ever warmer and whiter in hue, while flocks of gigantic white birds pass overhead crying *Tekeli-li!* At last they find themselves driven towards a silent cataract of white vapor.

> And now we rushed into the embraces of the cataract, where a chasm threw itself open to receive us. But there arose in our pathway a shrouded human figure, very far larger in its proportions than any dweller among men. And the hue of the skin of the figure was of the perfect whiteness of snow.[16]

Thus the *Narrative* ends; a Postscript apologizes for the loss of the "few remaining chapters" upon Pym's recent death.

There is little doubt that the Symmes Theory furnished Poe with the unacknowledged basis for his story. The Antarctic hole would have to be far smaller than the 6000-mile diameter Symmes gave to it—about 500 miles would fit Pym's bearings. But Poe could well be describing the unknowing traversal of its rim and the entry into an inner world which, like Symmzonia, is entirely white.

One person who could not bear to leave Pym's narrative unfinished was Jules Verne (1828–1905). In his *Le Sphinx des Glaces* (The Sphinx of the Icy Regions, 1897), he reintroduces Dirk Peters on a voyage to Antarctica whose secret object is the rescue of Arthur Gordon Pym—not returned and dead as Poe's informant had it, but abandoned and perhaps still alive in that mysterious polar land.

Verne's story takes his characters on open sea to the same black land, now devoid of its inhabitants who have perished in an earthquake. Still seeking Pym, they proceed northwards on the other side of the Pole until they find the curtain of mist which lifts to reveal the Sphinx of the title, presumably identical to the giant white figure of Poe's conclusion. It is a mountain shaped naturally into a crouching sphinx—but a magnetic mountain, so powerful as to suck every piece of iron out of a ship. There they find Pym's last and tragic resting-place, pinioned to the rock by his own musket. Dirk Peters dies of a broken heart at thus finding his "poor Pym"; the others just manage to clear the ice-barrier before winter freezes it, and so they come home.

In a typically didactic digression, Jules Verne's narrator tries to account for this magnetic mountain:

> The Trade-winds bring a constant succession of clouds or mists in which immense quantities of electricity not completely exhausted by storms, are stored. Hence there exists a formidable accumulation of electric fluid at the poles, and it flows towards the land in a permanent stream. [...] it would suffice that a block of iron should be subjected to [these currents'] action for it to be changed into a magnet of power proportioned to the intensity of the current, to the number of turns of the electric helix, and to the square root of the diameter of the block of magnetized iron.[17]

The turns of the coil of this giant electro-magnet are supplied, he supposes, by the windings of a metallic lode in the ground, connected with the base of the block. So the south polar vortex in this case is not a watery but an electrical one.

We will return in Chapter Thirteen to Jules Verne and the secret agenda of his works. Now we turn to the inheritor of Poe's literary mantle, Howard Phillips Lovecraft (1890–1937). This writer of fantastic literature sketched in a handful of stories a whole mythological complex dealing—as any complete mythology must—with the origins of the human race. After Lovecraft's death it was elaborated by other writers, especially August Derleth, into what the latter called the "Chthulhu Mythos," after the monstrosity let loose upon the world in Lovecraft's *The Call of Chthulhu* (1926). So far this resembles the continuation of Poe's tale by Jules Verne. But in Lovecraft's case there is more: the mythology which he himself regarded as no more than dream-inspired fiction was accepted as factual by the afficionados of the Shaver Mystery on the one hand, and, on the other, by certain highly educated practioners of the "Magick" of the Left Hand Path, led by the prestigious mage of the O.T.O., Kenneth Grant.

One of Lovecraft's longest and by general consent finest tales, *At the Mountains of Madness* (written 1931, published 1936), is set in Antarctica, whither the narrator has gone on an expedition sponsored by the fictitious Miskatonic University. As Peter Cannon points out,[18] Lovecraft had been fascinated by the Antarctic since boyhood; he was surely inspired by the recent expedition of Richard Byrd, who in 1929 was the first to fly over the South Pole; and he pays explicit tribute in the story to Poe's *Narrative of Arthur Gordon Pym.*

At the Mountains of Madness tells of the discovery of the star-headed, barrel-bodied, five-winged Old Ones,[19] who came to earth before there was any life upon it, and when the continents had not yet drifted apart (Lovecraft was an early follower of Wegener's theory). They created life on earth and built on the Antarctic "Plateau of Leng" a gigantic city of obsidian, which the explorers discover by airplane. Landing there at the risk of their lives, the narrator and one companion explore the city and learn from elaborate bas-reliefs of the incredible history of the Old Ones and the planet for which they have cared; of the other races that have evolved or arrived from elsewhere, usually to the detriment of the Old Ones' utopian civilization. Lovecraft evokes sympathy for these primordial beings, gentle scientists and historians by nature, and for the pathetic end of the ones awoken by the explorers from their age-long sleep, only to be eaten by their own creations, the ghastly Shoggoths.

Lovecraft's mythopoeic methods were the antithesis of those of a Tolkien, who supported his mythology with carefully worked-out philological and geographical documents. This is why August Derleth took it upon himself to improve the Chthulu Mythos through his own fictional contributions, filling out gaps and giving it a tighter organization. A case in point is the "Plateau of Leng."[20] In *The Hound* (1922), just after the first mention in any of Lovecraft's works of the grimoire *Necronomicon*, comes an allusion to "the corpse-eating cult of inaccessible Leng, in Central Asia."[21] A few years later, in *The Dream-Quest of Unknown Kadath* (1927), the Plateau of Leng is a dream-place where the protagonist confronts a high priest masked in yellow silk. Finally, in *At the Mountains of Madness*, the explorers find an endless plateau and identify it as the true Plateau of Leng. "Mythologists," explains the narrator, "have placed Leng in Central Asia; but the racial memory of man—or of his predecessors—is long."

It is with no conscious intention that we have also moved, in the present book, from a mythological Agartha in Central Asia, through one that seems rather to exist in dream and vision (Shambhala), to the Antarctic. Two of Lovecraft's friends completed the cycle by setting their fantasy-novels in the uttermost North: Robert E. Howard, with his series on Conan the Barbarian, and Clark Ashton Smith, with his Commorian legends also set in frozen Hyperborea. A separate study would have to be made on the archetypes of Hyperborea and Thule in modern fantasy-literature and games (for example, *Dungeons and Dragons*): a study for which the present book might provide some anchoring points.

Lovecraft's ancient civilization in Antarctica is placed so far back in time that those who wish can actually reconcile it with geology. I follow here the scientific account of Margaret Bradshaw,[22] who writes that Antarctica, as part of the supercontinent of Gondwana, was probably in equatorial latitudes during the Cambrian Period (about 500 million years ago). By the beginning of the Permian Period (300 my), Gondwana was polar, the South Pole migrating in the course of twenty million years from the region that would later become Africa / South America, across Antarctica, to Australia. In the Triassic Period (240–190 my),

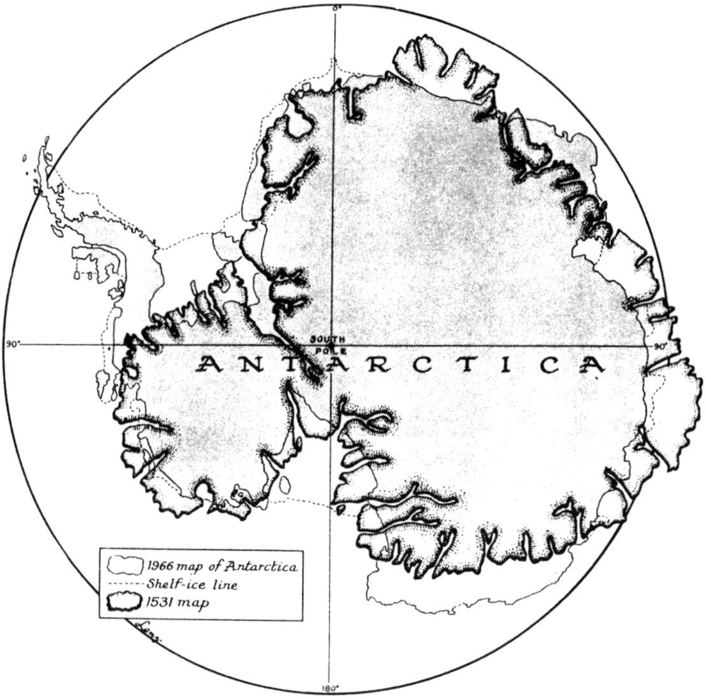

Illustration 11: Oronteus Finaeus' 1531 map of Antarctica superimposed on a modern one, showing the Ross Sea unglaciated

Antarctica was richly forested and inhabited by reptiles. After that came the period of violent volcanic activity that eventually led to the breakup of Gondwana and the beginning of the continents' progress to their present situations. In the course of the Tertiary Period (65–1.5 my), the major mountain chains were built on the continent, and the present ice-sheet was formed. The continent has been thoroughly glaciated for about twenty million years, so any later habitation is out of the question.

While this is the large-scale story, there may have been variations within shorter spans of Antarctic history. Charles Hapgood, in his *Maps of the Ancient Sea Kings* (1979), reproduces the findings of geologists of impeccable credentials that show, in his words, that "during the last million years or so there have been at least three periods of temperate climate in Antarctica when the shores of the Ross Sea must have been free of ice."[23] In particular, there was a longish warm period that ended about 4,000 BCE. Hapgood's book is subtitled *Evidence of Advanced Civilization in the Ice Age*, and presents a wide variety of ancient maps that show uncannily accurate knowledge not only of lands undiscovered until the modern age, such as the Antarctic coast, but also of lands invisible at any age of human existence, namely the shores of the Ross Sea. Alas, history has no room in its limited imagination for theories such as Hapgood's, however persuasively argued and well-documented, because they would require too thorough a revision of the status quo. It is one thing for analyses of Antarctic sea-floor cores to be published in the *Journal of Geology*; it is quite another to ask prehistorians to imagine a civilization 6,000 years ago which was capable of mapping the whole globe. Like the cardinals who refused to look through Galileo's telescope, lest they should see what he saw and suffer the same delusions, most prehistorians simply do not read books with subtitles such as Hapgood's.

Polarity of North and South

The mythology surrounding the North Pole has tended to be positive: it is always the Arctic that is imagined as the location of the endless springtime and the cradle of noble races. The Antarctic, on the other hand, is negative: it evokes tales of gloom and destruction, and is populated by primordial horrors, or else by their recent representatives, the Nazis. If the Arctic Ocean is still imaginable as open to the world within, from which the Aurora Borealis streams in all its wonder and beauty, any hole at the South Pole is firmly shut with a lid of ice three miles thick. In short, the North is the positive and the South the negative pole of the earth.

In the accounts of this from "illumined" sources, there seems either to be confusion of the physical with the non-physical—magnetism and electricity with the soul, for instance—or else there is evidence of some occult unity which modern science, ignorant of the ways of souls, cannot fathom. For example, in 1845 an uneducated girl gave in mesmeric trance a number of answers to questions of cosmology and occultism that have a bearing on our subject. Her answers were recorded by Zadkiel (Richard Morrison) in his *Almanac*, and reprinted in Peter Davidson's *Occult Magazine*.[24] One of them states:

> The magnetism of the Earth is another modification of electricity, and also circulates through the system. It passes off from the Earth at the North Pole, producing the *Aurora Borealis*, circulates through the other planets, and returns to the Earth in a purified state [...]

And another, which seems to refer to Mackey's "Age of Horror" (see Chapter Fifteen):

> [Question] Will you look at the Earth and say whether the pole be turned away from its course—the same as it was 10,000 years ago—or be less turned away?
> [Answer] Yes, it is less turned away. The Sun once went over the Pole of the Earth, but that was a long time ago—that was before Adam—there were other kinds of men on the Earth then.

In *Ghostland*, the anonymous author writes of the great spirit Metron, tutelary angel of this planet. (Possibly he means Metatron, who in Kabbalah is the spirit of the Primum Mobile.) Metron governs the "electric life evolved from the galvanic action of metallic lodes threading their way like a gigantic nervous system through every globe; vast reservoirs of polar force generated in the Arctic North and Antarctic South."[25] These regions, we are told, "form the brain and feet of the living earth,"[26] but Metron's station is in the "brain regions of the polar North."[27]

H. P. Blavatsky concurs with this polarization of the earth. She writes in *The Secret Doctrine* of how when the first Atlanteans were born on Lemuria, they very soon began to divide into those who worshipped "the one unseen Spirit of Nature, the ray of which man feels within himself," and those who offered "fanatical worship to the Spirits of the Earth, the dark Cosmic anthropomorphic Powers, with whom they made alliance."[28] It was the latter, one understands, who gravitated to the South Pole, called "the *pit*, cosmically and terrestrially—whence breathe the hot passions blown into hurricanes by the cosmic Elementals, whose abode it is."[29] Elsewhere she explains that the earth's seven zones correspond to the Seven Principles of man, Mount Meru or the North Pole answering to the Seventh principle, "the region of Atma, of pure soul, and Spirituality."[30] Therefore the South, although Blavatsky does not spell it out, is probably to be taken as corresponding to the physical body, the lowest of the principles.

We meet an interesting reference to Meru in Saint-Yves d'Alveydre's *Mission de l'Inde*:

> Everything has been plumbed [by the Agarthians], from the fiery entrails of the Globe to its subterranean streams of gas and water, both fresh and salt, even to the living beings who inhabit these flames, gases, and waters.
>
> Everything has been plumbed across the breadth and depth of the oceans, even the role of magnetic currents which interfere with one another longitudinally from pole to pole, and latitudinally from tropic to tropic. [...]
>
> Everything has been revealed, even to the universal harmonies that produce the terrestrial seasons, and the ascending migrations of souls by the North Pole: that unfindable Mount Meru and that undecipherable Alborj of the Vedic and Pahlevi books.[31]

Movement of souls, it seems, is from South to North, and that is what one would expect if the North is the closer to the spiritual world.

Among more recent philosophers whose polar theory is in accord with that of Theosophy, Schwaller de Lubicz compares the poles to the active (North) and passive (South), or male and female principles.[32] Commenting on ancient Egyptian symbolism, he depicts the movement from one to another as literally as the circulation of Kircher's oceans:

> Let us note something not generally known: that is, that the North Pole attracts and the South Pole repels, with respect to the masses of these rotating bodies [planets, etc.]. Our North Pole *hollows out the earth* and it can be said to absorb the continents, whereas the South Pole extrudes earth and it can be said to create the continents. The entire mass of our continents is projected in a spiral motion toward the North Pole.[33]

This passage, written in 1949, bears study in the context of what is now known of Continental Drift. In the scientists' reconstruction of Gondwana, Antarctica lies between Africa, India, and South Australia. The other continents have gradually moved away from it to their present positions surrounding the Arctic Ocean. As for the extrusion and absorption of earth, one can at least say that ancient maps of the North Atlantic and Arctic Oceans record islands and mainland regions that have since disappeared.[34]

The reversal of the two poles of the earth relative to the celestial poles, as imagined by several of the theorists in Part Five, naturally raises questions about this matter of polarity. Does the negativity of Antarctica derive from its position on earth, or from its orientation in space? Miguel Serrano thought that the reversal of the poles during the cataclysm of Hyperborea had raised Antarctica to the place of honor, and that for the "Last Avatar" to take up residence there in a revived Hyperborea was absolutely appropriate. But being Chilean must give one a certain *parti-pris*, which in Serrano's case goes to the logical extreme of making his homeland, the southernmost country on earth, into the refuge for the Kali Yuga and the spiritual center of the New Age.[35]

Another aspect of reversal occurs in Kenneth Grant's work, dedicated to the exaltation of the god Set, or Shaitan, or Satan. "Shaitan," he says in *The Magical Revival* (1972), "is the God of the South, yet his votaries face North when invoking him." He explains this by the fact that "on entering Capricorn, the zodiacal house of Shaitan [Saturn], the sun turns northward. Consequently the worshipper identifies himself with the sun—Horus—which is *therefore not the object of worship*, for he is the god that dies and is reborn on entering the House of Set (Capricornus)." Grant also hints at a physical reversal of poles as he continues: "There was a time when the South had precedence and was the primary station of the Pole Star."[36] Later he says that Set "was Lord of the (South) Pole, first born of the seven sons, or stars, represented by the Northern Constellation of Typhon, the Great Bear. When primitive man moved northward from Equatoria, the Star of Set in the South sank beneath the horizon and was supposed to have 'fallen.' "[37]

It is a small step from Antarctica as the house of Satan or of the Führer, alive or dead, to the myth of the lurking Old Ones and Shoggoths of Lovecraft's fantasy—and from there to the astonishing number of people who take this kind of myth literally. Here is an account of the "arch enemies of mankind" as presented by Robert Ernst Dickhoff in his *Agharta*:

> Agents of Venus are hidden in places on earth and in the earth, only known to themselves, which are at present in suspended animation, awaiting the coming of their rescuers from Venus when they are sure of success. [...]
>
> If Kadath is one of the remaining ice-bound cities in Antarctica, of which there were an original seven, including Rainbow City now open for operation, and nature turns the keys of release at a time yet to come, it will reveal of what Rhani Khatani speaks, when she hints that there too will be found rows upon

> rows of crypts filled with serpents, awaiting this release from the strange gas which keeps them alive in suspended animation. They should be destroyed if found, before they are released by sympathetic humans obeying serpent commands.[38]

Dickhoff was not making this up. He was merely reproducing and elaborating on the Rainbow City myth, which has its roots in a document known as the Hefferlin Manuscript, circulated privately since the 1940s.[39] In a summary of this work by Timothy Green Beckley, we read that William C. and Gladys Hefferlin are now believed to be living in this Antarctic refuge, described as:

> an ancient center of culture called "Rainbow City," which currently is in the hands of reincarnated descendants of the first colonizers from outer space who made tropical Antarctica the "Mother Land of the World" some two and a half million years ago. There also exist six other cities (all connected by vast underground tunnels), completely dormant, while "Rainbow City" is protected on all sides by warm hot springs. However to prevent its being discovered, and exploited by outsiders, ice walls some ten thousand feet high have been built around the city so that it can be reached only by those who know its exact location.[40]

Rainbow City derives its name from its construction, which, like some monstrous Legoland, is entirely out of colored plastic blocks. It is part of the network of underground cities founded aeons ago by Martians, the first colonizers of our planet. Rani Khatani, mentioned by Dickhoff, is one of the "Ancient Three," Martians reincarnated in human form. (One notices a correspondence to the triple rulership of Agartha's Brahmatma, Mahatma, and Mahanga.) The serpent or crocodile-people are later interlopers from the planet Venus, enemies of the Martians and hostile to mankind whom they have periodically forced or tricked into worshipping them.[41] It is H. P. Lovecraft who supplies the name of Kadath, and, in *At the Mountains of Madness*, anticipates the pattern of good colonizers usurped by evil ones; while in *The Nameless City* (1921) he describes a crypt-passage leading to an inner earth, lined with caskets holding the bodies of an unknown, pseudo-crocodilic race. The entrance to the Nameless City is in "the desert of Araby"; others place it at the North Pole, or under Mount Shasta—but that is another story.[42] It little matters, if as the Hefferlins say the whole earth is honeycombed with passages through which trains pass at 2,000 M.P.H.[43]

The study of myths leads inevitably to mysteries: that seems to be its nature. To take an example more familiar to serious readers than Rainbow City: if one makes a scholarly study of one of the Greek myths, say that of Apollo, one soon finds oneself in an inextricable jungle of contradictory theories, facts, and fictions. Is Apollo the Sun-God? All well and good—but he was born on the island of Delos. Is he the god of Delphi and the Navel of the Earth? Yes, but he also comes from Hyperborea. Does he rule music, archery, and the clear arts of reason? Yes, but he prophesies from chthonic depths. Yet there is something Apollonian that is unviolated by these contradictions. It is the same with the myths treated in this book: there is no clear definition possible of what the myth of Antarctica is, but the continent is as mythopoeic as any place on earth. Fully discovered only in the twentieth century, it is the ideal location for the favorite myths of our time: those of extraterrestrial visitations, secret technology, the eternal war of good against evil, and the coming New Age.

Even as I write, the Antarctic myth is taking on other accretions. What could be more appropriate than the reflection of the fabled hole at the South Pole in the ozone layer, allowing the ingress of evil influences which threaten us with cancer, and the whole region with the demise of its sustaining krill? What more symbolic than the placing of a United States base under a giant geodesic dome at the South Pole, where it can study impotently the rent in the sky, and, if the reports in the tabloids are to be believed, the chasm opening beneath its feet?[44] And what exactly prompts the United States to dissent from the community of nations and refuse to sign an agreement to ban Antarctic mining for fifty years?[45]

PART IV:
Arcadia Regained

Chapter Eleven:
The Symbolic Pole

The more one learns about the myths, legends, and religions of the human race, the more imperative is the demand that one somehow make sense of them as a whole. Their competing voices, their incompatible dogmas, call for the stern hand of a moderator who will bring meaning and unity to the whole assembly.

The first tentative efforts of this kind were those of the medieval mythographers, as they tried to make something of the literary and archeological débris of classical civilization. One landmark is Boccaccio's *Genealogy of the Gods*, a marvel of erudition for its time (the second half of the fourteenth century). Following the interpretive procedure of the Christian Fathers, for whom paganism had no spiritual value save a certain ethical uprightness, Boccaccio used moral edification as his key. The heathen gods and goddesses, demigods and heroes, appeared to him as allegories of the virtues and vices; their myths, as improving tales of the sort we know from Aesop's Fables—and the *Decameron*.[1]

Once an interpretive decision has been made, it can be fitted with more or less tailoring to any situation. But so simple-minded an interpretation as Boccaccio's could not survive the discovery in the fifteenth century of the works of Plato, Plotinus, Hermes Trismegistus, Orpheus, the Chaldean Oracles, and the Kabbalah. Texts like these, so obviously the fruit of profound thought and genuine spiritual experience, called for a deeper response. Marsilio Ficino, Giovanni Pico della Mirandola, and the other Platonists who enjoyed the protection of the Medici of Florence worked under the assumption that these works, while not Christian, nevertheless embodied the wisdom of a *prisca theologia*: a "primordial theology" that had been revealed by God to the pagan nations as well as to the Jews, and which was true in its own terms and its own time. The Renaissance Platonists made the important leap of accepting spiritual instruction from sources outside the Judeo-Christian tradition, though to do so was to run severe political risks.

The Florentine enterprise, as Emanuela Kretzulesco-Quaranta has shown in her beautiful study of *The Dream of Poliphilo*, *Les Jardins du Songe* (The gardens of the dream, 1986), was soon driven underground.[2] It was too inimical to the ambitions of the Borgias, who were coming increasingly to dominate the Roman church and to claim for it temporal as well as spiritual power. Later, the atmosphere engendered by the Counter-Reformation made open enquiry into ancient paganism impossible in the Catholic countries. In the Protestant ones, historical curiosity as to how a primordial theology might have been revealed to different peoples at different times was checked by a biblical fundamentalism that set the Creation of the world circa 4000 BCE, and the universal Deluge about 1650 years later. As a result, scholars of the sixteenth and seventeenth centuries did not make much advance on the model of the Florentines.[3] Not being Platonists by inclination, most of them were more inclined to interpret the pagan pantheon as deified human beings than as divine hypostases. Saturn, Jupiter, Osiris, and others, when they were not actually condemned as demons, became kings who had reigned shortly after the Deluge, and their myths were read as memories of historical facts.

Florentine Platonism, with its respect for the feminine principle, for Nature, and for a spiritual quest fired by erotic love that owed nothing to the biblical Christ, disappeared from the circles of free discussion, to surface only in the disguise of symbolic works of literature and art. The *Dream of Poliphilo* (also called the *Hypnerotomachia*, or "Strife of Love in a Dream") was one of the first of these secret manifestos; the pagan allegories of Botticelli, more familiar to most readers, are another.

During this period, however, there took place a twofold expansion of the European imagination. The first aspect was geographical, associated with the names of the great navigators from Vasco da Gama to Drake. The more the world was discovered, the more imperative became the need to understand why these Asians, Africans, and Americans were not Christian, and what destiny God had envisaged for them. If one were to be a better missionary to them than the Spaniards in the New World, it would be advisable first to find out what they already believed, and why. Thus the learned Jesuits, around 1600, began their tremendous work of studying the myths and religions of the people they intended to convert.

The second expansion was cosmological, the work of Copernicus, Kepler, and Galileo. Their new cosmologies swept aside the tidy system of nesting spheres, turned by the hand of God, that had served so well since the time of Aristotle. Breaking the bounds of the Ptolemaic cosmos required a new imagining of space, while the infinite vistas revealed demanded a new scale of time. Isaac Newton himself, largely responsible for the consecration of the former, was incapable of the latter. But all efforts at universal explanation had to be revised in the face of the new knowledge, and this was one of the foremost tasks that the philosophers of the eighteenth-century Enlightenment set themselves.

The first attempt at a universal theory of comparative religion held that all traditions and myths derive ultimately from sun-worship. Perhaps credit should go first to Macrobius, who in his *Saturnalia*, in the fourth century CE, explained that all the gods of the pantheon were but aspects of the Sun, and all the goddesses aspects of the Moon. But it was long before anyone could dare to say the same of the Christian god, and interpret the life of Christ, along with the myths of Jason and Hercules, as a personification of the sun's annual journey through the twelve signs of the zodiac. The ground-breaking work in this regard was the *Origine de tous les cultes* (Origin of all religions, 3 vols., 1795) of Charles François Dupuis, whose publication was possible because of the atmosphere of freedom and skepticism following on the French Revolution. Since Dupuis' time, the solar myth theory of religious origins has had many adherents who have restated it in the light of ever-increasing knowledge and sophistication.

The second universal theory was the phallic one: it says that most mythology and religion can be traced to what Richard Payne Knight called "the worship of the generative powers," in his pioneering work of 1785, *A Discourse on the Worship of Priapus*. This was so shocking to most nineteenth-century minds that it could not possibly enjoy the wide dispersion of the solar model. Not long after Dupuis, J. A. Dulaure published *Des divinités génératrices, ou du culte du phallus* (Of the generative divinities, or the cult of the phallus, 1805). Dulaure reckoned that the phallic theme had come out of the original solar worship at the epoch when the spring equinox was in the sign of the virile Bull. Phallicism is mentioned discreetly in Godfrey Higgins' *Anacalypsis* (1836), but only later in the century were such writers as Thomas Inman and Hargrave Jennings able to write more openly about "lingam" and "yoni" worship, either concealing their theories under deceptive titles (Jennings: *The Rosicrucians: Their Rites and Mysteries*, 1870; Inman: *Ancient Faiths Embodied in Ancient Names*, 2 vols., 1872), or else cultivating the collectors of erudite pornography with the limited editions of the "Phallic Series," in the 1880s and 1890s. The phallicists were soon to see themselves triumphantly vindicated by Siegmund Freud, whose discoveries in the psychology of the unconscious seemed to justify their readings.

The third example of mythic explanation is directly relevant to the present work, and for its most exhaustive treatment I turn to *The Night of the Gods* (2 vols., 1893, 1897), by John O'Neill. This treats the myths, symbols, and legends of the whole world as referring to the revolution of the heavens around the celestial pole. O'Neill was a retired British civil servant and diplomat, and enough of an Orientalist to write a Japanese language textbook. His theme is that "the Most High, the deity symbolically worshipped on High Places, was the God of the Polestar, who was seated at the Highest celestial spot of the Cosmos, the North Pole of the heavens."[4]

Starting from this point, O'Neill finds that his archetype is capable of absorbing and explaining all the myths, legends, and folkloric practices that have to do with trees, spears, stakes, rods, and of course poles: all these symbolize the axis that joins (or separates) earth and heaven. Primordially, as he reads the myths, earth and heaven were not apart: their sundering was the first act of creation. The mutilation of Kronos by Zeus is one account of this separation,[5] whilst the phallus, far from being a primary symbol, is just another emblem of the axial pillar that was erected after the event. One might adapt to O'Neill's theory the quip uttered in mockery of the phallic symbolists and Freudians: that anything longer than it is wide is an axial symbol.

O'Neill's ingenuity goes far beyond this. He writes, for example, of sacred stones that fall from the sky, which are often found to be of magnetic iron. Three of his many examples are the Stone of the Great Mother at Pessinus in Phrygia; the Stone of Emesa, which the Emperor Heliogabalus brought to Rome; and the stone set in the corner of the Ka'aba at Mecca. Their celestial origin shows that such meteorites come from the Most High God, whose seat is the Pole star; also they point to the north when suspended or floated. And at the terrestrial North Pole, does not legend tell that there is a whole mountain of lodestone? This mountain, at the navel of the earth, is the prototype of all sacred rocks and navel-stones, like the Omphalos at Delphi, and the precedent for practices such as the navel-contemplation of the Hesychast monks, which led them to behold a dazzling light.[6] All cities and other locations regarded as umbilical—and O'Neill names Cuzco, the Mississippi mounds, Jerusalem, Babylon, Athens, Delphi, Paphos, Samarcand, and Boston—"may very well be offshoots from a lost primeval cosmic conception [...] of the northern terrestrial navel or nave, which turned on the cosmic axle-tree."[7]

The Pole is the supreme *Arcanum* or "secret," for *Arx* is the celestial pole, from which (in a reversal of the conventional etymology) O'Neill derives the Latin word for summit, high hill, and citadel. All arks, sacred chests, and boxes then become repositories of the secret of the polar sanctum—of *Arcadia*.

> Arkas, son of Kallistô by Zeus (who changed son and mother into the Great and Little Bears) was also placed in the heavens as Arktouros and, by another legend, as Arktophylax. Arkas [...] was the father of the Arkades or Arcadians, who claimed to be the first men. Hermês, born on Mount Kullenê (Cyllene) in Arcadia—that is on the hollow (*kula*) or the rolling (*kuliô*) mountain of the heavens—was *the* Arcadian [...]; and the caduceus of Mercury was therefore called the Arcadian rod.[8]

The god who rules the universe from the celestial pole is above and beyond the contrarieties of his progeny and creation. The Chinese Taoists know him in the symbol of the *Tai-Ki*, the "Great First," which divides into the dual powers of Yang and Yin. From this model, O'Neill develops a polar interpretation for all trinities and triple figures; one such is the fleur-de-lys, which aptly enough is habitually drawn at the north point of the compass.[9] Gods who come in pairs fall into place as symbols of the dual powers beneath the One, while all symbols of justice, balance, and harmony are related to the same complex.

In arithmology, the axial model serves O'Neill wonderfully well: all fours and their multiples (including twelves) are symbols of the directions of space around the Pole, while all sevens refer to the twice-seven stars of the Great and the Little Bears (*arktoi*). Domes and rounded hats (especially winged ones like Mercury's) are emblems of the celestial vault, while all wheels, swastikas, and other spinning and rotating objects and persons show the cosmic machinery in motion.

John O'Neill's study falls short in one glaring respect: his avoidance of the issue of solar symbolism. One of his weakest chapters, admittedly from the second volume that was assembled from his notes after his sudden death, is that in which he seeks to explain the solar worship of Egypt as a late substitute for their original cosmic religion. The sign for the sun, a circle with a dot at its center, becomes instead the symbol of "the Universe-heavens and its omphalos."[10] When something does not fit his theory, O'Neill, who has a ready Irish wit and a command of picturesque language, becomes sarcastic and contemptuous.

Perhaps it requires the obsessional type, with a one-track mind and an utter conviction of his own rightness, to pursue such studies through hundreds of sources in a dozen languages. But the great temptation to such a person is to become so enraptured by his own theory that he uses it as a Procrustean bed onto which all the world's myths, legends, and religions are to be accommodated. The situation is exacerbated if his theory has come to him not by simple thinking but through some illuminative or mystical experience.

For all his monomania, O'Neill has brought into focus a most valuable and neglected element of ancient mythology. Early observers of the phenomenal world must have regarded the nightly circling of the starry sky around the polar point to be one of the most awe-inspiring evidences of divinity—second only to the daily journey of the sun across the sky. The polar model requires the solar for completion, as the night needs the day. The phallic model, too, has something to offer in the way of explanation, as does the corresponding symbolism of the Great Mother. Nor can one discount the interpretations of Sir James Frazer's *The Golden Bough*, based on fertility symbolism and the succession of sacred kingship. Memories of deified men and women must also have entered into the making of myths, as have the letter and number combinations studied by kabbalists and arithmologists. Nothing, in short, is unworthy of notice when it comes to the Sisyphean task of understanding mythology, except the raucous claim to exclusivity and a monopoly of the truth.

The Swastika

How does the celestial pole appear to the watcher in the night? For inhabitants of the Northern Hemisphere during the last 6,000 years, the most prominent constellation in the north part of the sky has been Arktos, otherwise known as the Great Bear, the Plough, the Big Dipper, and Charlie's Wain. Everyone knows the shape of these seven stars. Each night they are seen to swing counter-clockwise around the polar point, which is currently close to the star Polaris. Naturally the whole circle can only be inferred, as the sun's rising obscures the daytime motion of the stars.

Nearby there is another seven-star group of remarkably similar shape, but reversed: the Little Bear. This also swings around Polaris, which is the last star of its tail. In between the two Bears is Draco, who may be imagined as the dragon or serpent guarding the Apples of the Hesperides which grow on the axial tree.

Dante urges the reader of his *Paradiso* to hold on to this image, firm as a rock:

> The fifteen stars, that in their divers regions
> The sky enliven with a light so great
> That it transcends all clusters of the air;
>
> Let him the Wain imagine unto which
> Our vault of heaven sufficeth night and day,
> So that in turning of its pole it fail not;
>
> Let him the mouth imagine of the horn [Little Bear]
> That in the point beginneth of the axis
> Round about which the primal wheel revolves...[11]

As one follows the round-dances of the Bears, night after night, one notices that they do not always start in the same place. In winter, the Great Bear appears low in the northeast; in summer, high in the northwestern sky and the other way up. With the rest of the stars, they are all making a secondary circle, also counter-clockwise, that takes a year before it brings them back to their starting-points. As modern people, we know that it is not the stars that are moving, but the earth; we may also understand that these twin counter-clockwise motions are the reflections of the earth's daily rotation and its annual revolution around the sun. (The earth's motions are counter-clockwise when the earth is viewed from above the North Pole, but clockwise from the viewpoint of observers in the Northern Hemisphere looking up at the sky.)

If one wanted to record in graphic form the nightly or yearly cycle of the Great and Little Bears, it would be enough to show them in four positions, corresponding to the four directions of space and the four seasons (see diagram). These diagrams are so strongly suggestive of the swastika in all its varieties, that it is not surprising that the latter has been used as a symbol of the Pole and of motion around it.

Anthropological studies have shown that the swastika is a well-nigh universal symbol, being found from the Bronze Age onwards throughout the Old and New Worlds. To judge from its usage as a decorative mark on household objects of every kind, its meaning was simply "good luck," as later acknowledged by its Sanskrit name: *su* (equivalent of Greek *eu*, "good"), *asti* (like Greek *estô*, "be"), *ka* (a suffix);[12] compare the Sanskrit-Tibetan word *Swasti*, "May It Be Auspicious," used at the beginnings of texts.[13] Only in Buddhism and, to a much slighter degree, in Christianity, has it been used it as sacred symbol: it appears notably on the soles of the Buddha's feet, and in the Catacombs of Rome.

The swastika dropped out of use in the fine and decorative arts of Europe from the Middle Ages onwards. It has no place in the iconography of alchemy, Rosicrucianism, or Freemasonry. It began to reappear as the result of nineteenth-century scholarship in two fields: comparative ethnology, and Oriental

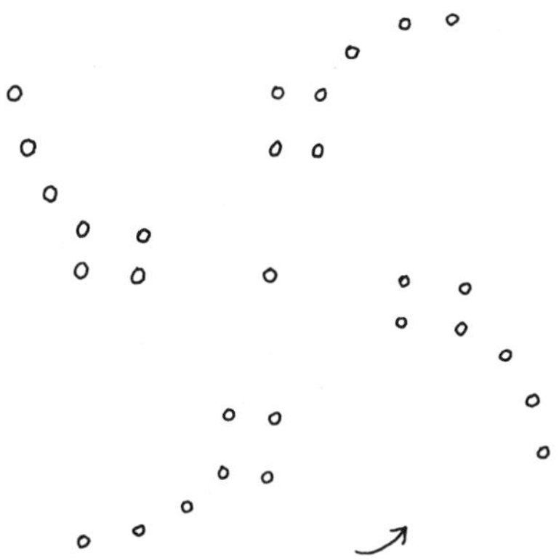

Illustration 12a: 4000 BCE, Seasonal positions of Ursa Minor around Thuban (alpha Draconis), then Pole-star

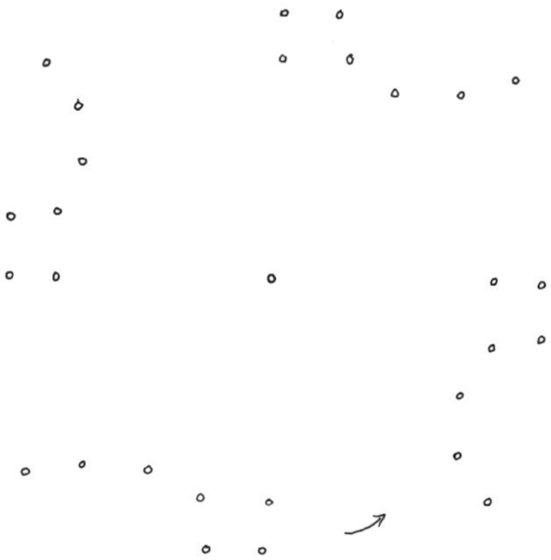

Illustration 12b: Present, Seasonal positions of Ursa Major around Polaris

religion. The first discovered that the swastika, despite its wide distribution, was conspicuously absent from Egypt, Chaldea, Assyria, and Phoenicia. This led many scholars to identify it as an Aryan sun-symbol, and its presence as the indication of the Aryan migrations or influences that they were so keen to trace. The orientalists discovered the symbolic and ritualistic use of the swastika by the Buddhists, the Jains, and the magician-priests (*Tao shih*) of Taoism. Reports were published of an order of *'Tao-sse*, called "Doctors of Reason" or followers of the "Mystic Cross," which was the swastika, in pre-Buddhist China and India.[14]

One person who caught at the idea was the astrologer Richard Morrison (1795–1874), who as "Zadkiel" published a regular spate of almanacs and astrological literature. In 1870 he announced the intention to "resuscitate in England, and spread throughout Europe, India and America—The Most

Ancient Order of the Suastica; or, The Brotherhood of the Mystic Cross," in three degrees of Apprentice Brothers, Tao Sze or Doctors of Reason, and Grand Master. The Order, he said, had first been founded by Foe, "in the confines of Tibet," in about 1027 BCE.[15] Zadkiel displayed the swastika prominently on his publications, as did many other authors who may or may not have had connections with the Brotherhood in question, or with its offshoot, the Brotherhood of Luxor.[16] One of these was Madame Blavatsky, who incorporated the swastika in the seal of the Theosophical Society, as symbolizing the centripetal and centrifugal powers that "preserve harmony and keep the Universe in steady, unceasing motion," including that of the earth upon its axis.[17]

In the early years of the twentieth century, the swastika was familiar throughout the English-speaking world from its appearance on the covers of Rudyard Kipling's books. He later had it removed, for obvious reasons, but it remains in the illustration to his *Just So Story*, "The Crab that Played with the Sea," where he calls it "a magic mark." So innocent were the "good luck" associations of the swastika that during World War I, it was used as the emblem of the British War Savings Scheme, appearing on coupons and stamps.[18]

Much has been written about the symbolic significance of so-called right- and left-handed swastikas, especially in the light of the Nazis' adoption of the former. To avoid ambiguity, I use "left" and "right" to refer only to the direction taken by the arms outward from the center. André Brissaud, the most reliable of the French writers on the Nazis and the Occult, says that the left-handed swastika turns in the direction of the earth's rotation: hence it symbolizes the solar wheel, the benefic fire of heaven, expansion, creation, evolution, fertility, and is the "Wheel of the Golden Sun." The right-handed swastika, on the other hand, is the "Wheel of the Black Sun" representing the earthly fire recreated by man and the quest for political hegemony in opposition to the Fire of Heaven.[19] Miguel Serrano writes that the left-handed, clockwise-turning swastika symbolized the ancient exodus of the Aryan Race from the North Pole, while the right-handed, counter-clockwise one of the Nazis stands for the return of the race to its esoteric center at the South Pole.[20] The Hopi Indians have an equally ingenious myth: they tell of how their clans originally issued forth from the central *omphalos* of the Americas, Tuwanasavi. As Nigel Pennick relates the story, half of the clans turned to the right. "This transformed the cross of energies into a great swastika rotating anti-clockwise to indicate the Earth. These clans possessed high knowledge and in turning right were claiming the land for their people in accordance with the plan of the Creator." The others turned to the left. "These clans were less well developed. They did not possess complete rituals; instead they greeted the sun in prayer, lit fires at their shrines for the four elements and directions and supported the other clans. By turning left they made a swastika rotating clockwise with the sun, symbolizing their faithfulness with the Creator."[21]

Whatever the validity of these theories, the ancient decorative swastikas show no preference whatsoever for one type over the other.[22] The place where the left-right distinction is supposed to be most significant is Tibet, where both Nicholas

a b

Illustration 13: a) "Left-handed" Swastika (presumed rotation clockwise); b) "Right-handed" Swastika (presumed rotation counterclockwise)

Roerich and Anagarika Govinda observed that the swastika of the ancient Bön-Po religion points to the left, the Buddhist one to the right.[23] Now it is true that the Bön-Pos perform ritual circumambulations counter-clockwise, the Buddhists clockwise,[24] but almost all the Buddhist iconography collected by Thomas Wilson shows left-handed swastikas, just like the ones on the Bön-Pos' ritual scepter, their equivalent of the Buddhist *vajra*.[25] One can only say that the swastika should perhaps be left-handed if (as in Bön-Po) it denotes polar revolution, and right-handed if (as in Buddhism) it symbolizes the course of the sun.[26] But the root of the problem is probably the inherent ambiguity of the symbol itself, which makes the left-handed swastika appear to be rotating to the right, and vice versa.

The Caduceus

If the swastika is the prime symbol of the Pole in its aspect as center of the celestial or terrestrial circle, then the caduceus is the prime symbol, in the West, of the World Axis that joins the two. Together, the symbols of center and axis contain the basis for an entire body of metaphysical teaching.

The symbol of the World-Axis embodies the archetypal experience of Up and Down, felt most concretely in our physical bodies. Before we were born, most of us were carried upside-down in our mothers' wombs, and emerged into this world head first. Many myths represent the human soul as looking down from the heavens to earth, before diving through the spheres into incarnation. As invariably happens, the great events and formations of Nature mirror metaphysical truths. Another example: humans are unusual among mammals for their upright stance, which makes each of us a miniature of the Axis. The quadrupeds have all four feet on the earth (the foursquare place, made from the four elements), the axes of their spines are horizontal, and their heads look down or along its surface. Unlike the animals, whose development proceeds in parallel with that of the earth, the human being has the possibility of making deliberate progress upwards, from earth towards heaven. Our two feet base us in the world of duality, but the domes of our skulls replicate the single vault of the sky. Thus the yogi's ascent to samadhi through the seventh chakra (Sahasrara, the "thousand-petalled lotus" at the crown of the head) is identical to the Hermetic adept's penetration beyond the vault of heaven into the eighth sphere.

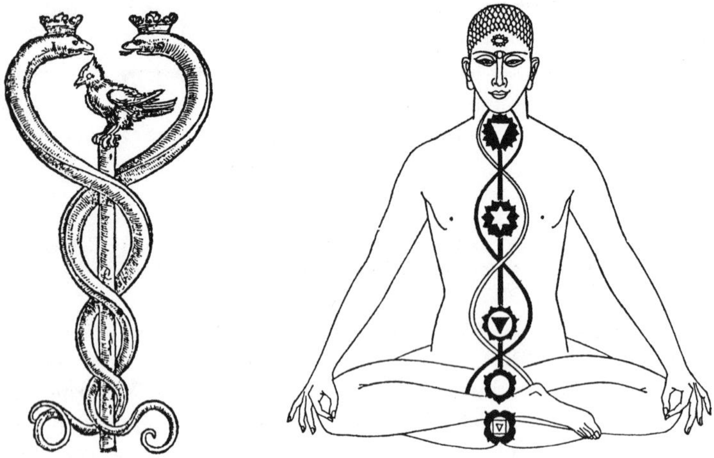

a b

Illustration 14: a) The staff of Hermes, or caduceus, from a drawing by Hans Holbein the Younger; b) yogic anatomy.

The human being, like the World-Axis, is a link between heaven and earth, and human life can be lived at every intervening degree, from the virtually animal to the virtually divine. Through the subtle body course the dual currents known and studied in Yoga as *Ida* and *Pingala*, which also travel in serpentine vortices around the macrocosmic axis. One current is negative, the other positive. We have encountered the same pattern in the body of the earth itself, with Arctic and Antarctic as the opposite ends of an axis of polarity. But it would be silly to leap too soon to the conclusion that one current or pole is good and the other evil. Although in a sense this is true, it all depends on one's standpoint.

As we know from innumerable myths, it is the business of certain gods to look down from heaven and create worlds. Viewed from their point of view, at the heavenly summit of the cosmic axis, the downward current is expansive, outbreathing, creative, and hence "good." It builds planets, populates and sustains them. The upward current is the contrary: a contractive inbreathing, sucking creation back and in effect destroying it, which seems "evil." The whole of Hermetic philosophy is based on the interplay of these contraries, which have been treated with especial profundity by Robert Fludd and Jacob Boehme.

We know the dual currents quite intimately in their manifestations as birth and death, twin events without which existence as we know it would be impossible. It is natural for us to favor the downward, expansive, creative current: to rejoice at a birth and to mourn a death. However, there are those—and both Buddha and Christ seem to have been among them—who have preached the virtues of the upward current that leads away from earthly existence, obedient to the upward pull of the celestial magnet which tends to draw all things back into itself. From the earthly and physical point of view, ascesis and death belong to the contractive, destructive current; yet do they not involve a corresponding expansion in the spiritual domain?

The fabric of our experience is tightly woven out of both tendencies, Yang and Yin; we feel the outbreathing and the inbreathing, the downward and the upward attractions simultaneously. Among esoteric practitioners, some work exclusively upward toward *samadhi*, the blissful detachment from all conditioned things that is supposedly the state of the gods. This "Right-hand path" tends to use asceticism, detachment, and continence as its allies, to withdraw the soul from the sense-world. Other methods accept the conditioned and created world, especially its most powerfully creative elements, the sexual powers, and take a "Left-hand path" that affirms creation—indeed, plumbs it to illuminate its very depths with the heavenly ray.[27] And this, they assure us, leads ultimately to the same goal. Both paths have their characteristic pitfalls, though those of the Left are more obvious. We will have a last look at these issues in Chapter Thirteen.

The Will of Heaven

For a fuller understanding of the other aspect of polar symbolism, which concerns the intersection of the axis with the earth, we return to René Guénon, especially to his *Symbolism of the Cross*, *The Great Triad*, *The King of the World*, and the essays collected posthumously as *Symboles fondamentaux de la science sacrée* (Fundamental Symbols of Sacred Science). In the geometrical schemata which Guénon used with such mastery to teach metaphysical concepts, human existence is sometimes represented by a horizontal circle transfixed by a vertical axis. On this field are played out all the possibilities of the human being—multifarious but not infinite, because bounded by the circumference. At the center is the "Celestial Ray," the axis that exerts a magnetic pull on the being, which may respond to it or resist. The nearer the being comes to the axis, the nearer its condition to the ideal or complete human state. Guénon placed a low value on human life lived in ignorance of this center: he says that "the aggregate of the being's possibilities properly constitutes only a chaos 'without form and void,' wherein there is nothing but obscurity until the moment of illumination which determines its harmonious organization in the passage from potency to act."[28] Evidently the spiritual centers of the various traditions exist to awaken and facilitate this awareness of the Celestial Ray at the center of one's own being.

> This principle, of divine essence and indwelling in beings [...], is again, in the Vedic symbolism, *Agni* [fire, the active principle] manifesting itself at the centre of the *swastika*, which as we have seen is the cross traced on the horizontal plane, and which, by its rotation about that centre, generates the evolutive cycle that constitutes each of the elements in the universal cycle. The centre, the only point that remains motionless in this rotary movement, is by very reason of its immobility (an image of the principial immutability) the mover of the "wheel of existence"; it contains within it the "Law" [...], that is, the expression or

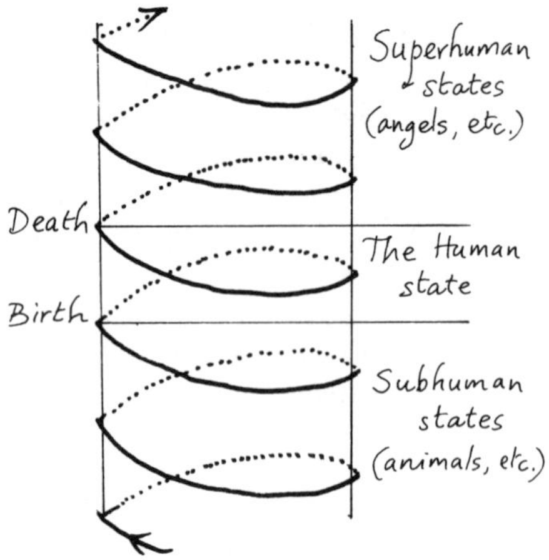

Illustration 15: The evolutive helix (Matgioï)

> manifestation of the "Will of Heaven" for the cycle corresponding to the horizontal plane in which the rotation takes place, and, following what was said before, its influence is measured—or rather, would be measured if we had the faculty of doing so—by the pitch of the evolutive helix on the vertical axis.[29]

Guénon is here using the language of Taoism, for he was influenced, and perhaps even initiated, by the French Taoist philosopher Matgioï (=Albert de Pouvourville). Now he develops what one might call an axial cosmology in three dimensions. He asks us to imagine a rising helix or spiral, of which each turn represents a different state: for example, the human one. A being makes the circuit of a given state, then returns to the place where it started—but since it has traversed not a flat circle but one helical turn, it finds itself at another level, beginning life at another state of being. Thus death to one state is birth into the next one. The progress made between birth and death in a given cycle is measured, as Guénon puts it in the quotation above, by the "pitch of the evolutive helix." So in a sense, Guénon's famous pessimism and fierce opposition to modern theories of evolution is not absolute. Although he believed the present world-cycle to be in the last throes of its decline, from a larger viewpoint the cosmos and its inhabitants are subject to evolution and, dare one say, progress.

Matgioï himself, in the book that Guénon frequently quotes (*La Voie métaphysique*—The metaphysical way), describes how not only the individual, but also the collective evolution of humanity follows this spiral of universal becoming, which he imagines as rising around a cylinder. He reminds us that all parallels meet at infinity, so that eventually the cylinder, having become a cone, vanishes in a point. "Thus," he says, "it is *precisely* at infinity that *the evolved Universe becomes indistinguishable from Perfection.* [...] The reintegration into the bosom of Perfection is the total and inevitable fate of all beings."[30]

All swastikas, crosses within circles, omphaloi, sacred stones and cities here find their highest significance: they are symbols of the Center, on whatever plane, wherever the Will of Heaven is felt as the Unmoved Mover. Likewise, all towers, cones, lances, obelisks, and other symbols of the World-Axis do not merely figure forth the space between the North Pole and the Pole Star, however many light-years that might be: they symbolize the total evolution of the universe, proceeding in cycles that defy the imagination towards the culminating point of perfection and reabsorption in the One. As Matgioï says:

> Let us then greet confidently the plans of the *Will of Heaven*, as yet unknown, but logical and intelligible; and let us be fearless about the course and the end, inevitably happy ones, of the Destinies of the Universe.[31]

Chapter Twelve: *Solar and Polar Traditions*

René Guénon's prehistory of our cycle, as related in Chapter Two, told of a very early Hyperborean culture which was forced to leave the North and disperse into Asia and Europe, in much the same way as the "Aryan Race" is supposed to have done; and of a somewhat later Atlantean culture which, after the destruction of its homeland, spread across the sea westward to the Americas and eastward to Egypt. In his fascinating essays "Le Sanglier et l'Ourse" (The Boar and the She-Bear) and "La Terre du Soleil" (The Land of the Sun),[1] Guénon writes of the corresponding transition from the Primordial tradition of Hyperborea to the Atlantean tradition: a change from a fundamentally polar tradition to a solar one.

Before the time of this change, Guénon says, the constellations we know as the Great and Little Bears were together called the Scales:[2] *Tûla*, in Sanskrit—which may give a clue to the origin of the name Thule. Only afterwards, with the new emphasis on the sun and its course, was that name transferred to the constellation in the zodiac which we know as Libra. True, it is recognized in the history of astronomy that Libra was a late addition to the zodiac, taking over the stars that had formerly been called the Scorpion's Claws.[3] No one claims to know much about the situation prior to this, except a few esotericists of the nineteenth century of whom Guénon was certainly aware, and who assert that the zodiac formerly had only ten signs. One of these, they say, was a compound sign of Virgo and Scorpio (whose astrological symbols are certainly alike); it was split, and Libra inserted, to give the new total of twelve.[4] I have found no early corroboration for this story, which may have some relation to the Pythagorean conception of the heavenly sphere as a dodecahedron, whose equator would naturally divide into ten sectors. It more likely refers to the time when the vague star-pictures known to the earliest cultures were tabulated, measured, and adapted to become the regular zodiac of twelve signs, each spanning exactly thirty degrees of the celestial equator.

Along with the transference of Libra to the zodiac, Guénon mentions that of the "Seven Rishis," ancient Indian sages elevated to the heavens. In the Vedic period, this name was given to the seven stars of the Great Bear. Guénon explains that the function of these beings is to give the wisdom of previous cycles to the present one;[5] therefore one might suppose that they will take on different forms as the source of wisdom migrates. Guénon's account in "The Boar and the She-Bear" is very rich in implications:

> In a certain period, the name of *sapta-riksha* [Seven Rishis] was no longer applied to the Great Bear, but to the Pleiades, which also number seven stars. This transference from a polar to a zodiacal constellation corresponds to a passage from solsticial to equinoctial symbolism, implying a change in the starting-point of the yearly cycle, as well as in the order of predominance of the cardinal points which are related to the different phases of this cycle. [Guénon's note: The transference of the Scales into the zodiac naturally has a similar significance.] The change here is from the North to the West, which refers to the Atlantean period; and this is aptly confirmed by the fact that, for the Greeks, the Pleiades were the daughters of Atlas, and, as such, also called Atlantides.[6]

Writing of another significant change in the Great Bear's name, Guénon says that it was formerly called the Boar, a word whose roots he associates with the "Boreal" pole and with the sky gods Varuna and Ouranos. He says that our entire cycle or Kalpa is called the "Cycle of the White Boar," and that the polar "sacred land," the seat of the primordial spiritual center of this Manvantara, is also called the "Land of the Boar."[7] Guénon attributes the change of animal to the usurpation of the Brahmins (priestly caste), whose sign was the Boar, by the Kshatriyas (warrior caste), whose sign was the She-Bear.[8] In Greek mythology, this is figured in the Calydonian hunt of the White Boar: the beast is killed by Atalanta, who had been raised by a bear. This, he says, shows that the revolt took place in Atlantis, or among descendants of the Atlantean tradition:[9] an early symptom of the spiritual decline that is the mark of the Hindu conception of time-cycles, as explained in Chapter Two. We can therefore glean a more or less complete picture from Guénon's hints of a time of transition from Hyperborean to Atlantean influence; from polar to solar tradition; and from priestly authority to aristocratic power.

The Beginning of the Zodiac

Nomadic peoples, such as the Hyperboreans must necessarily have been during their long wandering from the North, live by hunting and herding, not by agriculture. They have no reason to develop the mathematical arts which settled peoples need for the surveying of land and the measurement of time. As Voltaire wrote to Bailly, the Scythian tigers did not carry astrolabes! Agriculture, on the other hand, requires a calendar, and one of the most challenging tasks of the priestly caste in a settled culture is to provide one. To do so it is necessary somehow to reconcile the two great phenomena mentioned in the previous chapter: the movement of the sun, observable only in the daytime, and that of the stars, observable only at night. This requires a mathematical system that can be applied to the celestial movements, and an observatory (which may be as simple as a flat plot of high ground) where the movements can be marked and recorded from year to year.

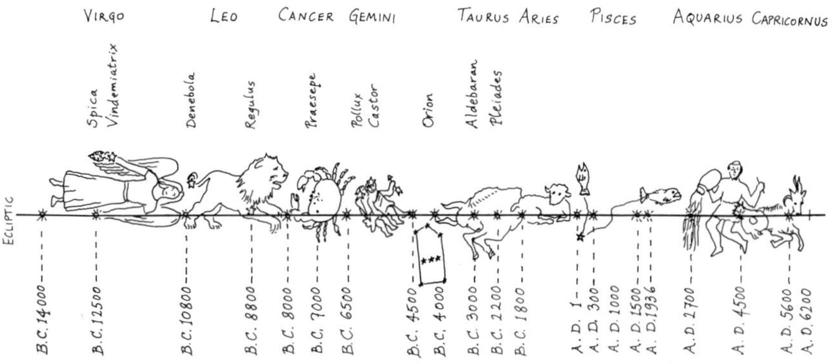

Illustration 16: Historical positions of the equinox (*Hamlet's Mill*)*

When did this first occur? The general consensus seems to place it in Mesopotamia, during the "Geminian Age" (sixth and fifth millenia BCE). Giorgio de Santillana and Hertha von Dechend come to this tentative conclusion in *Hamlet's Mill* (1969), a heroic attempt at universal mythography whose keystone is the early discovery and widespread knowledge of the precession of the equinoxes. They describe this earliest period as a Golden Age; a "Time Zero," whose special characteristic was that the ecliptic points in Gemini and Sagittarius also marked the ends of the Milky Way. Therefore "the exceptional virtue of the Golden Age was precisely that the crossroads of ecliptic and equator coincided with the crossroads of ecliptic and Galaxy."[10] This was also the Age of Saturn, presumably because at that time, Saturn's thirty-year orbit was the longest-known astronomical cycle.

The discovery of precession fell like a bombshell into this prematurely ordered world:

> The equinoctial sun had been gradually pushed out of its Golden Age "sign," it had started on the way to new conditions, new configurations. This is the frightful event, the unexpiable crime that was ascribed to the Children of Heaven. They had nudged the sun out of place, and now it was on the move, the universe was out of kilter and nothing, nothing—days, months or years, the rising or setting of stars—was going to fall into its rightful place any more. [...] The infernal pushing and squeezing of the Children of Heaven had separated the parents, and now the time machine had been set rolling forever, bringing

---

* Reprinted with permission from the Harvard Common Press. Copyright © 1969. By Giorgio Santillana and H. von Dechend.

> forth at every new age "a new heaven and a new earth," in the words of Scripture.[11]

A new, "astronomical" era then took shape, Santillana and Dechend say, around 4,000 BCE,[12] along with the myths that sought to explain what had happened.

For the next stage of the story, I turn to a project on an even more ambitious scale, the *Archetyp und Tierkreis* (Archetype and Zodiac, 1951) of Julius Schwabe, who tried to do for astronomy and astrology what Jung had done for alchemy. This Swiss author sees the transition of 4,000 BCE as a calmer one: it was then, according to his account, that the Sumerians accomplished the adaptation of the simple star-pictures into a mathematically exact zodiac. In so doing, these admirable people created the coordinated systems of measurement which we still partially use: the 360 degrees of the circle (which cannot but recall the 360 days of the "ideal" or mythological year mentioned in Chapter One); the division of time into months, hours, and minutes; and weights and measures based on factors of 12, 60, etc.

Once the stars had been accommodated to a mathematical system, the sun's annual course could be aligned to them via the solstices and equinoxes which mark the seasons. In about 4,000 BCE, the summer and winter solstices found the sun respectively in Leo and Aquarius; the spring and fall equinoxes, in Scorpio and Taurus. Schwabe points out how appropriate at least three of these are:[13] Leo, with its prominent star Regulus, puts the solar animal and the symbol of kingship at the point of the sun's greatest power and elevation; Scorpio is the beast which "kills" it in the autumn; Taurus, the symbol of new life, virility, and blood-sacrifice in the spring. Aquarius, he adds with less conviction, always has to do with resurrection from the depths.

In the symbolism of the zodiac, these four "fixed" signs are often given a prominence in excess of the "cardinal" signs. Most notably, they appear in the Bible as the Four Beasts of Ezekiel's vision,[14] and of the Apocalypse[15] (Scorpio having become the Eagle, and Aquarius simply the Man). Occultists identify them with the four great angelic beings who govern the destinies of the earth. Schwabe shows what he reckons to have been the original set-up of the zodiac, with these signs at the compass points: Leo, at the North, because the sun reaches its northernmost point at the summer solstice; Taurus, at the East, where the sun rises in the spring; Aquarius at the South, where the sun is confined in winter; and Scorpio in the West, as the place of the autumnal equinox. This arrangement has the signal advantage of allowing the rest of the zodiac to align neatly and logically in solar and lunar columns, each containing a sign ruled by one of the other five planets (see diagram).

This primordial zodiac, as Schwabe points out, puts Heaven in the North and the Underworld in the South.[16] His book is rich in consequences to be drawn from this. I would comment that it shows a more "polar" than "solar" way of thinking, with its privileged placement of the North. However, it involves a

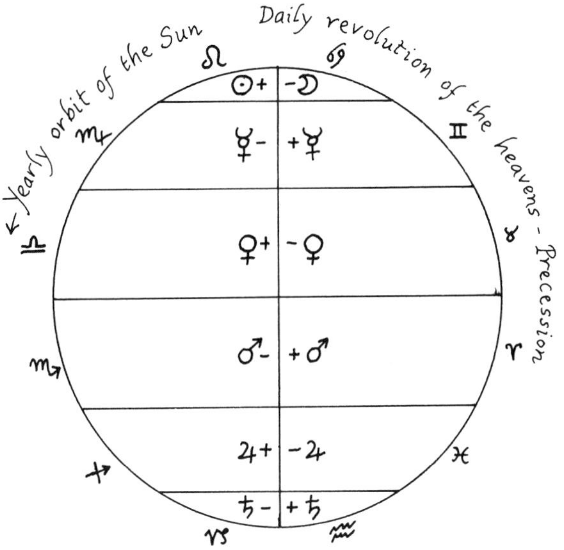

Illustration 17: Original arrangement of the Zodiac, c. 4000 BCE (Schwabe)

contradiction that must have troubled those in search of a system that would unite heaven and earth. For while the sun is at its midsummer culmination in Leo, the "autumnal" constellation of Scorpio is rising in the East, and the "spring" one of Taurus is setting in the West. The heavenly directions appear to be the reverse of the earthly ones—which is only to be expected, since the diurnal movement of the zodiac is from East to West, whereas the annual movement of the sun through the signs is from West to East.

The traumatic event took place, according to Schwabe, not at the beginning of this "Taurian" age but towards 2,200 BCE, when it was realized that the original zodiac would no longer serve: precession had moved the sun's seasonal points relative to the constellations, and the summer solstice was no longer taking place in Leo, but in Cancer. The priests entrusted with the revision of the zodiac decided also to cure the anomaly of East and West. Consequently, as Schwabe says, the whole cosmos was "stood on its head." [17] Cancer became the southern constellation, which was justifiable if one considered that it now partook of the sun's midsummer glory, and Capricorn became that of the cold North. The spring constellation Aries was now in the East, and the autumnal Libra in the West, giving the zodiac with which astrologers today are familiar. At the same time, the beginning of the year was shifted to the spring equinox, so that this became the Age of Aries. The polar orientation, which naturally privileges the north-south axis, had given way to the solar one, which favors east and west.

Although precession has naturally continued since that time, astrology has elected to take no notice of it, realizing that, in Schwabe's words, *Der Tierkreis*

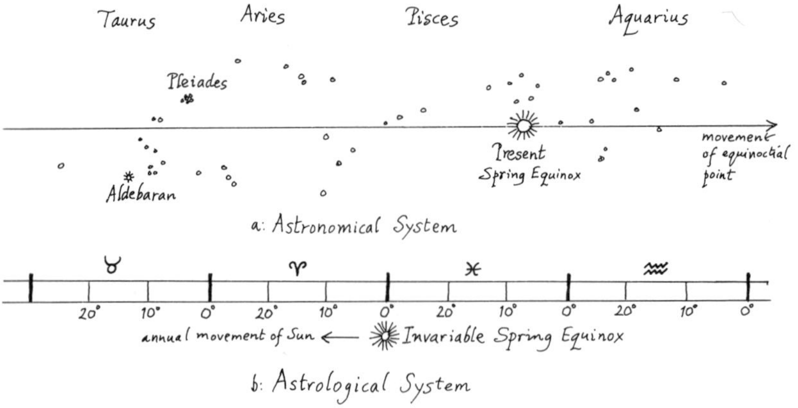

Illustration 18: Placement of the Sun at the spring equinox

ist der Jahreskreis der Sonne:[18] "The zodiac is the sun's annual course," and has nothing whatever to do with stars outside our solar system. The assignment of degrees to the signs of the zodiac derives from Ptolemy (mid-second century CE), who called the spring equinoctial point the first degree of Aries. Now the sun's annual journey through the zodiac is from west to east (right to left in the northern hemisphere), so that the first degree of any zodiacal constellation is at its right-hand end. But the sun's precessional cycle is from east to west, or from left to right, so that it enters each successive sign in the thirtieth degree and works backwards. Thus while Ptolemy called the spring point 1° Aries, within a few centuries it had moved into the "latter" degrees of Pisces. Because the constellation of Pisces covers well over one-twelfth of the zodiacal circle, it is anyone's guess when exactly the "Age of Pisces" began. Carl Jung's discussion in *Aion* is probably the most intelligent study of the subject.[19] But, as said before, none of this affects practical astrology. To say that Venus is in the first degree of Aries means simply that Venus is at the point of the sun's spring equinox—no matter that it can be seen plainly shining among the western stars of Pisces.

The new zodiac of the Arien Age spread throughout the Old World, and with it a solar tradition that became well-nigh universal. Writings on this zodiac and its putative history and symbolism are legion; here I mention only two independent sources that seem to bear especially on the event to which Guénon has alluded. One is Jean Richer's *Géographie sacrée du monde grec* (Sacred geography of the Greek world, 1967), which shows how the symbolism of the "new" zodiac permeated Greek culture and, which is more surprising, Greek geography. Richer ties in the cycles of Greek mythology with locations that reproduce a zodiac on an enormous scale, covering the whole Peloponnese and Greek mainland and stretching to the islands and Asia Minor. Another is the recent work of John Michell and Christine Rhone,[20] who in *Twelve-Tribe Nations and the Science of Enchanting the Landscape* (1991) trace the foundation, all over the world, of cultures whose symbolism is solar and based on the number twelve. Michell writes that in Britain, it "appears to have risen some 4,000 years ago, at the beginning of the age of Aries. Its religion was based on a solar myth within the twelve-part framework of the zodiac, and the leader of its twelve ruling gods was a British version of Apollo, namely Arthur."[21] Michell then refers to the earlier, Polar tradition:

> The origins of Glastonbury's Round Table lie in times before civilization, when Arthur was Arcturus, the keeper of the Great Bear formed by Glastonbury's seven sacred islands. With solar civilization came a highly structured social order, dominated throughout by the number twelve. The earthly Round Table was converted from a stellar landscape into a giant zodiac with twelve sectors round the Isle of Avalon, and Arthur with twelve companion knights was recast as a solar hero. The Great Bear was then seen as the vehicle in which the sun god circled the heavens. Thus it acquired its old English name—Arthur's chariot.[22]

Guénon, whose knowledge of Glastonbury was restricted to Katherine Maltwood's 1935 announcement of her discovery of the zodiac formed by the surrounding landscape, interpreted it in his essay on "The Land of the Sun" as a ten-signed zodiac, hence as a relic of the primordial pattern of the heavens. He believed that the Celts had preserved something of the great Hyperborean tradition,[23] and that the figure of King Arthur was rooted there: he expands on the etymology of Arthur-Arktos, son of Uther Pendragon, whose name, in turn, recalls the polar constellation Draco.[24] We note that the prominent star Alpha Draconis was the Pole Star for the centuries around 3,000 BCE.

Arthur's transformation from polar to solar hero is parallel to that of Apollo, who came to Greece as a Hyperborean and ended as the Sun. But not all cultures experienced this transition at the same time, or at all. We have already mentioned pre-Buddhist Tibet, where in Lama Govinda's words, "the main deities of the Bön-pos were originally those of the sky, the embodiments of space and light, of infinity and purity."[25] The cosmology of the Bön-po's shamanistic brethren, the native North Americans, is likewise polar, and dominated by the characteristic symbols of the axial tree at the center of the world and the swastika-cross of the four directions. In imperial China, the whole astronomical system was developed around the celestial pole and equator, rather than around the planets and the ecliptic, as in Babylon and its heirs. Whereas the warring Roman Emperors increasingly accepted an identification with the unconquered Sun-God, the Chinese Emperor was likened to the Pole Star, the unmoving center of a vast "revolving" state of peasants and bureaucrats.[26]

Mithras

The Mithraic mystery religion is a remarkable instance of the Polar tradition's revival in Hellenistic times. Appearing shortly before the time of Christ,

Mithraism spread throughout the Roman Empire in the wake of conquering armies, and before it disappeared in the fourth or fifth century CE, bequeathed much of its symbolism and ethos to Christianity—not, perhaps, to the benefit of the latter.[27]

The origins of Mithraism and the nature of Mithras have troubled scholars for a hundred years. The great Theosophical scholar G. R. S. Mead already sensed that Mithras was not simply the Sun, but a supra-cosmic divinity, as shown in Mithras' birth out of a rock; Mead shows that this is not the rock of earth, but the firmament of heaven, "which was thought of as solid or rigid by the ancients."[28] The recent work of David Ulansey (*The Origin of the Mithraic Mysteries*, 1989) confirms Mead's intuition by associating the foundation of Mithraism with the rediscovery of the precession of the equinoxes [see Chapter Fifteen for an explanation] by Hipparchus in the second century BCE: an event that brought with it the awesome realization that even the axis of the universe was not fixed. Ulansey cannot believe that precession could have been discovered earlier, an anathema to classicists though commonly accepted by historians of science.[29] If there is any truth in his theory, we must assume that the questions which caused such anguish in 4,000 or 2,000 BCE had long been forgotten, probably during the "dark age" consequent on the Santorini eruption in the fifteenth century BCE.

The precessional movement, which in the geostatic cosmology of Antiquity was ascribed to the stars, required a supra-cosmic divinity to move it, and according to Ulansey it was the Persian god Mithra who was adapted to this role. Already in Zoroastrianism, Mithra dwelt "above Harâ, the lofty, gleaming [mountain] round which circles many [a star], where there is neither night nor darkness."[30] Thereupon all his attributes fall into place more or less tidily. The primary icon of Mithraism is the Tauroctony or bull-slaying scene, which we encountered in the place of honor in Wilhelm Landig's "Point 103" temple (see Chapter Six). Mithras is shown kneeling on the back of a bull, which he is stabbing with a knife; lower down are a scorpion, a snake, a raven, a cup, a lion, and a dog (or some of these). The bull is of course Taurus, the other creatures or attributes correspond to the constellations nearby (Scorpio, Hydra, Corvus, Crater, Leo, Canis minor), while Mithras himself is the pseudo-Persian hero Perseus, visible directly above the Bull. By killing the celestial Bull, Mithras asserts his power over the entire cosmos, and enables the next sign, that of Aries the Ram, to become home to the Sun at the spring equinox, as was the case during the two millenia BCE. Ironically enough, by the time that Mithraism was fully established, the equinoctial point was already moving out of Aries and into Pisces: an event celebrated by such words as "Worthy is the Lamb that was slain" (Apocalypse 5.12) and "Behold, I shall make you fishers of men" (Matthew 4.19).

Two powerful symbolic figures associated with the Mithraic monuments are Phanes and Aeon. Phanes is the first-born god of light in the Orphic cosmogony, who broke out of the two halves of the cosmic egg that subsequently became heaven and earth. The well-known relief sculpture in Modena shows him as a beautiful young god with wings and a serpent entwined around him, standing in the circle of the zodiac and holding a staff. In a previous work (*Mystery Religions of the Ancient World*, 1981), I suggested a Platonically-influenced interpretation of the Modena Phanes as the power that infuses the visible cosmos with the archetypal ideas.[31] He could equally well be seen as a theophany of the god who directs the universal order from beyond the Pole Star, holding the axis-staff, with the serpent round his body denoting the path of the stars—and of the initiate.

Aeon is shown in ancient iconography with a male human body, wings, and a lion's head, similarly wound round with a serpent. Mead quotes the following definition of Aeon from Macrobius:

> He who made all things and governs all things, joined together by means of the surrounding Heaven the power and nature of Water and Earth, heavy and downward, flowing down into the Depth, and that of Fire and Spirit, light and rushing upward to the measureless Height. It is this mightiest power of Heaven that hath bound together these two unequal powers.[32]

Far from being a god of time, Mead says, Aeon is "the Paradigm thereof—Eternity."[33] Without going into the many arguments and sources gathered by Mead in support of this, I point out that this binding of opposites, this spanning of heaven and earth, and this combination of the winged power of movement with the serpentine power of ascent, make Aeon a perfect figuration of our axial divinity. As for the lion's head, which makes the Aeon statues so numinous and awesome to look upon, it is a reminder of what was said in the previous chapter about the negative aspect of the upward path: it is a destruction and a devouring, as the person is assimilated to the god. Howard Jackson writes, in his study of the lion-headed figure, of how it is sometimes called "Ahriman"—who would seem to be the power of evil if one follows too slavishly the dualism of Persia. This, he says, is not so:

> The leontocephaline, as the distillation of celestial power, cannot, then, have been an irredeemably oppressive force but, as it embodies souls, so it might aid—by initiation and not by compulsion—in freeing them from that embodiment.[34]

The polar cult also survived in classical times in popular religion and magic. The Greek magical papyri contain many spells addressed to the Great Bear,[35] for example:

> Bear, Bear, you who rule the heaven, the stars, and the whole world; you who make the axis turn and control the whole cosmic system by force and compulsion, I appeal to you, imploring and supplicating that you may do the [thing I desire], because I call upon you with your holy names at which your deity rejoices, names which you are not able to ignore...[36]

In the next quotation, the seven Greek vowels (aeêiouô) are sounded to represent the seven stars of the Bear: another ambiguous legacy of the polar-solar transition, for the more typical use of the vowels in Antiquity was as symbols of the seven planets.[37]

> Thôzopithê, Bear, greatest goddess, ruling heaven, reigning over the pole of the stars, highest, beautiful-shining goddess, incorruptible element, composite of the all, all-illuminating, bond of the universe aeêiouô, you who stand on the pole, you whom the lord god appointed to turn the holy pole with a strong hand.[38]

There is evidently some uncertainty in the spells as to whether the Bear is the Supreme God of the cosmos, or whether the She-Bear is a goddess subordinate to him. But this probably did not concern the magician, any more than the average Christian worried about whether the cosmos was turned by the Father or the Logos.

The Ascent of the Spheres

Somewhere between the secret initiations of the Mithraic cult and these commonplaces of folk-magic comes the so-called "Mithras Liturgy" in the great Paris magical manuscript (fourth century CE). It is not a liturgy but a theurgic evocation, which (in the author's words) "the great god Helios Mithras ordered to be revealed to me by his archangel, so that I alone may ascend into heaven as an inquirer and behold the universe."[39] The instructions are interlarded with descriptions of the visions consequent on them, first of which is the sun's disk from which hangs a pipe (*aulos*), "the origin of the ministering wind" that wafts to east and west. This puzzling image fascinated Carl Jung, one of whose patients had independently had a similar vision.[40] Doors in the sun's disk open to reveal the world of the seven planetary gods, then comes forth the youthful Helios. Evidently we are dealing with an ascent through the planetary spheres. Helios is seen to "come to the celestial pole, and you will see him walking as if on a road."[41] Keeping in mind the source of the evocation, "Helios-Mithras," this is presumably where the god transmutes from his solar to his polar, supra-cosmic form.

Now doors open again and the seven Fates appear as virgins who, in keeping with Egyptian symbology, have the faces of asps. Then come another seven gods, probably the seven stars of the Great Bear,

> who have the faces of black bulls, in linen loincloths, and in possession of seven golden diadems. They are the so-called Pole Lords of heaven, whom you must greet in the same manner, each of them with his own name: 'Hail, O guardians of the pivot, O sacred and brave youths, who turn at one command the revolving axis of the vault of heaven...'

Lastly, with thunderings, lightnings, and earthquakes, comes the god Mithras himself, garbed in Persian fashion and holding the bull's foreleg, Egyptian

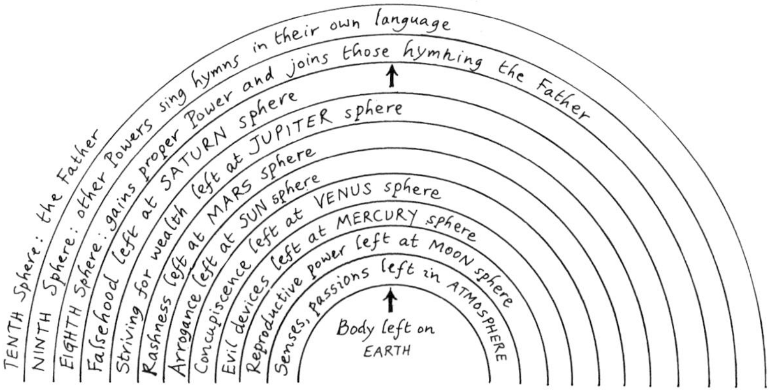

Illustration 19: The Hermetic ascent of the soul

symbol of the Great Bear. The theurgist will see:

> a god descending, a god immensely great, having a bright appearance, youthful, golden-haired, with a white tunic and a golden crown and trousers, and holding in his right hand a golden shoulder of a young bull: this is the Bear which moves and turns heaven around, moving upward and downward in accordance with the hour. Then you will see lightning bolts leaping from his eyes and stars from his body...[42]

The theurgist of the Mithras Liturgy has followed the typical path of the Polar initiate: up the world-axis, through the realm of the sun and planets, past the stars, to the supra-cosmic reality. This is the place of utter immobility, which paradoxically enough is also that of absolute power, by whose fiat the two Bears and all the heavens are turned.[43]

The classic description of this path is in the *Pomandres*, best-known of all the treatises attributed to Hermes Trismegistus. In accordance with the Ptolemaic cosmology, the simple dichotomy ("cutting-in-two") of heaven and earth is there resolved into a system, at once astronomical and psychological, of intervening spheres. The ancient astronomer imagined that between himself and the Pole Star were the transparent spheres of the seven planets: Moon, Mercury, Venus, Sun, Mars, Jupiter, and Saturn. The Hermetic philosopher taught that these have to be crossed one by one on the upward, as on the downward journey: at each sphere, one had to lay aside the negative tendencies ruled by the planet in question. Perhaps this is why the upward trajectory of the soul is not an unimpeded straight line, but a serpentine path.

The crossing of the planetary spheres is described in the *Poimandres* as occurring after death, but the preparation for it takes place in the course of life. It is what Jung called the "integration of the personality" or the "way of individuation," and the planetary portals are the challenges thrown to us both by life and by the archetypal contents of the unconscious. The Pole Star, shining from the Eighth Sphere, is a symbol of the Self: the all-but-inaccessible Center, where the keystone of the heavenly vault opens to give access to another order of existence. Jung cautioned against the too presumptive assimilation of one's human ego to this transcendent Self, just as we have offered for consideration the examples of men who aimed at transcendence without having first cultivated psychological balance and the virtues.

If Mithraism borrowed something from the religion of Persia, it seems to have returned the loan. In the Sassanian dynasty (226–652 CE), a sect arose within Zoroastrianism which centered on the god Zrvan (written also Zarvan, Zervan, and Zurvan), "Infinite Time."[44] A god of this name already existed in the Avesta, but the peculiarity of the Zurvanists was to regard Zurvan as the source both of Ormazd, the principle of good in Persian dualism, and of Ahriman, the principle of evil. Zurvan was a god beyond the cosmic circuit and beyond time as we know it, which points clearly enough to the supra-cosmic divinity.

Zaehner says that the Zoroastrians "turned the planets into demons because their irregular motions could not be explained. When, however, they came into contact with the Babylonians, they learnt the 'science' of astrology."[45] The planets remained in Zurvanism as creatures of Ahriman, while the constellations were on the side of Ormazd. Zurvan was mightier than both, but as such he was synonymous with death: the death of the macrocosm as well as of the human microcosm.

The esotericist will recognize here the "death" of Non-Being or of the Unmanifest, into which the whole created universe must be dissolved, and to which the polar initiate surrenders his being. Here, as in the Hermetic ascent, the seven planets—not excluding the Sun—are but obstacles: they are like the demons encountered in the posthumous or initiatic journey, the "guardians of the threshold" who are not intrinsically evil, but appear as such to test the voyager. In the next chapter we will see how this experiential polar tradition survived after the fall of the classical world in the very heart of Islam.

Chapter Thirteen:
The Spiritual Pole

It is in Medieval Iran that we find the fullest literature on the spiritual Pole and the experience of mystical ascent to it. The Iranian Sufis drew not only on Islam, but on the Mazdean, Manichean, Hermetic, Gnostic, and Platonic traditions that all flourished on the hospitable soil of Persia. (One recalls that the Athenian Academy, founded by Plato, took refuge there after its suppression in 529 CE) In the intellectual ferment of the Islamic Middle Ages, these were blended in a "theosophy": a science of divine knowledge that was at once mysticism and the highest form of practical philosophy. It is thanks to the work of Henry Corbin, the French scholar who made this literature available to Westerners, that I am able here to give a slight impression of it.

The medieval Persian sages, of whom the chief was Sohrawardi the Martyr (1153–1191), were called in their day "Philosophers of the Orient." The Orient is where the sun rises, and for this reason the East symbolizes the place from which light of every kind is to be expected: *ex oriente lux*. Thus so great a Sufi as Mohyiddin Ibn 'Arabi regarded his eastward voyage from Spain to Syria and Arabia as a symbolic ascent to the source of light.[1] And it is evident that for the Jews and Christians of Europe, and the Muslims of Egypt and the Mahgreb, their religious capitals of Jerusalem and Mecca have always lain eastwards.

Esoterically, however, the Persian theosophers situated their "Orient" neither to the East, nor to the South, whither they faced in prayer towards the Ka'aba. "The *Orient* sought by the mystic, the Orient that cannot be located on our maps, is in the direction of the *north*, beyond the north."[2] About this Pole reigns a perpetual Darkness, says the *Recital of Hayy ibn Yaqzan*, one of the visionary recitals of Avicenna (Ibn Sina). "Each year the rising sun shines upon it at a fixed time. He who confronts that Darkness and does not hesitate to plunge into it for fear of difficulties will come to a vast space, boundless and filled with light."[3] This Darkness, says Corbin, is the ignorance of the natural man. "To pass through it is a terrifying and painful experience, for it ruins and destroys all the patencies and norms on which the natural man lived and depended..."[4] But it must be faced consciously before one can acquire the saving gnosis of the light beyond.

The Darkness around the Pole, annually pierced by the sun's rays, is at once terrestrial and symbolic. On the one hand, this is the situation at the North Pole, where there are six months of night and six of day. It is characteristic of esoteric tradition that the same image is valid on two or more levels. But as Corbin and Guénon never tired of pointing out, the symbolic level is not a fanciful construct on the basis of hard terrestrial fact: it is quite the other way round. In the present case, the mystical experience of penetrating the Darkness at the Pole is the fundamental reality and the authentic experience of the individual. The fact that the set-up of the material world reflects the celestial geography is what is contingent. In brief, in this teaching as in Platonism, it is the supersensible realm that is real, and the material realm that is a shadow of it.

By the same token, the Aurora Borealis of the Arctic regions, meaning literally the "northern dawn," is another visible image of the Midnight Sun that dawns in the mystical consciousness; Corbin reminds us of the prominence of inner light in the rituals of the mystery religions.[5] Charles Fourier's "boreal crown," which will be described in Chapter Fifteen, is perhaps a faint intuition of the same illumined state, which Fourier foresaw as the destiny of the whole of humanity.

The individual who, through deep meditation and the practice of active imagination, succeeds in entering the real world of such theosophic visions, is making a pilgrimage to the polar "Orient" that is not found on maps. This is the place of the soul's origin, and of its return. In between, the person is in exile in the "West," that is to say, in the material world, which opinion mistakes for the only reality. The journey to this pole is sometimes illustrated as the ascent of a column of light, which extends from the depths of Hell to the lucid paradise in the cosmic north.[6] There is darkness at both ends: at the bottom, the darkness of the extreme of non-being, the absence of light which is pure matter; at the top, the luminous darkness of the impenetrable beyond-being, the divine night of origins. In this higher darkness, the midnight sun blazes forth, as the being enters the state of superconsciousness, overcoming its own darkness to realize its own light.[7]

Again, in the Iranian visions there may be a cable let down from the cosmic pole. Hermes, according to Sohrawardi's *Book of Elucidations*, climbed this cable of light, and found himself with both heaven and earth beneath his feet.[8] This means that he had gone beyond the eight spheres described in his *Poimandres*, beyond the furthest objects visible to the bodily eye—the fixed stars—to the realm that medieval cosmology imagined to surround the entire visible cosmos, where God and the angelic hierarchies have their dwelling.

This cable or column of light is also Homer's Golden Chain of Jupiter that holds the worlds together, Plato's Spindle of Necessity on which all the worlds are threaded and spun, and the Taoists' Celestial Ray that René Guénon has shown us transfixing the levels of existence. There are further symbols for it in Sufism. The nomadic imagination sees it is the central pole of the tent of Heaven, surrounded by four subsidiary posts that are the pillars of the Earth.[9] While simple souls may conceive of heaven or earth as actually resting on four pillars—and even on elephants and a turtle, if they are Hindus—these pillars symbolize the locations in space of the two solstices and the two equinoxes, together forming a cross within the circular orbit of the earth and their ruling angels.

The Pole is also a mountain, called Mount Qaf, whose ascent, like Dante's climbing of the Mountain of Purgatory, represents the pilgrim's progress through spiritual states.[10] We know by now that it is not necessary to think of this as a physical mountain in the Arctic Ocean. Geographically speaking, the mountain of ascent is wherever the pilgrim begins his journey to the "Orient," and its symbol could be the local zenith of every place on earth.[11] For the more settled peoples of the Middle East, Mount Qaf was symbolized very adequately by the Babylonian ziggurats, tall towers with a spiral path of ascent, at the top of which is a platform for the observation of the heavens. The aspiration of the builders of the Tower of Babel, in nearby Iraq, to raise a tower "with its top in the heavens" (Genesis 11.4) was not so stupid, nor so arrogant, as Yahweh and his followers thought. The same desire to imitate the axial mountain of the Pole emerges in Chinese pagodas, in the piled-up towers of Hindu temples, and in the spires of Christian churches. Wherever inspired architecture has placed the image of the polar mountain, there the esoteric pilgrim can read the invitation to a spiritual ascent. And where it has not, nature offers the same invitation in the clear air of mountaintops, or in the contemplation of the stars themselves.

In the Iranian theosophy, the heavenly Pole, the focal point of the spiritual ascent, acts as a magnet to draw beings to its "palaces ablaze with immaterial matter."[12] Here again one can see a concordance with the physical pole which attracts the loadstone and the compass needle. The Occidental Exile of Sohrawardi is "summoned at last to return *home*, to return *to himself*."[13] This magnetism is the work of the divine Compassion, that (like Matgioï's "Destiny," mentioned at the end of Chapter Eleven) eventually draws all its creatures to itself. In a passage that might seem contradictory to the above, Corbin calls the Mountain of Qaf the "Sphere of Spheres surrounding the totality of the visible cosmos; an *emerald rock*, casting its reflection over the whole of the mountain of Qaf, is the keystone of this celestial vault, the pole."[14] The mountain here becomes assimilated to the symbol of the heavenly tent, which must logically be spherical if the earth is so. It is the level of being superior to the visible world, thus the same as the angelic realm that extends infinitely beyond the visible boundary of the fixed stars. There is only one way through the latter, and that is at the celestial pole. The spiritual pilgrim finds there the Emerald Rock, the threshold of the beyond.

Najm Kobra, who wrote in detail on the colors and lights seen on the theosophic journey, speaks of green as the color of the pole.[15] The pilgrim at first finds himself in a deep well—evidently the World Axis experienced from within in the unillumined state—that is suddenly illuminated by an extraordinary green light that first shines at the mouth, then, in the course of ascent, suffuses the whole of the well so that one is traveling up a luminous shaft. "Dark at the beginning, because it was the dwelling-place of devils, it is now luminous with *green light*, because it has become the place to which descend the Angels and the divine Compassion."[16]

There is no place to digress on the prevalence in the hollow earth literature of green lights, green children, etc.[17] But the Iranian theosophers refer continually to this color: to emerald rocks, giving access to emerald cities, and to the Green Island where the hidden Imam dwells.[18] All these appear to be transcripts of the same *visio smaragdina* (emerald vision), an experience of immaterial light, that as Corbin says may either precede or succeed the "darkness at the approach to the pole." [19] That the cosmology of Hermes Trismegistus was written on an "emerald tablet" is surely no accident; for such visions are not merely entertainments, like their drug-induced imitations. They bring an initiation of knowledge, both cosmological and theosophic. The pilgrims are not only the richer for the experience, but also the wiser. They are henceforth "Hyperboreans," whose soul has "reached such completeness and harmony that it is devoid of negativity and shadow; it is neither of the east nor of the west." [20]

This Iranian theosophy could scarcely be further from the narrow and oppressive exotericism for which Iran has temporarily become notorious. We are speaking of a tradition that is Islamic only by accident, as it were, having existed long before Muhammad. Nevertheless, the Shi'ite branch of Islam has contributed richly to the lore of the Pole by identifying with it the hidden Imam. Each prophet-messenger, in Shi'ite doctrine, is followed by twelve Imams who continue his theophanic function. The Twelfth Imam of the Islamic line disappeared in 940 or 941 CE. According to some Sufis he died, and his function has been held ever since by a line of Sufi shaykhs whose names and number are known to initiates. The *Ishraqiyun* or Oriental theosophers, on the other hand, believe that the Twelfth Imam has not died, but is "occulted," residing in the intermediate world to which access is given as described above. He is and remains the "mystic Pole," until the Resurrection, because he is the last Imam of Islam, and Islam is the last revelation of the prophetic series.[21] He does not need to be recognized by mankind to fulfil his function, which is not a social one but a sacral and metaphysical one.[22] He is the "perfect Sage, whose mere secret presence, unknown to the multitude of men, at once suffices and is necessary for the leaven of Wisdom to continue to ferment among them and for the perpetuation of a humanity of which the Imam is the 'pole' (*qutb*)." [23] As such, he sounds very much like Guénon's King of the World.

Following Sohrawardi, Corbin explains that around the "hidden Pole" of the Imam is a whole group who are the columns sustaining the world, "since it is through them that the effusion of divine grace still arrives in this world; and if it should ever happen that an epoch were deprived of them, the world would perish in an irreversible catastrophe." [24] The numbers of this hierarchy vary; sometimes they are equated with the fourfold columns, but more often with the stars that surround Polaris in the northern sky. Ruzbehan of Shiraz (died 1209), whom Corbin calls "the *imam* par excellence of the '*Fedeli d'amore*' in Iranian Sufism, [...] had a series of visions referring to the heavenly Pole; it was by meditating on these that he finally understood how he was personally and secretly connected with the group of the masters of initiation symbolized by the stars stationed in the immediate vicinity of the Pole Star."[25]

This again underlines the essentially individual, not social nature of theosophy. Yet it is far from being useless to the community. Just as the Platonic world of Forms gives being to the material world, so the influence of the esoteric masters and the access to them, one by one, of their destined pupils is the magnetic influence that keeps humanity from falling into complete abandonment and self-destruction.[26]

Ruzbehan, in his vision, was "given oil from the constellation of the Bear," which he seems to have recognized as an anointing, admitting him to the rank of the seven masters of initiation. On turning his attention to the Great Bear, Ruzbehan saw its seven stars as seven apertures through which God was showing himself.[27] One should note the language here: in Islam there is no incarnation, as there is in Hinduism and Christianity, but there is theophany, in which God, in Ruzbehan's anthropomorphic terms, "shows himself."

Apart from the obvious analogy with the Seven Rishis of the Vedas, Corbin finds parallels in Zoroastrianism and Taoism to the Sufi's vision of the Great Bear as a constellation of great beings attendant on their polar head.[28] In particular, he notes a Taoist tradition of "*seven* spiritual rulers 'localized' in the constellation of the Bear." This comes from a book called *The Classic of the Pivot of Jade*, which is the Taoist designation for the Pole Star—jade being, aptly enough, a green stone. The Confucians, being more exoteric, called Polaris the Emperor, and the Great Bear his chariot.[29] The Buriats and Mongols apparently saw the stars of the Great Bear as "seven old men" or "seven Tengris" (gods or deified patriarchs),[30] which is close to the Hindu designation of them as the Seven Rishis, ancestral heroes or sages translated to the heavens.[31]

Among those peoples who turned to the Pole Star for their prayers, Corbin names the Mandeans, the Sabeans of Harran, the Manicheans, and the Buddhists of Central Asia.[32] The Brethren of Purity of Basra, an isolated community of pious scholars who inherited some of the Sabean practices, held a monthly ritual in which "a *cosmic text* was read under the starry heavens facing the polar star."[33] All in all, the sacred character of the celestial Pole and its attendants seems to have filtered down into the religions of many peoples of Central and Western Asia, but to the "Oriental theosophers" of Iran and their modern spokesman, Henry Corbin, goes the eternal credit of having explored and mapped this place of theophanies and spiritual transmutations.

Dante and the Polar Tradition

Dante's journey through Inferno, Purgatory, and Paradise is the most shining example in Christendom of a theosophic ascent such as the Iranians describe. In the *Inferno*, Dante and Virgil travel from Jerusalem, the "polar" city of the Judeo-Christian tradition, gradually downwards through the subterranean pit, shaped like a funnel, which ends with Lucifer at the center of the earth. They continue in the same direction, passing rapidly through a tunnel to emerge at the foot of the Mountain of Purgatory, from which they can see the stars of the Southern

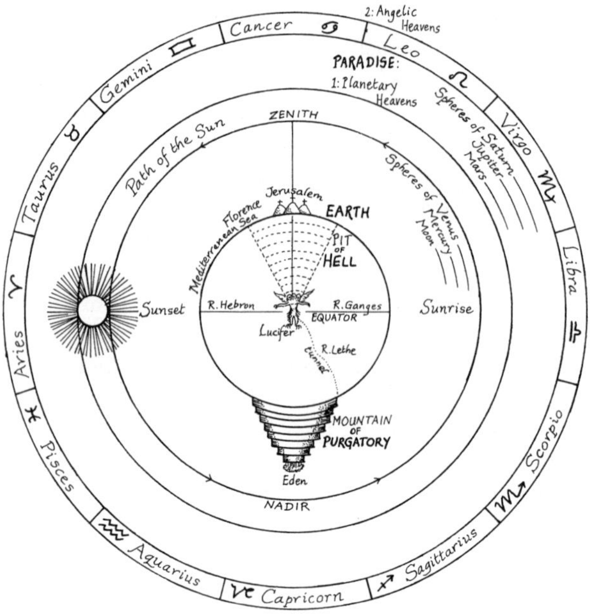

Illustration 20: Dante's cosmos

Cross. Like Meru or Sinai, this is the archetypal mountain with its spiral stages of ascent that join earth to heaven. Being opposite Jerusalem, it must be in the southern hemisphere; one might assimilate it to the negative currents mentioned in our study of the Antarctic (see Chapter Ten). But somehow in the course of the *Purgatorio* the travelers accomplish a "reversal," for when they reach the Earthly Paradise at the top of the mountain, the stars they see are the *Septentrion*, the Seven Stars of the Little Bear, that announce the coming of Beatrice on the Griffin Chariot—the Great Bear.[34] Beatrice is robed and veiled in green, and her eyes are like emeralds,[35] which to the reader schooled in the Iranian theosophy is not simply an emblem of Hope, but an announcement of the "Smaragdine Vision" that is presumably the common experience of all who rise so far.

Whereas the ascent of the *Poimandres* situated the purgations of the soul in the seven planetary spheres, omitting any detail of celestial geography beyond the entry into the Eighth Sphere, Dante has them on a mountain which reaches only to the First Heaven, that of the Moon. The planetary spheres are then available as a variegated setting for the *Paradiso*. Throughout the work, stars are much more important than planets, even including the Sun: as every student of the *Divine Comedy* knows, the word *stelle* ends each of the three parts of the poem.

Dante's way to Paradise was through his love for Beatrice, and hers for him. Titus Burckhardt (1908–1984), the Swiss scholar and Muslim, in his essay "Why Dante was right," says:

> That Dante should have bestowed upon Divine Wisdom the image and name of a beautiful and noble woman is in accordance with a compelling law, not merely because Divine Wisdom, insofar as it is the object of knowledge, includes an aspect which precisely is feminine in the highest sense, but also because the presence of the divine Sophia manifested itself first and foremost to him in the appearance of the beloved woman. Herein a key is provided that enables us to understand, at least in principle, the spiritual alchemy whereby the poet is able to transpose sensory appearances into supra-sensory essences: when love encompasses the entire will and causes it to flow towards the center of the being, it can become knowledge of God. The means that lies between love and knowledge is beauty: upon experiencing its inexhaustible essence—which confers release from all constraints—an aspect of Divine Wisdom is already within it, so that even sexual attraction may lead to knowledge of the Divine, to the extent that passion is absorbed and consumed by love, and passion likewise transformed by the experience of beauty.[36]

Although everyone can find in Dante, as in the Bible, something to support their own agenda, I venture to point out two further appearances of Arktos that seem to bear directly on Burckhardt's theme. One of these occurs during the visit to the Seventh Circle of Purgatory, where the sin of Lust is punished: the souls in their hymn of penitence choose, of all the myriad tales of lust from the pagan repertory, to mention that of Helice (another name for Callisto): "To the wood/ Diana ran, and drove forth Helice/Therefrom, who had of Venus felt the poison."[37] The second is near the culmination of Paradise, where the angels form themselves into a white rose. Dante likens his amazement to that of

> ...the barbarians, coming from some region
> That every day by Helice is covered,
> Revolving with her son whom she delights in,
> Beholding Rome and all her noble works...[38]

The name of *Helike*, one of the Greek terms for the Great Bear, refers directly to its "helical" spiralling around the celestial Pole; its two appearances in the *Paradiso* mark precisely the contrast between carnal and spiritual love. With the exception of a mention of Phoebus later in the same canto, this is the last classical reference in the *Divine Comedy*. At the very least, one can say that Dante was alert to the archetypes with which we have been dealing.

According to the mid-nineteenth century studies of Eugène Aroux—though conventional scholarship seems to know nothing of it—Dante was a member of a secret society called the *Fedeli d'Amore*, the "Faithful of Love." In one direction, this points back to the "courts of love" of the Troubadours, suppressed in the Albigensian Crusade a century before Dante. In the other, it points forward to the rather watered-down conventions of courtly love which dominate the music and poetry of the fourteenth and fifteenth centuries, if not long after that. The whole subject is too large and too well-explored for any summary to be desirable here; but the essential thing to be retained is the idea of a spiritual eroticism, or of an erotic spirituality, known in the Bible from the Song of Solomon but rigorously excluded from dogmatic Christianity. Its symbolism is polar because it links heaven and earth, and because its practices concern the axial currents of the human body. There is a Right-handed version, to which Dante adhered, in which the transmutation of carnal love requires its renunciation. And there is a Left-handed version, more secret by far, in which it does not. Possibly some of the alchemists were practicing the latter with their *sorores mysticae*.

This brings us again to the *Dream of Poliphilo* and the group of *quattrocento* philosophers whose ideals were enshrined in that work during the period of their enforced silencing by the Church. The first letters of each chapter make an acrostic, saying that Francesco Colonna (the protector of the work), was a lover of Polia, who appears in the book as the feminine symbol for Divine Wisdom as revealed through Nature. One notices in passing the fact that Francis "column" was thus the lover of a feminized "pole"! With the *Dream* as its literary vehicle, the liberal Platonic philosophy survived through the difficult times of the sixteenth and seventeenth centuries. Its symbolism calls, as Dante's does, on the rich fund of archetypes from classical mythology; on the idea of a sacralized Nature, studied through the Quadrivium and the new science; and on sexual love as the spur to, or image of, the assimilation to the Divine.

The English-speaking world knows this body of thought through the works of Shakespeare and Bacon; the French, through Rabelais, then through the artists around the early court of Louis XIV; the Germans, through the Rosicrucians and alchemists; and the Italians, as we now know from Kretzulesco-Quaranta's work, through the ultra-concealed medium of symbolic garden-design. One of its mottos is *Et in Arcadia ego*, inscribed on the tomb in Nicolas Poussin's famous painting of that name. Is it merely a nostalgic sigh, as it is usually understood today, meaning "I, too, have been in Arcadia"; or is it a *memento mori*, meaning "I [Death] exist even in Arcadia"; or is it a password of those who know or aspire to the realm of Arcas, son of Jupiter and Callisto, who circles the Pole as the Little Bear?

The Two Paths and their Dangers

Our study of the polar archetype has now brought us, with many a detour, from the lowest to the highest of which the human being is capable: a journey that some may have found more troubling than entertaining. One of the things that the "Thulean" movement has forced us to recognize is the existence of spiritual aspirations and awareness in such men as Lanz von Liebenfels, Rudolf Hess, Miguel Serrano—and even Adolf Hitler himself. Although one hesitates to pass judgement on so large and terrifying a phenomenon as they represent, it seems important to clarify their relationship to the two paths: those of the Right hand and of the Left.

To equate the Left-hand path with evil and "black magic" is too simplistic.

True, there was a black magic at work in the Nazi movement, in the sense of occult operations performed with intent to harm. The Nuremberg rallies were one manifestation of these, *Kristallennacht* one of their effects, and the defeat and disgrace of the Nazi leaders the inevitable rebound. But however nefarious their political actions, some of those men had a spiritual dimension to their lives and were, in their way, religious. One sees this at its clearest in Miguel Serrano, the most erudite and articulate spokesman for Nazi spirituality, if one dare employ the term.

This type of spirituality perverts both paths. In its asceticism it tends to the Right-hand path, which is furthered by abstinence from meat, tobacco, drugs and alcohol, by sexual continence, the observance of ethical rules, and a concern with purity of every kind. Hitler's tendencies in that direction are well known. Serrano, following Otto Rahn, sees the neo-Aryans as the inheritors of the world-rejecting Cathars ("Pure Ones") of the Middle Ages. He says that the Aryan warrior is naturally continent, transmuting the sexual energies and substances into spiritual ones.[39]

The besetting sins of the Right-hand path are pride, and the tendency to set oneself apart from humanity. What better way of doing this than to claim that one's own race comes from the heavens, all others from the dirty earth? The more fanatical the quest for purity, the worse the consequences for anyone who gets in the way. If Aryans alone can tread the path to Deliverance, those who are disqualified by blood, race, or caste from this high destiny are an unfortunate nuisance, to be shunned, enslaved, or exterminated, while the masters set their steely eyes in nostalgia for the cold purity of their Hyperborean home.

The corresponding fault of those who take the Left-hand path is to misunderstand the famous motto of Aleister Crowley's Thelema: "Do what thou wilt shall be the whole of the Law." In a sense, but a very precise and restricted one, this implies freedom from ethical restraints. But it is all too tempting to identify one's "will" with one's basest impulses of indulgence and selfishness. Hitler invariably acted as if everything were permitted him: no amount of suffering and death mattered so long as it served his purposes, and he set an example of how a whole people can be willed into a frenzy of hatred and nationalism. The second part of the motto of the left-hand path, "Love is the law, love under will," became for the Nazis: "Hatred is the law, hatred under will"—a powerful formula indeed.

The inescapable historical parallel to all of this is to be seen in the innumerable cruelties committed by Christians against Jews, pagans, witches, heretics, and each other: a disgrace to the Solar tradition, as the Nazis are to the Polar. Yet many of the worst offenders were pious, and believed themselves to be sincere Christians; some of them were even mystics. All this goes to show that any religious tradition can do more harm than good, unless it is tempered by the simple humanity and compassion that come more readily to women than to men. When the Dalai Lama says with his characteristic smile, "My religion is Kindness," he is pointing the way to the Golden Age more surely than any priest, shaykh, or esoteric pundit.

The Underground Stream

We have periodically hinted at the continuation of a Polar tradition as an underground current in Christendom and Islam. Michel Lamy, in his remarkable book *Jules Verne, Initié et Initiateur* (Jules Verne, initiate and initiator, 1984), brings more of this current to light and shows how Verne's work, "entirely dedicated to the transmission of a message, must have reflected the thought not of a single man, but of a community."[40] Lamy found the signpost to this community in the strange writings of Grasset d'Orcet, a late nineteenth-century writer on cryptography. He quotes from an article of 1881 by Grasset d'Orcet:

> There are certain literary names which will never disappear from the great honor-roll of humanity. They are those of the artists whose work unites a wisdom sufficiently profound with a form sufficiently moving, to interest all social classes in at least one aspect of their creations. In modern times, such are Dante, Rabelais, Cervantes, and Goethe. It is quite intentionally that I thus unite these four geniuses, otherwise so very different from each other. All of them have delivered to the public only half of their secret, reserving the complete understanding of their oeuvre for an infinitely restricted circle of affiliates. Goethe is the last of them, dying well on in the nineteenth century. A host of special signs indicate that he belonged to the same mysterious society as his illustrious predecessors.[41]

To this Lamy adds:

> This society is the Angelic Society, and to the list drawn up by Grasset d'Orcet, which stops at the beginning of the nineteenth century, we must add Dumas, Nerval, George Sand, Jules Verne, and a few others, as well as numerous painters and artists of all nationalities. One might find it surprising that Grasset d'Orcet makes no allusion to Shakespeare, nor to painters such as Nicolas Poussin, Eustache Lesueur, Guercino, Claude Lorrain, Leonardo da Vinci, Watteau.[42]

Another name for this *Société Angélique*, according to Lamy, was *Le Brouillard*, meaning "mist" or "fog," probably alluding to its occluded status as a persecuted "Church of Light." He finds its characteristic symbols strewn throughout Jules Verne's novels, often concealed in word-plays of which the most obvious is the name of Phileas Fogg, the hero of *Around the World in Eighty Days*: "Fogg" is evident enough, while "Phil-eas" has the same meaning as Poli-philo, "lover of all." The multiple signatures which Lamy discovers in Verne, Maurice Leblanc, and Maurice Barrès, as well as in earlier work by Nerval, Nodier, and George Sand, are astounding, and his book deserves to be taken as seriously as Kretzulesco-Quaranta's, even though its presentation is less scholarly.

One of the pervasive themes treated by Lamy is the subterranean kingdom, immortalized in Verne's *Journey to the Center of the Earth*. Another is the Pole itself, a theme to which Verne returned more than once, as we have seen. Lamy pushes the connections forward in history and across the Rhine, to involve the Thule Society and even the Nazi program of Jewish extermination, codeworded *Nacht und Nebel* ("night and fog"). While his proofs are only circumstantial, we have seen in the present book how intrinsic the Polar tradition is to Nazism. Lamy's study concludes with reflections on the mysterious assassination attempt on Jules Verne in 1887, and on his repudiation of the *Brouillard* and its methods—hence, in a way, of his life's work in its service—during his last years.

Works of virtuoso interpretation like Michel Lamy's are a speciality of the French, who cannot resist *calembours* (puns and plays on words). In the esoteric field, this tendency was encouraged by Fulcanelli's *Le Mystère des Cathédrales* (1925), which suggested that a language of hidden puns concealed the secrets of the alchemical work. In 1987, at Cérisey la Salle in Normandy, I heard a lecture by Claude Gaignebet, the Rabelais scholar, which included a reading of Poe's *The Raven* that placed its 108 verses (a magical number!) firmly in this tradition. "The Raven" became a bilingual pun concealing the poem's true title, *rêve* (dream); the bird, speaking of course the *langue des oiseaux*, quoth "Never-*mours*!" (never die); Poe's radiant maiden Leonore was *Le Nord* (the North), center of the world; and his "book of ancient lore" really concealed *l'or* (the ancient or alchemical gold). This astonishing performance raised the eternal question of interpretation: should one draw the line between what one can read into an author's work, given a certain key (alchemy, numerology, Marxism, Freudianism, deconstruction), and what the author actually wrote into the work? All interpreters must face this question, though few are entirely honest about answering it. Because their key has given meaning to their own world, they feel justified in assuming its presence even when the author does not know or believe as they do. Never is this more true than in the case of esoteric interpreters, whose world-view may allow such possibilities as authors acting intuitively in response to archetypes, or mediumistically in response to promptings from elsewhere, when they are not actually credited with membership of a secret society.

The postulate of an underground group of writers and artists surviving for centuries and deliberately planting certain symbols in the popular mind raises another question: *cui bono*? Whom does it profit to acquaint millions of otherwise innocent readers with the archetypes of the Subterranean World, the Polar Center, the Black Sun, the Green Flash, the survival of ancient races, the Mystery of Blood and of the Holy Grail? What patient program of universal education could it be that has received the support of churchmen and skeptics, royalists and anarchists alike? Did a common purpose link the pious Rosicrucians of the early seventeenth century with the secular Illuminati of Bavaria at the end of the eighteenth? Should one pay any attention to the mystery of Rennes-le-Château and the Priory of Sion, which Lamy regards as central to the *Brouillard* Society?

Yes and no. History is not as tidy as the conspiracy theorists would have it, nor is the solution to the world's ills—or their cause—to be found in any one group or nation. One notices the very special role which many of our authors ascribe to France, as the nation which will eventually lead the world to salvation; Parvulesco, for instance, says that France has inherited the spiritual leadership of Tibet.[43] On the other hand, we have heard more than enough about those who attributed a sacred mission to the German people. In Britain, a strong movement clings to the national myths of King Arthur and Glastonbury: Britain, they say, will answer the call to lead a spiritual instead of an earthly empire. In Italy, Evola believed in the sacrality of the Caesars, and hoped for its revival in the next-best form of Fascism. American philosophers such as the late Manly Palmer Hall write of the secret destiny of the United States, laid down by those masonic illuminates, the Founding Fathers. Theosophists look for the Sixth Root Race to appear on the beaches of California, or Australia. Miguel Serrano puts his trust in Chile and its South American neighbors, obedient to a reversal of polarities in a world that has too long been north-heavy. Père Martin seems to think that the "*Grande Monarque*" will come from French Canada. And what of Holy Russia? What of the inhabitants of Poland who think that they are under the special patronage of the Virgin? What of Prague, capital of alchemy and Kabbalah, heart of Europe and best hope of the former Communist satellites?

One could go on and on. Nearly everyone touched by the archetype of the New Age sees it refracted through their national, racial, or religious consciousness. The *Brouillard* turned sour as it got itself involved in politics and self-important obsessions with Gallicanism and the bloodline of French royalty. Some of the neo-Arthurians in Britain and the spiritual sons of the American Revolution make ready bedfellows with racist and anti-Judaic elements. But the Pole Star and its guardians, like the Sun and its planets, is sublimely indifferent to these provincial nuances. One must seek for what is truly universal about the Polar tradition, and beware of any movement that, while claiming allegiance to it, cherishes the least element of nationalism and separatism. The Thulean episode should have been enough to warn us: the Pole is not political!

PART V:
The Tilt

Chapter Fourteen:
The Catastrophists

At the beginning of this book we heard something of the mythical Golden Age, supposedly caused by the earth's axis being upright, and of the succeeding ages which followed on its fall from perfection. We know very well that the axis is now inclined at 23 1/2° to the perpendicular; that we have seasons, and days and nights which vary in length according to the time of year and the latitude. The coming chapters treat the question of how and when the earth's situation may have shifted, calling on scientific as well as esoteric sources.

The two main schools of thought on this matter parallel those of geology. One, the catastrophist school, believes that at some time in prehistory, though not necessarily beyond the memory of mankind, a cataclysmic event took place that tilted the earth and caused it to take up its present angle. The second, uniformitarian school, believes that the axis has always been shifting, but too slowly to be perceptible except by civilizations able to make observations over thousands of years. A third group blends the two explanations, or confuses them. And there are further complications, bearing on the question of what it is that changes position: the whole earth, or merely its surface?

The early Greek philosophers agreed in recognizing the earth's tilt as an irregular condition: not as something fixed since the beginning of all things, but as having occurred at some definite point in prehistoric time. Most of them assumed the earth to be flat, or shaped like a shallow drum. Empedocles (circa 493–433 BCE) possibly believed that the northern end of the disk had risen as the result of the sun's influence on its air, and that the south had consequently fallen.[1] Leucippus (flourished circa 440–430) proposed that the apparent tilt of the zodiacal belt was caused by the sinking of the frozen northern parts of his drum-shaped earth.[2] Democritus (born circa 460) thought, on the contrary, that the fertile south had become heavier and outweighed the barren north,[3] tilting the earth like the bar of a balance.

The most authoritative voice in this chorus of pre-Socratic philosophers is that of Anaxagoras (circa 500–428). He visualized the situation not from space looking down on a flat earth, but from the earth's pole looking up at the stars, as we have described it above; thus his observation is valid irrespective of the shape of the earth. Anaxagoras says: "In the beginning the stars moved in the sky as in a revolving dome, so that the celestial pole which is always visible was vertically overhead; but subsequently the pole took its inclined position."[4] At about the same time, in the second half of the fifth century BCE, Oinopides of Chios identified the ecliptic as the sun's oblique path. Eratosthenes, two centuries later, became the first to measure it.[5]

These philosophers were evidently catastrophists. Blissfully innocent of any concept of gravitation, they thought it sufficient for one end of the earth simply to become overweight and sink. Plato's own ideas might seem just as naive if as little of his writing had been preserved as has been of the pre-Socratics'; but here we are more fortunate. Plato's dialogue *The Statesman* develops the idea of a periodic reversal of the rotation of the world, possibly meaning the entire cosmic machinery rather than just our earth. The Stranger tells the young Socrates an "old story" about the alteration in rising and setting of the sun and the other planets. "The story tells us that on this famous occasion [during the quarrel between Atreus and Thyestes] these all set where they now rise and rose where they now set. Afterwards, however, when he had testified by this miracle to the justice of Atreus's claims, Zeus restored all these heavenly bodies to their present system of motion." He goes on, a little later: "All these stories originate from the same event in cosmic history."[6] Then follows the explanation given in Chapter One, of how the world's governance is alternately under God's power and under its own, and the description of the state of humanity in the first Age, that of Cronus. At the appointed close of that era,

> ...the gods of the provinces, who had ruled under the greatest god, knew at once what was happening and relinquished the oversight of their regions. A shudder passed through the world at the reversing of its rotation, checked as it was between the old control and the new impulse which had turned end into beginning for it and beginning into end. This shock set up a great quaking which caused—in this crisis of the world just as in the former one—destruction of living creatures of all kinds. Then, after the interval needed for its recovery, it gained relief at last from its clamors and confusion, and attaining quiet after great upheaval it returned to its ordered course and continued in it, having control and government of itself and of all within it [...][7]

Where did the Greek philosophers get such ideas? Probably from the scientifically more advanced cultures of Chaldea and Egypt. Herodotus (484–before 420 BCE), the "Father of History," writes one of the most famous passages on our subject, whose almost verbatim resemblance to Plato's suggests a common source. Herodotus had been told by the hierophants of Egypt about the sequence of their kings, which covered 341 generations. This he estimated as a duration of 11,340 years,

> ...in all which time (they said) they had had no king who was a god in human form, nor had there been any such thing either before or after those years among the rest of the kings of Egypt. Four times in this period (so they told me) the sun rose contrary to his wont; twice he rose where he now sets, and twice he set where now

> he rises; yet Egypt at these times underwent no change, neither in the produce of the river and the land, nor in the matter of sickness and death.[8]

Plato describes the event as if seen from outside, the earth changing its direction of rotation; Herodotus, as seen from the surface, where the sun's behavior indicates what has happened. Both are explicit about the double nature of the phenomenon. In the account given by the priests to Herodotus, the whole process occurred twice, while Plato's Stranger presents it as an ever-recurrent cycle.

There are several possible explanations of what the Egyptians told Herodotus. First, there is the one favored by modern catastrophists: that the earth's axis tumbled through 180° and back again, reversing the direction of the earth's rotation and hence the apparent rising-place of the sun. Second, there is the uniformitarian explanation, usually based on some consideration of the precession of the equinoxes (see next chapter). According to this, the change in the sun's rising would refer not to its daily but to its annual cycle, the place in question being not a direction of the compass but a sign of the zodiac. Thirdly, there is the possibility considered by Wilford and, after him, Daniélo: that there was confusion in ancient times as to whether the North and South are right and left, or vice versa, this leading to the periodic re-naming of the directions.[9] In that case, nothing cosmic need have happened at all.

Sacred Theories of the Earth

The Greeks had spoken variously of the Golden Age, and of the uninclined ecliptic, but had not, so far as we know, recognized the interdependence of the two. Only in the seventeenth century, as European culture strove to digest the new discoveries in astronomy, did the full implications emerge. John Milton writes in *Paradise Lost* X (completed 1665) of how God used this device to bring an end to the Edenic state:

> Some say he bid his Angels turne ascance
> The Poles of Earth twice ten degrees and more
> From the Suns Axle; they with labour push'd
> Oblique the Centric Globe...
>
> ...to bring in change
> Of Seasons to each Clime; else had the Spring
> Perpetual smil'd on Earth with vernant Flours,
> Equal in Days and Nights, except to those
> Beyond the Polar Circles...

A little later in the century, two English divines developed in more prosaic form the idea of an axial tilt having occurred since the creation of the earth. Thomas Burnet (1635?–1715), in his *Sacred Theory of the Earth* (1681), agrees with the "doctrine of the Ancients" according to which, in his words:

> *The Poles* of the World did once change their situation, and were at first in another posture from what they are in now, till that inclination happen'd [...] the Earth chang'd its posture at the Deluge, and thereby made these seeming changes in the Heavens; its Poles before pointed to the Poles of the Ecliptick, which now point to the Poles of the Aequator, and its Axis is become parallel with that Axis [...] And I am apt to think, that those changes in the course of the Stars, which the Ancients sometimes speak of, and especially the *Aegyptians*, if they did not proceed from defects in their Calendar, had no other Physical account than this.
>
> And as they say the Poles of the World were in another situation at first, so at first they say, there was no variety of seasons in the Year, as in their Golden Age.[10]

As for the cause of the Deluge, Burnet supposes that a huge piece of the earth's crust collapsed, allowing the "waters under the earth" to come gushing out like a burst water-main.[11] The axis was thereupon toppled by the planet's loss of equilibrium, one pole being more attracted to the sun than the other, "in which skew posture it hath stood ever since, and is likely to do for some ages to come."[12] Then, as an afterthought, he adds that a change in its magnetism might also have contributed to the same effect. Burnet was uneasy about his "most obvious" explanation because he realized that the earth does not always incline the same pole to the sun: in the northern winter, it is the South Pole that leans toward it; in the summer, the North Pole. But he had more glamorous matters to attend to, such as the Golden Age, so the physics of the tilt are not dwelt upon further in *Sacred Theory of the Earth*. At the end of time, Burnet expected the cycle of the earth's history to close with a restitution of its perfect state.

Like Burnet, William Whiston (1667–1752) spurned the literal reading of the Genesis creation story in order to extract from it a "New Theory of the Earth" (the title of his book of 1696) more in keeping with modern astronomy and the common sense of the dawning Enlightenment. The Mosaic account of creation is true in essence, says Whiston, but the form it takes is an adaptation for "dense and unphilosophical people"; also it only concerns this earth, whereas there may well be other humanities.[13] The natural state of a planet, according to Whiston, is to have its day and year identical, rotating once on its axis while it orbits once around the sun,[14] just as the moon does with regard to the earth. This annual motion began as the earth emerged from the state of a comet: the "chaos" of the Mosaic account of creation. Later, at the Fall of Man, the earth acquired its secondary, diurnal rotation, and at the same time the tilt of its axis, bringing about the seasons.[15] The classical authorities mentioned above are marshalled in support of the theory.

In dedicating his book to Sir Isaac Newton, Whiston must have known the opinion of that great man on the topic, which was that the inclination of the axis and the precession of the equinoxes are fixed by the mechanics of the solar system. (I will explain this in the next chapter.) But this did not eliminate the

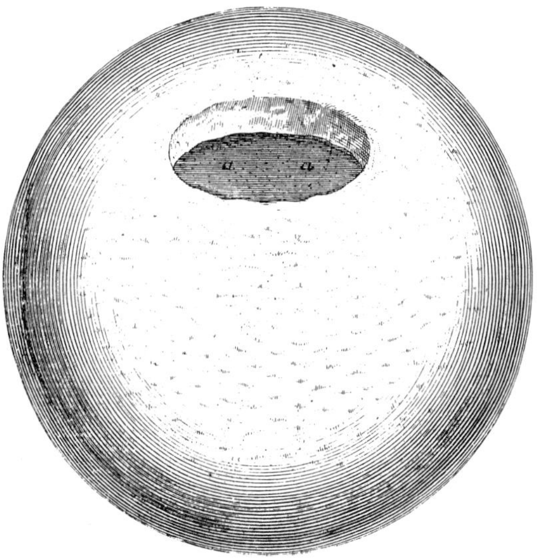

Illustration 21: The Hole at the North Pole (Burnet)

possibility of the rare intervention of the Lord of Hosts.

William Whiston seems to have been content to leave the tilt to God, though he transcribes the reasons given for it by the pre-Socratic philosophers. The only question for him was whether it occurred at the Fall of Man, or at the Deluge. In deciding for the earlier date, he points out that before the tilt, the equator would have been too hot to allow for the peopling of the southern hemisphere. This is a reference to the theory consecrated by Aristotle, according to which the earth is divided latitudinally into five zones. The polar ones are supposedly too cold for human life, the tropical one too hot. Therefore the only two populated zones are the north and south temperate belts, which have no possible communication with one another. Whiston, living well after the modern voyages of discovery, knew that this is not the case, but nevertheless believed that if the earth were upright and without seasons, the equatorial region would be too hot for habitation. Besides, he says, there would have had to be seasons for the antediluvians to have been so long-lived.[16] Here he flatly contradicts Burnet, who thought that it was the absence of seasons before the Flood that allowed them to live hundreds of years. Left with the necessity for accounting physically for the Deluge, Whiston allows a secondary cause in the form of the great comet (Halley's) of 1682, which he calculates would have met the earth on 17 November 2349 BCE (New Style).[17]

As we proceed, we will find an astonishing variety of theories to account for an event that so many people are certain took place. Besides the unanswerable accusation of the hand of God, we will find the blame put variously on the moon (either joining or leaving the earth), Venus, Mars, a defunct planet (now the asteroids), a comet, the earth itself, and even on human behavior. Some of these, of course, are not mutually exclusive.

Early Scientific Theories

The first scientific catastrophist was Comte George Louis Buffon (1707–1788), whose illustrated *Histoire naturelle* did much to popularize the natural sciences. It was he who initiated the theory of catastrophic polar wandering (to which we will return in Chapter Seventeen), not to justify the biblical stories but in order to account for the evidence of a warm climate having once existed in the Arctic, as shown by the fossils of trees and the bones of now tropical creatures. Jean-Jacques Rousseau (1712–1778) was a believer in the sudden, single tilt of the earth's axis away from the perpendicular. This brought to an end the stasis of the Golden Age and, by initiating the seasons, forced the human race to build shelters, develop skills, migrate, and intermingle. In his *Essai sur l'origine des langues* (Essay on the origin of languages, written circa 1761, published 1781) he paints a sentimental picture of the axial shift as the cause of civilized, as opposed to pastoral life:

> Imagine a perpetual spring upon the earth; imagine everywhere waters, cattle, pasturage; imagine mankind, issuing from the hands of nature, once dispersed among all this. I cannot imagine how they would ever have renounced their primitive liberty and quit their isolated, pastoral life, so comfortable to natural indolence, to impose on themselves unnecessarily the servitude, the labors, and the miseries which are inseparable from the social state.
>
> Whoever wanted mankind to become sociable touched with his finger the axis of the globe, and tipped it relative to the axis of the universe. At this slight movement, I see the face of the earth changing and determining the vocation of the human race: I hear from afar the cries of joy of a mindless multitude; I see palaces and towns being built; I see the birth of arts, of laws, and of commerce; I see peoples forming, spreading, dissolving, and succeeding one another like the waves of the sea; I see men gathering at certain points of their dwelling to devour one another, to make a frightful desert of the rest of the world: a worthy monument of social union and of the usefulness of the arts! [18]

A persistent current of speculation links this event to the destruction of Atlantis, whether or not that is identified in turn with Noah's Flood. The philosopher and philologist Fabre d'Olivet (1767–1825), who wrote one of the most stimulating books of esoteric history (*Histoire philosophique du genre humain*, Philosophic history of the human race, 1822), reviews the explanations given by other savants to account for the end of Atlantis: the eruption of a volcano, an earthquake, the overflowing of a lake, an inland sea, or the tail of a comet.[19] The error of all these, says Fabre d'Olivet, induces him to unveil the true cause of the catastrophe:

> The frightful cataclysm that submerged Atlantis was caused by a sudden movement of the terrestrial globe, which, suddenly raising the Boreal pole, which had become lowered, caused it to take a contrary position to what it had formerly. In this movement, which perhaps had many oscillations, the mass of waters, which had been upon this pole, rolled with violence towards the Austral pole, returned to the Boreal pole, and back again many times towards the opposite pole, where it finally became fixed, overpowered with its weight. The earthwork gave way in many places, particularly where it covered caverns and deep anfractuosities and, in falling, opened immense abysses where the waves rushed furiously, engulfing the débris which they had drawn after them and the multitude of victims whom they had deprived of life. The Eastern Hemisphere resisted longer and was only washed, so to speak, by the waves which crossed over it without stopping; but the other was everywhere sunk and covered with stagnant waters which remained there a long time. All the Austral lands, where Atlantis properly so-called was, disappeared. At the opposite pole, the Borean [sic] lands emerged from the depths of the waters and became the cradle of the White or Borean Race, whence we issued. Thus it was to the disaster of Atlantis that we own in a way our existence. The Black Race, that I have named *Sudeen*, of African origin, being born, as I have said, in the neighbourhood of the equinoctial line, suffered much from this catastrophe, but infinitely less than the Red or Austral Race which perished almost entirely.[20]

This is not the delicate touch of the finger of God, but an abrupt and devastating pitching of the earth, apparently through 180°, which set the seas rolling in one tidal wave after another. Its result was the opposite of the busy commerce that Rousseau imagined, namely depopulation and the ruin of flourishing civilizations. No wonder that Fabre d'Olivet, in interpreting the Hindu system of the Four Yugas, reversed the traditional ordering and called the first one (Satya Yuga) the Age of Iron, as the human race struggled to recover from the Deluge; the subsequent Yugas then got progressively better, until the Kali Yuga, in which we find ourselves, which is the Golden Age![21] (Saint-Yves d'Alveydre would also adopt this extremely heterodox interpretation.[22]) Yet Fabre d'Olivet, in pretending at last to unveil the cause of Atlantis' fall, has done nothing of the kind: he has only pushed the problem back one step, leaving unanswered the question of what brought about the "sudden raising of the Boreal pole," or, for that matter, its declination. We will perhaps find an answer to this in the theory of Saint-Yves, to be treated in Chapter Sixteen.

Fabre d'Olivet was out of tune with his time, in which official science was moving from the catastrophism of Buffon to the steady-state universe as described in the *Mécanique céleste* (1799–1825) of Pierre-Simon Laplace, and the correspondingly calm earth of Sir Charles Lyell's *Principles of Geology* (1830–1833). Henceforth one can say, in general, that the illuminates have been catastrophists, while the spokesmen for material science have been uniformitarians, at least as regards the period of human existence on this planet. Our study is therefore less an investigation of the truth about the past than a survey of intellectual history. Our question is not: Did the earth's axis shift? but: What have people believed about its shifting, and why? The polar tilt is an archetype that has prompted such different reactions and conclusions that one can only class it among those formative myths, analogous to those of Creation, Fall, and Deluge, around which human understanding and imagination crystallize as best they can, limited by their expectations and prejudices; a myth whose reflection in terrestrial reality is, perhaps deliberately, occluded from our view.

In the nineteenth century, fringe science eagerly adopted the tilt as an explanation for the universal or partial deluge. The dark cloud of biblical authority loomed over the entire debate, obfuscating scientific attempts to arrive at an independent estimate of the age of the world or the extent of any flood: a fundamentalist shadow that is still very much with us. It would take us too far astray to go into the question of the Deluge and the various attempts to account for it; it has been treated very adequately in a recent book by the British geographer and scholar Richard Huggett.[23] An axial shift is indeed a tempting explanation for it; it only requires a melting of the polar icecaps by increased exposure to the sun, and there is all the water needed for a flood of legendary, if not quite of biblical proportions.

Louis Michel (1816–1883), sometimes called "de Figanières" after his birthplace, was speculating on the subject around mid-century, but since he was an uneducated psychic, his results were very different from those of Fabre d'Olivet and the scientists.[24] Figanières' theory would probably not have survived if it had not been embraced and enthusiastically explained by the famous occultist Papus.[25] He had found, since his boyhood, that in a state of "magnetic lucidity" he could penetrate space, water, earth, and other planets, and bring back precise information. He discovered that the earth had been formed originally from four different planets that were in the course of disintegration. These were to have become four continents, but one of the planets refused to join in, and was consequently expelled into space. The process caused the frightful cataclysm of the Deluge, as the waters of the pole swamped the inhabited continents, and the inclination of the ecliptic was caused then and there. The miscreant body is still with us: it is none other than our moon.

A more respectable French savant, Alphonse-Joseph Adhémar, in *Révolutions de la Mer* (Revolutions of the sea, 2nd ed., 1860),[26] offered a theory of not one, but a perpetual series of catastrophic floods. Given that the autumn and winter in the southern hemisphere are a week longer than in the northern, he assumed that there was a consequent increase each year in the coldness of the South Pole. Over 10,500 years, ice accumulates at the south at the expense of the north, until the earth's center of gravity is displaced. A massive readjustment follows, after which the other pole becomes the colder one, and the cycle begins again. This again suggests the 180° pole-flip which several of our authorities have favored. Adhémar's theory would be revived by Hugh Auchincloss Brown and Richard Noone (see Chapters Seventeen and Eighteen).

Cometary Cataclysms

The theory of the earth's encounter with a comet is probably the most persistent of all the catastrophic agents suggested over the years. Ignatius Donnelly, the Minnesota congressman who wrote noteworthy books on Atlantis and on the Bacon-Shakespeare mystery, devoted his *Ragnarok: The Age of Fire and Gravel* (1882) to this theme. Donnelly's comet caused the end of the Golden Age, laid down the accumulations of gravel known as the Drift, and plunged the earth into an Ice Age. But as Donnelly rejects the tilt of the axis as either cause or result of this,[27] his work does not concern us here. The same theory was also proposed in *The Mysterious Comet* (1932) by William Comyns Beaumont: a highly articulate and educated man with the strangest of historical ideas. The whole of the Bible, he believed, tells of events that actually took place not in the Middle East but in Britain, whose once flourishing civilization was destroyed by a comet that landed just outside Edinburgh (the "Jerusalem" of the Bible). Thereupon much of the land sank (which explains the Atlantis myth), and lost its semi-tropical climate, while the year changed from 360 to its present 365 1/4 days.[28]

Neither of these authors was acknowledged by Immanuel Velikovsky, though his polymathic reading must have brought him into contact with their works. One of the unspoken intentions of Velikovsky's books seems to have been to prove the veracity of the Hebrew Bible, but without bringing on himself the stigma of the religious zealot, much less the psychic visionary. The crucial premise of his *Worlds in Collision* (1950) is that in the second millenium BCE, the earth encountered a "comet" extruded from Jupiter. The near-collision that ensued might, according to Velikovsky, have caused the earth to slow down or even stop its rotation, and its axis to be tilted out of position.[29] Several centuries later, the earth had a near-miss with Mars that likewise disturbed its axial tilt, but restored it again to its previous position.

One of Velikovsky's primary exhibits in support of the Venus catastrophe is the account in Joshua 10.13, which tells of how at the Battle of Gibeon, in response to Joshua's prayer, "the sun stood still and the moon halted until a nation had taken vengeance on its enemies, as indeed it is written in the Book of Jashar [another, lost Book of Joshua]. The sun stayed in mid heaven and made no haste to set for almost a whole day." This had already been the object of a celebrated interpretation on the part of Galileo, in his *Letter to the Grand Duchess Christina* (1615). Biblical fundamentalists, such as Charles Totten, had achieved marvels of ingenuity in their struggles to reconcile it with scientific knowledge.[30] *Worlds in Collision* pretended to place it, at last, on a scientific basis: the sun had "stood still" because the earth had temporarily ceased to rotate.

When Carl Sagan tried to quantify the results of Velikovsky's suggestion,[31] he found that the earth's rotation could have stopped "unnoticeably" in a little over an hour, but that stopping and starting again in a single day would have imparted an average temperature increase of 100°K (comparable to the difference between the freezing and boiling points of water). "The deceleration might be tolerable, if gradual enough," writes Sagan, "but not the heat." [32] Sagan also points out what any careful reader of Velikovsky will have noticed: that he is very vague and difficult to follow when he comes to the exact mechanics of the earth's braking. This raises extremely grave problems of physics, not least of which is the absence of any magnetic record of the event in the earth's rocks.[33] Velikovsky himself says: "Whether there was a complete reversal of the cardinal points as a result of the cosmic catastrophe of the days of the Exodus, or only a substantial shift, is a problem not solved here."[34] Yet nothing cries out more urgently for solution and reconciliation with the principles of celestial dynamics. Consequently, even Velikovsky's best friends, the contributors to the short-lived magazine *Pensée*, have had difficulty in answering the physical problems posed by his theories.

Lunar Encounters

We now return to the moon as the cause of catastrophe. The cosmological theory of Hans Hoerbiger, known today mainly because of its adoption as orthodox science by the Nazis, is based on a succession of moons that have been captured by the earth. Hoerbiger's primary assumption is that planets do not move in circular ellipses, but in elliptical spirals tending inward.[35] The smaller the planet, the more rapid its spiralling; consequently, if it begins outside the orbit of a larger planet, it will eventually intersect with the latter. Thereupon, the smaller planet may be captured to become the moon of the larger one.

According to Hoerbiger, this is exactly what happened about 14,000 years ago to our present Luna, formerly a small planet orbiting the sun between Earth and Mars. His theory goes on to explain that once acquired, the satellite continues to spiral gradually inwards around its partner. As it goes, its surface becomes coated with ice. The closer it comes, the shorter its "month" and the stronger its gravity, until the encircled planet's tides rise miles high and its creatures grow to extraordinary dimensions. Finally the moon flies apart under the pressure from the larger body, and its fragments crash onto the surface of the earth: mud, rocks, the metallic core, and finally a thick coating of ice. In this paroxysm, virtually all life on earth is annihilated and an Ice Age supervenes. But eventually plants and creatures stir again from the seas, and the planet teems with life again—until the next moon comes along.[36]

The "World-Ice Theory" (*Welteislehre* or simply WEL) accounts for the ice ages, and for the deluges, giants,[37] and other phenomena recorded in myth. It also explains the polar shift, for once a moon is captured, Hoerbiger explains, its pull causes the crust of the earth to slide around, shifting the poles.[38] Thus are explained all the changes in climate of the past, as also the disappearance of oceans in some places (for example, the Gobi Desert and the Sahara) and their invasion in others (for example, Atlantis).

While Hoerbiger's premises, like Velikovsky's, offer solutions for a certain number of historical enigmas, they leave coolly unanswered enormous questions of celestial and terrestrial dynamics. Hoerbiger's theory found few followers outside the Third Reich: two notable exceptions were Denis Saurat, the distinguished professor and war-time friend of General de Gaulle, and H. S. Bellamy, for whom the Book of Revelation was not a prediction of the future but a record of past catastrophe. Saurat and Bellamy made much of the myth of giant races as the previous inhabitants of the earth, explaining their hypertrophy by the upward pull of the last approaching moon.

The eccentric French prehistorian Marcel Boscher (whose work I know only through Robert Charroux' summary[39]) joins this group with his postulate of an early humanity living in a state of perfect equilibrium, endowed with psychic powers and a nine-foot stature. He offers an alternative picture of the Golden Age as ended by the intervention of a wandering moon, which is not a dead planet in Boscher's scenario but the home of another highly-developed race: the Selenites. Finding themselves in peril because their excessive closeness to the sun was rarefying the lunar atmosphere, the Selenites decided to invade Earth when the opportunity of a close approach presented itself.

> As the moon's orbiting became ever closer, the earth suffered from tidal waves, volcanic eruptions, then a terrific catastrophe caused by the swinging of the poles, which also had the result of increasing the velocity of gravitation and increasing the forces of attraction. [...]
>
> The invaders, of gigantic stature and armed with atomic weapons, had no trouble in vanquishing the Earthlings, and appeared in the latter's eyes as gods descended from heaven. [...]
>
> Continents were engulfed, others emerged from the oceans. The equator, which had formerly passed through Siberia, now became fixed beneath Asia.

Boscher offered no scientific or scholarly support for his theory, of which, however, every element is a familiar part of the popular mythology of extra-terrestrial visitation and cataclysmic history. The interbreeding of the Selenites with the inferior Earthlings, which Boscher says resulted in the Yellow Race, can be justified with reference to the famous passage on the "Sons of God" mating with the "Daughters of Men" in Genesis 6.2. Robert Charroux' books exploit these themes to sensational effect, and we will be hearing more about them in due course.

Neither Hoerbiger nor Velikovsky claimed any psychic, spiritual, or revealed source for their theories: quite the contrary, they wanted to be recognized as scientists in the modern sense. In a far different setting, a more moderate version of the Hoebigerian theory has been put out by "Helio-Arcanophus, Guide and Founder of The Atlanteans," an entity who spoke to a community in Cheltenham, England:

> The catastrophe which brought about the sinking of Atlantis was caused by the capture of the planet Lucifer into the gravitational field of the Earth, making it the Moon you see today. There was a complete tilt of the Earth's axis causing many lands to rise and many to sink. The poles appeared where the equator had

> been and land which had been warm became cold and *vice versa*. People are inclined to forget when endeavouring to assess the exact position of Atlantis that the continent lay in the southern zone of the Earth, as did the country now known as England, for such was the angle of the Earth's axis in those days. [...]
>
> How long did this fabulous civilisation last? Approximately 10,000 years, reckoning years as we know them today, for years were shorter before the capture of the Moon.[40]

Even if no two sources seem to agree about when and how it happened, the flipping-over of the earth's axis is a pervasive theme. This chapter has dealt with versions of the myth that put it in a sudden and catastrophic context. In the next, we will find that there are gentler ways of attaining the same result.

Chapter Fifteen:
The Uniformitarians

The seeds of the theory of a gradual shift in the obliquity of the ecliptic were sown in the early sixteenth century, as astronomers compared their own measurements with those they had inherited from Ptolemy. Dominicus Maria Novara[1] (died 1504), one of Copernicus' teachers, was aware that Ptolemy's figure was 23° 51', while he estimated it to be 23° 29': he therefore concluded that it had altered in the intervening years. But his figures, and Ptolemy's, were too vague for astronomy as it had developed two centuries later. To make a true comparison between an ancient measurement and a modern one, they should ideally have been made from exactly the same place.

The experiment that determined this was the work of Jacques Eugène d'Allonville, Chevalier de Louville (1671–1732).[2] A professional soldier who retired in 1713 to devote himself to mathematics and astronomy, de Louville was an austere, stoical figure, respected by his colleagues in the Académie des Sciences and in the Royal Society of London. Upon his retirement, he settled temporarily in Marseille, with the express intention of measuring the height of the north celestial pole as seen from there, and consequently (the latitude of Marseille being known) calculating the precise obliquity of the ecliptic.

De Louville chose Marseille for his experiment because of a previous resident of the ancient harbor-city, Pytheas of Massilia. In the late fourth century BCE, Pytheas had calculated accurately the local latitude and the obliquity of the ecliptic. It was he, too, who first determined that the pole of the heavens does not coincide exactly with any star, and was the first of the Greeks to understand the connection of the tides with the moon. In Chapter Five we mentioned Pytheas' remarkable voyage to the North.[3]

The Chevalier de Louville, observing the obliquity of the ecliptic from Marseille, found it to be 23° 30'; his findings were confirmed by other astronomers. Pytheas' figure was 20' less (23° 50'). Hence, de Louville concluded, the obliquity must have been diminishing at the rate of one degree every 6,000 years,[4] and might be assumed to continue thus indefinitely.

Jean-Sylvain Bailly, who's speculations on an Arctic homeland were reviewed in Chapter Three, discussed de Louville's findings at length.[5] He himself had read the figure of 24° for the obliquity in the *Mathematics Useful for the Study of*

Plato by Theon of Smyrna,[6] and more than 25° reported by the Brahmins of India. Both of these, being larger than the current measurement, seemed to support the Chevalier's theory of a steady diminution in the angle since the creation of the world. But Bailly was not willing to entertain, at least in print, an earlier date for the Creation than circa 6000 BCE. Thus any prehistory of the declining angle was a closed book to him.

Voltaire (1694–1778) treated de Louville's discovery in one of his works of scientific popularization, *Dissertation sur les changemens arrivés dans notre globe* (Dissertation on the changes that have happened on our globe, 1749), observing that if the Chevalier's conclusions were correct, one would have to add a further motion to the ones that the earth was hitherto known to have. Voltaire was not frightened by large figures, so was able to come closer to the modern idea of the earth's age. He points out that, given the rate of declination as one degree in 6,000 years, every climate would come by turns into the torrid and the glacial zones over a period of two million years or so (6,000 x 360°).[7] But Voltaire reminds us that "the philosophers relish great changes on the world scene, just as the populace desires spectacular entertainments."[8] Once the obliquity is shown to be inconstant, he says, it remains to be seen whether it revolves continuously; or goes in a to-and-fro motion; or whether it has a tendency to approach the plane of Jupiter's or of Saturn's orbit. He cautions that it is impossible to be certain of the answer while we have only a century of observations to go on, and have only been considering these matters for thirty years.[9] Voltaire, with his common-sensical approach, is as different as could be from those who see in the gradual axial shift a revelation of the controlling forces behind the scene of world history, sending it from civilization to chaos and back again.

The Prophet of Montmartre

Or is civilization just another form of chaos, as Jean-Jacques Rousseau had implied? The philosopher Charles Fourier (1772–1837) was in no doubt of it. Living in Napoleonic France, he saw around him the most civilized society the world had ever known: yet what had it brought the human race besides war, want, economic folly, and the repression of all natural feelings? Civilization, he decided, was little better than the state of barbarism it pretended to cure. All of history, in fact, testified to nought but "ages of perfidy, injustice, oppression, poverty, revolutions and bodily weakness."[10] Believing as he did in a beneficent Providence, Fourier could not imagine that the human race and its globe were in anything but their tiresome infancy, suffering a chaotic and painful period of adjustment analogous to teething, which would eventually be succeeded by a saner and healthier maturity.

One argument for his theory, Fourier thought, was the misplacement of the earth's axis.[11] Why ever should God have put the North Pole in such a position as to make useless the valuable lands and seas of northern Asia? To all appearances, it would have been much better placed a little south of the Bering Straits, where only the most useless part of the globe would have been sacrificed

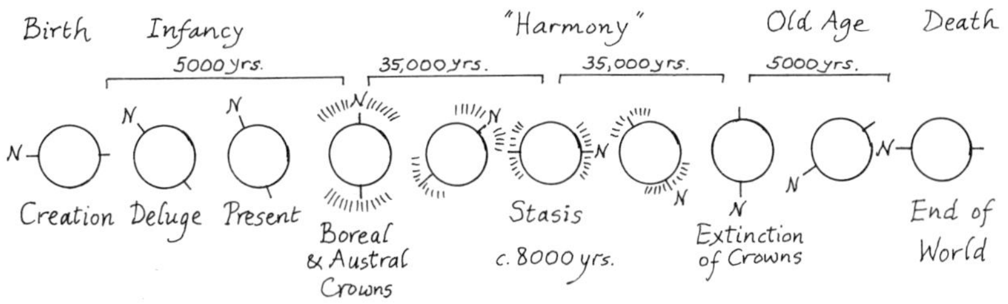

Illustration 22: Cycle of axial inclination (Fourier)

to the ice-cap. Then the present Arctic ocean could be a region of flourishing maritime trade. Fourier, however, was reluctant to criticize the wisdom of God, and so he proposed a compromise solution. Although the polar regions are currently out of commission, he says, they will quite soon be heated and illuminated, for the earth is destined to acquire a "Boreal crown": an immense Aurora Borealis visible as far as the sixtieth degree of latitude, that will channel the sun's energy to earth. Then the pole will enjoy a climate comparable to that of Andalusia or Sicily, and the whole northern hemisphere will become fertile.[12]

Fourier warned that this phenomenon, although cosmic in origin and inevitable in the long run, depends for its exact time of arrival on humanity's own progress towards social maturity. The Boreal crown, he reckoned, will appear four years after the foundation of "Harmony,"[13] his name for the ideal social state which he devoted his whole life to planning and imagining. A few centuries later, the South Pole will acquire in its turn an "Austral crown," and the whole globe will come under cultivation. Once established, the happy state of Harmony will last about 70,000 years: a duration which makes light of the 5,000 or so years of preliminary chaos in which we are currently stuck. Finally there will come 5,000 years of senility and decline, followed by the planet's natural death. Thus Fourier envisages a world-cycle of some 80,000 years, analogous to the fourscore years of human life.

There is no philosopher remotely like Charles Fourier. He earns a footnote here and there as the inventor of Socialism—scarcely a small achievement, one would have thought—and as a Utopian whose vision inspired the early communes of the United States. His ideas, which include a marked element of eroticism, were sufficiently bizarre to attract the attention of the Surrealists. But the plinth of his monument in Montmartre has long since lost its statue, melted down to support some one of civilization's wars, and now his very name is scarcely legible upon it. Is it some occult link that fills the solitary researcher with a genuine affection for him, as for other all-but-forgotten figures who tried to recreate the universe in the image of their own inspired intelligence?

Fourier developed the essentials of his theory, including the Boreal crown, from 1799 to 1807, publishing them the following year in *Théorie des quatre mouvements* (Theory of the four movements). In later years his cosmological thought developed to embrace a theory of alterations in the obliquity of the earth's axis. He noted these in manuscript on the great chart of the world's 80,000-year history which had appeared in his book of 1808; when the book was reissued in 1841, after his death, the additions were included.[14] The first note is of the "Earlier decrease in the obliquity of the ecliptic," occurring in the early, chaotic stage of the earth's history along with the poisoning of the seas, the death of the moon, and the universal deluge. Before the Flood, presumably, the earth's axis was even more tilted than it now is. Fourier's second note goes along with the establishment of Harmony and the Boreal crown: "Earlier increase in the obliquity of the ecliptic." Around the center of the 80,000-year cycle there is a "pivotal period" of about 8,000 years, the "apogee of happiness," when Fourier notes a "Temporary station of the ecliptic." Next comes the "Later decrease in the obliquity of the ecliptic" during the declining millenia of Harmony; "Later increase in the obliquity of the ecliptic" during the 5,000 year death-agony of the globe; and, at the end, "Spiritual death of the globe; end of the nutation and rotation of the axis; overturning of the pole of the globe to the equator; hemispheric fixation on the sun; natural death; fall and dissolution into the Milky Way."

From these brief comments it seems that Fourier was imagining the earth's axis as making one complete rotation, relative to the ecliptic, in the course of its life-cycle (see diagram). He gives no reason for this movement, any more than for the other events of the earth's symmetrical evolution and devolution: we are to accept it as an innate law, implanted by the fiat of God and only discovered by Fourier. To all appearances, the axis begins and ends parallel to the equator; at the establishment of Harmony and at its end, it is perpendicular; at the midpoint of the cycle it is static, again parallel to the equator. Why it will not then adversely affect the inhabitants, we cannot say: perhaps their "apogee of bliss" will suffice to preserve them from alternate freezing and roasting.

Fourier scholars have virtually despaired of tracking down any sources for his cosmological ideas, of which this specimen is by no means the oddest. He did have a copy of Johannes Kepler's *Harmonices Mundi Libri V* (Five books on the harmony of the world, 1619), but lifelong poverty kept him from owning a library, and a paranoid sense of his own mission prevented him from giving credit to anyone else. His habitual reading was limited to newspapers, where he picked up many an idea that was colorfully developed in his own writing.

The Shoemaker of Norwich

If Fourier hatched his theory of the axial tilt in hermetic isolation, he was not alone in his interest. At exactly the same time, a shoemaker in Norwich, England, was thinking along very similar lines.[15] This was Sampson Arnold Mackey.

Mackey, one of the most endearing autodidacts, must somehow have learned of de Louville's gradual diminution of the ecliptic angle, an astronomical commonplace by the early nineteenth century. But instead of merely comparing the present inclination with some other one given in the past, Mackey works

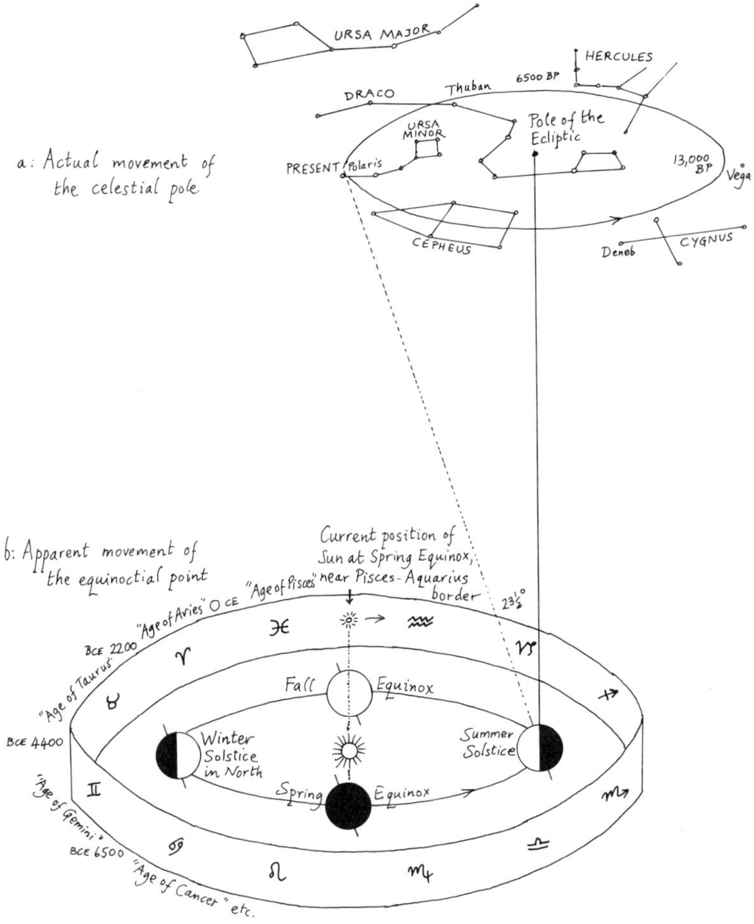

Illustration 23: The Precession of the Equinoxes

both forward and backward to explore the ultimate consequences of such a motion. His conclusions are grand, sweeping, and simple, but in order to follow them it is necessary to explain briefly the phenomenon known as the "precession of the equinoxes," known to the ancients, rediscovered by Hipparchus in the second century BCE, and explained mathematically by Isaac Newton.

In his *Principia Mathematica*,[16] Newton demonstrates that the precession of the equinoxes is the result of the earth's shape, which is not a perfect sphere but an oblate spheroid: in other words, it bulges about twenty-seven miles around its middle. Because of gravitational pressures exerted by the sun and moon on this bulge, the axis of the earth describes a very gradual circle in relation to the stars. Consequently, in the course of nearly 26,000 years, the loci of the celestial poles,

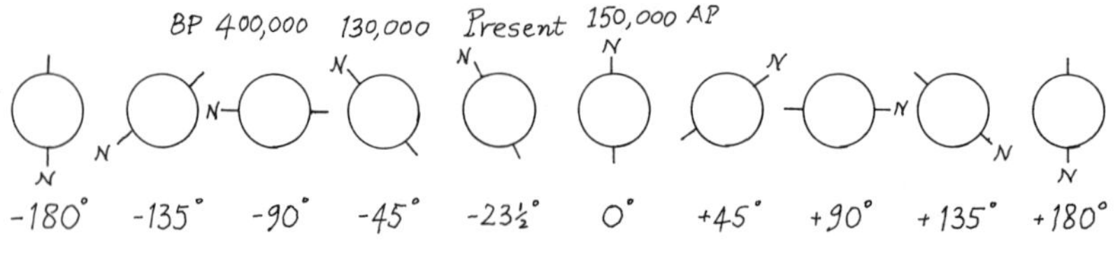

Illustration 24: One cycle of axial inclination (Mackey)

as determined from the earth, move around a central axis in the heavens. At some epochs the earth's axis points to a star, then there is a Pole Star. In past millenia it has pointed approximately to Vega and to Deneb, and also to starless regions. Currently it points to within a degree of Polaris, the last star in the tail of the Little Bear or Dipper.

One consequence of this motion is that the intersection of the earth's equatorial plane with the ecliptic (the plane of its orbit around the sun) describes a corresponding circle, and with it go the spring and autumn equinoxes that occur when the sun stands at these two points of intersection. Hence the position of the sun at the spring equinox is slightly different every year, moving backwards through the zodiac at the rate of one sign in about 2160 years.

Mackey assumes that the precessional cycle takes 25,000 years, in which the north polar axis describes a circle around a fixed celestial pole in the head of the constellation Draco. He likewise accepts the diminution of the angle of inclination at the rate of one degree in about 6,000 years. The combination of the two movements means that the axis describes not a circle but a diminishing spiral, which will end by pointing it directly at the heavenly pole (see diagram). Mackey believes that each precessional turn alters the angle of obliquity by exactly four degrees. Consequently it will take a little less than six precessional cycles to diminish the present obliquity to nothing. Therefore the "Golden Age" position will be reached about 150,000 years hence.

Casting his mind's eye far back into the past, Mackey could imagine the horrifying consequences of this movement for life on the planet. The further back one goes, the wider will have been the angle, and consequently the more intense the alternations of summer and winter. At present the Arctic Circle and the Tropic of Cancer are far apart: the one at latitude 66° 33' (23° 27' from the North Pole), the other 23° 27' from the equator. Somewhat more than five precessional cycles ago, the angle of obliquity would have been 45°, with the consequence that the Arctic Circle and the Tropic of Cancer would have coincided. This means that in the latitude of Ottawa or Turin the sun would have stood directly overhead at noon on the summer solstice, and just grazed the horizon at midnight, while on the day of the winter solstice it would not have appeared at all. Over much of the globe, a more-than-tropical summer would have alternated with a bitter winter.

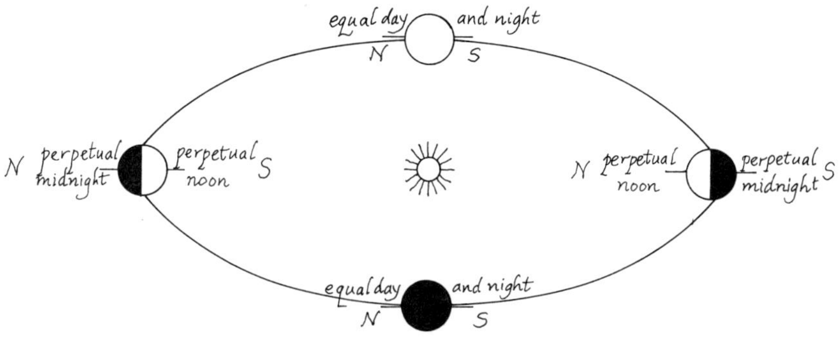

Illustration 25: The "Age of Horror" (Mackey)

Earlier still, the polar and tropical circles would have overlapped, and several days of sunless winter would have occurred, while at midsummer an increasing number of days would have enjoyed—if that is the word—perpetual sunshine. As the spiralling of the axis brought it closer and closer to the ecliptic, both conditions would intensify. When it actually lay in the same parallel as the ecliptic, what Mackey calls the "Age of Horror" would have ensued for several thousand years. In the northern summer, the sun would have shone night and day, not with the pale rays of Saint Petersburg's "white nights," but with the full force of equatorial heat as it stood still at the celestial pole. Months of intolerable heat would have been succeeded each year by a winter of utter darkness, while the opposite hemisphere had its turn in the solar oven.

Counting back 6,000 years for each degree of latitude traversed by the spiralling motion of the axis, we reach an approximate date of 400,000 BP for the Age of Horror. And before that? The axis must have traversed an analogous path, though in the southern hemisphere, as the (now) North Pole made its way from pointing due south, spiralling up to the equator. Mackey gives us no reason to believe that the earth's axis has ever done otherwise than to repeat this expansive and contractive motion, taking ninety turns to get from one pole to the other and back again.

Mackey's own explanation of the axial motion is not quite so clear as I have tried to make it, because he never states it outright. For one thing, he follows the bad example of Erasmus Darwin and a few other scholars of the time in casting his findings in verse, then follows his poem with four times its length in explanatory notes. The poem is pure allegory: the notes, a treatise in comparative mythology. The twin gods of the Samothracian Cabiri, Axieros and Axikersa, whose images stood head-to-tail,[17] are only one of the many instances in ancient mythology and symbolism which seem to Mackey to refer to the double axial movement. Any mythological reference to fire or disaster he takes as a memory of the Age of Horror. Mackey is, moreover, subject to the besetting weakness of mythologists with esoteric leanings, namely that of inventing fantastic word-derivations. Not all of his observations are as crass as the association of the Seven Rishis or Rachas of the Vedas with "rashers" of bacon[18]—both of them representing strips or zones. But many are just as implausible.

Apparently Mackey conceived his theory in virtual isolation, then tentatively circulated his poem among friends. He thought that his boldest step was "taking such a vast retrospective view of antiquity,"[19] hence calling into question the orthodox Creation date of around 4000 BCE. He intended to follow his poem with a work called *The Theory of Time*, which would presumably have defended his views. His admirers, however, urged him to go ahead and publish the poem independently, with "a few explanatory notes."

The appearance in 1826 of a popular work by the Rev. C. C. Clarke,[20] *The Wonders of the Heavens Displayed*, which modified the biblical text to allow for the age of the earth to be at least 140,000 years,[21] gave Mackey the courage to publish his own. Clarke was convinced of the earth's age by the evidence of animal and vegetable remains found outside their current climates, which he felt required the tropics to have once been much wider than they are at present; he suggests 45°. As we have seen above, using de Louville's figures for the rate of change in the angle of the ecliptic, this would have been well over a hundred thousand years ago.

Mackey had his poem published on 16 July 1822, by a local printer, as "*The Mythological Astronomy of the Ancients Demonstrated, by restoring to their Fables and Symbols their original meaning*. By Sampson Arnold Mackey, Shoe-maker." To the poem and notes, he adds an Appendix on the "Hindoo Registers of Time," which he based on the best sources available to him: articles in *The Evangelical Magazine* and *Missionary Papers*, and *Studies of Nature* (English edition 1796) by Rousseau's friend, Bernadin de Saint-Pierre. Publication brought the learned artisan to wider notice, and, as he says, gave him access to the libraries of several gentlemen in Norwich, who directed him—one can well imagine with what condescension—to read the *Asiatic Researches*, Bryant's *Ancient Mythology*, Parkerson's *Organic Remains*, and Volney's *New Researches*. But far from being overwhelmed by the discovery of all this higher erudition, Mackey was shocked by the ignorance shown by Volney and Dupuis, and by the Christian prejudices of the *Asiatic Researches* scholars, who had missed so much through not knowing Mackey's all-explaining theory. He launched forthwith into "Part the Second" of his *Mythological Astronomy*, calling it *The Key of Urania, the wards of which will unlock all the Mysteries of Antiquity* (1823). After dealing with the Hindus, he added "The Analyzation of the Writings of the Jews, as far as they are found to have any connexion with the sublime Science of Astronomy." Here he shows that he had benefited from reading the Frenchmen's allegorical treatment of ancient epic tales—especially those of Hercules, Samson, and Christ—as descriptions of the sun's passage through the zodiac. Mackey makes his own versions of them, anticipating the Hoerbigerians by reading the ever-adaptable Book of Revelation as a historical description of the different conditions of the earth in the distant past.

Like Dupuis and Volney, Mackey was a religious skeptic: not averse to a broad and humanistic Deism, but fiercely contemptuous of the dogmas of the Church. He belongs within a freethinking movement of the 1820s and 1830s in England that included such defenders of freedom of speech as William Hone, author of *Ancient Mysteries Described* (tried for political satire and blasphemy in 1817 but acquitted); Richard Carlile (jailed 1819–25 for publishing the works of Thomas Paine and other offensive literature); Robert Taylor, the preacher of Dupuis' doctrines from "The Devil's Pulpit" (jailed 1827–28 and 1831–33 for blasphemy); and Godfrey Higgins, author of *The Celtic Druids* (1829) and *Anacalypsis* (1833–36). Mackey probably did not know these people, but he was subject to the same movement of the human spirit as they: eager to do away with the mind-control of state and church, and to use the freedom thus gained to cultivate a more generous sense of the cosmos. The astronomical theory of ancient religion, expounded by Dupuis, Volney, Robert Taylor, Mackey, and Higgins, was in itself an invitation to expand the imagination by ranging over all the earth's religions, and then over all of space and time.

Mackey's anti-orthodoxy is balanced by a pro-Indian sentiment quite unusual for his colonial times: a preference that he finds justified, above all, by the fact that the Indians were learned in astronomy hundreds of thousands of years ago. "The Hindoos were a learned and polished people while we lived in forests and cloathed ourselves with skins," he says in 1823;[22] and three years later: "It is well known, that at Cassimere, [Kashmir] there is still preserved a vast body of ancient science, undisturbed by either Jews, Turks, or Monks; and, I think I may say, by modern Missionaries. Even the Greeks, in the time of Alexander, dared not pollute that sacred soil of Art and Science."[23]

H. P. Blavatsky called Mackey "the self-made adept of Norwich,"[24] and, as we shall see, cited some of his theories with approval. Perhaps she had come across them during her membership of the "Brotherhood of Luxor," or as it was later known the "Hermetic Brotherhood of Luxor" or simply the "H. B. of L."[25] This esoteric order taught Mackey's doctrine in the form of a short essay issued to neophytes, called "The Hermetic Key," by Thomas H. Burgoyne, secretary of the Brotherhood.[26] Mackey's poem is quoted, but he is not named except as "an initiate of our Noble Order."[27] There are two changes to Mackey's scheme. First, the amount of latitude covered by each turn of the spiral is changed from 4° to 3° 36', so that the complete cycle of 360° takes one hundred turns, not ninety as in Mackey's version. Second, the period of one turn is given the traditional precessional number of 25,920 years. These changes undermine most of Mackey's mythological supports, which are based on specific latitudes and, in the case of the Hindu sources, on a cycle of only 24,000 years.

The Occult Magazine, the organ of the H. B. of L., reprinted Mackey's poem in 1886, but ceased publication before it could add the explanatory notes.[28] The Editor (Peter Davidson) notes that "S. A. Mackey was *the Neophyte of an Initiate of the H. B. of L.*, and it was from this source that he acquired his knowledge of the Ancient Astronomy, consequently we had active Outer workers, long antecedent to the establishment of our Exterior Circle [in 1884]."[29] One does not know what to make of this: whether it is a case of posthumous enrollment of a person in no position to confirm or deny it (a common procedure in some secret societies), or whether it is true that Mackey was involved with some esoteric order of his own day which already espoused the theory. The scholar must incline to the first option until other evidence appears.

At any event, Mackey was a remarkably original thinker, responsible for the most elaborately worked-out of all theories of axial motion. Its adoption at the end of the century by the H. B. of L. ensured that it passed beneath the eyes of such initiates as Papus, Barlet, and (at second hand) René Guénon in France; Theodor Reuss and Karl Kellner (founders of the Ordo Templi Orientalis or OTO) and Rudolf Steiner in Germany; most of the founding members of the Theosophical Society in the U.S.A.; and several members of the Golden Dawn in England.

Modern Geological Theory

One would have thought that theories such as Fourier's and Mackey's could only arise in the minds of illuminates who believed themselves to have been granted a God's-eye view of cosmic history. How amazing it is, then, to find a modern scientist of unimpeachable respectability proposing much the same thing! This is the Australian geologist George E. Williams, editor of a large volume of papers on *Megacycles*.[30] Williams's own paper of 1972, collected in that book, sets out with great simplicity a vision of universal history worthy of Mackey himself. It holds that the earth started out at its formation about 4,500 million years ago with its axis parallel to the ecliptic. Gradually it rose (or fell), until it was perfectly upright. Then it continued its path, descending again to the horizontal. After 2,500 million years, it had come full circle, back to its starting-point. Then the cycle began again. In 500 million years or so, the earth will have completed two cycles in the course of its existence. So this is a very long-term change indeed.

The evidence put forward by Williams includes the long interval from about 230 million to 10 million years ago, in which "much of the world enjoyed a warm, tropical to subtropical climate"[31] without apparently any ice-ages intervening. It could have been the consequence of the last period of a vertical and near-vertical position of the axis. That would account for the penetration into the polar circles of exotic vegetation that needs twelve hours of sunlight each day, on which several scientific papers have been written. Williams also mentions that the time of 0° obliquity (that is, the "Golden Age" position), about 120 million years ago, coincides with the Late Jurassic and Early Cretaceous eras, "when the sauropods, the greatest of all dinosaurs, attained their maximum dimensions." The onset of varying seasons, of course, spelled the extinction of these unadaptable beasts.

Further back in time, Williams cites evidence for glaciations as having occurred at precisely the appropriate epochs, when the earth was neither too upright nor too horizontal. During the period when the axis coincided with the ecliptic, there would have been a dramatic contrast of climates every year, and it is exactly this that Williams suggests as the cause for certain geological phenomena, notably the Precambrian banded iron formations, "the rhythmic and laterally persistent microbanding of which has previously defied interpretation using uniformitarian principles."[32] These formations are found in the Western Australian desert, and date back 2,000 million years, that is, to the "Age of Horror" before last, according to Williams's reckoning. As for the future, he says that in the coming 500 million years "most terrestrial life will gradually migrate equatorward in pace with the shift of equable environments."[33]

An obvious objection to Williams's immensely long cycles is that the angle of the ecliptic is known to shift at a faster rate than the 0.05" of arc per century required by them, and in the opposite direction. Williams himself, in editorial comments, admits that his rate of change is undetectable, and contrasts it with the observed rate of 47"; but he carefully calls the latter "obliquity oscillation," to distinguish it from the secular change that he is positing. In this geologist's view, then, the tumbling earth of the occultists is still with us; but it tumbles exceedingly slowly, and on the way it suffers many an incidental shudder.

Chapter Sixteen:
Composite Theories

Another person beside Sampson Mackey for whom a connection with the Brotherhood of Luxor is claimed—indeed, who may be near the root of it[1]—is the American mulatto medium and sex-magician Paschal Beverly Randolph (1825–1875). The only one of his many books that has any pretention to scholarship, *Pre-Adamite Man* (1862), was written expressly to prove that the world is far older than the six thousand years allowed by biblical literalists, and that there is ample evidence for humans having existed long before our present races. Randolph's contribution to one of the liveliest debates of the nineteenth century went into at least six editions.

The calculation of the date, nature, and extent of the biblical Deluge is obviously an important feature of any such book. Its cause is a still more sensitive matter, if the whim of an angry Yahweh is discounted. Here Randolph is squarely on the side of Science, and assures us that "The catastrophe was the result of natural law, totally independent of any miraculous element whatever."[2] He goes on to explain:

> It may not be known to the general reader, but it is a well-attested fact, nevertheless, that, in addition to the diurnal and orbital motions of the earth, there is a third, an oscillating motion, requiring vast periods of time for the accomplishment of one movement. This movement is that of the deviation of the earth's axis, and by means of it the poles, and therefore the equator also, are shifted, and a great change takes place in the temperature, not only in polar, but in all other regions of the globe; and the cold is greater or less, for a period, at the middle of one of these oscillations, than at the end. It is believed that when this movement of the earth reaches one extreme, there is a terrible degree of cold at the poles, and consequently vast accumulations of ice are gathered there; and it is certain that the poles have been permanently shifted more than once. The greatest recent degree of heat occurred at the poles not less than twenty-two thousand years ago, in consequence of the deviation of the earth's axis; and the melting of the ice on that occasion may have been the cause of Noah's Flood.[3]

Randolph's ideas are far from lucid. At first he appears to be speaking of the precession of the equinoxes (the third motion of the earth), and his later mention of 22,000 years indicates a cycle of that order of magnitude. But he turns out to be imagining a shifting in the angle of the ecliptic, though how far, and what he means by its "extremes," it is impossible to guess. His mention of heat and cold makes no sense; nor can a number of "permanent" shifts be reconciled with a regular oscillating motion. In short, one wonders whether Randolph is not himself confusing precession with some hearsay, based perhaps on Mackey.

But Noah's was not the only flood. Randolph is perfectly justified in deducing from the myths of ancient peoples that there were several inundations, large and small, in prehistoric times. Long before Noah (or Adam, for that matter), "there occurred the most tremendous event this earth ever witnessed, or ever will witness, until a final convulsion shall hurl it out of being—as a habitable globe." [4] Randolph dates this to between 42,000 and 58,600 years before the present, favoring the more distant date. As he describes it,

> the planet of this system then revolving on its axis in an orbit between those of Mars and Jupiter, BURST asunder [...and produced the asteroid belt]. As the result of this bursting, I conceive that this earth suddenly changed its axis and its angle toward the ecliptic pole; the sun melted the ice at the earth's poles; the melted mass in the earth's bowels became disturbed, and it vomited forth fire and flame from a hundred volcanic mouths [...] That climates changed at that time, is proved by the bones of tropical animals, and remains of tropical plants now found in frozen regions [...][5]

Randolph has had it both ways: his version of prehistory includes both the progressive axial movement, and the sudden catastrophic one provoked from outside. His picture is a vivid one (especially in the pages of death and destruction, omitted here), but he avoids explaining exactly how the shifts could have caused these climatic conditions.

The last third of the nineteenth century was particularly rich in speculations about how to "save the appearances" of different recorded obliquities, climate changes, and catastrophes evident from the geological record. One of the most ingenious theories was that of Major-General Alfred Wilks Drayson, who had trained at Greenwich Observatory.[6] Drayson was teaching at the Royal Military Academy at Woolwich in about 1870, when a cadet asked him whether the distance between the pole of the heavens and the pole of the ecliptic had always been the same. Drayson replied that it was formerly somewhat greater, and that it diminishes at the rate of about half a second per annum, this being known as the "Decrease in the Obliquity of the Ecliptic." Where then, asked the bright cadet, is the center of the circle that the pole of the heavens describes around the pole of the ecliptic? Drayson realized in a flash that there can be no center to a diminishing circle, and set to work to devise a theory that would account for both precession and the decrease in the obliquity.

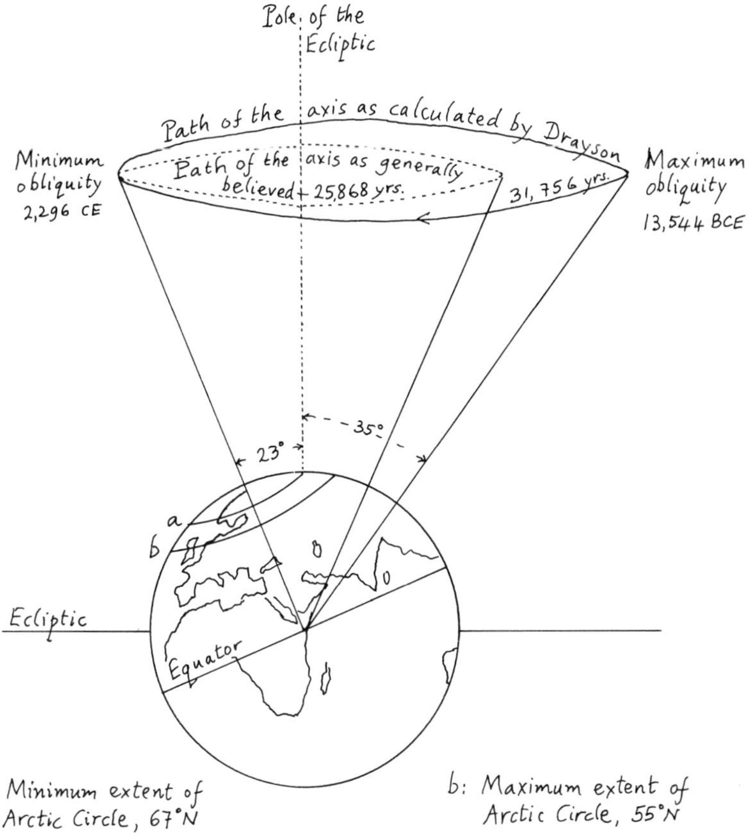

Illustration 26: The Drayson Theory

Drayson's theory was based on collecting figures for the angle of obliquity from the fifteenth century onwards (he did not trust the Greeks to be accurate enough). It had the unique virtue of explaining both the precessional movement and the decrease in obliquity by a single motion (see diagram). The course of the pole is a circle round a point 6° from the pole of the ecliptic, traversed in about 32,000 years. Part of this circle is so close to the smaller one around the pole of the ecliptic that for centuries it has been assumed that the earth's pole has been traveling around the latter, in the precessional cycle timed traditionally at 25,920 and scientifically at 25,868 years. Drayson's larger circle would of course take longer: he calculated it, on the basis of the observed precessional speed, as 31,756 years. But the major, experiential difference between the two cycles is that the Drayson cycle would have "seasons," because as the earth's pole followed it, its tilt would gradually rise and fall within a range of about twelve degrees.

The point of minimum obliquity, Drayson calculated, will be reached quite shortly, attaining exactly 23° in the year 2,295. The Arctic and Antarctic Circles will then be at their smallest, with the least differentiation of seasons throughout the globe—though still far from the Golden Age position of absolute verticality. His follower of the 1920s, Alfred Barley, saw in Drayson's cycle the explanation of the steadily warmer winters reported over the past 2,000 years. The other extreme, that of maximum obliquity, was supposedly reached in 13,584 BCE, when the angle between axis and ecliptic had increased to 35°. The Arctic Circle would then have descended as far as the North of England—but only for the winter, to be followed by a tropical summer. The alternate freezing and melting, Drayson believed, were the true explanation for the relics of the Ice Age that had occurred fifteen thousand years ago, and would recur whenever the extreme part of the 32,000-year cycle was attained. Drayson's theory is thus gradualist in its cosmic aspect—since the earth goes quietly on its precessional course—but periodically catastrophic in its consequences for the surface of the planet. It would find confirmation, up to a point, in the Milankovitch Cycles of modern geology (see Chapter Eighteen), which include a 41,000-year cycle of variation for the obliquity of the axis.

Blavatsky's Cataclysmic History

We return now to H. P. Blavatsky, the most fecund source of ideas on our subject. In her first major work, *Isis Unveiled* (1877), she wrote of the catastrophe that closes each Great Year (*Magnus Annus*) of earth history: "The polar and equatorial climates gradually change places; the former moving slowly toward the Line [equator], and the tropical zone, with its exuberant vegetation and swarming animal life, replacing the forbidding wastes of the icy poles. This change of climate is necessarily attended by cataclysms, earthquakes, and other cosmical throes."[7] She cites as "nearer the truth" two of the periods assigned in antiquity to the Great Year: 10,800 years (Herodotus) and 13,894 years (Linus), vaguely approximating to half the precessional period (about 12,960 years).[8]

When Blavatsky came to write *The Secret Doctrine* in 1885–1888, she was far more explicit on the matter of cataclysmic history and its causes. It was not a fortuitous outside agency, such as de Boucheporn's comet (which she specifically rejects[9]), nor a mindless, mechanical motion, but a divinely ordered plan for the development of the human race. "Fohat," she says, naming the executive or demiurgic power within our solar system, "is as good as any comet, having, in addition, universal intelligence to guide him!"[10]

As outlined in Chapter Two, the "divinely ordered plan" of Blavatskian Theosophy comprises a Round of seven Root-Races, each appearing on a different continent with a different configuration of land and sea. These changes are part of the economy of the planet, for "as land needs rest and renovation, new forces, and a change for its soil, so does water. Thence arises a periodical redistribution of land and water, change of climates, etc., all brought about by geological revolution, and ending in a final change in the axis."[11]

In Blavatsky's scheme of things, "there is a secular change in the inclination of the earth's axis, and its appointed time is recorded in one of the great Secret Cycles."[12] Of the seven *pralayas*—periods of rest or void—that conclude the seven Root-Races, three of them are occasioned by a change in the inclination of the earth's axis.[13] The first of these, we read, came at the close of the Second Race. The earth's tilt swept beneath the seas the whole Second Continent (Hyperborea), with its races; then came another lurch, as the axis returned rapidly to its previous degree of inclination, raising the earth once more out of the waters to become home to the next Root Race,[14] the Third or Lemurian.

A later disturbance of the axis is described in the "traditional commentary" on the Stanzas of Dzyan, which Blavatsky often cites in order to elucidate—or to further complicate—those cryptic verses. When the Third Race was at about the middle point of its development, says the ancient text,

> The axle of the Wheel tilted. The Sun and Moon shone no longer over the heads of that portion of the Sweat Born [early Lemurians]; people knew snow, ice, and frost, and men, plants, and animals were dwarfed in their growth. Those that did not perish, remained as half-grown babes in size and intellect. This was the third pralaya of the races.[15]

What is supposed to have been the position of the axis when the sun and moon still shone over the scarcely physical heads of the early Lemurians? Blavatsky says repeatedly—and the geologists agree—that there was once a semi-tropical climate in the Arctic regions. It is here, she says, that the ultimate physical transformation of the Third Race into nascent physical mankind began.[16] But the reader who has followed the argument thus far will realize that, given the current locations of the north and south polar regions (and Blavatsky says that these have not changed[17]), any inclination of the axis that brings them a warmer summer will only entail a longer and colder winter. Extraordinary as it may seem, another Commentary dealing with this period suggests that the earth was indeed in the position of Mackey's Age of Horror, with the axis horizontal to the celestial pole, and that this is its natural position:

> When the Wheel runs at the usual rate, its extremities (the poles) agree with its middle circle (equator), when it runs slower and tilts in every direction, there is a great disturbance on the face of the Earth. The waters flow towards the two ends, and new lands arise in the middle belt (equatorial lands), while those at the ends are subject to pralayas by submersion...[18]

Of course, the poles could never agree with the earth's "equator," as Blavatsky's explanatory parentheses state; it is with the ecliptic, or the celestial equator, that they coincide. Given that, the Lemurians in the Arctic would certainly have had the sun and moon above their heads—for the summer. Then they would have had a long, dark winter as the North Pole pointed away from the sun. Each year would comprise, as it were, a single day and night.

Blavatsky was more generous to Mackey than to many of her predecessors and most of her contemporaries. She calls his explanation of the polar motion "ingenious, even if it is not altogether free from occult heresy. Yet it is nearer the truth than many of a more scientific and especially theological character."[19] Here is the version preferred by her authorities:

> According to the old teaching, the axis of the earth gradually changes its inclination to the ecliptic, and at the period referred to [early Third Race], this inclination was such that a polar day lasted during the whole period of the earth's revolution about the sun, when a kind of twilight of very short duration intervened; after which the polar land resumed its position directly under the solar rays. This may be contrary to astronomy as now taught and understood: but who can say that changes in the motion of the earth, which do not take place now, did not occur millions of years back?[20]

The only way for such an annual day and night not to be equal would be for the earth's axis to change its orientation in the course of its orbit around the sun, that is, to point at the sun, rather than at some star. No one among our sources has yet suggested anything of the kind; it presumes conditions and motions which astronomy would be very hard put to imagine. The moon, certainly, always turns the same face to the earth, but not its axis. Possibly one should suppose that the precessional cycle coincided with the annual revolution. But even then, the brief twilight remains to be explained, and the whole situation is most puzzling.

After the axis had shifted out of this inexplicable position, putting an end to the early Third Race, Blavatsky says that the polar lands became uninhabitable and a new continent formed between Africa and Australia. The peoples that survived, being now fully physical, were divided into two distinct classes, we are told: the Sons of Night (or Darkness) and the Sons of the Sun (or Light). There were terrible battles between them, as the Sons of Night left their inhospitable land, from which the sun now departed for months on end, and invaded the equatorial regions of their more fortunate brethren.[21] This is not hard to understand, as it seems to refer to a situation not much different from our present one: the inhospitable lands are the extreme Arctic or Antarctic regions, with their sunless winter months.

The Third Continent of Lemuria was destroyed in its turn, but this time not through what Blavatsky calls the "sidereal phenomenon" of an axial shift: it perished through a "geological phenomenon," as the result of subterranean convulsions and the breaking of ocean floors. Blavatsky is explicit about the two distinct types of cataclysm,[22] which nowadays are called "exogenic" (caused from outside the earth) and "endogenic" (caused from the earth itself).

The Fourth Continent of Atlantis was, for a time, a "land of bliss," and one passage in *The Secret Doctrine* points to its having enjoyed the perpetual spring of an upright axis.[23] About halfway through its course, there were begun the "astronomical records of Universal History,"[24] which seem to have included the invention or discovery of the zodiac. Atlantis was brought to an end by a series of disturbances in the axial motion, which caused the bulk of it (the island-continents Ruta and Daitya) to sink beneath the Atlantic. This was towards the close of the Miocene Age,

850,000 years ago.[25]

Blavatsky makes it plain that although the seven Root-Races have succeeded each other on the scale of millions of years, elements of them and their continents continually overlap. Substantial Atlantic islands persisted right up to the inundation recorded by Plato, which took place in about 11,000 BP (Before Present),[26] leaving now only the slightest remnants in the Azores, the Canaries, Bermuda, etc.

The axial motions, however, did not cease with the destruction of Greater Atlantis, but have continued well into the period of our own Fifth Race. "Occult data show that even since the time of the regular establishment of the Zodiacal calculations in Egypt, *the poles have been thrice inverted*,"[27] and a new zodiac has had to be invented each time. Blavatsky allows between 75,000 and 80,000 years of age to their last (and our present) zodiac, which suggests that since then there has been no major axial disturbance, only precessional movement.[28]

The crucial question, as we move from those unimaginably early races to times more relevant to our own, is whether Blavatsky is now referring to sudden inversions of the poles, or to a gradual motion of the kind imagined by Mackey, or to both. In one place, she plainly states that "Every sidereal year the tropics recede from the pole *four degrees* in each revolution,"[29] which concurs with Mackey. Likewise, she speaks of myths of "the age when the gods forsook the earth and were said to ascend into heaven," that is, when the signs of the zodiac did not surround the horizon, but arched over the zenith from north to south, and "the ecliptic had become parallel with the meridian."[30] This occurs when axis and ecliptic coincide. She then invites the student to "exercise his intuition by placing these facts together; no more can be said."[31]

Blavatsky is unstinting with her information, but unfortunately her chaotic presentation leaves the student, once the labor of sorting it out is done, to the mercies of his or her own intuition. If a summary can be attempted, it is this. Her secret doctrine teaches that the past history of the earth's behavior is anything but regular and tidy, and that situations have obtained in the past which have not the slightest resemblance to anything known to science. At the same time, her past races did not resemble us, either, so that it would be wrong to project onto them the sensations that we would experience under the same circumstances. The epoch of *homo sapiens* as recognized by science—say the last million years—has suffered periodic topplings of the globe, of which the latest one has left us in the situation commemorated by the Egyptian zodiac and the Great Pyramid, both of which date from the seventieth millenium BP.[32] Since then the earth has followed a precessional cycle of something under 26,000 years (nobody doubts that) and a gradually diminishing angle of inclination (de Louville's theory). For this comparatively recent period, then, Blavatsky agrees with Mackey, but without projecting these movements back, as he does, into the more distant past.

As far as the future is concerned, Blavatsky does not give us much to worry about in our time. She says that the tropic has still 2 1/2° to run before the end of the Sidereal Year (for which her figure is 25,868 years); "which gives humanity in general, and our civilized races in *particular*, a reprieve of about 16,000 years."[33]

This implies that at the end of the Sidereal Year the earth will indulge in another convulsion, with cataclysmic results for its creatures.

Papus and Saint-Yves d'Alveydre

The French occultist Papus (1865–1916, born Gérard Encausse) was for a time an admirer of Madame Blavatsky and a member of her society. But by the time *The Secret Doctrine* was available to him, he had become disillusioned with Theosophy.[34] Consequently, when he wrote the first of his encyclopedic works, *Traité élémentaire des sciences occultes* (Elementary treatise on the occult sciences), he took little notice of any theories she might have put about. Papus turned instead to Louis Michel de Figanières, one of a number of seers with whom this highly intelligent man became infatuated, and whose moonstruck theories were outlined in Chapter Fourteen. Papus writes:

> If the equator and the ecliptic were to coincide, the earth would be in a state of physical harmony, from the point of view of seasons and climates, of which it would know nothing.
>
> Since this harmony does not exist, the terrestrial poles oscillate periodically; and it is from this oscillation that the subtle transformations derive that are felt by the continents and engraved on the memories of mankind in the form of geological cataclysms and deluges.
>
> Each terrestrial pole, according to secret tradition and not to current science, may occupy *eight successive positions* with regard to the equator. This is the *law of eight terrestrial poles*, which we are content to name, without going any further.
>
> Whence comes this inclination of the ecliptic with regard to the equator? All the initiations are unanimous in this regard: it comes from the MOON.[35]

We saw in Chapter Fourteen how Michel de Figanière's visions had given him the idea of a moon reluctant to take its place with the other masses that made up the primitive earth. But what are these "eight terrestrial poles" of which no one else appears to have spoken? It is possible that Papus had gleaned them from Mackey, if he looked no further than the diagram in *Mythological Astronomy* called "Cyclobthiad," which does show only eight turns of the spiral. He could have learned about Mackey from his colleagues in the Hermetic Brotherhood of Luxor. In a later essay he was a little more explicit, saying that as one pole succeeds another, the various land masses sink beneath the ocean, leaving behind only their mountains as islands. Papus adds the interesting note that England will never disappear in this way, because the English represent the "adventurous nation *par excellence*," and the spirit of adventure will always manifest somewhere—notably in the English colonization of these remnants of sunken continents.[36]

When Papus was preparing his popular book for its seventh edition, in 1896–97,[37] he must have mentioned the subject of catastrophic changes to his "intellectual master" Saint-Yves d'Alveydre, who in January 1897 decided to make a confidential revelation to his disciple. Saint-Yves was by this time living in virtual seclusion at Versailles, at least as regards the Parisian occultists who would have been all too eager to lionize him and enrol his prestigious name for their enterprises. Papus urged him, during this year, to make good the omission of a chapter on Jesus Christ, which Saint-Yves had withdrawn before publishing his longest work, *Mission des Juifs* (Mission of the Jews, 1884). Saint-Yves wrote back with candor about his devotion to Christ and to the principle of Love, which put him regrettably at odds with Fabre d'Olivet and other non-Christian esotericists; but he doubted that his thoughts were for this age of the world.

In this correspondence, Saint-Yves also touched on the Brahmanical wisdom that lay at the base of his great scheme of universal correspondence, the *Archéomètre*. The passage in which he explains the changes of the earth deserves to be read in full:

> The 11,500 years of which you speak are the result of a calculation on the Brahminical astronomical cycles. And, after the cycle concerned, maritime Europe, as our geographers know it, will have the same fate as Atlantis, about a dozen centuries from now. The Law of this cycle is inherent in the fact of a fourth terrestrial movement, as yet unknown to scientists. The fact, and its Law, are the consequence of a spiritual Principle of beneficence and general order, violated from age to age by the perversity of the dominant races. This Principle, divine in its nature, tends to maintain or restore the Earth to equilibrium, i.e. with its axis coinciding with that of the heavens, and hence in the planet's normal biological state. Now, the deviation in the human substance brought about that of the entire planetary substance—of the whole planet: the rapid mobilization of the magnetic meridian in little cycles, ending with a cycle of eighteen years; the inclination of the Poles (third large-scale movement); and finally the polar subversion and recension, sending Cain to the Land of Nod, precipitating the summit from its zenith to its nadir; in a word, burying beneath the seas the impious race and its continent. Keep to yourself, dear Sir, these redoubtable secrets of the ancient university of the Patriarchal Church, a terrible secret among many others, also known to the Prophets and disciples of Our Lord Jesus Christ. More than ever, the truth must be kept from the reach of the profane: not only for love of the truth, but also out of charity towards those who would desecrate it.[38]

In the above quotation, Saint-Yves first defines the "normal" state of the globe, namely with its axis perpendicular to the ecliptic, which the Spiritual Principle is concerned to maintain. There ensues a deviation, increasing the obliquity of the ecliptic *pari passu* with human decadence; this is the third large-scale movement (*mouvement séculaire*), presumably after the annual orbit and the precessional cycle. Finally comes the sudden fourth movement, unknown to science, governed by a cyclical law that makes it occur every 11,500 years: a catastrophic reversal of the poles.

As far as is known, Saint-Yves never said another word on this subject. Papus was enough of a gentleman to keep the contents of this letter to himself, much as it would have adorned subsequent editions of his treatise.

Saint-Yves' letter must be understood in the light of a megahistorical view which, as mentioned in Chapter Fourteen, was the reverse of the traditional Greek or Hindu one. Like Fabre d'Olivet, he saw the four Yugas as ascending, not descending in quality. By applying the 11,500-year cycle which he confides to Papus in the above letter with the scheme given in *Mission des Juifs*, one arrives at the following tentative reconstruction:

circa 8400 BCE: Deluge. Destruction of Atlantis. Restoration of vertical axis.

8400–3800 BCE (4 x 1150 years): Satya Yuga: Iron Age. Axis becomes oblique through human vice.

3800–350 BCE (3 x 1150 years): Treta Yuga: Bronze Age. Axis gradually returning towards vertical (de Louville's movement).

350 BCE–1950 CE (2 x 1150 years): Dvapara Yuga: Silver Age.

1950–3100 CE (1 x 1150 years): Kali Yuga: Golden Age "opening before us" [in 1884]. Marked by establishment of Synarchy, world government, unified religion.

circa 3100 CE (about 1200 years after 1897): Reversal of poles at end of 11,500-year cycle, leading to Deluge and a new Iron Age.

Comparing this with the Guénonian timetable of Jean Phaure on the one hand, and with that of Blavatsky on the other (see Chapter Two), shows how little consensus there is in esoteric chronology. Yet a consensus is beginning to emerge from our illuminates, to the effect that Atlantis perished in a pole-flipping cataclysm, and that the next one is due to finish off our present civilization, be it "iron" or "golden" in character.

Chapter Seventeen:
Polar Wandering

While the people mentioned in the previous three chapters have been eager to propound their various theories of the earth's shifting axis, very few of them have been willing to give a physical explanation of how this happened. This is probably because most of them were without scientific training, and were either unaware of the physical problems posed by their theories, or else indifferent to that level of discourse. It is quite another matter with our final group of authorities. In this chapter we turn largely to the scientists, to see how they have handled our subject over the past hundred and fifty years.

Their consensus is that whether or not the poles of the earth move relatively to the stars, they do move relatively to the earth's own surface. Some of them call their theory by the gentle name of "polar wandering," or the apologetic "pole slippage," while others prefer the more vigorous "earth tumble." The founder of this school of thought seems to have been Sir Isaac Newton, who explained in *Principia Mathematica* what it would take for the axis of the spinning earth to change:

> [...] let there be added anywhere between the pole and the equator a heap of new matter like a mountain, and this by its perpetual endeavour to recede from the centre of its motion will disturb the motion of the globe, and cause its poles to wander about its surface, describing circles about themselves and the points opposite to them.[1]

In other words, if a sufficiently large mountain were suddenly to arise, the earth would move into equilibrium around a new pair of poles. Looked at from the surface, the poles would have wandered to a new geographical location, though they would still point to the same stars.

It was long before the consequences of such an event were seriously considered, probably because the sudden emergence of mountains had no place in early modern geology, which was strictly uniformitarian. Probably the first extensive treatment was that of Frederic Klee (1808–1864), a Danish scholar who published a book on the *The Deluge* in Copenhagen (1842). Klee's approach blends geology with the study of mythological sources; his attitude to the Bible is respectful but not fundamentalist. For reasons quite different from those of today's scientists, he nevertheless came to the conclusion that originally the lands of the earth had formed a single continent: "Europe, Asia and North America were joined at the North Pole so as to form a continent of prodigious size, stretching towards the South Pole in three peninsulars: South America, Africa, and Oceana."[2] After reviewing the different lands that have disappeared since that time, as the result of the Deluge, Klee concludes that the only satisfactory way to account for all the changes is by assuming that there was a displacement of the earth's rotational axis. Formerly, he says, it was probably on the equator, between the longitude of Hierro Island (18° W) and the opposite point, while the present poles were then equatorial.[3]

Klee's is not an axial shift, but a change in the locations on earth through which the axis passes. As for the cause of this displacement, which he believed to have been sudden and quite violent, Klee was not prepared to specify it. In the French edition of his book, he gives ample space to the theory of Baron René de Boucheporn, who had suggested in 1844 that the cause of the axis shift was a comet.[4] Nevertheless, he himself was certain that the cause was to be found within the earth, rather than outside it; it was, he thought, a natural event, foreseen in the Creator's plans with the intention of bringing about a more perfect order of things.[5]

Much of Klee's book is devoted to comparative mythology and to theories about the migration of races. Like many other believers in historic or prehistoric catastrophe, he finds ample support for his theory in ancient writings, including the Edda, Genesis, and the Apocalypse. Changes in the sun's direction or rising place, for example, are easily accounted for, as are the great migrations which, as we saw in Chapters Three and Four, were a burning issue of contemporary science. But Klee's pre-catastrophic phase, although highly civilized, is not a Golden Age.

Unable to find a physical explanation for polar shifting, Klee was content to persuade scientists first that it must have happened; finding the cause could come later. In 1848, John Lubbock took up the torch in a paper presented to the Geological Society of London "On Change of Climate Resulting from a Change in the Earth's Axis of Rotation."[6] He showed how the centrifugal force that presently swells the oceans of the earth around the equator would, if the poles shifted, cause the bulge to change position. Some lands would emerge, others would disappear beneath the sea. What could cause this? Lubbock thought that the axis might be shifted by changes occurring in the distribution of land, perhaps brought about by the dislocation of strata as the earth cooled.

There was so much interest in Lubbock's theory that George Darwin (son of Charles) set out to control it in an article of 1877, the first of his many papers on cosmology.[7] Darwin thought that the poles might wander indefinitely if the earth were more or less plastic, but not if it were rigid, as he believed it to be. It was Darwin's colleague Lord Kelvin who had persuaded him that the earth is indeed rigid, yet even Kelvin believed that there might have been gradual polar wanderings in ancient times, amounting to as much as 40°. Darwin himself allowed that the pole could have worked its way 10°–15°, with a maximum of 3° for any one geological period. His study was meant to limit speculation, but it had quite the opposite effect, launching a new wave of enthusiasm for large-scale polar displacements.

A group of Germans, working in the first years of the twentieth century, went much further than Darwin and Kelvin by proposing "polar pendulation." [8] This concept, coined by Reibisch in 1901, posited an axis of oscillation that passed through Ecuador and Sumatra, which never changed their latitude; around this, the poles swung up and down, north and south, along the 10th meridian east of Greenwich. In 1902, Kreichgauer produced a map that had the North Pole migrating from the Antarctic in the Precambrian era, through the Pacific Ocean, across Alaska and Greenland, to its current position.

The object of pendulation theory was to explain the distribution of certain plants and animals. For instance, as Heinrich Simroth demonstrated in *Die Pendulationstheorie* (1907), the Tertiary flora of Ecuador and Sumatra was apparently not modified right through the Pleistocene (Ice Age) era. This implied that in those places the climate had not changed, while obviously it had altered greatly in most other parts of the world. But these scientists, overwhelming the opposition with the weight of their learning, did not trouble to explain how and why the pole had behaved thus: they were geologists and biologists, after all, not astronomers.

As Sir George Darwin pointed out, a planet whose crust was filled with fluid would have a far better chance than our solid earth of adjusting its shape to achieve equilibrium around its axis. It would also be easier for its continents to float around on the surface. However, the astronomical orthodoxy of the early twentieth century favored the rigid model of the earth. Thus when Alfred Wegener (1880–1930) proposed the theory of Continental Drift in 1915, he was regarded as something of a crank, especially by American geologists. Wegener conceived of the continents as plates floating on the softer body of the earth, rather like pieces of shell on a hard-boiled egg. Their direction was dictated by two forces, *Polfluchtkraft* (pole-fleeing force) and *Westwanderung* (westward motion), caused by the earth's rotation. In order to account for their present situation, Wegener had to locate the poles from which they had "fled" in different places from the present ones, and this made his speculative maps of the ancient continental formations rather different from those accepted today.[9]

Wegener's ideas were so out of line with contemporary geological theory that he was long dismissed as of no more significance than Hoerbiger. Thirty years after his death on an expedition in Greenland, the accepted wisdom had changed, and the earth was again considered fluid enough, beneath its crust, for Wegener's ideas to be reconsidered. Today every student of geology is familiar with plate tectonics and with the map of "Pangaea," the primordial continent into which all the present ones are ingeniously fitted in jigsaw fashion, its shores washed by the waves of "Panthalassa," the one primordial ocean. Later the land masses are believed to have fragmented, first into super-continents with names like Gondwana and Laurentia, then eventually into the six or seven continents of today.

If the very continents have drifted about on the surface of the globe, then large-scale polar adjustments are quite thinkable. Wegener himself allowed for 60° of polar wandering between the Carboniferous and the Quaternary epochs.[10] These shifts, he said, would have been followed by gradual adjustments in the earth's shape in order to keep its bulge at the equator. The oceans, on the other hand, could adjust their levels much more quickly, resulting in massive inundations in certain places, compensated by withdrawal of the seas in others. All this Wegener found confirmed by the geological record.

The wandering of the poles and the redistribution of land and sea are the "chicken or egg" problem of paleogeology. They seem to be causally linked, but which came first, and why? No one is quite sure.

Two other pioneering figures are worth a brief mention before we turn to current ideas on the subject. The engineer Hugh Auchincloss Brown (1879–1975) made a certain name for himself in the 1940s by getting very worried about the imminence of a major rearrangement of the poles.[11] He built on A.-J. Adhémar's idea: that the South Polar icecap was growing and causing a serious imbalance to one side of the South Pole. This would act like Newton's "heap of new matter," forcing the earth to slide itself around its axis and to find more comfortable places for the poles on its surface. Its axis would continue to point to the same stars, but the icecaps would now be near the equator, and would consequently melt. The 27-mile differential between the polar and equatorial diameters would reassert itself with regard to the new position, causing unimaginable upheavals. The results of such a shift—Brown was afraid that it would happen in a single day—would be so catastrophic for humanity that he proposed a typical engineer's solution: the South Polar icecap should be prophylactically blown apart by nuclear explosions. Thus modern man would call a halt to a natural cycle which Brown thought to have repeated itself in the past every seven thousand years or so.

Brown called his first treatise *Popular Awakening Concerning the Impending Flood* (1948), a title that did not inspire confidence on the part of scientists, nor of anyone else when the flood failed to materialize. But he had one sympathetic reader in Charles Hapgood, a New England college teacher. After ten years of research, Hapgood produced a book called *Earth's Shifting Crust* (1958), to which none less than Albert Einstein contributed two letters and a Foreword. Hapgood's point of departure was the known problem of ice ages having occurred, long ago, in India, Africa, and other now tropical latitudes. His solution began from the observation that the only places currently having ice ages are the North and South Poles. Hence it seemed to him that "the best theory to account for an ice age is that the area concerned was at a pole."[12] This would also explain the anomalous fauna and flora found beneath the present icecaps: they had once been in the tropics. As for Brown's theory, Hapgood had gone far beyond it in the course of his meticulous and sober research, coming to the conclusion that it is not the whole body of the earth that shifts relative to its axis, but only the crust; and that this happens relatively slowly, from the human point of view (no single day of terror occurs), though very rapidly in terms of geological time.[13] The last shift, moving the North Pole from Hudson's Bay to its present position in the Arctic Ocean, occurred, according to Hapgood's reckoning, between 18,000 and 12,000 years ago.

Modern Geological Theory

The dating suggested by Hapgood was far too recent for his theory to impress geologists, who find evidence for the slippage of the earth's crust hundreds of millions of years ago, but not within human memory. Yet the theory itself was certainly in the air. In 1955, the astronomer Thomas Gold proposed an elegant solution to the "chicken or egg" problem. The earth, he wrote, has enjoyed long periods of stasis, alternating with short ones of comparatively rapid change. The motive force is within the earth itself, as the periodic redistribution of matter—Gold speaks of "tectonic change"—calls for a different equilibrium around the axis. He makes the often-quoted suggestion that if South America were suddenly to be raised by 30 meters, the earth would topple over to compensate, at the "rapid" rate of one degree per millenium.[14] Gold continues with the following picture of the earth's possible behavior:

> It is thus tempting to suggest that there have been just a few occasions when the axis has been 'free' and has swung around as rapidly as would be given by the stiffness of the earth and the rates of tectonic movement, leading to a time-scale of the order of 10^5 or 10^6 years, but scarcely longer. But then in its rapid movement it has encountered a trap where it was caught within a small angle by the shifts in masses which its movement itself induced. It must then have remained in that neighbourhood until either there was a sufficient tectonic change to lead to an unbalance greater than could be compensated by glaciation or atmospheric effects, or until the distribution of land and water had been so modified as to destroy the mechanism of the trap. Then would have followed another period of hunting until a new trap became operative.[15]

The scientists of today can be fully as imaginative as the seers of yesteryear, once they yield to the temptation of visualizing the past from a God's-eye view! In Gold's system, neither pole-shift nor surface change has to come first; like a good marriage, they are in a perpetual state of mutual adjustment. W. H. Munk, author of the standard textbook on the rotation of the earth,[16] welcomed Gold's 1955 article as the first "serious study" of the subject since George Darwin's of 1877.[17]

By the time Charles Hapgood published a revision of his book on polar wandering, *The Path of the Pole* (1970), his Wegenerian belief in a shifting crust had come to be shared by a large body of geologists, though since he was an "amateur," and had proposed an unacceptable time-scale, he did not receive much recognition. The study of polar wandering is still a young one, and based less on the humanistic approach of Hapgood than on the new science of Paleomagnetism.[18] This is the study of the magnetic orientations of ancient rocks and artefacts. To invent a simple example, let us suppose that successively older layers of rocks in a given place are found to have their "north" magnetic poles pointing to the northwest, the west, and the southwest. This could mean at least two different things. Perhaps the north magnetic pole of the earth once lay to the southwest of this place, then moved successively northwards until reaching its present position. That would be a case of "True Polar Wander" (TPW). On the other hand, perhaps it was the place in question that moved, drifting over the earth's surface in the course of billions of years and changing its orientation in the process. That would be "Apparent Polar Wander" (APW), in which case the earth's magnetic poles could have remained constant.

But have the poles truly wandered? No one is quite sure. Peter Goldreich and Alar Toomre, in an article of 1969, showed once again that they could have; that, given a quasi-rigid model of the earth, "quite modest redistributions of mass within the earth can give rise to large excursions [as much as 90°] of the rotation axis relative to the entire crust and mantle."[19] Goldreich and Toomre believed that large displacements had happened on a geological time scale, but did not say where, when, or exactly how large.

True Polar Wander itself comes in three different forms, as explained by Donna M. Jurdy.[20] First, the lithosphere (crust) can slip around the mesosphere (mantle), so that the surface will have new poles, but not the core of the earth (see diagram). Alternatively, the mesosphere can slip round inside the crust, betraying its activity by the movement of "hotspots"—places like volcanoes, where the magma penetrates the crust. As a third possibility, both lithosphere and mesosphere can wander relatively to the axis of rotation. Jurdy deduced that there had been a modest TPW of 5.7° from the late Cretaceous to the early Tertiary eras (80–53 million years ago), and a lesser one of 3 1/2° from that time to the present.

Low estimates of polar wandering are the norm, so long as continental drift is the preferred explanation for it. As D. H. Tarling says, "it is impossible to distinguish between 'true' polar wandering and continental (plate) motions unless it can be shown that there are systematic differences between the palaeomagnetically determined pole and palaeoclimatic indicators."[21] In other words, one should not assume that it was the poles that moved, unless there is evidence that climates have also changed. Nor should one assume too readily that the crust can slip over the mantle of the earth, according to recent geological theory. Jean A. Andrews, in 1985, found it hard to accept the decoupling of the earth's crust and mantle as implied by the idea of "mantle roll." She thought that instances of true polar wandering were more likely caused by the whole earth tumbling, or the shifting of the lithosphere and the mantle together. Thus her position comes back to that of Hugh Auchincloss Brown. Looking back over the history of the globe, Andrews found some periods of little or slow polar motion, then, for example between 65 and 50 million years ago, a rapid movement of 8

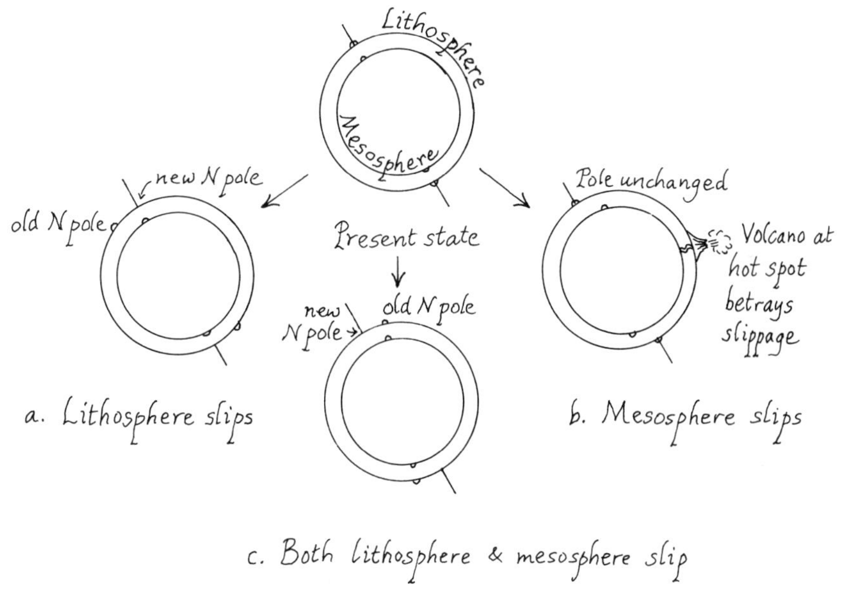

Illustration 27: Three forms of "True Polar Wander"

or 10 centimeters a year—this being faster than any present-day velocities of the continental plates. Another rapid period seems to her to have occurred 5 million years ago, coinciding with the unusual ice sheets of the Pleistocene.[22]

Tarling, for his part, rejects polar wandering as an explanation of the ice ages. "There seems little doubt," he writes, "that the fundamental control on such advances and retreats [of ice sheets] is related to regular cycles in the obliquity of the Earth's axis to the solar plane." [23] So we are back to a true axial shift, moving the whole earth with it, as the cause of the most widespread and documented catastrophe of recent epochs, namely the glaciation of much of the northern hemisphere that ended only about ten thousand years ago.

Yet the climates definitely have changed, and changed radically, in the course of the geological record. This was the starting point for W. L. Donn,[24] who in a posthumously published article of 1989 used Goldreich and Toomre's figures to justify a bold proposal: that the poles had, in fact, wandered to their present positions from what are now tropical marine latitudes. It is accepted that from the Triassic to the Eocene periods, the tropical Pacific temperatures were considerably colder than they are today, while the Arctic and Antarctic regions were temperate and even semitropical. During this period, according to Continental Drift theory, the land mass of Pangaea was in the course of breaking up, but was far more compact than the continents of today. All over it are found the remains of dinosaurs—right up to Spitzbergen, which is within 10° of the present North Pole. The virtually universal distribution of the giant reptiles—

a class not known for liking cold weather—is indeed one of the greatest problems of the past, if the continents are imagined as spreading through every temperature zone. What is more logical than to assume that Pangaea was then spread around the equator, while the poles were in the oceans? Donn shows a map of the later part of this period, the Paleocene (60 million years ago), when the continents were separated but still far closer than today; he draws one pole a few hundred miles off the coast of California, and the other east of Madagascar. This explains how a luxurious fauna could have flourished from Ellesmere Island in the Canadian Arctic to the capes of Africa and South America.

I have given only a small sampling of recent scientific theory. But the reader who has persisted through it may have noticed a certain similarity between these competing theories of the scientists, on the one hand, and those of the "illuminates" on the other. Within each group there is little consensus, and the scientists are each enclosed in their intellectual bubbles, as surely as poor Fourier or Mackey were. Each has a pet theory, backed up with a chart of figures obtained at great trouble and expense, which he or she proposes apparently without any sense of how it fits into a general world-view. The largest questions of cosmology are subjects for agnosticism. Just occasionally, one comes across a bold and sweeping theory like Williams' or Dodd's, which literally turns the world upside-down; but even these have not become received wisdom in the sense, for example, that continental drift has.

One has to conclude that the geological or cosmological theories about polar wandering and axial shift are no more proven than those of the illuminates, or of the humanists whose suppositions are based on ancient texts. All are in quest of the theory that "saves the appearances," whether these be the readings of paleomagnetism or the myths of the earliest civilizations. No two theories agree with one another, and most of them are mutually incompatible.

Should one, then, throw the whole idea overboard and join the majority of the human race in agnosticism or indifference? Only if one is unmoved by the persistence of this archetype in the collective imagination. The myth of a pole shift has haunted the Western mind from its beginnings, surfacing sporadically like an underground stream, only to sink out of sight again for a few hundred years. Over the past two centuries it has fascinated a small group of illuminates and cranks, and an equally small group of scientists, while mischievously eluding the firm grasp of any one of them. This book does not pretend to succeed where so many experts have failed; but if the archetype has not yet been hunted down, at least I think that we have surrounded it, and that the reader has been given a fair chance to decide whether or not to believe in its existence.

Chapter Eighteen:
The Restoration

The early chapters of this book presented the twin myths of a Golden Age in the more or less distant past, in which the earth's axis was perfectly vertical, and of its current 23 1/2° inclination as coeval with the fall of humanity into its present condition. We have also reviewed theories of historical cycles, which hold that now, at the end of the twentieth century, we are nearing a crucial juncture. In closing, we turn to the prophecies and predictions concerning an imminent restoration of the pole to its original position, with all its consequences for good and ill.

Not so long ago, bewitched by burgeoning technology, people began to think that there was nothing of which humanity might not be capable one day, even as far as bringing about a pole shift themselves. Jules Verne wrote his novel *The Purchase of the Pole* as a warning against such technocratic arrogance. The story tells of a consortium that buys up enormous areas of the Arctic regions, very cheaply because they are thought to be worthless. The cunning speculators then install a gigantic cannon in Mount Kilimanjaro (Tanzania), intending to push the earth sufficiently off its axial tilt to bring those polar regions within a temperate zone, thus making them inestimably valuable. When the cannon fires, however, nothing significant happens. Someone had blundered in his calculations, leaving off three crucial zeros, thus underestimating by a factor of one thousand the amount of force needed!

Such an enterprise is more feasible now than it was a hundred years ago, since atomic fusion can produce a burst of energy fully equal to a thousand Vernian cannons. It would not work at Mount Kilimanjaro, but it could be used at the Antarctic ice-cap, as Hugh Auchincloss Brown suggested. However, at the time of writing this does not seem very likely.

The manuscripts of the Black Order captured by La Boucane in Père Martin's story tell of a similar instance of titanic ambition. The writer is a Dutch scientist, Willibrod, who has been working at the secret base in Canada. A former collaborator with Hoerbiger, Kiss, and Planck, he has created a "reflector of telluric waves, controllable at will." [1] The history of the project is as follows:

> Some years ago, the Führer asked Hoerbiger if it would be possible for him to displace the North magnetic Pole. "Certainly," replied my master. "How soon

would you estimate that you could make the first experiments?" "Perhaps in a year, if I had everything necessary at my disposal, and co-workers trained for this kind of research." "Very well, then: draw up your list and get to work," concluded Hitler with the same simplicity.[2]

Obviously this is the sensitive point at which the two major themes of this book meet: the polar shift, and the Black Order. Since the very existence of the latter is debatable, most normal people will not want to dwell seriously on this possibility, and will accept that Martin's story is as fictitious as Jules Verne's—an ironic variation on the same theme of the earth's fall and restoration. In purely natural terms, however, there is cause for alarm if there is any truth in the theory that the reversal of the earth's magnetic poles coincides with that of its geographical poles relative to the ecliptic. The magnetic field of the earth is very low indeed at present, and no one knows for sure whether another reversal of polarity is not in preparation.

We may receive some comfort from the views of official science, which is uniformitarian unless faced with indisputable evidence to the contrary. As far as the behavior of the earth's axis is concerned, the scientific position is defined by a refined version of the three cycles formulated by Milutin Milankovitch in the 1920s and 1930s:[3]

1. The obliquity of the ecliptic, or the tilt of the earth's axis, which fluctuates from about 21° 55' to about 24° 18' over a cycle of about 41,000 years. On 1 January 1950 the angle was 23° 26' 45", and it is currently diminishing by about 0.47" annually. No return to the "Golden Age" position is allowed for here.

2. The shape of the earth's orbit, which stretches into a more or less eccentric ellipse, completing its cycle in about 100,000 years. This does not directly concern us.

3. The precession of the equinoxes, which Milankovitch calls a 23,000-year cycle. I have seen in scientific journals figures as various as 21,000[4] and 26,000.[5] The traditional number is 25,920, divided into twelve astrological "months" of 2,160 years each.

Broecker and Denton have drawn the boldest conclusions from the Milankovitch cycles, in attributing to their interaction the major changes of climate and glaciation that occurred between 14,000 and 13,000 years ago. They wonder tentatively whether the system might alter again as a result of the carbon dioxide emitted through human agency.[6] But a sudden or imminent pole shift is beyond the calculations of these or of any geologists.

There would be no point here in duplicating the findings of John White, author of *Pole Shift* (1980), a book of superlative value to researchers which assembles and summarizes a large number of scientific and occult sources. At the end of it, White concludes soberly that a pole shift *might* occur before the end of the century, and that it would be prudent to open one's mind to the possibility.[7] Thus he avoids both the fault of materialistic science, which refuses even to consider the scenarios envisaged by the illuminates, and also the fault of the prophets of doom who have been blowing the whistle since time immemorial. Naturally, like all researchers who dare to cross the iron curtains of human thought, White has come in for criticism from both sides, for contrary reasons, and, as he later said, was "often appalled by the ignorance and prejudice [he] found."[8]

A decade later, in an article "Is a Disastrous Pole Shift Inevitable?"[9] White reviewed his findings in the light of the new data that had appeared in the 1980s. These included new analyses of the frozen mammoths of Siberia (a classic locus for theorists of a sudden polar and climactic shift); the refutation of Hapgood's theory of an unglaciated Antarctica, as supposedly mapped before recorded history; and the final quietus to the Velikovsky controversy. Summarizing, White calls the case for pole shifts in the past "virtually nonexistent,"[10] and reassures the reader that "On the basis of this information and a decade's hindsight, I think that the possibility of a catastrophic pole shift at the end of this century is increasingly unlikely."[11]

John White was writing for the readers of a journal published by the Association for Research and Enlightenment and the Edgar Cayce Foundation, institutions which had made a best-seller of his *Pole Shift* book.[12] In that book he had naturally given ample space to the well-known predictions of Cayce's source (whatever it was) concerning the coming "earth changes," of which this is the most extensive:

> The earth will be broken up in the western portion of America. The greater portion of Japan must go into the sea. The upper portion of Europe will be changed as in the twinkling of an eye. Land will appear off the east coast of America. There will be the upheavals in the Arctic and in the Antarctic that will make for the eruption of volcanoes in the Torrid areas, and there will be the shifting then of the poles—so that where there have been those of a frigid or semi-tropical will become the more tropical [sic], and moss and fern will grow. And these will begin in those periods in '58 to '98, when these will be proclaimed as the periods when His Light will be seen again in the clouds.[13]

Cayce's "life-readings," which produced material on his querents' past lives, also touched occasionally on pole shifts as having marked the end of prehistoric epochs.[14] A professional geologist who commented on them, anonymously, in the Cayce Foundation's book *Earth Changes* concluded warily that "it is perhaps not too dangerous to at least speculate that the earth's rotational axis followed closely the movements of the geomagnetic-dipole axis."[15] Thirty years later, it is still not possible to say much more, except that the Cayce source's record for dated predictions is not good: 1936 was supposed to see not only wars but "upheavals in the interior of the earth, and the shifting of same by the differentiation in the axis as respecting the positions from the Polaris center."[16]

On the other hand, it may just be the timing that is inaccurate—something to be expected, perhaps, when there is communication from the timeless—for numerous other people have been told in dream, trance, or the waking state that something of the kind is soon to occur. John White has collected a number of these, to which I add that of Viola Petitt Neal, an unusually well-educated medium whose "night classes" were taken down by Dr. Shafica Karagulla:

> January 18, 1962. There are movements in the earth crust all over the world and, as in the time of ancient Atlantis there were many warnings—earthquakes, changes in climate and volcanic eruptions, so today, for the last few years, especially the last year, there have been many earthquakes in different parts of the world which indicate the shift of continents and of the earth's crust.
>
> The spin of the earth will change. Not in time of rotation, although there will be a disturbance in the time of rotation for a while. The axis of rotation will change. The North axis will move toward Siberia, the South axis into the South Pacific. This will cause considerable disturbance in the whole atmosphere which will produce storms and winds of great velocity and climate changes.
>
> The Southern part of the United States will move closer to the equator, and the equator will move closer to the Southern part. The whole Pacific Coast will be changed right down through South America because of various sinking and rising of land. Much of California, quite a bit of it, can come down and there could be an island of California. A part of California will become a large island.
>
> There will also be changes in the Atlantic including the St. Lawrence area and Maine. New York and Manhattan will be broken up. The rainfall will be different in various parts of the world. Many places that are deserts will become very fertile with plenty of rainfall. For example, the Sahara Desert in North Africa will become a very populous area and, with lots of rainfall and vegetation, will become more fertile.
>
> The climate of Arabia will be colder, more temperate, but it will also be a more fertile country—Southern Arabia especially. There was a great map there or rather a globe of the world; from time to time places that have changed were indicated.
>
> This will not come all at once. There is a gradual move up in the shifts here and there. There will come a time when there will be tremendous shifts at once and suddenly. This is not too far off, but it was not indicated how soon it would be. We seem to be already in this process of change.[17]

Two other books deserve mention along with John White's for their attempts to combine scientific with psychic data. Jeffrey Goodman's *We are the Earthquake Generation* (1978) takes Cayce's predictions as its starting-point; its warnings of earthquakes in California and elsewhere are obviously worth taking seriously. Goodman writes an excellent chapter on "Shifting of the Poles"[18] which considers the possibility of this as either the cause or the result of major earthquakes. Richard W. Noone's *5/5/2000; Ice: the Ultimate Disaster* (written in

1982) favors the imbalance of the Antarctic icecap as a probable trigger for a pole shift. Noone's rather journalistic book takes a wandering course through the familiar halls of ancient cataclysms, secret societies, unexplained high technology, and pyramidologists, from whom he gets his date of 5 May 2000 for the "ultimate disaster" that is supposed to end our cycle. More confirmation is available for the list of evidences he draws up for "some extraordinary activity"—possibly a pole shift—having taken place on earth between 4,500 and 4,000 BCE.[19] This would mark the beginning of the "Age of Taurus"; it is the epoch of the foundation of the Egyptian calendar; of the beginning of the world in the Biblical chronology; and of datable records of historic civilizations.

All of these writers—the Cayceans, John White, Goodman, and Noone—share the opinion that earth changes and their attendant cataclysms are not inevitably written in the heavens, and that the behavior of the human race has a lot to do with when and how they might take place. The more sophisticated astrologers teach, likewise, that while the horoscope can be used to predict events, the nature of these events and the level on which they happen—physical, psychic, etc.—are determined by the individual's free will. By "right living"—which does not require any attention to astrology—one can be sure that every happening will contribute to one's overall development, rather than just confirm the law of cause and effect.

The same is likely to be true on a collective scale: the "horoscope" of the earth, namely its cycles and ages, are fixed, but the overall tone of human thought and feeling will determine the immediate destiny of our species on it.

That destiny, however, does not necessarily include the continuation of life as we know it. We scarcely need the illuminates telling us that we are reaching the end of the Piscean Age, the end of the Kali Yuga, and the end of Adamic humanity, to be aware that the present time is unique. Whether the "overall tone of human thought and feeling" is better or worse than in past ages, I would not like to say; but the overall tone of global life has never been worse. It is hard to imagine a more poetically just way for much-abused Earth to reassert its rights over us than to execute a sudden, or even a gradual return to its Golden Age position. That would certainly put us in our place! But such an event is past planning for. In one sense, it is much too large to worry about; yet in another sense, even that would be but a twist on the spiral path that leads every creature eventually to Arcadia.

Notes

CHAPTER ONE

1. Phaure 1988, 255.
2. See "Ages of the World" in Hastings I, 183–210.
3. H. Jacobi, "Ages of the World (Indian)," in Hastings I, 201.
4. Hesiod, *Works and Days*, 117–120, trans. R. Lattimore.
5. Plato, *Statesman* 272a, trans. J. B. Skemp.
6. Ovid, *Metamorphoses* I, 122.
7. Plato, *Statesman* 270a.

CHAPTER TWO

1. See Blavatsky 1888, II, 6.
2. Blavatsky 1888, II, 310.
3. Blavatsky 1888, II, 401.
4. Blavatsky 1888, II, 249.
5. Blavatsky 1888, II, 138.
6. Blavatsky 1888, II, 7.
7. Blavatsky 1888, II, 401–402.
8. Blavatsky 1888, II, 138.
9. Blavatsky 1888, II, 138.
10. Blavatsky 1888, II, 7.
11. Blavatsky 1888, II, 273.
12. Blavatsky 1888, II, 132.
13. Blavatsky 1888, II, 173.
14. Blavatsky 1888, II, 250.
15. Blavatsky 1888, II, 273.
16. Blavatsky 1888, II, 8–9.
17. Blavatsky 1888, II, 404.
18. Summary in Daniélo 1840, 413n, 417.
19. Blavatsky 1888, II, 6.
20. *Asiatic Researches* 8:302ff.
21. See Thompson 1989, 43, 57.
22. See, however, Johnson 1990.
23. Guénon 1970, 40–41. The "archeologist" in question is Paul Le Cour, founder of the review *Atlantis*.
24. *Sûrya Siddhânta* I, 18.
25. Guénon 1970, 24.
26. Guénon 1970, 38, quoting from Guénon 1983, 56.
27. Guénon 1970, 48.
28. Guénon 1970, 50.
29. Collected in Guénon 1962.
30. Guénon 1970, 36n.
31. Guénon 1953b, 140ff.
32. Guénon 1953b, 144.
33. See Negus 1969, 54.
34. See also Blavatsky 1888, II, 289.
35. Blavatsky 1888, II, 135.
36. Phaure 1988, 263.
37. Phaure 1988, 280–281.

CHAPTER THREE

1. Pierre Joseph Marie Amiot, editor of *Mémoires concernant l'histoire, les sciences et les arts des Chinois* (1776–1791).
2. Editor of *Asiatic Researches* (1788–1839).
3. Title of Smith 1954.
4. Bailly 1781, 95.
5. Bailly 1781, 74, and notes on 480–482.
6. Bailly 1781, 79–80.
7. Bailly 1781, 98, after Olaus Rudbeck.
8. Bailly 1781, 99.
9. Bailly 1781, 326.
10. Bailly 1781, 325–326.
11. Bailly 1781, 104.
12. Buffon 1939, 112.
13. Buffon 1939, 122.
14. Buffon 1939, 284.
15. Bailly 1781, 103 and note.
16. Bailly 1781, 103–104.
17. Bailly 1781, 105.

18. Warren 1885, 47.
19. Warren 1885, 65.
20. Warren 1885, 68.
21. Warren 1885, 70.
22. Warren 1885, 194.
23. Warren 1885, 357–358.
24. Dates *sic*. See Bennett 1965, 21, for reference to Tilak.
25. See Tilak 1903, i–iv.
26. Summarized from Tilak 1903, 453–454.
27. Tilak 1903, 22–29.
28. Tilak 1903, 69.
29. Tilak 1903, 86–109.
30. Tilak 1903, 125–128.
31. Tilak 1903, 73–75.
32. See Spencer 1965, 122.
33. Spencer 1965, 126.
34. Spencer 1965, 207, 291.
35. Spencer 1965, 210.
36. Spencer 1965, 352, 353.
37. Spencer 1965, 352.
38. Broecker & Denton 1990, 54.
39. Broecker & Denton 1990, 55.

CHAPTER FOUR

1. Poliakov 1974, 183–185.
2. Voltaire 1785, Vol. 63, 163 (letter of 19 January 1776).
3. Voltaire 1785, Vol. 63, 135 (letter of 15 December 1775).
4. Herder n.d., 206, 211.
5. Poliakov 1974, 186–187.
6. On the Schlegels' contribution, see Poliakov 1974, 190–193.
7. Schlegel 1849, 472–473, 516.
8. Schlegel 1849, 514.
9. Herodotus VII, 62.
10. Poliakov 1974, 193.
11. Poliakov 1974, 195–198.
12. Poliakov 1974, 255.
13. "The Veda and Zend-Avesta," in Müller 1881, I, 62.
14. Renan, 116.
15. Renan, 117, 120.
16. *La Doctrine secrète*, 1899; *Die Geheimlehre*, 1897–1901.
17. Blavatsky 1877, I, 589.
18. Blavatsky 1877, I, 590.
19. Blavatsky 1877, I, 241.
20. Blavatsky 1877, II, 426.
21. *Mahatma Letters* XVIII, 121.
22. *Mahatma Letters* XVIII, 121.
23. *Mahatma Letters*, XXIIIB, 154.
24. *Man* 1885, 94.
25. The view of Mommsen and Hale, according to Taylor 1906, 9.
26. Cited from Taylor 1906, 46.
27. Schrader 1890, 432–433.
28. Fabre d'Olivet 1915, 6–7 and throughout.
29. Fabre d'Olivet 1915, 121n, 144n.
30. Saint-Yves d'Alveydre 1928, 137.
31. Rhys 1888, 636–637.
32. Rendall 1889, 53.
33. Morris 1888, 28.
34. Morris 1888, 42–51.
35. Müller, *Good Words*, Aug. 1887, cited in Taylor 1906, 53.
36. Taylor 1906, 47.

CHAPTER FIVE

1. See Voltaire's four letters to Bailly in his *Oeuvres* LXIII, and Bailly's Letters 11–24 to Voltaire in Bailly 1779.
2. Bailly 1779, 430 and note.
3. Bailly 1781, 286, 323.
4. Bailly 1779, 293–334 (letter of 20 April 1778).
5. For Pytheas's voyage, see Stefansson 1940.
6. See Strabo I.4.4–5; II.5.8; IV.5.5; Diodorus Siculus V.21.
7. *Germania* 2.
8. Stefansson 1940, 233.
9. Stefansson 1940, 263.
10. *Germania* 4.
11. See Goodrick-Clarke 1985, 90–122 and bibliography, 275–280.
12. Blavatsky 1888, II, 685–689.
13. Bronder 1964, 229–230; Goodrick-Clarke 1985, 97.
14. Goodrick-Clarke 1985, 55.
15. Goodrick-Clarke 1985, 127ff.
16. Mabire 1986, 336ff.
17. Goodrick-Clarke 1985, 129.
18. Goodrick-Clarke 1985, 142.
19. Goodrick-Clarke 1985, 142.
20. See Goodrick-Clarke 1985, 135–143.
21. Mabire 1986, 247.
22. Mabire 1986, 339–340.
23. See Goodrick-Clarke 1985, 145.
24. Bronder 1964, 240.
25. Goodrick-Clarke 1985, 149–151.
26. See illustration in Sokoloff 1924, fig. 21, opposite p. 81.
27. Rollin 1939, 69–71.
28. Rollin 1939, 75–76.
29. Rollin 1939, 77.
30. Rollin 1939, 72, 78.

31. For more detail, see Webb 1981, 213–344.
32. Rees 1948, 35.
33. Hieronimus 1975, 44–45.
34. Frère 1974, 97.
35. Dumas 1975, 61.
36. Brissaud 1969, 54.
37. Ley 1947, 92.
38. Pauwels & Bergier 1968, 216.
39. Pauwels & Bergier 1968, 283.
40. Walsh 1948, 32.
41. Guénon 1982, 262, 368.
42. Schwaller de Lubicz 1916, 42.
43. See especially VandenBroeck 1987, 163ff., 268f.
44. VandenBroeck 1987, 166.
45. Douglas-Hamilton 1971, 25.
46. Goodrick-Clarke 1985, 145.
47. Schwaller de Lubicz 1963, 106, citing *Cahiers du Sud*, no. 358.
48. Mariel 1964, 154, cited in Saunier 1971, 177.
49. See VandenBroeck 1987, throughout.
50. See Milosz 1985, 26.
51. Milosz 1985, 453; *La Revue Baltique*, Sept.–Oct. 1918.
52. Exegetic notes to *Les Arcanes*; see Milosz 1985, 371.
53. Wirth 1928, 55–56; Wirth 1931, 1146–1148.
54. Serrano 1984, 261–262.
55. On Rosenberg, see especially Angebert 1974, 216–224; Bronder 1964, throughout.
56. Bronder 1964, 292.
57. Rosenberg 1936, 24.
58. See Hitler 1951, 275 (11 April 1942).
59. See Mabire 1986, 249.
60. Mabire 1986, 254–255.
61. Mabire 1986, 59.
62. Quoted in Baillet 1987, 55.
63. Fabre d'Olivet 1915, 151ff.
64. See Evola 1983.
65. Evola 1951, 253–254.
66. Evola 1951, 260.
67. Evola 1951, 263.
68. Evola 1951, 272.
69. Evola 1951, 279–280.
70. Evola 1951, 281.
71. Baillet 1987, 57.
72. Baillet 1987, 58.
73. Information from Eliade's student John Patrick Deveney, New York, July 1991.
74. *The Doctrine of Awakening* and *The Metaphysics of Sex*.

CHAPTER SIX

1. Kafton-Minkel 1989, 217–242.
2. Landig 1971, note before title-page.
3. Landig 1971, 132–133.
4. Landig 1971, 158–162.
5. See Fuchs & Kölper 1958, under "Fliegende Scheibe" and "Ufo"; Mattern 1974; Harbinson 1982, 587–605.
6. Landig 1971, 114–117.
7. Landig 1971, 134, 137f., 251.
8. Landig 1971, 51, 131, 251, 472, 497, 544.
9. Landig 1971, 253–258.
10. Landig 1971, 138–139.
11. Landig 1971, 317.
12. Landig 1971, 314ff., 373.
13. Landig 1971, 319.
14. Landig 1971, 169–170.
15. Landig 1971, 374.
16. Landig 1971, 368.
17. Landig 1971, 471–472.
18. Landig 1971, 169.
19. Landig 1971, 367, 735.
20. Landig 1971, 619.
21. Landig 1971, 629.
22. Landig 1971, 630.
23. Landig 1971, 631.
24. Landig 1971, 637.
25. Landig 1971, 742, 747.
26. Landig 1971, 261, 748.
27. Landig 1971, 709.
28. See the analysis in Robin 1986, 359.
29. Parvulesco 1986, 126–140; Robin 1986, 331–362; 1989, 159–184.
30. Martin 1984, 261–266.
31. Martin 1984, 228–229.
32. Martin 1984, 314.
33. Serrano 1984, 199.
34. Serrano 1984, 146.
35. Serrano 1984, 150.
36. Serrano 1984, 196.
37. Serrano 1984, 238.
38. Serrano 1984, 196–198.
39. Serrano 1984, 265.
40. Serrano 1984, 190–191.
41. Serrano 1984, 255.
42. Serrano 1984, 239.
43. Serrano 1984, 192.
44. Serrano 1984, 198, 260.
45. Serrano 1984, 256.
46. Serrano 1984, 98.
47. Serrano 1984, 150, 260.
48. Serrano 1984, 256–257, 265.
49. Serrano 1984, 95.

50. Serrano 1984, 115.
51. Serrano 1984, 606–607.
52. Serrano 1984, 116.
53. Serrano 1984, 250.
54. Serrano 1984, 592–597.
55. Serrano 1984, 339–342.
56. Serrano 1984, 597.
57. Serrano 1984, 602.
58. Serrano 1984, 615.
59. Serrano 1984, 387.
60. Serrano 1984, 615–616.
61. Serrano 1984, 617.
62. See in Bibliography under Friedrich and Mattern.
63. Published Bogotá: Editorial Solar, 1987 or 1988.
64. Parvulesco 1986, 121.
65. See the chapter "Uomo e donna" in Evola 1951, 217–227.
66. Milosz 1985, 64.
67. Serrano 1984b, 147.
68. Mundy 1967, 320–321.
69. Parvulesco 1986, 345–346.
70. Parvulesco 1986, 137.
71. Parvulesco 1986, 206.

CHAPTER SEVEN

1. Pauwels & Bergier 1968, 282.
2. See Dumas 1975, 99; Brissaud 1969, 58–59.
3. Frère 1974, 118–120.
4. Frère 1974, 120.
5. Jacolliot 1873, 237.
6. Jacolliot 1873, 264; an abbreviated version also in Jacolliot 1901, 24–26.
7. Jacolliot 1873, 309–311.
8. Jacolliot 1873, 326–327.
9. Ghostland 1897, 258–259.
10. Ghostland 1897, 267.
11. Ghostland 1897, 265.
12. Ghostland 1897, 270.
13. See the editorial material, with photographs, in Saint-Yves 1981.
14. For further details, see Godwin 1986.
15. For publication history, etc., see Saint-Yves 1981.
16. Jean Saunier's 1981 edition is more complete.
17. Saint-Yves 1892.
18. Saint-Yves 1981, 77–78.
19. See Saint-Yves 1928, 102–121.
20. Guénon 1983, 48.
21. See Blavatsky 1877, II, 31.
22. Mani XXV/44: 482.
23. Ossendowski 1922, 314.
24. Guénon 1925, 210.
25. Guénon 1958, 9.
26. Guénon 1958, 96.
27. Laurant 1975, 136.
28. Pallis 1983.
29. For further details, see Cooke 1968, 18–22, 185–188.
30. *Bulletin des Polaires* 1 (May 1930).
31. Cooke 1968, 23.
32. Bhotiva 1929, 11.
33. Bhotiva 1929, 15.
34. Bhotiva 1929, 26.
35. Cited from Parvulesco 1986, 83.
36. Bhotiva 1929, 86.
37. Bhotiva 1929, 51.
38. Guénon in *Le Voile d'Isis*, February 1931, quoted in Guénon 1982, 447–448.
39. Bhotiva 1929, 74–75.
40. Bhotiva 1929, 85.
41. Saunier 1971, 178.
42. Girodias 1980, 260.
43. Cooke 1968, 26.
44. Cooke 1968, 38.
45. Cooke 1968, 186.
46. Cooke 1968, 39.
47. Bernadac 1978, 208.
48. See Bernadac 1978, 209–210.
49. Geyraud 1938, 65.
50. This is the theme of Bernadac 1978.
51. Rahn 1974, 34.
52. Bernadac 1978, 48.
53. Rahn 1974, 116.
54. Information from *Cahiers de la Fraternité Polaire*, n.s., 1 (March–April 1936).
55. Bernadac 1978, 206.
56. Bernadac 1978, 207.
57. This summary is taken from Allilaire 1973, various pages.
58. Titles from Dickhoff 1965, 6, 7, 21.
59. Dickhoff 1951, 36.
60. See Kafton-Minkel 1989, 182–187.
61. Dickhoff 1965, 1.
62. See Dickhoff 1965, 21.
63. Cherenzi-Lind 1948, title page.
64. Cherenzi-Lind 1948, 95.
65. See Bernard 1960.

CHAPTER EIGHT

1. Gyatso 1985, 166–167.
2. Gyatso 1985, 63.
3. Tomas 1977, 168.
4. Panchen Lama 1915, 10.
5. Panchen Lama 1915, 70–71.

6. Gyatso 1985, 60–61.
7. Gyatso 1985, 59.
8. Panchen Lama 1915, 70.
9. Tomas 1977, 168.
10. Blavatsky 1877, I, 589.
11. Blavatsky 1888, II, 319.
12. Blavatsky 1888, II, 220.
13. See Tillett 1982, 114–115.
14. Besant & Leadbeater 1913, 249–251.
15. Fuller 1988, 26.
16. Bailey 1974, 33.
17. Bailey 1974, 107.
18. Bailey 1974, 105.
19. See MacLellan 1983.
20. Angebert 1973.
21. See Roerich 1930a, 179; 1930b, 104.
22. Ravenscroft 1973, 255.
23. Roerich 1930c.
24. Roerich 1930b, 160.
25. Roerich 1930b, 111.
26. Roerich 1930a, 37; 1930b, 158–159; 1930c, 213.
27. Blavatsky 1877, I, 590.
28. Roerich 1930c, 42.
29. Roerich 1930a, 37–38; 1930b, 140; 1930c, 210–214.
30. Roerich 1930c, 217, 218.
31. Roerich 1930c, 218–222.
32. Roerich 1930a, 373; 1930b, 83–84; 1930c, 24–26, 36, 55.
33. See Wilson 1894, 799–801, for Buddhas with swastikas in both directions, also Pennick 1979.
34. See Mahatma Letters 1924, 284.
35. Roerich 1930a, 359; 1930b, 79.
36. Roerich 1930c, 28.
37. Roerich 1930b, 163.
38. Roerich 1930a, 359; 1930c, 296.
39. Roerich 1930a, 361–362.
40. Roerich 1930c, 244.
41. See Roerich 1930a, 391; 1930b, 101, 116, 122; 1930c, 11, 44; Saint-Hilaire 1930, 149.
42. Saint-Hilaire 1930, 145.
43. Roerich 1930b, 105.
44. Roerich 1930a, 343; 1930b, 144; 1930c, 22, 245; Saint-Hilaire 1930, 131–141.
45. Roerich 1930b, 144.
46. Roerich 1930c, 245.
47. Tomas 1977, 61–63.
48. Ossendowski 1922, 285.
49. Roerich 1930c, 245.
50. Roerich 1930a, 354; 1930b, 141.
51. Roerich 1930a, 352; 1930b, 143.
52. Roerich 1931, 156, 158.
53. See Kafton-Minkel 1989, 133–153.
54. See Palmer 1975, 36–41.
55. See Wentworth 1973, 119.
56. Wentworth 1973, 89, 105.
57. Agni Yoga 1980, 351.
58. See Beckley 1985, 19–20.
59. See especially Palmer 1975, 25–28.

CHAPTER NINE

1. Hieronimus 1975, 40.
2. *Sun* 9/16, 16 April 1991.
3. Kircher 1678, 171.
4. Kircher 1678, 169, 171.
5. Howell 1894, 6n. I have not found Colcott's book.
6. This summary is from de Camp and Ley 1952, 305. See also Kafton-Minkel 1989, 53–55.
7. Included in Lacassin 1990, 985–1018.
8. Cited in Lamy 1984, 194.
9. Cited in Kircher 1678, 172.
10. References from de Camp and Ley 1952, 304. On Klim, see Kafton-Minkel 1989, 254–256.
11. Cited in Lamy 1984, 194–195.
12. For further instances, see Walton 1985; Kafton-Minkel 1989, 243–273.
13. Symmes 1878, from which this biography is taken.
14. MacBride 1826, 165.
15. MacBride 1826, 162–163.
16. See Reynolds 1827.
17. See Symmes 1878, 18–19.
18. MacBride 1826, 37.
19. Matthews 1824, 8.
20. Matthews 1824, 4–6.
21. Matthews 1824, 4–11.
22. Macdonald 1969, 4.
23. Denton 1888, 139–140.
24. Denton 1873, II, 76–78.
25. Denton 1873, II, 91–92.
26. Denton 1873, II, 81–82.
27. Howell 1894, 6.
28. Symmes 1878, 67–68.
29. Gardner 1957, 23.
30. Koresh 1898, 5.
31. Koresh 1898, 13.
32. Koresh 1898, 22.
33. Koresh 1898, 24.
34. Kafton-Minkel 1989, 90–107.
35. Gardner 1957, 22–27.
36. Michell 1984, 41–56.

37. Michell 1984, 45.
38. Lyon 1971, 9.
39. Lyon 1971, 15.
40. Lyon 1971, 51.
41. Lyon 1971, 401.
42. Questions quoted from Reed 1964, 16–17. Answers summarized from ibid., 21–26.
43. Giannini 1959, 20.
44. Giannini 1959, 46–51.
45. Giannini 1959, 162.
46. Giannini 1959, 52–53.
47. Giannini 1959, 57.
48. Giannini 1959, 151.
49. Giannini 1959, 14.
50. Letter to the author from NYU Records, 9 January 1991.
51. MacLellan 1983, 149.
52. Beckley 1985, 41–42.
53. On all of these, see Kafton-Minkel 1989.
54. Sullivan 1957, 226–234.
55. Sullivan 1957, 340–344.
56. Kafton-Minkel 1989, 196.
57. See Montague 1971.

CHAPTER TEN

1. Stefansson 1924, 19.
2. Fort 1941, 732.
3. Sullivan 1957, 125–126; Friedrich 1979, 60–72, with illustrations.
4. Serrano 1984, 288.
5. McKale 1981, 62–63.
6. See Harbinson 1982, 589–605; also Kafton-Minkel 1989, 217–242.
7. Robin 1989, 231.
8. Robin 1989, 232.
9. Robin 1989, 257.
10. Robin 1989, 261.
11. Sullivan 1957, 199, 341.
12. See Mattern 1974, 98; Friedrich 1979, 106, 111, with maps.
13. Poe 1984, 199.
14. Poe 1984, 199.
15. Kirwan 1960, 69.
16. Poe 1984, 1179.
17. Verne 1911, XIV, 385.
18. Cannon 1989, 101.
19. See the analyses in Joshi 1980, 148–151; Cannon 1989, 102–105; Lévy 1988, 69–71.
20. See Burleson 1983, 85.
21. Lovecraft 1947, 158.
22. M. A. Bradshaw, "Geological History," in Hatherton 1990, 42–63.
23. Hapgood 1979, 82.
24. "Truths from humble sources," *The Occult Magazine*, I/8 (September 1885): 58.
25. Ghostland 1897, 262.
26. Ghostland 1897, 291.
27. Ghostland 1897, 293.
28. Blavatsky 1888, II, 273.
29. Blavatsky 1888, II, 274.
30. Blavatsky 1888, II, 403.
31. Saint-Yves 1981, 89–90.
32. Schwaller 1978, 67.
33. Schwaller 1977, 85.
34. See Hapgood 1979, 132.
35. Serrano 1984, 50.
36. Grant 1972, 55.
37. Grant 1972, 61.
38. Dickhoff 1951, 75–76.
39. See Kafton-Minkel 1989, 154–167; X 1969, 14–18.
40. Beckley 1985, 56. See also Godwin 1972, 177–178.
41. Dickhoff 1951, 28.
42. See Kafton-Minkel 1989, 119–132.
43. Beckley 1985, 62.
44. See unidentified newspaper report in publisher's appendices to Beckley 1985.
45. *New York Times*, 23 June 1991.

CHAPTER ELEVEN

1. See Seznec 1972, 225.
2. See Kretzulesco-Quaranta 1986, 29–45.
3. For exceptions, see Walker 1972.
4. O'Neill 1893, 486.
5. O'Neill 1893, 88.
6. O'Neill 1893, 375.
7. O'Neill 1893, 360.
8. O'Neill 1893, 395.
9. O'Neill 1893, 62.
10. O'Neill 1897, 800.
11. *Paradiso* XIII, 7–15, trans. Longfellow.
12. Wilson 1894, 768–769.
13. Evans-Wentz 1958, 251.
14. Wilson 1894, 774, with references.
15. Zadkiel 1870, 66.
16. See Godwin 1991a.
17. Blavatsky *Collected Writings*, II, 145.
18. See illustration in Pennick 1979, 6.
19. Brissaud 1969, 23–24.
20. Serrano 1984, 603.
21. Pennick 1979, 8.
22. See the hundreds of illustrations in Wilson 1894.
23. See Govinda 1969, 223; also Hastings II, 122.

24. See Govinda 1969, 223.
25. See illustration in Norbu 1986, 18.
26. On the Buddhist swastika as solar, see Wilson 1894, 800.
27. Compare the "pyramid" symbolism of Robert Fludd.
28. Guénon 1958, 105–106.
29. Guénon 1958, 107–108.
30. Matgioï 1956, 83.
31. Matgioï 1956, 83.

CHAPTER TWELVE

1. Guénon 1962, 177–183, 114–119; see also translation of the first article as "The Wild Boar and the Bear" in *Studies in Comparative Religion* I/1 (1967): 36–41.
2. Guénon 1962, 116.
3. Gleadow 1968, 169.
4. See Jennings 1870, 65ff.; Blavatsky 1877, II, 456ff.
5. Guénon 1962, 180.
6. Guénon 1962, 180–181.
7. Guénon 1962, 178.
8. Guénon 1962, 181.
9. Guénon 1962, 181.
10. Santillana & Dechend 1969, 63.
11. Santillana & Dechend 1969, 154.
12. Santillana & Dechend 1969, 340.
13. Schwabe 1951, 30–36.
14. Ezekiel 1.10.
15. Revelation 4.7.
16. Schwabe 1951, 43.
17. Schwabe 1951, 44.
18. Schwabe 1951, 31.
19. See Jung, *Collected Works* 9/II: 72–74, 149–150.
20. See Michell 1990; Michell & Rhone 1991.
21. Michell 1990, 62–63.
22. Michell 1990, 63.
23. See Guénon 1962, 19.
24. Guénon 1962, 116.
25. Govinda 1969, 224.
26. See J. Needham, "Astronomy in Ancient and Medieval China" in Hodson 1974, 67–82.
27. See Wynne-Tyson 1972, which is devoted to this subject.
28. Mead 1949, I, 95.
29. See Krupp 1979, 218.
30. Zaehner 1961, 112, quoting *Yasht* 10.50.
31. See Godwin 1981, 170, with illustration.
32. Mead 1949, I, 403–404; *Saturnalia* I, ix.
33. Mead 1949, I, 405.
34. Jackson 1985, 33.
35. See Betz 1986, I, 52, 62–64, 137–138, 299.
36. Betz 1986, I, 137 (PGM VII, 686–692).
37. See Godwin 1991b, 22.
38. Betz 1986, I, 63 (PGM IV, 1301–1307).
39. Betz 1986, 48.
40. See Jung, *Collected Works* 5: 101–102.
41. Betz 1986, 51.
42. Betz 1986, I, 51–52; see also Mead 1949, I, 176n.
43. See *Hermetica* II ("Universal Discourse of Hermes to Tat"), sect. 7.
44. On Zurvan, see Zaehner 1961, 236–247.
45. Zaehner 1961, 238.

CHAPTER THIRTEEN

1. Corbin 1978, 58.
2. Corbin 1978, 2.
3. Corbin 1980, 142.
4. Corbin 1980, 159.
5. Corbin 1978, 45.
6. Corbin 1978, 5.
7. See Corbin 1978, 6–7.
8. Corbin 1978, 46.
9. Corbin 1977, 158, 315n.; 1978, 56–57.
10. Corbin 1978, 44.
11. Corbin 1978, 42.
12. Corbin 1978, 11.
13. Corbin 1978, 43.
14. Corbin 1978, 43.
15. Corbin 1978, 78.
16. Corbin 1978, 79.
17. See Maclellan 1982, 17–18; Kafton-Minkel 1989, 30–34.
18. Corbin 1978, 58.
19. Corbin 1978, 11.
20. Corbin 1978, 40.
21. Corbin 1971, II, 73–74.
22. Corbin 1971, II, 72n.
23. Corbin 1980, 249.
24. Corbin 1971, II, 69.
25. Corbin 1978, 8.
26. For an unusual view of the Axis' activities, see Noone 1986, 269–277.
27. Corbin 1978, 52 and 149n.
28. See Corbin 1978, 56–57, 149n.
29. Hastings, XII, 77.
30. Hastings, III, 11.
31. Hastings, XII, 84.
32. Corbin 1978, 50.
33. Nasr 1978, 35.
34. *Purgatorio* XXX, 1.
35. *Purgatorio* XXX, 32; XXXI, 82, 116.

36. Burckhardt 1987; cited from *Avaloka* I/2 (1987): 11.
37. *Purgatorio* XXV, 130–132.
38. *Paradiso* XXXI, 31–34.
39. On "Aryan" sexuality, see Serrano 1984, 559.
40. Lamy 1984, 218.
41. Cited from Lamy 1984, 225.
42. Lamy 1984, 225–226.
43. Parvulesco 1986, 82ff.

CHAPTER FOURTEEN

1. Cited in Whiston 1978, 95, but not in the extant *Fragments of Empedocles*.
2. Diogenes Laertius IX, 33, Dicks 1970, 80, 83.
3. Diels-Krantz A96; Dicks 1970, 83.
4. Diogenes Laertius II, 9 (trans. R. D. Hicks, Loeb edition).
5. Dicks 1970, 88, 157.
6. *Statesman* 269a, b.
7. *Statesman* 272e–273a.
8. Herodotus ii, 142, trans. A. D. Godley.
9. Daniélo III, 392–394.
10. Burnet 1965, 192–193 (Book II, ch. 8).
11. Burnet 1965, 64–66.
12. Burnet 1965, 147.
13. Whiston 1978, Preface, 91.
14. Whiston 1978, 53.
15. Whiston 1978, 79, 96.
16. Whiston 1978, 96–99.
17. Whiston 1978, 123, 127.
18. Rousseau 1821, XIII, 180–181.
19. Fabre d'Olivet 1915, 348.
20. Fabre d'Olivet 1915, 348–349.
21. Fabre d'Olivet 1915, 30–31.
22. Saint-Yves d'Alveydre 1928, 60–61.
23. Huggett 1989.
24. This account is drawn from Michel 1897.
25. See Papus 1897, 238ff.
26. Summary from Warren 1885, 75.
27. Donnelly 1887, 58.
28. See Michell 1984, 136–143.
29. Velikovsky 1955, especially 113–129, 361.
30. See Totten 1968.
31. Carl Sagan, "An Analysis of *Worlds in Collision*" in Goldsmith 1977, 41–104.
32. Goldsmith 1977, 100.
33. Goldsmith 1977, 64–65.
34. Velikovsky 1955, 123.
35. See summary in Bellamy 1936, 26.
36. Bellamy 1936, 35–36.
37. See Saurat 1957.
38. Bellamy 1936, 232, 279.
39. Charroux 1963, 140–142.
40. *Atlantis past and to come* 1978, 18.

CHAPTER FIFTEEN

1. See Thorndike V, 234–235.
2. See *Biographie Universelle* XXV, 285, under "Louville."
3. On Pytheas' voyage, see Stefansson 1940, 2–24; Singer 1959, 58.
4. See Voltaire 1785, XXXI, 375ff.
5. Bailly 1781, 255–256, 333, 406.
6. Theon 1979, 98–99.
7. Voltaire 1785, XXXI, 380.
8. Voltaire 1785, 381.
9. Voltaire 1785, 380–381n.
10. Fourier 1967, 94.
11. Fourier 1967, 100–101.
12. Fourier 1967, 98–99.
13. Fourier 1967, 98n.
14. For the two versions of the chart, see Fourier 1967, 94–95 and 338–339.
15. The best source on Mackey is in Blavatsky *Collected Writings* XIV, 545–549.
16. Second Edition, Bk. III, Prop. XXXIX, Prob. XX; see Newton 1934, 489–491; for further explanation, see Cohen 1971, 197.
17. Mackey 1973, I, 18, 38ff.
18. Mackey 1973, III, 74.
19. Mackey 1973, I, i.
20. Pseudonym for Sir Richard Phillips, a popular science writer.
21. Mackey 1973, I, ii.
22. Mackey 1973, III, 138.
23. Mackey 1826, 111.
24. Blavatsky 1888, II, 362n.
25. See Godwin 1991a, part 4.
26. See "La clef hermétique," (in English) in Burgoyne 1969, I, 86–102.
27. Burgoyne 1969, I, 92.
28. *Occult Magazine* II/15–23 (1886).
29. *Occult Magazine* II/15 (April 1886):25n.
30. Williams 1981.
31. Williams 1981, 347.
32. Williams 1981, 351.
33. Williams 1981, 353.
34. Williams 1981, 334.

CHAPTER SIXTEEN

1. See Guénon 1982, 36.
2. Randolph 1888, 116.
3. Randolph 1888, 116–117.
4. Randolph 1888, 134–135.

5. Randolph 1888, 135–7.
6. See Barley 1922; Huggett 1989, 141–145.
7. Blavatsky 1877, I, 30–31.
8. Blavatsky 1877, I, 30–31.
9. Blavatsky 1888, II, 330.
10. Blavatsky 1888, II, 330.
13. Blavatsky 1888, II, 329; emphases omitted.
14. Blavatsky 1888, I, 369.
15. Blavatsky 1888, II, 329.
16. Blavatsky 1888, II, 329.
17. Blavatsky 1888, II, 776.
18. Blavatsky 1888, II, 324–325; parentheses original, emphases omitted.
19. Blavatsky 1888, II, 357–358.
20. Blavatsky 1888, II, 292.
21. Blavatsky 1888, II, 772.
22. Blavatsky 1888, II, 314.
23. Blavatsky 1888, II, 356.
24. Blavatsky 1888, II, 353.
25. Blavatsky 1888, II, 433.
26. Blavatsky 1888, II, 433.
27. Blavatsky 1888, II, 353.
28. Blavatsky 1888, II, 436.
29. Blavatsky 1888, II, 331.
30. Blavatsky 1888, II, 785.
31. Blavatsky 1888, II, 786.
32. Blavatsky 1888, II, 432, 436.
33. Blavatsky 1888, II, 331.
34. See Godwin 1989 for a chronicle of these events.
35. Papus 1897, 237–238.
36. Papus 1954, 133.
37. See Papus 1897, 242, 366, for confirmations of these dates.
38. Letter of Saint-Yves d' Alveydre to Papus, dated 28 January 1897; MS. in Fonds Papus of the Bibliothèque Municipal, Lyon.
39. Saint-Yves 1928, 60.

CHAPTER SEVENTEEN
1. Newton 1934, 188–189 (Sect. 1, Prop. 66, Theo. 26, Cor. 22).
2. Klee 1847, 83.
3. Klee 1847, 85.
4. Klee 1847, 70–75n.
5. Klee 1847, 119.
6. Lubbock 1848; see Huggett 1989, 118–20.
7. On Darwin and Kelvin, see Munk 1960.
8. For the following account, see Barrell 1914.
9. See Ley 1969, 86–87.
10. Wegener 1929, 159, cited in Huggett 1989, 122.
11. See White 1980, 65–87, for a summary of Brown's theories.
12. Hapgood 1958, 56.
13. See White 1980, 99.
14. Gold 1955, 528.
15. Gold 1955, 528–529.
16. Munk & MacDonald 1960.
17. Munk 1960, 551.
18. See Tarling 1983 for an introduction to the field, its history, and for cautions against premature conclusions (pp. 265ff).
19. Goldreich & Toomre 1969, 2563.
20. Jurdy 1981.
21. Tarling 1983, 284.
22. Andrews 1985, 7746.
23. Tarling 1983, 295.
24. See Donn 1989.

CHAPTER EIGHTEEN
1. Martin 1984, 244.
2. Martin 1984, 243.
3. Figures from Broecker & Denton 1990, 49; *Facts on File*.
4. Hays et al. 1976, 1121.
5. Munk & McDonald 1960, 7.
6. Broecker & Denton 1990, 56.
7. White 1980, 386.
8. White 1989, 21.
9. White 1989.
10. White 1989, 42.
11. White 1989, 20.
12. Reprinted Virginia Beach: A. R. E. Press.
13. Cayce reading no. 3976–15, 19 January 1934, cited from Cayce 1980, 87.
14. See Cayce 1980, 60–63, 69.
15. Cayce 1980, 62.
16. Reading no. 5748–6, 1 July 1932; cited from Cayce 1980, 84.
17. Neal & Karagulla, 1983, 267–268.
18. Goodman 1978, 149–176.
19. Noone 1986, 329–331.

Bibliography

Agni Yoga. 1929. 1980. New York: Agni Yoga Society. (1st ed. 1952)

Allilaire, Jean François. 1973. *Etude d'un délire d'imagination dans ses rapports avec la question de déterminisme en psychopathologie.* M.D. Thesis, University of Paris VI (Pitié-Salpetrière).

Andrews, Jean A. 1985. "True polar wander. An analysis of Cenozoic and Mesozoic paleomagnetic poles." *Journal of Geophysical Research* 90: 7737–7750.

Angebert, Jean. 1973. "Le Agartha et les mondes souterrains." *Conférences des Lundis de l'Institut d'Herméneutique* 36 (14 May): 1–20.

Angebert, Jean-Michel [Michel Bertrand and Jean Angelini]. 1974. *The Occult and the Third Reich.* New York: McGraw Hill. (1st ed. 1971)

Atlantis past and to come. An examination from legendary, historical, scientific and psychic sources. 1978. Third Series. Cheltenham: Atlanteans Association.

Bailey, Alice A. 1974. *Initiation, Human and Solar.* New York: Lucis Publishing Co. (1st ed. 1922)

Baillet, Philippe. 1987. "Les rapports de Julius Evola avec le fascisme et le national-socialisme." *Politica Hermetica* 1, 49–71.

Bailly, Jean-Sylvain. 1779. *Lettres sur l'Atlantide de Platon et sur l'ancienne histoire de l'Asie.* London: M. Elmesly.

Bailly, Jean-Sylvain. 1781. *Histoire de l'astronomie ancienne depuis son origine jusqu'à l'établissement de l'école d'Alexandrie.* Paris: De Bure. (1st ed. 1775)

Barley, Alfred H. 1922. *The Drayson Problem. His important astronomical discovery.* Exeter: William Pollard.

Barrell, Joseph. 1914. "The Status of hypotheses of polar wanderings." *Science* n.s. 40: 333–340.

Beckley, Timothy Green. 1985. *The Shaver Mystery and the Inner Earth.* Mokelumne Hill: Health Resarch. (1st ed. 1967)

Bellamy, H. S. 1936. *Moon, Myths and Man. A Reinterpretation.* London: Faber & Faber.

Bennett, J. G. 1965. *Long Pilgrimage. The Life and Teachings of Sri Govindananda Bharati, known as the Shivapuri Baba.* London: Hodder & Stoughton.

Berger, A. et al. 1982. *Milankovitch and Climate.* Dordrecht: D. Reidel.

Bernard, Raymond. 1960. *Agharta, the Subterranean World.* Mokelumne Hill: Health Research.

Bernard, Raymond. 1969. *The Hollow Earth. The Greatest Geographical Discovery in History, Made by Admiral Richard E. Byrd in the Mysterious Land Beyond the Poles—The True Origin of the Flying Saucers.* New York: University Books. (1st ed. 1964)

Bernardac, Christian. 1978. *Le mystère Otto Rahn: du catharisme au nazisme.* Paris: Eds. France Empire.

Besant, Annie, and C. W. Leadbeater. 1913. *Man: Whence, How and Whither. A Record of Clairvoyant Investigation.* Adyar: Theosophical Publishing House.

Betz, Hans Dieter, ed. 1986. *The Greek Magical Papyri in Translation, including the Demotic Spells.* Chicago: University of Chicago Press.

Bhotiva, Zam [Cesare Accomani]. 1929. *Asia Mysteriosa.* Paris: Dorbon Ainé.

Biographie Universelle. 1811–28. Paris: L. G. Michaud.

Blavatsky, H. P. 1950–1991. *Collected Writings.* Ed. Boris de Zirkoff. 15 vols. Wheaton: Theosophical Publishing House.

Blavatsky, H. P. 1877. *Isis Unveiled.* 2 vols. New York: Bouton. (Facsimile reprint, Los Angeles: Theosophy Co., 1931.)

Blavatsky, H. P. 1888. *The Secret Doctrine.* 2 vols. London: Theosophical Publishing Co. (Facsimile reprint, Los Angeles: Theosophy Co., 1982.)

Bradshaw, M. A. 1990. "Geological history." In *Antarctica: the Ross Sea region.* Ed. Trevor Hatherton. Wellington, NZ: DSIR Publishing, 42–63.

Brissaud, André. 1969. *Hitler et l'Ordre Noir: Histoire secrète du national-socialisme.* Paris: Perrin.

Broecker, Wallace S., and George H. Denton. 1990. "What drives glacial cycles?" *Scientific American* 262/1: 49–56.

Bronder, Dietrich. 1964. *Bevor Hitler kam. Eine historische Studie.* Hannover: Hans Pfeiffer Verlag.

Buffon, Georges-Louis Leclerc, Comte de. 1939. *Morceaux choisis.* Ed. A.-M. Petitjean. Paris: Gallimard.

Burckhardt, Titus. 1987. *Mirror of the Intellect: Essays on Traditional Science and Sacred Art.* Trans. William Stoddart. Cambridge: Quintessentia.

Burgoyne, Thomas A. 1969. *The Light of Egypt, or The Science of the Soul and the Stars.* Portland, OR: Green Dolphin Bookshop. (1st ed. 1889)

Burleson, Donald R. 1983. *H. P. Lovecraft: A Critical Study.* Westport: Greenwood Press.

Burnet, Thomas. 1965. *Sacred Theory of the Earth.* Carbondale: Southern Illinois University Press. (1st ed. 1681)

Cannon, Peter. 1989. *H. P. Lovecraft.* Boston: Twayne Publishers.

Cayce, Hugh Lynn. 1980. *Earth Changes Update.* Virginia Beach: A. R. E. Press.

Charroux, Robert. 1963. *Histoire inconnue des hommes depuis cent mille ans.* Paris: Robert Laffont.

Cherenzi-Lind, Om. 1948. *Tourmente et Terreur sur le Monde.* Montrouge: Editions de l'Aghartha.

Cooke, Ivan. 1968. *The Return of Arthur Conan Doyle.* Liss: White Eagle.

Corbin, Henry. 1971. *En Islam Iranien. Aspects spirituels et philosophiques.* Vol. 2, *Sohravardî et les Platoniciens de Perse.* Paris: Gallimard.

Corbin, Henry. 1977. *Spiritual Body and Celestial Earth from Mazdean Iran to Shi'ite Iran.*

Trans. Nancy Pearson. Princeton: Princeton University Press. (1st ed. 1960)

Corbin, Henry. 1978. *The Man of Light in Iranian Sufism.* Trans. Nancy Pearson. Boulder: Shambhala. (1st ed. 1971)

Corbin, Henry. 1980. *Avicenna and the Visionary Recital.* Trans. Willard R. Trask. Dallas: Spring Publications. (1st ed. 1954)

Danielo, J.-F. 1840. *Histoire et Tableau de l'Univers*, Vol. 3. Paris: Gaume Frères.

de Camp, L. Sprague, and Willy Ley. 1952. *Lands Beyond.* New York: Reinhart & Co.

Denton, William, 1873. *The Soul of Things; or, Psychometric Researches and Discoveries.* Vols. 2, 3. Wellesley: Mrs. E. M. F. Denton.

Denton, William and Elizabeth M. F. 1888. *The Soul of Things; or, Psychometric Researches and Discoveries.* Vol. 1. Wellesley: Denton Publishing Co. (1st ed. 1863)

Dickhoff, Robert Ernst. 1951. *Agharta.* Boston: Bruce Humphries.

Dickhoff, Robert Ernst. 1965. *The Eternal Fountain. A Kaleidoscope of Divine Inspired Thought Sparks.* Mokelumne Hill: Health Research. (1st ed. 1960)

Dicks, D. R. 1970. *Early Greek Astronomy to Aristotle.* Ithaca: Cornell University Press.

Donn, W. L. 1989. "Paleoclimate and polar wander." *Palaeogeography* 71: 225–236.

Donnelly, Ignatius. 1887. *Ragnarok: The Age of Fire and Gravel.* New York: D. Appleton. (1st ed. 1882)

Douglas-Hamilton, Lord James. 1971. *Motive for a mission: the story behind Hess's flight to Britain.* London: Macmillan.

Dumas, François Ribadeau. 1975. *Hitler et la Sorcellerie.* Paris: Plon.

Evans-Wentz, W. Y. 1958. *Tibetan Yoga and Secret Doctrines.* London: Oxford University Press. (1st ed. 1935)

Evola, Julius. 1951. *Rivolta contro il mondo moderno.* rev. ed. Milan: Fratelli Bocca. (1st ed. 1934)

Evola, Julius. 1983. *The Metaphysics of Sex.* New York: Inner Traditions International. (1st ed. 1969)

Fabre d'Olivet, Antoine. 1915. *Hermeneutic Interpretation of the Origin of the Social State of Man.* Trans. Nayán Louise Redfield. New York: Putnam's Sons. (1st ed. 1822; also titled *Histoire philosophique du genre humain*)

Fort, Charles. 1941. *The Books of Charles Fort.* New York: Henry Holt.

Fourier, Charles. 1967. *Théorie des quatre mouvements et des déstinées générales.* Ed. Simone Debout. Paris: Pauvert. (1st ed. 1808)

Frère, Jean Claude. 1974. *Nazisme et sociétés secrètes.* Paris: Culture, Arts, Loisirs.

Friedrich, Christof. 1979. *Germany's Antarctic Claim: Secret Nazi Polar Expeditions.* Toronto: Samisdat Publishers Ltd.

Fuchs, K. H., and F. W. Kölper. 1958. *Militärisches Taschenlexikon.* Bonn: Athenäum Verlag.

Fuller, Jean Overton. 1988. *Blavatsky and her teachers. An investigative biography.* London: East-West Publications.

Gardner, Martin. 1957. *Fads and Fallacies in the Name of Science.* New York: Dover. (1st ed. 1952)

Geyraud, Pierre [Raoul Guyader]. 1938. *Les sociétés secrètes de Paris.* Paris: Emile Paul Frères.

[Ghostland]. 1897. *Ghostland.* Chicago: Progressive Thinker. (1st ed. 1876)

Giannini, Amadeo. 1959. *Worlds Beyond the Pole*. New York: Vantage.

Girodias, Maurice. 1980. *The Frog Prince. An Autobiography*. New York: Crown Publishers. (1st ed. 1977)

Gleadow, Rupert. 1968. *The Origin of the Zodiac*. London: Jonathon Cape.

Godwin, John. 1972. *Occult America*. New York: Doubleday.

Godwin, Joscelyn. 1981. *Mystery Religions in the Ancient World*. London: Thames & Hudson.

Godwin, Joscelyn. 1986. "Saint-Yves d'Alveydre and the Agarthian Connection." *Hermetic Journal* 32:24–34; 33:31–38.

Godwin, Joscelyn. 1989. *The Beginnings of Theosophy in France*. London: Theosophical History Centre.

Godwin, Joscelyn. 1991a. "The Hidden Hand." *Theosophical History* n.s. 3/2–5.

Godwin, Joscelyn. 1991b. *The Mystery of the Seven Vowels: In Theory and Practice*. Grand Rapids: Phanes Press.

Gold, Thomas. 1955. "Instability of the Earth's axis of rotation." *Nature* 175: 526–529.

Goldreich, Peter, and Alar Toomre. 1969. "Some remarks on polar wandering." *Journal of Geophysical Research* 74: 2555–2567.

Goldsmith, Donald, ed. 1977. *Scientists Confront Velikovsky*. Ithaca: Cornell University Press.

Goodman, Jeffrey. 1978. *We are the Earthquake Generation. Where and When the Catastrophes Will Strike*. New York: Seaview Books.

Goodrick-Clarke, Nicholas. 1985. *The Occult Roots of Nazism. The Ariosophists of Austria and Germany 1890–1935*. Wellingborough: Aquarian Press.

Govinda, Lama Anagarika. 1969. *The Way of the White Clouds: a Buddhist Pilgrim in Tibet*. London: Hutchinson. (1st ed. 1966)

Grant, Kenneth. 1972. *The Magical Revival*. London: Frederick Muller.

Guénon, René. 1925. "Le Roi du Monde." *Les Cahiers du Mois* 9/10: *Les Appels de l'Orient*. Paris: Emile Paul Frères.

Guénon, René. 1953a. *L'Erreur spirite*. Paris: Editions Traditionnelles. (1st ed. 1923)

Guénon, René. 1953b. *The Reign of Quantity and the Signs of the Times*. Trans. Lord Northbourne. London: Luzac. (1st ed. 1945)

Guénon, René. 1957. *La Grande Triade*. Paris: Gallimard. (1st ed. 1946)

Guénon, René. 1958. *Symbolism of the Cross*. Trans. Angus Macnab. London: Luzac. (1st ed. 1931)

Guénon, René. 1962. *Symboles fondamentaux de la science sacrée*. Paris: Gallimard.

Guénon, René. 1970. *Formes traditionnelles et cycles cosmiques*. Paris: Gallimard.

Guénon, René. 1982. *Le Théosophisme, Histoire d'une pseudo-religion*. enl. ed. Paris: Editions Traditionnelles. (1st ed. 1921)

Guénon, René. 1983. *The Lord of the World*. Trans. Anthony Cheke et al. Ellingstring: Coombe Springs Press. (1st ed. 1927)

Gyatso, Tenzin [Dalai Lama XIV]. 1985. *The Kalachakra Tantra*. Trans. Jeffrey Hopkins. London: Wisdom Publications.

Hapgood, Charles H. 1958. *Earth's Shifting Crust*. New York: Pantheon.

Hapgood, Charles H. 1970. *The Path of the Pole*. New York: Chilton Book Co.

Hapgood, Charles H. 1979. *Maps of the Ancient Sea Kings. Evidence of Advanced Civilization in the Ice Age*. rev. ed. London: Turnstone Books. (1st ed. 1966)

Harbinson, W. A. 1982. *Genesis*. New York: Dell Publishing. (1st ed. 1980)

Hastings, James. 1908–1926. *Encyclopaedia of Religion and Ethics*. 13 vols. Edinburgh: T. & T. Clark.

Hatherton, Trevor, ed. 1990. *Antarctica: the Ross Sea Region*. Wellington, NZ: Dept. of Scientific and Industrial Research.

Hays, J. D., J. Imbrie, and N. J. Shackleton. 1976. "Variations in the earth's orbit: pacemaker of the Ice Ages." *Science* 194:1121–1132.

Herder, Gottfried von. n.d. *Ideen zur Philosophie der Geschichte der Menschheit*. In *Deutsche National-Litteratur*, vol. 77. Stuttgart: Union Deutsche Verlagsgesellschaft. (1st ed. 1785)

Hesiod. 1959. *Works and Days*. Trans. R. Lattimore. Ann Arbor: University of Michigan Press, 1957.

Hieronimus, Ekkehard. 1975. *Der Traum von den Urkulturen. Vorgeschichte als Sinngebung der Gegenwart?* Munich: Carl Friedrich von Siemens Stiftung.

Hitler 1951. *Hitlers Tischgespräche im Führerhauptquartier 1941–42*. Ed. Gerhard Ritter. Bonn: Athanäum-Verlag.

Hodson, F. R., ed. 1974. *The Place of Astronomy in the Ancient World*. London: Oxford University Press.

[Howell, H. M.?]. 1894. *The Kosmic Problem solved, and Paradise found*. New York: Mount Hope Publishing. Co.

Huggett, Richard. 1989. *Cataclysms and Earth History. The Development of Diluvianism*. Oxford: Oxford University Press.

Jackson, Howard. 1985. "The Leontocephaline in Roman Mithraism." *Numen* 32/1 (1985): 17–45.

Jacolliot, Louis. 1873. *Le Fils de Dieu*. Paris: Lacroix.

Jennings, Hargrave. 1870. *The Rosicrucians, their Rites and Mysteries*. London: J. C. Hotten.

Johnson, Paul, 1990. *The Masks of the Masters. Beyond the Occult Myth*. South Boston: the Author.

Joshi, S. T., ed. 1980. *H. P. Lovecraft: Four Decades of Criticism*. Athens, OH: Ohio University Press.

Jung, Carl Gustav. 1956–1974. *Collected Works*. Trans. R. F. C. Hull. 18 vols. New York: Bollingen Foundation.

Jurdy, Donna M. 1981. "True polar wander." *Tectonophysics* 74: 1–16.

Kafton-Minkel, Walter. 1989. *Subterranean Worlds: 100,000 years of dragons, dwarfs, the dead, lost races & UFOs from inside the earth*. Port Townsend: Loompanics Unlimited.

Kircher, Athanasius. 1678. *Mundus Subterraneus*. Amsterdam: Jansson van Waesberghe. (1st ed. 1665)

Kirwan, Laurence P. 1962. *A History of Polar Exploration*. Harmondsworth: Penguin Books.

Klee, Frédérik. 1847. *Le déluge, considérations géologiques et historiques sur les derniers cataclysmes du globe*. Paris: Masson & Charpentier. (1st ed. 1842)

Koresh. 1898. *The Cellular Cosmogony, or The Earth a Concave Sphere*. Chicago: Guiding Star Publishing Co.

Kretzulesco-Quaranta, Emanuela. 1986. *Les Jardins du songe. "Poliphile" et la Mystique de la Renaissance*. 2nd rev. ed. Paris: "Les Belles Lettres." (1st ed. 1976)

Krupp, E. C., ed. 1979. *In Search of Ancient Astronomies.* New York: McGraw Hill. (1st ed. 1978)

Lacassin, Francis. 1990. *Voyages aux pays de nulle part.* Paris: Robert Laffont. (Includes *Le Passage du pôle arctique au pôle antarctique par le centre du monde*, 1st ed. 1721)

Lamy, Michel. 1984. *Jules Verne, initié et initiateur. La clé du secret de Rennes-le-Château et le trésor des Rois de France.* Paris: Payot.

Landig, Wilhelm. 1971. *Götzen gegen Thule. Ein Roman voller Wirklichkeiten.* Hannover: Hans Pfeiffer Verlag.

Laurant, Jean-Pierre. 1975. *Le Sens caché selon René Guénon.* Paris: L'Age d'Homme.

Lévy, Maurice. 1988. *Lovecraft: A Study in the Fantastic.* Trans. S. T. Joshi. Detroit: Wayne State University Press.

Ley, Willy. 1947. "Pseudoscience in Naziland." *Astounding Science Fiction* 39/3 (May): 90–98.

Ley, Willy. 1969. *The Drifting Continents.* New York: Weybright & Talley.

Lovecraft, H. P. 1947. *Cry Horror!* New York: Avon Books.

Lubbock, John. 1848. "On changes of climate resulting from a change in the Earth's axis of rotation." *Quarterly Journal of the Geological Society of London* 4: 4–7.

Lyon, William F. 1971. *The Hollow Globe; or The World's Agitator and Reconciler.* Mokelumne Hill: Health Research. (1st ed. 1871)

Mabire, Jean. 1986. *Thulé. Le soleil retrouvé des Hyperboréens.* Paris: Editions du Trident. (1st ed. 1978)

[MacBride, J.?]. 1826. *Symmes' Theory of concentric spheres... by a citizen of the United States.* Cincinnati: Mongan, Lodge & Fisher.

MacDonald, Edwin A. 1969. *Polar operations.* Annapolis: U. S. Navy Institute.

Mackey, Sampson Arnold. 1826. *The Mythological Astronomy in Three Parts.* London: Hunt & Clarke. (Different contents from the 1822 book of similar title.)

Mackey, Sampson Arnold. 1973. *The Mythological Astronomy of the Ancients Demonstrated.* Minneapolis: Wizards Bookshelf. (1st ed. 1822)

Maclellan, Alec. 1983. *The Lost World of Agharti. The Mystery of Vril Power.* London: Corgi Books. (1st ed. 1982)

Mahatma Letters. *The Mahatma Letters to A. P. Sinnett.* Ed. Trevor Barker. New York: Frederick Stokes, 1924.

Man. 1885. *Man: Fragments of Forgotten History.* By Two Chelas of the Theosophical Society [Mohini M. Chatterji and Laura Holloway]. London: Reeves & Turner.

Mani, Le Swâmî Narad. "Baptême de Lumière. Notes pour servir à l'Histoire de la Société dite Théosophique." *La France Antimaçonnique* 25/43, 44, 49, 50; 26/2, 9 (1911–1912).

Mariel, Pierre. 1964. *L'Europe païenne du XXe siècle.* Paris: La Palatine.

Martin, R. P. 1984. *Le Renversement, ou La Boucane contre l'Ordre Noir.* Paris: Guy Trédaniel.

Matgioï [Albert de Pouvourville]. 1956. *La Voie métaphysique.* Paris: Eds. Traditionnelles. (1st ed. n.d.)

Mattern, Friedrich. 1974. *UFOs, Nazi Secret Weapon?* Toronto: Samisdat Publishers Ltd.

Matthews, Thomas J. 1824. *A Lecture on Symmes's theory of concentric spheres.* Cincinnati: A. N. Deming.

McKale, Donald M. 1981. *Hitler: the Survival Myth*. New York: Stein & Day.

Mead, G. R. S. 1949. *Thrice-Greatest Hermes. Studies in Hellenistic Theosophy and Gnosis*. 3 vols. London: John M. Watkins. (1st ed. 1906)

Michel, Louis. 1897. "Louis Michel de Figanières." *L'Initiation* 36/10: 50–60.

Michell, John. 1984. *Eccentric Lives and Peculiar Notions*. London: Thames & Hudson.

Michell, John. 1990. *New Light on the Ancient Mystery of Glastonbury*. Glastonbury: Gothic Image Publications.

Michell, John, and Christine Rhone. 1991. *Twelve-Tribe Nations and the Science of Enchanting the Landscape*. Grand Rapids: Phanes Press.

Milosz. 1985. *The Noble Traveller. The Life and Writings of O. V. de L. Milosz*. Ed. Christopher Bamford. West Stockbridge: Lindisfarne Press.

Montague, Richard. 1971. *Oceans, Poles and Airmen*. New York: Random House.

Morris, Charles. 1888. *The Aryan Race. Its Origin and its Achievements*. Chicago: S. C. Griggs.

Müller, Max. 1881. *Chips from a German Workshop*. 4 vols. London: Longmans.

Mundy, Talbot. 1967. *Om*. New York: Ballantyne. (1st ed. 1924)

Munk, W. H., and G. J. F. MacDonald. 1960. *The Rotation of the Earth*. Cambridge: Cambridge University Press.

Nasr, Seyyed Hossein. 1978. *An Introduction to Islamic Cosmological Doctrines*. Boulder: Shambhala. (1st ed. 1964)

Neal, Viola Petitt, and Shafica Karagulla. 1983. *Through the Curtain*. Marina del Rey: DeVorss & Co.

Negus, Michael. 1969. "Man, Creation and the Fossil Record." *Studies in Comparative Religion* 3/1: 49–55.

Neuville, Pierre. 1976. *Les Dessous ténébreux de l'histoire*. Paris: Albin Michel.

Newton, Isaac. 1934. *Mathematical Principles of Natural Philosophy and his System of the World*. Trans. A. Motte. Berkeley: University of California Press. (From the 2nd ed. of 1729)

Noone, Richard W. 1986. *5/5/2000: Ice, the Ultimate Disaster*. New York: Harmony Books.

Norbu, Namkai. 1986. *The Crystal and the Way of Light. Sutra, Tantra and Dzogchen*. New York: Routledge & Kegan Paul.

O'Neill, John. 1893, 1897. *The Night of the Gods. An Inquiry into Cosmic and Cosmogonic Mythology and Symbolism*. 2 vols. London: B. Quaritch.

Ossendowski, Ferdinand. 1922. *Beasts, Men and Gods*. New York: Dutton.

Ovid. 1955. *Metamorphoses*. Trans. Mary Innes. New York: Viking Penguin.

Pallis, Marco. 1983. "Ossendowski's Sources." *Studies in Comparative Religion* 15/1–2: 30–41.

Palmer, Ray. 1975. *The Secret World*. Vol. 1, *The Diary Of A Lifetime Of Questioning The "Facts."* Amherst, WI: Amherst Press.

Panchen Lama III. 1915. *Der Weg nach Sambhala*. Trans. Albert Grünwedel. Munich: Verlag der Königlich Bayerischen Akademie der Wissenschaften.

Papus. 1897. *Traité élémentaire de science occulte*. 7th ed. Facsimile reprint. Paris: Dangles.

Papus. 1954. *Traité élémentaire d'occultisme*. rev. and enl. ed. Paris: La Diffusion Scientifique.

Parvulesco, Jean. 1986. *La spirale prophétique*. Paris: Guy Trédaniel.

Parvulesco, Jean. 1989. *Les mystères de la villa "Atlantis."* Paris: Guy Trédaniel.

Pauwels, Louis, and Jacques Bergier. 1968. *The Dawn of Magic.* Trans. Rollo Myers. New York: Avon Books. (1st ed. 1960)

Pennick, Nigel. 1979. *The Swastika.* Cambridge: Fenris-Wolf.

Phaure, Jean. 1988. *Le Cycle de l'humanité adamique. Introduction à l'étude de la cyclologie traditionnelle et de la fin des Temps.* rev. ed. Paris: Dervy-Livres. (1st ed. 1973)

Plato. 1957. *Statesman.* Trans. J. B. Skemp. New York: Macmillian.

Poe, Edgar Allen. 1984. *Poetry and Tales.* Ed. Patrick F. Quinn. New York: The Library of America.

Poliakov, Léon. 1974. *The Aryan Myth. A History of Racist and Nationalist Ideas in Europe.* Trans. E. Howard. New York: Basic Books. (1st ed. 1971)

Rahn, Otto. 1974. *La Cour de Lucifer dans l'Europe.* Paris: Claude Tchou. (1st ed. 1937)

Randolph, Paschal Beverley. 1888. *Pre-Adamite Man.* 6th ed. Toledo, OH: Randolph Publishing Co. (1st ed. 1862)

Ravenscroft, Trevor. 1973. *The Spear of Destiny. The Occult Power behind the Spear that Pierced the Side of Christ.* New York: Putnam's Sons.

Reed, William. 1964. *The Phantom of the Poles.* Mokelumne Hill: Health Research. (1st ed. 1906)

Rees, John Rawlings. 1948. *The Case of Rudolf Hess.* New York: Norton.

Renan, Ernest. n.d. *Dialogues et fragments philosophiques.* 6th ed. Paris: Calmann-Levy.

Rendall, Gerald H. 1889. *The Cradle of the Aryans.* London: Macmillan.

[Reynolds, Jeremiah N.?]. 1827. *Remarks on a review of Symmes' theory.* Washington DC: Gales & Seaton.

Rhys, John. 1888. *Lectures on the Origin and Growth of Religion as illustrated by Celtic Heathendom.* London: Williams & Norgate.

Robin, Jean. 1982. *Rennes-le-Château, la Colline envoûtée.* Paris: Guy Trédaniel.

Robin, Jean. 1986. *Les Sociétés secrètes au rendez-vous de l'apocalypse.* Paris: Guy Trédaniel.

Robin, Jean. 1989. *Opération Orth, ou L'incroyable secret de Rennes-le-Château.* Paris: Guy Trédaniel.

Roerich, George. 1931. *Trails to inmost Asia. Five years of exploration with the Roerich Central Asian Expedition.* New Haven: Yale University Press.

Roerich, Nicholas. 1930a. *Altai-Himalaya. A Travel Diary.* London: Harrolds.

Roerich, Nicholas. 1930b. *The Heart of Asia.* New York: Roerich Museum.

Roerich, Nicholas. 1930c. *Shambhala.* New York: Frederick Stokes.

Rollin, Henri. 1939. *L'Apocalypse de notre temps. Les dessous de la propagande allemande d'après des documents inédits.* Paris: Gallimard.

Rosenberg, Alfred. 1936. *Der Mythus der 20. Jahrhunderts.* Munich: Hoheneichen Verlag. (1st ed. 1930).

Rousseau, Jean-Jacques. 1821. *Oeuvres.* Vol. 13, *Ecrits sur la musique.* Paris: Lequien.

Saint-Hilaire, Josephine. 1930. *On Eastern Crossroads; legends and prophecies of Asia.* New York: Frederick Stokes.

Saint-Yves d'Alveydre. 1892. *The Poem of the Queen Victoria, Translated into English Verse from Le Poème de la Reine.* Trans. the Earl of Lytton. Paris: A. Lahure.

Saint-Yves d'Alveydre. 1928. *Mission des Juifs.* 2nd ed. Paris: Dorbon Ainé. (1st ed. 1884)

Saint-Yves d'Alveydre. 1981. *Mission de l'Inde en Europe; Mission de l'Europe en Asie.* Intro. J. Saunier. Nice: Bélisane. (1st ed. 1885/1910)

Santillana, Giorgio de, and Hertha von Dechend. 1969. *Hamlet's Mill. An essay on myth and the frame of time.* Boston: Gambit.

Saunier, Jean. 1971. *La Synarchie, ou le vieux rêve d'une nouvelle société.* Paris: Culture, Arts, Loisirs.

Saurat, Denis. 1957. *Atlantis and the Giants.* London: Faber & Faber.

Schlegel, Friedrich von. 1849. *The Aesthetic and Miscellaneous Works.* Trans. E. J. Millington. London: Bohn, 1849.

Schrader, O. 1890. *Prehistoric Antiquities of the Aryan Peoples.* Trans. F. B. Jevons. London: Charles Griffin. (1st ed. 1888)

Schwabe, Julius. 1951. *Archetyp und Tierkreis. Grundlinien einer kosmischen Symbolik und Mythologie.* Basel: Benno Schwabe.

Schwaller de Lubicz, Isha. 1963. "*Aor,*" *R. A. Schwaller de Lubicz, Sa vie—Son oeuvre.* Paris: La Colombe.

Schwaller [de Lubicz], René. 1916. *Etude sur les nombres.* Paris: n.p.

Schwaller de Lubicz, R. A. 1977. *The Temple in Man. The Secrets of Ancient Egypt.* Trans. Robert and Deborah Lawlor. Brookline: Autumn Press. (1st ed. 1949)

Schwaller de Lubicz, R. A. 1978. *Symbol and the Symbolic. Egypt, Science and the Evolution of Consciousness.* Trans. Robert and Deborah Lawlor. Brookline: Autumn Press. (1st ed. 1949)

Serrano, Miguel. 1984a. *Adolf Hitler, el último avatãra.* Santiago: La Nueva Edad.

Serrano, Miguel. 1984b. *Nos: Book of the Resurrection.* London: Routledge & Kegan Paul.

Seznec, Jean. 1972. *The Survival of the Pagan Gods.* Trans. Barbara F. Sessions. Princeton: Princeton University Press. (1st ed. 1940)

Singer, Charles. 1959. *A Short History of Scientific Ideas to 1900.* New York: Oxford University Press.

Smith, Edwin Burrows. 1954. "Jean-Sylvain Bailly, Astronomer, Mystic, Revolutionary." *Transactions of the American Philosophical Society* n.s. 44/4: 424–538.

Sokoloff, Nicolas. 1924. *Enquête judiciaire sur l'assassinat de la famille impériale russe.* Paris: Payot.

Spencer, H. S. 1965. *The Aryan Ecliptic Cycle.* Poona: H. P. Vaswani.

Stefansson, Vilhjalmur. 1924. *The Northward Course of Empire.* New York: Macmillan.

Stefansson, Vilhjalmur. 1940. *Ultima Thule. Further Mysteries of the Arctic.* New York: Macmillan.

Sullivan, Walter. 1957. *Quest for a Continent.* New York: McGraw Hill.

Surya-Siddhanta, a Textbook of Hindu Astronomy. 1978. Ed. Ebenezer Burgess. Minneapolis: Wizards Book Shelf. (1st ed. 1860)

[Symmes, John Cleves?]. 1965. *Symzonia; a voyage of discovery. By Captain Adam Seaborn.* Gainesville: Scholars' Facsimiles. (1st ed. 1820)

Symmes, John Cleves and Americus. 1878. *The Symmes Theory of concentric spheres.* Louisville: Bradley & Gilbert.

Tarling, D. H. 1983. *Paleomagnetism. Principles and Applications in Geology, Geophysics and Archaeology.* London: Chapman & Hall.

Taylor, Isaac. 1906. *The Origin of the Aryans.* 3rd ed. London: Walter Scott. (1st ed. 1888)

Theon of Smyrna. 1979. *Mathematics Useful for the Study of Plato.* Trans. J. Dupuis, Robert and Deborah Lawlor. San Diego: Wizards Bookshelf.

Thompson, Richard L. 1989. *Vedic Cosmography and Astronomy.* Los Angeles: Bhaktivedanta Book Trust.

Thorndike, Lynn. 1923–1958. *A History of Magic and Experimental Science.* 8 vols. New York: Columbia University Press.

Tilak, Bâl Gangâdhar. 1903. *The Arctic Home in the Vedas, Being also a new key to the interpretation of many Vedic Texts and Legends.* Poona: The Kesari.

Tillett, Gregory. 1982. *The Elder Brother. A biography of Charles Webster Leadbeater.* London: Routledge & Kegan Paul.

Tomas, Andrew. 1977. *Shambhala: Oasis of Light.* London: Sphere Books.

Totten, Charles A. L. 1968. *Joshua's Long Day and the Dial of Ahaz. A Scientific Vindication.* With *When the Earth Turned Over* by Howard B. Rand. Merrimac: Destiny. (1st ed. 1890)

Ulansey, David. 1989. *The Origins of the Mithraic Mysteries. Cosmology and Salvation in the Ancient World.* New York: Oxford University Press.

VandenBroeck, André. 1987. *Al-Kemi, a Memoir. Hermetic, Occult, Political, and Private Aspects of R. A. Schwaller de Lubicz.* Great Barrington: Lindisfarne Press.

Velikovsky, Immanuel. 1955. *Worlds in Collision.* London: Gollancz. (1st ed. 1950)

Verne, Jules. 1911. *Works.* New York: F. Tyler Daniels Co.

Voltaire. 1785. *Oeuvres.* Kehl: Société littéraire-typographique.

Walker, D. P. 1972. *The Ancient Theology. Studies in Christian Platonism from the Fifteenth to the Eighteenth Century.* London: Duckworth.

Walsh, Edmund A., S.J. 1948. *Total Power. A Footnote to History.* Garden City: Doubleday.

Walton, Bruce A. 1985. *A Guide to the Inner Earth.* Mokelumne Hill: Health Research. (1st ed. 1983)

Warren, William F. 1885. *Paradise Found.* 5th ed. Boston: Houghton Mifflin.

Webb, James. 1981. *The Occult Establishment.* Glasgow: Richard Drew.

Wentworth, Jim. 1973. *Giants in the Earth. The Amazing Story of Ray Palmer, Oahspe and the Shaver Mystery.* Amherst, WI: Palmer Publications.

Whiston, Thomas. 1978. *A New Theory of the Earth.* New York: Arno Press. (1st ed. 1696)

White, John. 1980. *Pole Shift. Predictions and Prophecies of the Ultimate Disaster.* New York: Doubleday.

White, John. 1989. "Is a Disastrous Pole Shift Inevitable?" *Venture Inward* 5/5: 18–21, 39–42.

Williams, G. E. 1975. "Late Precambrian glacial climate and the Earth's obliquity." *Geological Magazine* 112: 441–544.

Williams, G. E., ed. 1981. *Megacycles: Long-term Episodicity in the Earth and Planetary History.* Stroudsburg: Hutchinson Ross.

Wilson, Thomas. 1894. *The Swastika. The earliest known symbol, and its migrations.* Washington DC: Report of the National Museum, 757–1011.

Wirth, Herman. 1928. *Die Aufgang der Menschheit. Untersuchungen zur Geschichte der Religion, Symbolik und Schrift der Atlantisch-Nordischen Rasse.* Jena: E. Diederich.

Wirth, Herman. 1931. "Das Geheimnis von Arktis-Atlantis." *Die Woche* 35 (29 Aug.): 1144–1148, 1156, IV [sic].

Wynne-Tyson, Esmé. 1972. *Mithras, the Fellow in the Cap.* Fontwell: Centaur Press.

X, Michael [Michael Barton]. 1969. *Rainbow City and the Inner Earth People.* Clarksburg: Saucerian Books. (1st ed. 1960)

Zadkiel. 1870. *Zadkiel's Almanac for 1870.* London: Berger.

Zaehner, R. C. 1961. *The Dawn and Twilight of Zoroastrianism.* New York: Putnam's Sons.

Acknowledgment of Illustrations

3. Agartha and Shambhala. Used by Permission of Health Research, Box 70, Mokelumne Hill, California 95245 (from the book, *Agharta*, by Raymond Bernard, 1960)

4. The polar vortices. From Athanasius Kircher, *Mundus Subterraneus* (1665). By permission of Thames & Hudson, Ltd.

9. Nordic mythology and the hollow earth. Redrawn from Miguel Serrano, *Adolf Hitler, el último avatãra* (1984). By permission of the Author.

10. Richard Byrd's exploratory flights. From Walter Sullivan, *Quest for a Continent* (1957). By permission of the Author.

11. Oronteus Finaeus' 1531 map of Antarctica superimposed on a modern one, showing the Ross Sea unglaciated. From Charles Hapgood, *Maps of the Ancient Sea Kings* (1979). It has not been possible to trace the rights owner, who is hereby invited to contact Phanes Press.

14. a) The staff of Hermes; b) yogic anatomy. From Titus Burckhardt, *Alchemy: Science of the Cosmos, Science of the Soul* (1967). By permission of Mrs. Edith Burckhardt.

16. Historical positions of the equinox. Redrawn from Giorgio de Santillana and Hertha von Dechend, *Hamlet's Mill* (1969). By permission of Harvard Common Press.

Index

THE FANTASTIC INVENTIONS OF NIKOLA TESLA
by Nikola Tesla
with additional material
by David Hatcher Childress

This book is a virtual compendium of patents, diagrams, photos, and explanations of the many incredible inventions of the originator of the modern era of electrification. The book is a readable and affordable collection of his patents, inventions, and thoughts on free energy, anti-gravity, and other futuristic inventions. Covered in depth, often in Tesla's own words, are such topics as:

• His Plan to Transmit Free Electricity into the Atmosphere;

• How Anti-Gravity Airships could Draw Power from the Towers he was Building;

• Tesla's Death Rays, Ozone Generators, and more...

342 pp. ♦ 6x9 paperback ♦ Highly illustrated ♦ Bibliography & appendix ♦ $16.95

code: ***FINT***

EXTRATERRESTRIAL ARCHAEOLOGY
by David Hatcher Childress

With hundreds of photos and illustrations, Extraterrestrial Archaeology takes the reader to the strange and fascinating worlds of Mars, the Moon, Mercury, Venus, Saturn, and other planets for a look at the alien structures that appear there. This book is non-fiction! Whether skeptic or believer, this book allows you to view for yourself the amazing pyramids, domes, spaceports, obelisks, and other anomalies that are profiled in photograph after photograph. Using official NASA and Soviet photos, as well as other photos taken via telescope, this book seeks to prove that many of the planets (and moons) of our solar system are in some way inhabited by intelligent life. The book includes many blowups of NASA photos and detailed diagrams of structures—particularly on the Moon. Extraterrestrial Archaeology will change the way you think.

224 pp. ♦ 8½x11 paperback ♦ Highly illustrated with photos, diagrams & maps! ♦ Bibliography, index, appendix ♦ $18.95

code: ***ETA***

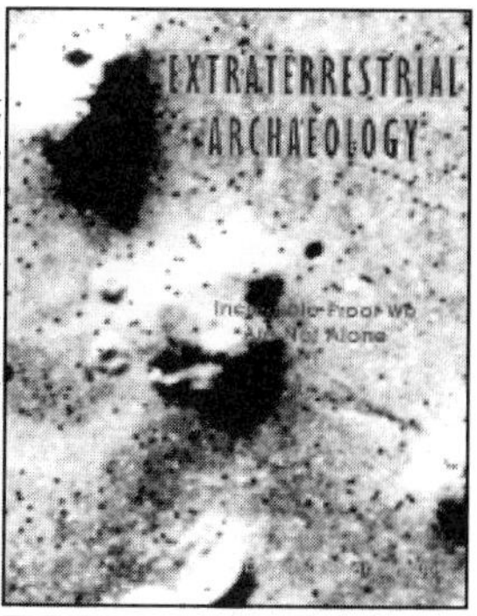

LOST CITIES OF ANCIENT LEMURIA & THE PACIFIC
by David Hatcher Childress

Was there once a continent in the Pacific? Called Lemuria or Pacifica by geologists, and Mu or Pan by the mystics, there is now ample mythological, geological and archaeological evidence to "prove" that an advanced and ancient civilization once lived in the central Pacific. Maverick archaeologist and explorer David Hatcher Childress combs the Indian Ocean, Australia, and the Pacific in search of the astonishing truth about mankind's past. Contains photos of the underwater city on Pohnpei, explanations on how the statues were levitated around Easter Island in a clockwise vortex movement, disappearing islands, Egyptians in Australia, and more.

379 pp. ♦ 6x9 paperback ♦ Photos, maps, & illustrations ♦ Footnotes & bibliography ♦ $14.95 ♦ *code:* ***LEM***

MAN-MADE UFOS: 1944-1994
50 Years of Suppression
by Renato Vesco & David Hatcher Childress

A comprehensive and in-depth look at the early "flying saucer technology" of Nazi Germany and the genesis of early man-made UFOs. From captured German scientists, escaped battalions of German soldiers, secret communities in South America and Antarctica to today's state-of-the-art "Dreamland" flying machines, this astonishing book blows the lid off the "Government UFO Conspiracy." Examined in detail are secret underground airfields and factories; German secret weapons; "suction" aircraft; the origin of NASA; gyroscopic stabilizers and engines; the secret Marconi aircraft factory in South America, and other secret societies, both ancient and modern, that have kept this craft a secret, and much more. Not to be missed by students of technology suppression, UFOs, anti-gravity, free-energy conspiracy, and World War II. Introduction by W.A. Harbinson, author of the Dell novels Genesis and Revelation.

440 pp. ♦ 6x9 paperback ♦ Packed with photos & diagrams Index & footnotes $18.95 ♦ *code:* ***MMU***

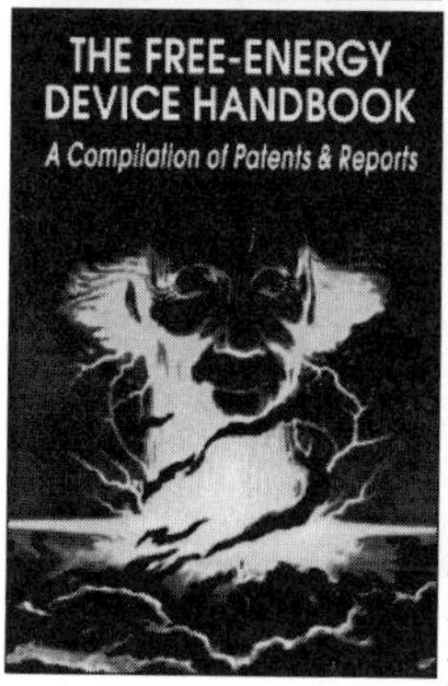

THE FREE-ENERGY DEVICE HANDBOOK
A Compilation of Patents & Reports by David Hatcher Childress

Large format compilation of various patents, papers, descriptions, and diagrams concerning free-energy devices and systems. The Free-Energy Device Handbook is a visual tool for experimenters and researchers into magnetic motors and other "over-unity" devices with chapters on the Adams Motor, the Hans Coler Generator, cold fusion, superconductors, "N" machines, space-energy generators, Nikola Tesla, T. Townsend Brown, the Bedini motor, and the latest in free-energy devices. Packed with photos, technical diagrams, patents, and fascinating information, this book belongs on every science shelf. With energy and profit a major political reason for fighting various wars, free-energy devices, if ever allowed to be mass-distributed to consumers, could change the world. Get your copy now before the Department of Energy bans this book!

306 pp. ♦ 7x10 paperback ♦ Profusely illustrated ♦ Bibliography & appendix ♦ $16.95 ♦

code: ***FEH***

THE HISTORY OF ATLANTIS
by Lewis Spence

Lewis Spence's classic book on Atlantis is now back in print. Lewis Spence was a Scottish historian (1874-1955) who is best known for his volumes on world mythology and his five Atlantis books. The History of Atlantis (1926) is considered his best. Spence does his scholarly best in such chapters as The Sources of Atlantean History, The Geography of Atlantis, The Races of Atlantis, The Kings of Atlantis, The Religion of Atlantis, The Colonies of Atlantis, more. Sixteen chapters in all.

240 pp. ♦ 6x9 paperback ♦ Illustrated with maps, photos & diagrams ♦ $16.95

code: ***HOA***

Adventures Unlimited Press

One Adventure Place
Kempton, Illinois
60946

24 Hour Telephone Order Line
815 253 6390

24 Hour Fax Order Line
815 253 6300

EMail orders
adventures_unlimited@mcimail.com

NEW BOOKS

UNDERGROUND BASES & TUNNELS

What is the Government Trying to Hide?
by Richard Sauder Ph.D.

Working from government documents and corporate records, Sauder has compiled an impressive book that digs below the surface of the military's super-secret underground! Go behind the scenes into little-known corners of the public record and discover how corporate America has worked hand-in-glove with the Pentagon for decades, dreaming about, planning-and actually constructing-secret underground bases. This book includes chapters on the locations of the bases, the tunneling technology, various military designs for underground bases, nuclear testing & underground bases, abductions, needles & implants; Is the U.S. Military Involved in "Alien" Cattle Mutilations? Includes a 50 page photo & map insert.

201 pages, 6x9 paperback. Well Illustrated. $15.95. code: UGB

COMMON SENSE SURVIVAL GUIDES

compiled by Albert Sindlinger

For virtually hundreds of thousands of people, Common Sense Survival Guides will serve as a valuable tool to dealing with many of life's challenges. Collected from a wide range of resources and based on years of experience, Common Sense Survival Guides will assist the reader in working out a plan to deal with personal survival in areas such as health, emergencies, natural disasters and victimhood. This handy, user friendly compilation offers tried and true suggestions that tie in with humankind's innate common sense and the need to become more self-reliant in today's ever changing world. Includes Natural Disaster Guides, First Aid Guides, Preparedness and prevention guides, Social and Spiritual guides, Checklists where necessary plus sources, Bibliography and where to get further information. The appendix includes all of the latest government and IRS forms relating to disaster and injury claims.

135 pages, 9x12 paperback. Illustrations and checklists. Bibliography & Appendix. $17.95. code: CSSG

24 hour credit card orders – call: 815 253 6390 • fax: 815 253 6300 • Email: aup@azstarnet.com

ANTI-GRAVITY

THE ANTI-GRAVITY HANDBOOK

Edited by David Hatcher Childress, With Arthur C. Clark, Nikola Tesla, T.B. Paulicki, Bruce Cathie, Leonard G. Cramp and Albert Einstein

The new expanded compilation of material on Anti-Gravity, Free Energy, Flying Saucer propulsion, UFOs, Suppressed Technology, NASA Coverups and more. Highly illustrated with patents, technical illustrations, photos and more, this revised and expanded edition has more material, including photos of Area 51, Nevada, the government's secret testing facility. This classic on weird science is back in a 90s format!

- How to build a flying saucer.
- Read about Arthur C. Clark on Anti-Gravity.
- learn about crystals and their role in levitation.
- Secret government research and developement.
- Nikola Tesla on how anti-gravity airships could draw power from the atmosphere.
- Bruce Cathie's Anti-Gravity Equation.
- NASA, the Moon and Anti-Gravity. Plus more.

230 pages, 7x10 tradepaper, Bibliography/Index/Appendix. Highly illustrated with 100's of patents illustrations and photos, $14.95. code: AGH

ANTI–GRAVITY & THE WORLD GRID

Edited by David Hatcher Childress

Is the earth surrounded by an intricate electromagnetic grid network offering free energy? This compilation of material on the earth grid, ley lines, and world power points contains chapters on the geography, mathematics, and light harmonics of the earth grid. Learn the purpose of ley lines and ancient megalithic structures located on the grid. Discover how the grid made the Philadelphia Experiment possible. Explore Coral Castle and many other mysteries; Including, acoustic levitation, Tesla Shields and Scalar Wave weaponry. Browse through the section on anti-gravity patents, and research resources.

274 pages, 150 rare photographs, diagrams and drawings, 7x10 paperback, $14.95. code: AGW

ANTI–GRAVITY & THE UNIFIED FIELD

Edited by David Hatcher Childress

Is Einstein's Unified Field the answer to all of our energy problems? Explored in this compilation of material is how gravity, electricity and magnetism manifest from a unified field around us. Why artificial gravity is possible; Secrets of UFO propulsion; free energy; Nikola Tesla and anti-gravity airships of the 20's and 30's; Flying saucers as superconducting whirls of plasma; anti-mass generators; vortex propulsion; suppressed technology; government cover-ups; gravitational pulse drive, spacecraft & more.

240 pages, 7x10 paperback,130 rare photographs, diagrams and drawings, $14.95. code: AGU

TAPPING THE ZERO POINT ENERGY

Free Energy & Anti-Gravity in Today's Physics
Moray B. King

The author, a well-known researcher, explains how free energy and anti-gravity are possible with today's physics. The theories of the zero point energy show there are tremendous fluctuations of electrical field energy imbedded within the fabric of space. This book shows how in the 1930s inventor T. Henry Moray could produce a fifty kilowatt "free energy" machine; how an electrified vortex plasma creates anti-gravity; how the Pons/Fleischmann "cold fusion" experiment could produce tremendous heat without fusion; and how certain experiments might produce a gravitational anomaly.

170 pages, 6x9 tradepaper, Illustrated with 60 diagrams and drawings. $9.95. code: TAP

MYSTIC TRAVELLER SERIES

IN SECRET MONGOLIA

Sequel to Men & Gods In Mongolia
Henning Haslund

Danish-Swedish explorer Haslund's first book on his exciting explorations in Mongolia and Central Asia. Haslund takes us via camel caravan to the medieval world of Mongolia, a country still barely known today. First published by Kegan Paul of London in 1934, this rare travel adventure back in print after 50 years. Haslund and his camel caravan journey across the Gobi Desert. He meets with renegade generals and warlords, god-kings and shamans. Haslund is captured, held for ransom, thrown into prison, battles black magic and portrays in vivid detail the birth of new nation. Haslund's second book Men & Gods In Mongolia is also available from Adventures Unlimited Press.

374 pages, 6x9 paperback. Illustrated with maps, photos and diagrams. Bibliography & Index. $16.95. code: ISM

MEN & GODS IN MONGOLIA

Henning Haslund

First published in 1935 by Kegan Paul of London, Haslund takes us to the lost city of Karakota in the Gobi desert. We meet the Bodgo Gegen, a God-king in Mongolia similar to the Dalai Lama of Tibet. We meet Dambin Jansang, the dreaded warlord of the "Black Gobi." There is even material in this incredible book on the Hi-mori, an "airhorse" that flies through the air (similar to a Vimana) and carries with it the sacred stone of Chintamani. Aside from the esoteric and mystical material, there is plenty of just plain adventure: caravans across the Gobi desert, kidnapped and held for ransom, initiation into Shamanic societies, warlords, and the violent birth of a new nation.

358 pages, 6x9 paperback, 57 photos, illustrations and maps. $15.95. code: MGM

DANGER MY ALLY

The Amazing Life Story of the Discoverer of the Crystal Skull
"Mike" Michell-Hegdes

The incredible life story of "Mike" Mitchell-Hedges, the British adventurer who discovered the Crystal Skull in the lost Mayan city of Lubaantun in Belize. Mitchell-Hedges was lived an exciting life: gambling everything on a trip to the Americas as a young man, riding with Pancho Villa, his personal quest for Atlantis, fighting bandits in the Caribbean and discovering the famous Crystal Skull.

374 pages, 6x9 paperback. Illustrated with maps, photos and diagrams. Bibliography & Index. $16.95. code: DMA

IN SECRET TIBET

Theodore Illion.

Reprint of a rare 30's travel book. Illion was a German traveller who not only spoke fluent Tibetan, but travelled in disguise through forbidden Tibet when it was off-limits to all outsiders. His incredible adventures make this one of the most exciting travel books ever published. Includes illustrations of Tibetan monks levitating stones by acoustics.

210 pages, 6x9 paperback, illustrated, $15.95. code: IST

DARKNESS OVER TIBET

Theodore Illion.

In this second reprint of the rare 30's travel books by Illion, the German traveller continues his travels through Tibet and is given the directions to a strange underground city. As the original publisher's remarks said, this is a rare account of an underground city in Tibet by the only Westerner ever to enter it and escape alive!

210 pages, 6x9 paperback, illustrated, $15.95. code: DOT

24 hour credit card orders – call: 815 253 6390 ▪ fax: 815 253 6300 ▪ Email: aup@azstarnet.com

Bruce Cathie's ENERGY GRID series

THE HARMONIC CONQUEST OF SPACE

Bruce L. Cathie

Bruce Cathie's research into the harmonic geometry of the Earth and its energy systems has been going on since he was an Air New Zealand pilot in the 1960s. His new book recaps and updates all his work to date, and takes the reader further into the realms which connect science with the unexplained. Chapters in this book include: mathematics of the World Grid; the Harmonics of Hiroshima and Nagasaki; Harmonic ttransmission and Receiving; the Link Between Human Brain-Waves, the Cavity Resonance between the Earth, the ionosphere and Gravity; Edgar Cayce-the Harmonicsof the subconscious;Stonehenge; the Harmonics of the Moon; the Pyramids of Mars; Nikola Tesla the Electric Car; The Robert Adams Pulsed Electric Motor Generator; Harmonic Clues to the Unified Fields, and more. Also included in the book are tables showing the harmonic relationship between the Earth's magnetic field, the 'speed of light,' and anti gravity/gravity acceleration at different points on the Earth's surface.

260 pages, 6x9. Tradepaper. Illustrated with diagrams a nd tables. Bibliography. $16.95. code: HCS

THE BRIDGE TO INFINITY

Harmonic 371244
Captain Bruce Cathie

Cathie has popularized the concept that the earth is criss–crossed by an electro-magnetic grid system that can be used for anti-gravity, free energy, levitation and more. The book includes a new analysis of the harmonic nature of reality, acoustic levitation, pyramid power, harmonic receiver towers, UFO propulsion. It concludes that today's scientists have at their command a fantastic store of knowledge with which to advance the welfare of the human race.

200 pages, 6x9 tradepaper, illustrated with photographs & diagrams. $11.95. code: BTF

THE ENERGY GRID

Harmonic 695 The Pulse of the Universe
Captain Bruce Cathie.

This is a compilation (updated and corrected) of Air New Zealand Captain Bruce Cathie's first three books. They are all rare, supagesressed and out of print. Exploring the energy grid in great detail there are chapters on unified equations, the mysterious aerials, Pythagoras & the Grid, Nikola Tesla, nuclear detonation & the grid, maps of the ancients, an Australian Stonehenge, & much more. Cathie explores the nature of Light Harmonics and how light hitting the earth creates an energy grid around the earth that is the very basis of physical reality. Cathie's books are a must for the serious student of Anti-Gravity and lost science.

255 pages, 6x9 tradepaper, illustrated with photographs & diagrams. ISBN 0-922-356-20-3. $13.95. code: TEG

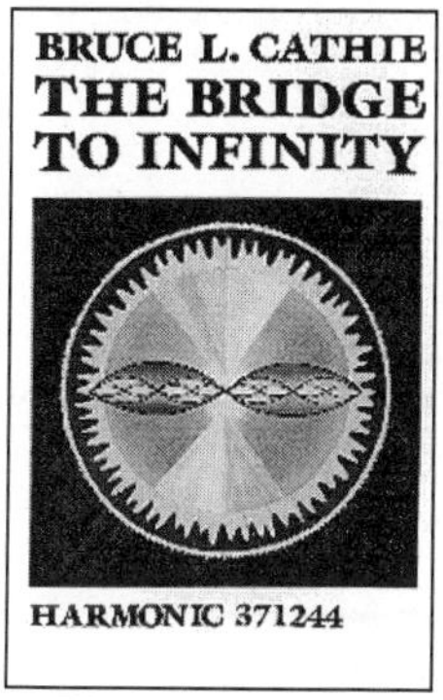

BRUCE CATHIE IN CONFERENCE EXPLAINING THE WORLD GRID

With Captain Bruce Cathie

New Zealand author and pilot Bruce Cathie on UFOs, the World Grid System, harmonic mathematics, Martian Pyramids, the Harmonics of the Moon, Anti-Gravity and Free Energy. He is the author of the underground best selling books THE ENERGY GRID and THE BRIDGE TO INFINITY and THE HARMONIC CONQUEST OF SPACE. In this video he explains his light-harmonic grid system, how antennas are used in this system, how various governments are already using a fantastic technology, UFO bases in New Zealand and Australia, more.

3 Hour video. VHS $29.95 code: BCV

Please use item codes when ordering http://www.azstarnet.com/~aup

THE LOST CITIES

LOST CITIES OF ATLANTIS, ANCIENT EUROPE & THE MEDITERRANEAN

David Hatcher Childress

Atlantis! The legendary lost continent comes under the close scrutiny of maverick archaeologist David Hatcher Childress. This sixth book in the internationally popular Lost Cities series takes us on quest for the lost continent of Atlantis. Childress takes the reader in search of sunken cities in the Mediterranean; across the Atlas Mountains in search of Atlantean ruins; to remote islands in search of megalithic ruins; living legengds and secret societies. From Ireland to Turkey, Morocco to Eastern Europe, or remote islands of the Mediterranean and Atlantic Childress takes the reader on an astonishing quest for mankind's past. Ancient technology, cataclysms, megalithic construction, lost civilizations and devastating wars of the past are all explored in this astonishing book. Childress challenges the skeptics and proves that great civilizations not only existed in the past, but the modern world and its problems are reflections of the ancient world of Atlantis.

524 pages, 6x9 paperback. Illustrated with 100s of maps, photos and diagrams. Bibliography & Index. $16.95. code: MED

LOST CITIES OF ANCIENT LEMURIA & THE PACIFIC

David Hatcher Childress

Was there once a continent in the Pacific? Called Lemuria or Pacifica by geologists, and Mu or Pan by the mystics, there is now ample mythological, geological and archaeological evidence to "prove" that an advanced, and ancient civilization once lived in the central Pacific. Maverick archaeologist and explorer David Hatcher Childress combs the Indian Ocean, Australia and the Pacific in search of the astonishing truth about mankind's past. Contains photos of the underwater city on Pohnpei, explanations on how the statues were levitated around Easter Island in a clock-wise vortex movement; disappearing islands; Egyptians in Australia; and more.

379 pages, 6x9, paperback. Photos, maps, and illustrations with Footnotes & Bibliography $14.95. code LEM

DAVID HATCHER CHILDRESS RADIO INTERVIEW

On the Lost Cities of North & Central America

In December of 1992, popular Lost Cities Series author, David Hatcher Childress, was interviewed live for six hours on the Laura Lee Radio Show, broadcast out of Seattle, Washington. The subject of the interview was David's book, Lost Cities of North and Central America, with special emphasis on the Smithsonian Institution's cover-up of American history. Other topics that were included in the interview, which also included live call-in questions, were pyramids around the world, the Rama Empire of India and Vimanas, Atlantis and Lemuria, UFOs, an Egyptian City in the Grand Canyon, and more! This audio interview comes on three high-quality 90 minute cassette tapes in boxes.

270 Minutes on 3 audio cassettes, $12.95 code: DHCR

ADVENTURES UNLIMITED

303 Main Street
P.O. Box 74
Kempton, Illinois 60946
USA
Tel.: 815-253-6390 ♦ Fax: 815-253-6300
Email: adventures_unlimited@mcimail.com

ORDERING INSTRUCTIONS

- Remit by USD$ Check or Money Order
- Credit Cards: Visa, MasterCard, Discovery, & American Express Accepted
- Call ♦ Fax ♦ Email Any Time

SHIPPING CHARGES

United States

- Postal Book Rate { $2.00 First Item, 50¢ Each Additional Item
- Priority Mail { $3.50 First Item, $1.50 Each Additional Item
- UPS { $3.50 First Item, $1.00 Each Additional Item

NOTE: UPS Delivery Available to Mainland USA Only

Canada

- Postal Book Rate { $3.00 First Item, $1.00 Each Additional Item
- Postal Air Mail { $4.00 First Item, $2.00 Each Additional Item
- Personal Checks or Bank Drafts MUST BE USD$ and Drawn on a US Bank
- Canadian Postal Money Orders OK
- Payment MUST BE USD$

All Other Countries

- Surface Delivery { $5.00 First Item, $2.00 Each Additional Item
- Postal Air Mail { $10.00 First Item, $8.00 Each Additional Item
- Payment MUST BE USD$
- Checks MUST BE USD$ and Drawn on a US Bank
- Add $5.00 for Air Mail Subscription to Future *Adventures Unlimited* Catalogs

SPECIAL NOTES

- RETAILERS: Standard Discounts Available
- BACKORDERS: We Backorder all Out-of-Stock Items Unless Otherwise Requested
- PRO FORMA INVOICES: Available on Request
- VIDEOS: NTSC Mode Only
  PAL & SECAM Mode Videos Are Not Available

European Office:
Adventures Unlimited, PO Box 372,
Dronten, 8250 AJ, The Netherlands

Please check: ☑

❒ This is my first order ❒ I have ordered before ❒ This is a new address

Name
Address
City
State/Province | Postal Code
Country
Phone day | Evening
Fax

Item Code	Item Description	Price	Qty	Total
CAT	Adventures Unlimited Catalog	N/C		N/C

Please check: ☑

❒ Postal-Surface
❒ Postal-Air Mail (Priority in USA)
❒ UPS (Mainland USA only)

Please Use Item Codes!

Subtotal ➤	
Less Discount-10% for 3 or more items ➤	
Balance ➤	
Illinois Residents 7% Sales Tax ➤	
Previous Credit ➤	
Shipping ➤	
Total (check/MO in USD$ only) ➤	

❒ Visa/MasterCard/Discover/Amex

#____________________ Exp. ______

Comments & Suggestions | **Share Our Catalog with a Friend**

10% Discount When You Order 3 or More Items!